D1551290

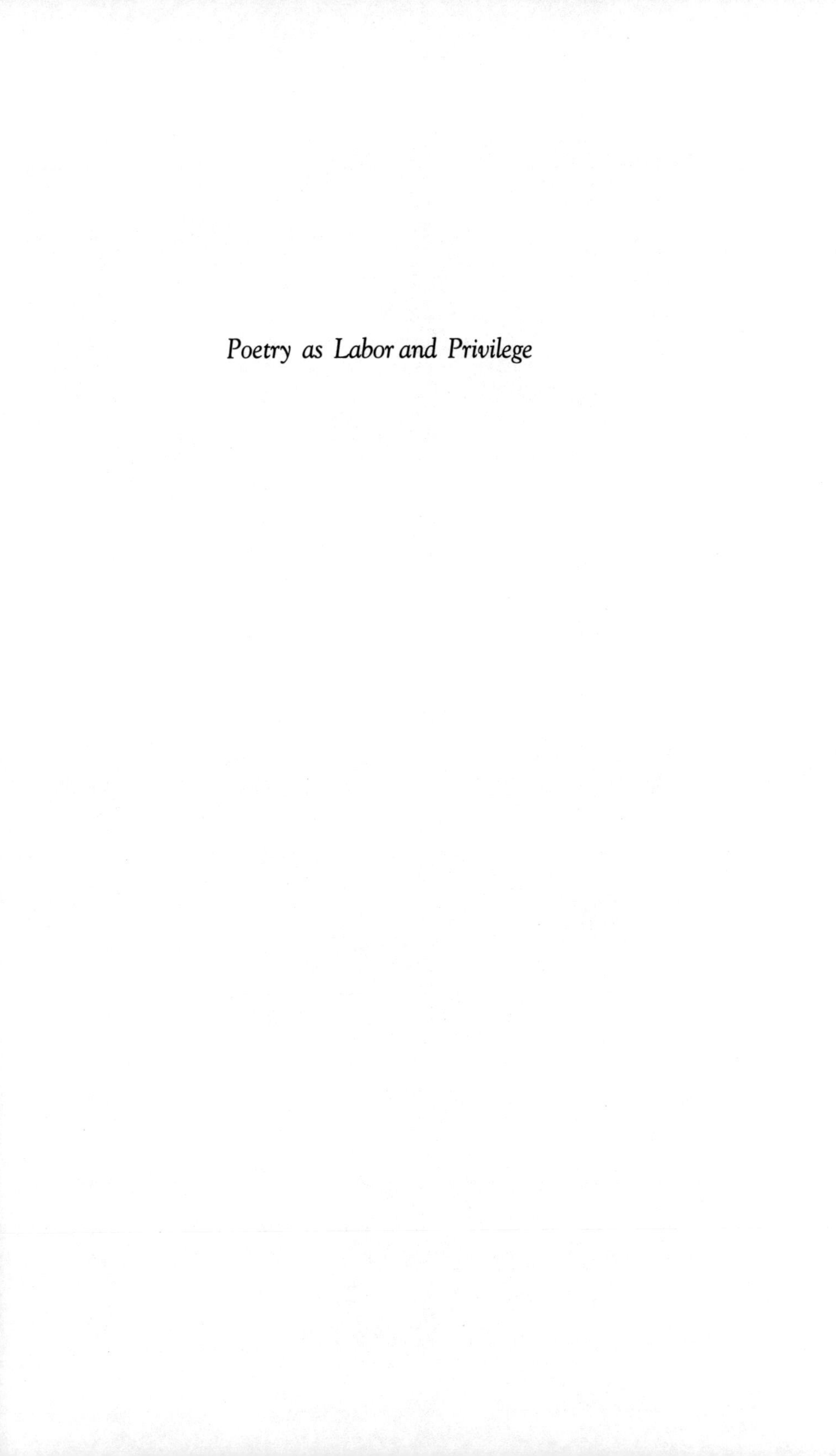

Poetry as Labor and Privilege

Poetry as Labor and Privilege

THE WRITINGS OF *W. S. Merwin*

EDWARD J. BRUNNER

UNIVERSITY OF ILLINOIS PRESS
Urbana and Chicago

Manufactured in the United States of America
C 5 4 3 2 1

This book is printed on acid-free paper.

Library of Congress Cataloging-in-Publication Data

Brunner, Edward J., 1946–
Poetry as labor and privilege : the writings of W. S. Merwin / Edward J. Brunner.
p. cm.
Includes bibliographical references and index.
ISBN 0-252-01775-7 (cl.)
1. Merwin, W. S. (William Stanley), 1927– —Criticism and interpretation. I. Title.
PS3563.E75Z62 1991
811′.54—dc20 90-48342
CIP

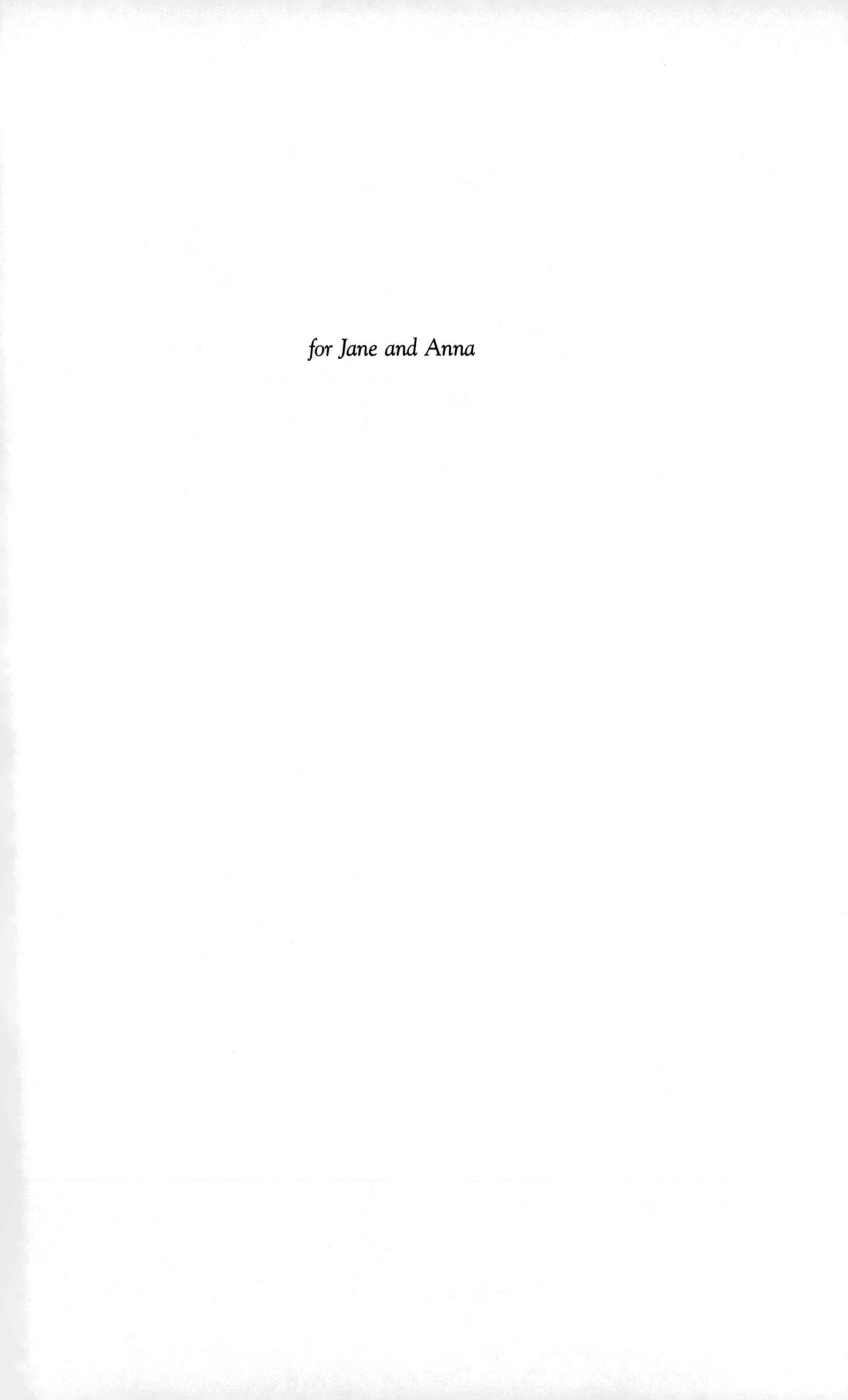

for Jane and Anna

The encouragement of poetry itself is a labor and privilege like that of living. It requires, I imagine, among other startlingly simple things, a love of poetry, and possibly a recurring despair of finding it again, an indelible awareness of its parentage with that biblical waif, ill at ease in time, the spirit. No one has any claims on it, no one deserves it, no one knows where it goes.

W. S. Merwin, "Notes for a Preface"

Contents

PART THREE

Chronicles

Preface

This study examines not the publications of W. S. Merwin but his *writings*, from "Meng Tzu's Song," completed in 1947 and the earliest poem in his first collection, *A Mask for Janus,* to work that appeared in magazines after *The Rain in the Trees* was published in 1988 (and that may or may not appear in a further collection of poetry). The study concentrates on poetry, but it continually draws upon the considerable amount of work Merwin completed in other forms, including drama, fiction, essays, and translations. Much of this other writing is not well known; some of it is entirely unknown. It ranges from work that appeared only in magazines of limited circulation to compositions begun but left unrevised or incomplete. This less-familiar material, when brought in line with the published work, presents a view of a whole career in evolution.

What happens to works that may be quite familiar to readers of contemporary literature when they are linked with unfamiliar writings produced at the same time or under similar circumstances? Such linking, on the one hand, is inevitably disruptive; on the other hand, these disruptions are stages toward reconstituting the works within a larger framework that may provide a greater clarity. This study employs such joining as its singularly modest method. It is no more controversial than other approaches that blend criticism with scholarship. If some conclusions result that are at odds with current conceptions of Merwin, it is perhaps because it is uncommon to apply, on the scope of a full-scale study, techniques of scholarly research to a contemporary writer. For one thing, it is usually impossible: the basic materials for such scholarship are generally unavailable. A writer's manuscripts alone, for example, are most likely beyond reach; if they have not been lost or destroyed, they may be preserved in a piecemeal fashion or uncatalogued or scattered in numerous locations with formidable prohibitions against their use.

None of this holds true for Merwin's manuscripts. The archives at the University of Illinois at Urbana-Champaign constitute a virtually complete record of his writing, from his years as a student at Princeton following World War II up to poems and fragments completed in February 1982. Included are drafts, revisions, and typescripts of all but a handful of poems over a period of more than thirty years; multiple versions and final scripts for four full-length plays and substantial drafts of three unfinished plays; drafts and revisions of short prose memoirs, fiction, travel writings, and personal essays; performance scripts for radio talks; manuscripts of book reviews, critical essays, and introductions; and two dozen notebooks, as well as perhaps five hundred pages of scattered notes. Moreover, the collection reveals that Merwin habitually composed on the reverse side of whatever scraps of paper were handy—including correspondence from editors, writers, and friends, as well as carbon copies of his own letters. This collection is not only an archive but a chronicle, albeit incomplete, of an extensive correspondence. Finally, all this material, including the correspondence, has been placed in a catalogue; identified, numbered, and briefly described, it is easily and rapidly accessible. So complete a record of a contemporary writer's work is extremely rare, perhaps even unique.

We are unaccustomed to having free access to such a wealth of material belonging to a contemporary writer. What occurs when an archive of such magnitude becomes available is that the process by which a literary identity is formed becomes enormously accelerated. Ordinarily, that process unfolds leisurely over the course of decades. The writer's identity is shaped at first by book reviewers, who offer a more or less immediate response to material as it appears. A further stage occurs if a writer has achieved a body of work substantial enough to warrant interpretation; then literary critics present their analyses of central works, usually in relation to what they discern to be the writer's outstanding work. The scholar enters at a later point, when a body of writing is complete and when enough background material has accumulated to allow the writer to stand in outline against his or her age. A writer who attracts enough interest to pass through all these stages has achieved a literary identity.

As a rule, a literary identity evolves gradually through each of these distinct stages. It is not surprising, therefore, for a writer's features to undergo significant change when passing through each. The T. S. Eliot of 1922 whom Conrad Aiken reviewed in the *New Republic* is considerably different from the Eliot whom Cleanth Brooks depicted in 1939 in *Modern Poetry and the Tradition;* this Eliot in turn is radically different from the one portrayed by Ronald Bush in 1983 in *T. S. Eliot: A Study in Character and Style.* With this study of Merwin, however, no lengthy grace period stretches between the depictions of literary critics and the findings of the scholar. The literary identity proposed by critics has not even had a chance to crystallize before the disruptions caused by the corrective scholar intervene.

But there is a further reason why the Merwin who appears in these pages sometimes assumes an appearance that can seem disconcertingly new, and it has to do with the difference between the requirements of the literary critic and those of the scholar. The essays literary critics write about contemporaries rarely take shape as their own direct response to the writer before them; only reviewers enjoy that luxury. Critics are almost always bent on effectively demonstrating a critical theory. Brooks's essay on *The Waste Land* is also a test of the procedures of the New Criticism. Eliot's work both validates and challenges a methodology that is in the process of being illustrated as Brooks applies it to Eliot. The same holds true for those essays on Merwin that prove strongest and most compelling. Cary Nelson's chapter on Merwin in *Our Last First Poets* is a bold mixture of two critical approaches not often considered compatible: he employs close phenomenological readings that register quite specific nuances of feeling, but within a framework of skepticism that constantly doubts, and informally deconstructs, the capabilities of language. One reason Nelson is able to go so far, farther than anyone else, in his readings, is that he invites Merwin's work to influence his own theoretical applications. Charles Altieri's treatment in *Enlarging the Temple* is insightful for a similar reason, though the space he opens for Merwin's work to impinge upon originates with Heidegger and existential moral philosophy. Somewhat more programmatic but still impressive applications of methodologies are Jan Gordon's variation on Heideggerian aesthetics in a study of *The Lice* (an approach Thomas B. Byers follows less broadly in an essay characterizing *The Miner's Pale Children* and *Houses and Travelers*) and the cross between Fredric Jameson's neo-Marxism and Merle Brown's neo-idealistic aesthetics in Evan Watkins's readings of Merwin's later free verse.

Our understanding of those contemporary writers that our age holds to be major is filtered through essays and book chapters that derive a portion of their authority from their ability to illustrate the workings of a specific theoretical method. They hold our attention as much for what they reveal about the usefulness and vitality and ingenuity of their method as for what they say about their subject. But their allegiance is inevitably divided, and their views cannot be entirely disinterested. Criticism, as a result, leaves an opening for the scholarship that follows. What the scholar is likely to know is what the critic can only guess at: the sequence in which a group of poems was written, or the chronology that underlies a volume of individual poems, or the poems that were omitted from a collection, or the poems that were dropped before they were finished. The scholar is aware of shifts in circumstance or new commitments that are apt to color a period of writing. The scholar has read the correspondence that confirms the influence of other writers or reveals unnoticed sources. Most notable of all, the scholar is trying hard to have a method that, as methods go, is as unbiased as it can possibly be.

The literary identity that the scholar portrays will never mesh cleanly with the one that the literary critic depicts, for each draws authority from singularly different areas. And as scholarship goes about establishing stable contexts for works, it necessarily destabilizes previous contexts assembled by critics from presumptions illustrating literary theory. If some of the readings in this study differ pointedly from the readings of previous critics, it is often because the context has been changed from one grounded in the speculations of theory to one established in a broader, more factual framework.

Some of the revisions are subtle, others dramatic. It seems questionable, for example, to give credence to the claim that through the 1950s Merwin pursued a rigorously formal poetry now that we have become aware of *The Ark of Silence,* a sprawling combination of prose and poetry assembled in 1957 and submitted as a fourth volume of poetry (but rejected by the publisher). The sequence of family poems assembled for the final pages of *The Drunk in the Furnace* (published in 1960) now appears to be closer to a commentary on America in general and its attitude toward the past, even though that commentary has particular reference to Merwin's own family. It also seems less likely that the four volumes of free verse published between 1963 and 1973 can be easily regarded as a single, unbroken unit expressing a profound pessimism, once the careful arrangements underlying each collection come under scrutiny. Even *The Lice,* Merwin's most celebrated volume, cautiously edges toward a number of modest but powerful affirmations that reveal an insistent movement away from a condition of outright despair. Interviewers in the 1980s often asked Merwin how he came to slip free of the sense of malaise that appeared to grip these four collections, to turn in *The Compass Flower* (1977) to a more expansive, all-embracing poetry. But this study suggests that long before this volume, he already had begun to shift his work in a direction that was deliberately more optimistic. Moreover, the change evident in *The Compass Flower* is itself complicated once that volume is understood as a record of the stages in his struggle to respond to the death of both his parents.

To compensate somewhat for introducing new and unfamiliar material, this study has been organized into chapters that consider Merwin's work according to the individual volumes. His collections deserve attention because they are in themselves important statements, usually marking the end of one cycle of poetry and the beginning of another; but they also serve as points of familiarity to the reader, points especially helpful when unfamiliar paths or alternate byways begin to emerge. This study, then, attempts to trace Merwin's career as it progresses—or digresses or stalls or loops back on itself to return to a site that he thought he had abandoned. It studies the choices he had before him, whether he was choosing to exclude a passage in an individual work, or to include a poem in a volume, or to end a cycle of poetry, or to make a major career shift (such as pursuing a second career as a translator rather than a playwright). It hopes to convey not only the sense in which he had intended his work to be known but also the process of thought that shaped his intention.

This kind of study would not have been possible outside of the superintending presence of the University of Illinois library staff, including the head of the Rare Book Room, Nancy L. Romero. Assistant Director for Special Collections Norman B. Brown and Director of Library Collections Carl W. Deal had the foresight to acquire the archives. Curator of Rare Books N. Frederick Nash and Curator of Special Collections Gene K. Rinkel always made themselves available for help. The process of cataloguing the manuscripts fell to Tom Callanan, who performed innovatively under conditions that would have frustrated a lesser man. With the support of subject specialists like Cary Nelson and Brian Daldorph, a microcomputer was used to sort manuscripts and correspondence (both recto and verso) according to date, genre, name, and title; the result stands as a model of manuscript cataloguing.

Carolyn Brown, Jane Cogie, Brian Daldorph, Ed Folsom, Steven Holmes, Cary Nelson, Robert Ober, and William Rueckert read all or parts of the manuscript and contributed considerably to its final form. Sherman Paul offered essential advice at every stage of the work. Ed Folsom encouraged the project when it was little more than two brief essays, sharing bibliographical materials and helping establish invaluable contacts. Both Carolyn Brown and Charles O. Hartman were involved from the start in ways that were most supportive; they offered insightful commentary at very early stages in the work. Brian Daldorph was a true ally in exploring the more vexing problems of Merwin scholarship, and I look with anticipation to the results of his own research. Innumerable visits to the University of Illinois library were transformed into occasions of pleasure and delight because of the hospitality and wit of Paula Treichler and Cary Nelson. Cary Nelson's 1977 essay awakened my interest in Merwin, and from that point on, he has been a guide both innovative and ingenious, whether discussing directions in a poem, details of manuscript identification, or elaborate strategies for guaranteeing the archives would be professionally catalogued. A small portion of chapter 14 survives from an essay, "W. S. Merwin and the Family Poems," which Cary Nelson and Ed Folsom edited for *W. S. Merwin: Essays on the Poetry* (Urbana: University of Illinois Press, 1987). I am grateful to the University of Illinois Press for permission to reprint it. W. S. Merwin's comments on that essay, as well as his hospitality during his April 1987 visit to the University of Iowa, arrived at just the right time.

A scholar unaffiliated with an academic institution necessarily creates problems whenever he or she wants to do academic things. To a publisher, the independent scholar's lack of formal status can be a headache; but here, as with a previous book of mine, Ann Lowry and the staff at the University of Illinois Press have been persistently helpful and clever in finding new ways to assure publication. Rob Schneider's careful and detailed editing improved my text considerably. I am especially grateful to the National Endowment for the Humanities, which awarded a one-year writing fellowship for work on the manuscript. That fellowship inevitably disrupted my duties as a Deputy Auditor for Johnson County, Iowa, but County Auditor Tom Slockett has at every moment enthusiastically supported this work and borne with utmost grace the complications it entailed; short of employment by a major research university, a better situation escapes my imagination, and it is a pleasure to acknowledge his help over the past eight years. In a similar way, present and past staff who have indirectly but immeasurably contributed to my work, answering office questions that kept my home phone from ringing, are Deputy Auditors Jeff McCullough and Sandra Steinbach, and Rhonda Yoder, Angie McIntire, and Kristen Esckilsen.

To my wife, Jane Cogie, who has read or heard every passage in this book at least twice and still responded with a thoughtful comment, and to my daughter, Anna, who entered this world when this work was halfway done, this study is dedicated, though nothing I could offer in writing would begin to convey my happiness for the pleasure of their companionship.

Acknowledgments

All manuscripts and unpublished works are quoted and reproduced from the W. S. Merwin Archive in the Rare Book Room, Special Collections, of the University of Illinois at Urbana-Champaign Library; W. S. Merwin retains all literary rights to these documents.

Excerpts from material by W. S. Merwin which has appeared in print in journals but has not been reprinted in books is published with the permission of W. S. Merwin.

In chapter 9, the translation of Sebastien Chamfort is excerpted from *Products of the Perfected Civilization,* translation copyright © 1969 by W. S. Merwin. Published by North Point Press and reprinted by permission.

In chapter 11, the translations are reprinted with permission of Atheneum Publishers, an imprint of Macmillan Publishing Company, from *(Asian Figures)* and *Selected Translations 1968–1978* by W. S. Merwin. Copyright © 1971, 1972, 1973 by W. S. Merwin.

In chapter 11, the prose is reprinted with permission of Atheneum Publishers, an imprint of Macmillan Publishing Company, from *Houses and Travellers* by W. S. Merwin. Copyright © 1977 by W. S. Merwin.

In chapter 15, selections from *The Rain in the Trees* are reprinted with the permission of Alfred A. Knopf, Inc., from *The Rain in the Trees.* Copyright © 1988 by W. S. Merwin.

Quotations from the following are reprinted by permission of Georges Borchardt, Inc., and W. S. Merwin:

For "Meng Tzu's Song," "Blind William's Song," "Anabasis (II)," "Carol of the Three Kings," "For a Dissolving Music," "A Dance of Death," "Herons," "Ode: The Medusa Face," "Hermione on Simulacra," and "Dictum: For a Masque of Deluge": © 1952, 1975 by W. S. Merwin.

For "Canso," "East of the Sun and West of the Moon," and "Fable": © 1954, 1975 by W. S. Merwin.

For "Leviathan," "The Mountain," and "Burning the Cat": © 1955, 1956, 1975, by W. S. Merwin.

For "Fog-Horn," "The *Portland* Going Out," "The Bones," "Cape Dread," "John Otto," "Grandfather in the Old Men's Home," "Grandmother Dying," "Grandmother and Grandson," and "Burning Mountain": © 1956, 1957, 1958, 1959, 1960, 1975 by W. S. Merwin.

For "Home for Thanksgiving," "The Nails," "Lemuel's Blessing," "Finally," "Route with No Number," "The Saint of the Uplands," "Departure's Girlfriend," "The Present," "Walk-up," "Air," "The Continuo," "The Way to the River," "The Students of Justice," and "For Now": © 1960, 1961, 1962, 1963 by W. S. Merwin.

For "A Glimpse of the Ice," "I Live Up Here," "Some Last Questions," "The Widow," "The Gods," "The River of Bees," "April," "The Room," "The Cold Before the Moonrise," "December Night," "New Moon in November," "Dusk in Winter," "The Asians Dying," "The Dry Stone Mason," "The Mourner," "For the Anniversary of My Death," and "Avoiding News by the River": © 1963, 1964, 1965, 1966, 1967 by W. S. Merwin.

For "Envoi from d'Aubigné," "February," "Lark," "Teachers," "The Birds on the Morning of Going," "Huckleberry Woman," "The Old Room," "Fear," "Pilate," "Psalm: Our Fathers," "Man With One Leaf in October Night," "Now It Is Clear," and "The Web": © 1967, 1968, 1969, 1970 by W. S. Merwin.

For "Within the Wardrobes," "Knives," "Unchopping a Tree," "The Songs of the Icebergs," "The Animal Who Eats Numbers," and "The Moles": © 1969, 1970 by W. S. Merwin.

For "A Door," "The Cry," "A Purgatory," "Instructions to Four Walls," "To the Hand," "The Initiate," "Folk Art," "The Day," and "The Diggers": © 1969, 1970, 1971, 1972, 1973 by W. S. Merwin.

For "The Heart," "Crossing Place," "The Drive Home," "The Snow," "The Arrival," "Robin," "Numbered Apartment," "St. Vincent's," "The Counting Houses," "The Estuary," "Kore," "Working into Autumn," "June Rain," "The Love for October," "Autumn Evening," "The Coin," "The Trestle," "Assembly," "The Banquet," "The Flight," and "The Windows": © 1977 by W. S. Merwin.

For excerpts from "Tomatoes," "Mary," "The Skyline," "Hotel," and "La Pia": © 1980, 1981, 1982 by W. S. Merwin.

For "Sun and Rain," "The Cow," "Questions to Tourists Stopped by a Pineapple Field," "Strawberries," "The Oars," "Sheridan," "Unknown Forebear," "Son," "Birdie," "Berryman," and "Yesterday": © 1983 by W. S. Merwin.

Abbreviations

AF	*(Asian Figures)*
CF	*The Compass Flower*
CL	*The Carrier of Ladders*
FF	*The First Four Books of Poems*
FI	*Finding the Islands*
HT	*Houses and Travellers*
L	*The Lice*
MPC	*The Miner's Pale Children*
MT	*The Moving Target*
OH	*Opening the Hand*
PPC	*Products of the Perfected Civilization* (selected writings of Sebastien Chamfort)
RM	*Regions of Memory: Uncollected Prose* (ed. Cary Nelson and Ed Folsom)
RT	*The Rain in the Trees*
STa	*Selected Translations 1948–1968*
STb	*Selected Translations 1968–1978*
UO	*Unframed Originals*
WUA	*Writings to an Unfinished Accompaniment*

PART ONE

The First Five Books of Poems

1

"Read Seeds Not Twigs"

A BEWILDERING ARRAY of forerunners have been adduced as influences on Merwin's early work. Glauco Cambon names Yeats and Pound plus Hart Crane, Valéry, and Auden; Cary Nelson agrees about Yeats but, in accordance with Harvey Gross, adds Keats; Richard Howard mentions St. John Perse, John Crowe Ransom, and Villon. Critics are united, however, in characterizing his first book, *A Mask for Janus* (published in the Yale Younger Poets Series in 1952). They have described its poetry as "formalist," "traditional," "elegant"—designations that fix this youthful work as typical of the academic poetry of the 1950s.[1] How can Merwin's early poetry emerge from such divergent sources yet present a unified facade? One answer is that critics only touch upon this early work while looking ahead to later, more problematic poetry, pausing just long enough to note features that signal its inconsequence. The critical tradition, then, inclines most commentators to dismiss Merwin's early writing as verse cut to a once-fashionable mode that bears traces of voices not fully assimilated.

Such a dismissal, however, is already a considerable misstep, for traits important to Merwin's later work exist embryonically in his earliest poetry. Rather than being highly formal or elegant, it displays a fondness for verse forms that are conspicuously rudimentary. Richard Wilbur deploys forms of elaborate refinement in "A Baroque Wall-Fountain in the Villa Sciarra," alternating meters in four-line stanzas while maintaining a strict rhyme scheme. By contrast, the forms in *A Mask for Janus*—the sonnet, the sestina, variations on the rondel, the epitaph, the *ubi sunt* poem, and the villanelle, as well as the carol, the song, and the ballad—are crude, even primal. They stand at the beginnings of European literature, among the earliest attempts to order language.

The influence weighing most heavily on Merwin's early work is Anonymous. No single forerunner accounts for its idiosyncrasies because it depends on a familiarity with medieval and pre-Renaissance verse, in English and the Romance languages. At Princeton, Merwin submitted his verse to John Berryman for commentary and attended R. P. Blackmur's seminars, but his field of study as a graduate student was Romance languages. In prefaces written in 1984 for *Four French Plays* and *From the Spanish Morning,* he recalled his early interest in "the origin of poetry," "the origin of drama," and "the origin of theater." A youthful enthusiasm for Pound focused on his early work of scholarship, *The Spirit of Romance* (1910). Pound sent a postcard in answer to Merwin's request for advice to the beginning writer: "Read seeds not twigs EP." Indeed, almost all of the literature Merwin would translate from 1947 to 1963 was either treated at length or noted in Pound's pages: *The Poem of the Cid* (1952–59), *Spanish Ballads* (1957–59), *Lazarillo de Tormes* (1960), *The Song of Roland* (1961), and drama by Lope de Vega and Lope de Rueda.[2]

Merwin's attraction to literature still in the process of finding its way, standing at the outset of a civilization, just beginning to take its shape even as it trails the disorder from which it is emerging, is a feature that endures throughout his work. It is the link between the ungainly, awkward poetry of his first collection and the sparse notations of his most celebrated volume, *The Lice* (1967); it is a connection that surfaces again in his experiments in the late 1970s with a "broken back line," a line interrupted with a prominent caesura like that displayed throughout *The Poem of the Cid.* It is an affinity registered in *(Asian Figures)* (1973), two- and three-line statements in the form of proverbs or riddles, and extending into the free verse of *Writings toward an Unfinished Accompaniment* (1973), where his interest lies in cultivating a wisdom literature that most closely resembles transcriptions of oral poetry from so-called primitive cultures. It is an interest that reappears in the poetry of *The Rain in the Trees* (1988), where he respectfully records his own limitations as a Westerner who stands outside the Hawaiian culture that Westerners have so heedlessly appropriated. And finally, it helps explain why the very lack of knowledge he has about the origins of his own family is ultimately not a barrier to the writing of his family memoirs but an impetus. Events in the past take on an air of compelling mystery once he realizes just how unshaped they remain, years after they have been complete.

The writer, for Merwin, should be a listener as much as an actor. The attentiveness that listening fosters becomes a natural limit on the writer's tendency to impose on material, to shape work in accordance with demands too exclusively his or her own. A danger Merwin never tires of appreciating is that language is always on the verge of losing its elements of transparency, on snapping its links with the actual world which, at its very best, it should reflect. Medieval and pre-Renaissance texts, shaped as they are by convictions of humility common to their time, are models of attentive propriety; they offer a tangential role, at best, to the sensibility of the narrator, who is engaged not in gestures of self-expression but in finding a description that will do justice to the intricacy in which he finds himself, not as a crucial instrument but as one ingredient among many. The extent to which Merwin is willing to stand aside, to evoke a world beyond himself, apart from his own sensibility, is the aspect of his work that remains most surprising, most idiosyncratic.

1

Just enough of that tendency is on display in *A Mask for Janus* that it remains uncertain how much the poetry's awkwardness stems from the clumsiness of a beginning poet and how much from Merwin's cultivating a way of listening that responds positively to the incomplete, the not-yet-fully shaped. Reviewing the volume, Richard Wilbur was left puzzled by what seemed odd infelicities. The appeal of "Blind William's Song" rests on the many different ways Merwin closes off each brief stanza: "Now he does it by rhyme, now word-repetition, now by alliteration, and one feels that the stanzas are all equally conclusive in form."[3] Yet Wilbur hesitates to suggest why such poetry needs a variety of closures; instead, he questions why Merwin cannot write more smoothly: "This makes one ask why he chooses to bother with syllabic verse, which seems to my thump-loving ear a rather weak formal device for English poetry (and especially for American) unless it is used in a strictly auxiliary way. One can't strain the lumps out of American and make it purl, and for me there is too frequent uncertainty, in the syllabic poems, as to where the thumps might fall." Wilbur's own writings utilize a strong, unhesitating iambic pressure, often in combination with pure rhyme. Merwin pointedly prefers short lines in slant rhyme. What Wilbur hears with some discomfort is a key to the oddity of this early work: slant rhyme expresses a wish to hear the line-ending close with authority, but the wish is never realized, only approximated, because the privilege of substantive closure is unavailable. Uncertainty prevails, since all order is provisional:

> How can the thin mind be able?
> How put off quaking only,
> Keeping all else simple,
> Even in wind steady? (FF, 20)

Characteristic of this early poetry, as in this stanza from "Meng Tzu's Song," is the firm line-ending. It is a gesture toward conclusiveness, an effort at completion that nonetheless fails to be satisfyingly complete. It can be heard as well in "Blind William's Song":

> Tuesday was dusty feet;
> I shall not be the first
> Who walked, and did not know
> The earth, the middle earth. (FF, 21)

Merwin's tropes replicate his own position as wanderer in search of an answer not forthcoming; he lights on points of rest that prove to be temporary. Inseparable from his unease is the hovering of the faint rhyme, marking a pause but never a conclusive halt. Closure remains tantalizingly out of reach. It is essential that the poem not flow: it is picking its way through a difficult field, choosing words with care.

Much that is open to criticism in Merwin's first book because it seems crude or awkward may be taken as a mark of his particular circumstances. The poetry is inherently discomforting, its speaker uneasy, a long way from home. In this respect, the volume's title proves misleading if it identifies Janus only as the god who represents two sides of truth. Janus is also the god of thresholds and beginnings who protects the wanderer. A typescript in an earlier, unpublished collection of Merwin's included a work addressed to Janus in his role as protector of voyagers.[4] In the two "Anabasis" poems Merwin presents voyages with no destination disclosed, as though his travelers had no choice but to embark on wandering. As wanderers they can neither stay at home nor discover a new home. Exiled, they are on their way toward realizing that their keen sense of being alien is the one true identity they will have. "Anabasis (II)" depicts a series of disappointing visits. Each begins promisingly but ends in dreariness:

> Our vision built on the approaching sand;
> We entered channels where the coral smiled,
>
> And but the countries of occasion found:
> There, at sundown, lodged where the tide lingers,
> Among the driftwood and the casual drowned,
> Slept on the lulled questions of those rivers. (FF, 8)

Disappointment after disappointment, always associated with arrival at port. Ultimately, these voyagers move on, with no certain end, growing accustomed to their rootless lot: "We turned from silence and fearfully made / Our small language in the place of night."

Along with the gentle, muted jarring of its slant rhymes, "Anabasis (II)" also expresses itself through an uneasy mixture of differing dictions, veering between the concrete and the abstract, vernacular statements and intellectual metaphors. Richard Howard identifies a similar shifting in other early Merwin poems and calls it "the Shakespearean doublet, violently yoking two nouns, one abstract, one concrete, into a resonant, unresolvable matrix: 'Wonder and white sheep lying like tombs.'"[5] But such yoking seems less ostentatiously dramatic than Howard makes out: it is as though the context is always shifting out from underneath. Just as contexts drop away, so slant rhymes continue to jar because nearly every stanza includes a pure rhyme with a slant rhyme. Finally, of the twenty quatrains in "Anabasis (II)" only two fail to end with a full stop; the majority end in a strong sentence with a period. But the poem itself is about restless wandering: "We seek a new dimension for the world," a sentence ends firmly, even as the statement belies any satisfaction. These ungainly, unlikely combinations guarantee the poem can never flow forward. They do not strike Merwin as inappropriate, for their awkwardness is in keeping with the anxiety that cannot believe answers are to be found yet keeps yearning for conclusiveness. The sensibility unfolding may be difficult to admire, but its presence is undeniably felt.

The quest that becomes an end in itself is a commonplace of modern literature. Merwin enhances it, though, by his tendency to minimize any lyrical outburst. With his reserve, the quest becomes a guarded undertaking in response to a constant menace. His early poems do not take wing and fly; they remain tight, clenched to themselves, taking small steps, and even the longest of them fail to develop. As variations on a theme, whole stanzas could be eliminated from both "Anabasis" poems without distortion.[6] His poems gain length by gathering a number of brief poems, each almost complete in itself but all dominated by a failure to be so (which in turn creates the need for another foray, the viewpoint restated from an additional perspective). Within his narrow rooms, he can be marvelously adept, precisely because he uses repetition to its fullest effect. In a situation that is fundamentally disturbing, repetition is not a sign of tedium but a mark of what little security is available.

With this attachment to repetition, it is proper that Merwin's two sestinas should be remarkable achievements, while his sonnets prove disappointing. The sestina is based upon remaining within a definite structure: the words that end every line in the six six-line stanzas are determined in the first stanza, and all six words must appear at the end of the other five stanzas, though in a different order, with the three-line envoi at the end using all six, two to a line. Yet within this patent limitation, Merwin is a success, in one sestina fluently generating variations on a line by Emerson, in the other summarizing a biography of Robert Graves. By contrast, his sonnets begin to crumble once the octet is passed, though the first eight lines can be stunning. Consider this early work, one of three published as a group:

> I trace a dark lie mastering the wall
> Till of an April day the wind is all
> And we are night, the coiled shadow, the stare—
> Withered tongues rattle the trellis air.
> Hours by their habit curve in the dark to lie
> Perfect as that blindness where we die.
> Now what man knows his bread from any stone?
> Each bone is fear and each dog barks alone.

In the sestet, the pace slows. Syntax coagulates, rhythms falter, and metaphors fatten obscurely:

Here while the deep hill like a finished sun,
Its dark perfection measuring yet the eye,
Heat exhales but no light I have begun
For the noisome pride a canon and charity
Lest fall the mind though from no lifted choir
To deafen in the rhetoric of fire.[7]

The sonnet form demands development; its organization is keyed by significant change past the octet. When he comes to the shift, Merwin rumbles and gasps. By contrast, the sestina plays lightly with any claim for development: it turns around its key words as it recovers them at the terminal point of each line. Yet no flamboyant digressions are permitted, for the end-words must be kept in focus, preparing for the envoi where all six will appear together. Within such constriction, Merwin moves adeptly, even expansively.

2

If these early works defer significant development, what keeps them from remaining hopelessly static? The answer lies in the shifting perspectives that Merwin discloses. The framework of the poem, hedged by its unyielding form, remains strictly limited, and opportunities for narrative are negligible. But it is possible, even necessary, to reconceive matters from a different perspective. That shift in point of view, even when it may yield a position of greater austerity, is the shift on which many poems depend. It is, moreover, a poetic signature that will reappear in subsequent poetry. Scale is never fixed with certainty in a Merwin poem: the significant may dwindle and the inconsequential may loom large. For one of the operations that makes poetry a valued art is that it constantly reclaims the power and authority of the mind in its ability to see beyond what had been accepted as an absolute assumption. Against such assumptions, evoked at first as solid barriers, Merwin frequently moves to suppose alternatives that are equally compelling. What appeared to be a barrier becomes, from another position, a threshold of new understanding. None of this unfolds dramatically; on the contrary, the supplanting of one perspective by another frequently occurs as a near-invisible change that is intended to seem inevitable.

Such a shift motivates "The Bones of Palinurus Pray to the North Star," one of Merwin's shortest poems. Its original introductory note was twelve words longer than its text: "Aeneas' pilot was swept at night from the stern of the vessel shortly before Aeneas reached Latium. He managed to get to shore, but was murdered by the inhabitants, and his body was left to the tide-water."[8] It is one of several epitaph poems in the volume, including a companion-poem of equal brevity, "Epitaph." "Epitaph," however, is a firm denial, rejecting any efforts at comprehension, while the address to the North Star is a consolation that pivots on accepting that there can be no consolation. Within its four lines, a subtle shift occurs that is a twist in perspective: the situation does not change but one's attitude toward it does. The poem moves from a figure of isolation to a figure of austerity, a movement that hinges on the idea of the candid, on clear and lucid speech. To model oneself not on the disorderly surface of a "night wake," a passage churned into scattered foam, but on the austerity of the constant pole star is to rise beyond self-pity into dignity; it allows the fragments to "gleam" like the stars even as they remain in pieces, scattered, pointing no direction. Beginning on a note of broken desperation ("Console us"), the poem allows constancy to be substituted for consolation. And behind this transformation is the example of the navigator, who has so often turned from the uncertainty of the moment, to look past disorder to the North Star, steadfast in its remoteness. The poem replaces the short view with the long view, the intensity of the moment with the spaciousness of the eternal. As the eternal achieves ascendancy, the fragmented bones no longer seem scattered but epitomize the finality of death, endured with stoic patience. Speaking out of that finality, they attain the steadfastness of a star.

This epitaph displays the attributes of Merwin's early poetry. The language is neither elevated nor demotic. Its poetic elements are modest to the point of invisibility: the assonance of "whiteness / night," the alliteration of "candor / constant" and "desolate / direction," and the syntactical pattern of two sentences end-stopped in contrast to the run-over last two lines. This last point may be the only dramatic technical effect, since it depends upon rhythm, line break, and repetition all working together. In the final line, "Us" receives an emphasis it did not when it appeared twice in the first line. The line break that follows "over" anticipates that the next word will be emphasized. Even when the first syllable of "desolate" receives a stress that undermines some of the strength in "Us," the word still rings out in contrast to its earlier appearances. The bones, if not exactly united, are no longer quite so dispersed. The undermining effect, along with the uplifting effect, accords with the idea that some consolation has been reached, though not enough, never enough.

Like many poems in *A Mask for Janus,* this poem takes death as an opportunity to expand understanding. Rarely is death conceived as a fearful presence. It can exist darkly and furtively, as though crouching among shadows; but if it is respected, embraced, acknowledged, then it opens onto a wider expanse. Then it ushers in the special presence Merwin associates with stones and explains why "stone" should be a key word in this poetry, defined in opposition to "shadow." A majority of the early poems employ one or both key terms.[9] Both shadow and stone are avatars of death, but they contrast with each other decisively. To be shadowed or in shadow is to be taunted by an uncertainty that is fearful; but to be a stone or among stones is to survey a chaotic vista from a calm distance. The modulation in "The Bones of Palinurus" from the disorderly wake of the sea to the remote austerity of the North

Star is, in fact, a paradigmatic shift, one that parallels contrasts elsewhere between the shadowy and the stonelike.

Shadows are not, as they might be, graceful; they tend to mask gestures of helplessness. In "Carol of the Three Kings," the speakers associate shadows with doubt and uncertainty:

> We have been a shadow
> Many nights moving,
> Swaying many nights
> Between yes and no. (FF, 51)

Shadows, like a dark animal side of ourselves, are all deception. There are "shadow-plays, / trepidation of fingers, / ruse of limbs" in "Canción y Glosa." When shadows are not delusive they are desiccating. "For a Dissolving Music" opens with:

> What shall be seen?
> Limbs of a man
> old and alone
> his shadow with him,
> going and gone. (FF, 23)

In "A Dance of Death," both desiccation and uncertainty are caught together in the scholar: "I sat like a shadow, / The light sallow, / Reasoning yes and no" (FF, 19).

Consistently, shadows figure as a negative element, creating irresolution, denying substantiality, frustrating clarity. These associations are not unlikely; what is surprising is Merwin's choice of stone as positive, as in "Herons": "I became the quiet stone / By a river where the winds / Favor honest thoughts" (FF, 44). To be stonelike is to enjoy the clarity of honest thoughts. Though associated with death, stone also stands for clarity, firmness, certainty—like the words of the stone that phrase the agreement or compact in "Epitaph." Unlike the shadow, torn between yes and no, the stone offers soothing completion. But the stone only resembles pure repose; it also looks back at life from within its own composure. The pure voice of sweet denial in "Epitaph" emanates from a profound composure, but it speaks in response to someone's agitated question. Rather than emblems of withdrawal, stones are participants sublimely at ease with themselves. Not all are as lucky as the quiet stone by the "river where the winds / Favor honest thoughts," but their presence introduces calm in disorderly scenes. The speaker in "Blind William's Song" asks:

> Lull the stones over me,
> I that on Saturday
> Closed about myself
> And raged and was the grave. (FF, 22)

Stones offset disorder, evoking a peace that stands in contrast to the violence of living. The speaker in "Ode: The Medusa Face" says: "I cannot tell if stone is upon me / Healing me, clotting time until I stand / Dead" (FF, 36). But a man who has been turned to stone may "stand in a sloth of stone," unaccustomed to the eternal perspective in which he now stands, the awesome lethargy of time. The agitation of the speaker's very question ("I cannot tell . . .") indicates he does not yet know what he may yet learn.

To be stone is not to be free of life, only to appreciate life from within a vast perspective. "Hermione on Simulacra" is spoken by the queen of *The Winter's Tale* who, to withdraw from her husband's violent jealousy, has become a statue. She begins by saying, "For comfort I became a stone." But that, as Merwin points out, is the wrong reason to become stonelike; one can long for silence and school oneself in discipline, and banish motion, but after all that, one will "have found / No simplicity in stone." For everything that is not stonelike gathers about what is stonelike, including the feverish thoughts of King Leontes, who exists in his own fantasies as "a prey / To the darkness of premonitions" and a "vagrant" only in the "shadow" cast by the statuelike Hermione. The queen finds no simplicity; rather, she discovers the strength to bear pain. Hermione, out of her deep placidity, becomes the widening, expansive complement to Leontes's desperation: "I am the night where he is blind / And I the orbit of his prayers." And in this she stands triumphant, her final lines quiet, authentic, approving, as she embraces all from within her strength:

> I had intended but to be
> My picture in a stone, but I
> Took shape of death and have become
> Death, and all things come to me.
>
> Death, in my varied majesty
> I am astonished in flesh and stone
> That you should be simplicity
> Whose visage so resembles me. (FF, 55)

This is the inner composure for which Merwin is striving in all his early work; his yearning for it helps explain why the poems often seem so raw, so edgy, so crude, even as they move with a steadfast care, attentive to rhymes just out of earshot.[10]

Within this unnerving world, which is actually a world of "varied majesty," a composure may be found—resting, perhaps, in the candor of a simple speech, avoiding pretension, speaking of generalized landscapes. One certainty is the inevitability of death, but even that, from a wider perspective, from the timelessness of the stones, is what all things come to. To bear such an eternal perspective in all its vastness demands a strong character—a virtue upon which Merwin will, in the course of his poetry, place a high premium. The poems move stiffly, but that is a mark of their restraint; if they seem prematurely aged that is a sign of the responsibilities they take upon themselves. They are not immediately appealing, offering an uneasy composure instead of elegance and felicity. When they are effective, it is because they evoke, without dramatically portraying it, a world whose disorder is positively menacing. Yet in their modesty, they achieve a homely grace more beguiling than it may at first seem.

3

Yet virtually every facet of Merwin's early work is absent from "Dictum: For a Masque of Deluge," the poem W. H. Auden singled out for praise in his foreword to the volume. The most recent poem in the collection, written in April 1951 and included at the last moment, it looks ahead to Merwin's next volume and differs from its predecessors in notable ways.[11] Its ten-line stanzas encourage a spaciousness not available in the tight four-line stanza previously preferred. Its metrical framework is a loose and fluent blank verse, a world remote from the painstaking five-beat line of "Anabasis (II)." Its final exception to rules otherwise enforced throughout the volume is that it takes place indoors: we witness a masque dramatizing the story of Noah and the Flood. Earlier poems depicted journeys through landscapes or seascapes, in contexts without clear boundaries, while "Dictum" highlights a play in production, under controlled circumstances. Before, journeys were open-ended and uncertain, prone to disconcerting shifts. Now, Merwin surrounds a familiar narrative, lavishing attention on details, each a delight in itself.

The immediate charm of the poem lies in the beguiling simplicity of the production it describes. The company has relied on its ingenuity. Noah's ark is a basket, and the creatures entering are represented by the shadows they cast, while those excluded appear painted on a wheel above the stage. The bareness of the stage is constantly present; the props display their origin: Noah appears, after the Flood, "under the all-colored / paper rainbow, whose arc he sees as promise." He must use his eye movements to indicate events. Since rain cannot fall upon the stage, the script replaces it with a special quality of speech: "So, with talk, like a blather of rain begun, / Weather will break" (FF, 38). Always in the foreground of Merwin's description is the resourceful way the performers adapt to limitations and transform them ingeniously. The obvious delight of the poem is to capture the audience's delight in witnessing so ingenious a performance. As the title indicates, we are presented not just with the play unfolding before us but with its "Dictum," the stage directions and production decisions that animate the play. We are in the audience, witnessing the familiar events, as well as backstage, appreciating the production itself as a performance.

This double perspective, however, is innovative in more than one respect. For one thing, it clearly acknowledges Merwin's own fascination with the art of drama. Play writing, in Merwin's earliest years, was no secondary occupation:

for every page of poetry in his 1949 and 1950 notebooks there is at least a page of dramatic dialogue, usually in verse.[12] These pages are not casual jottings but full-scale plans for productions, down to sketches that illustrate stage settings (fig. 1). Conceiving drama as production was nothing new for Merwin: what is new here is that his affection for theater should appear in his poetry. The effect is to introduce a clash of perspectives that calls into question attitudes previously on display in his poetry. His focus on the ingenuity of the production, on the dictum rather than the narrative, undermines the moralizing propensity of the story of Noah and the Flood. For the narrative of the Flood asserts the authority of a dour Creator who intervenes alarmingly in the course of human events. He exacts punishment for misdeeds by lowering the curtain on his earlier production and deciding that he will start over again with a smaller cast. By itself the narrative avers that human affairs are subject to abrupt reversals over which we can never have control; it is the sense of the world that underpins Merwin's voyagers who pick their way with caution through vast, uncertain landscapes. But "Dictum" splits off from supporting this version of a stage-manager God who works through Noah to achieve the effects he desires; instead, the poem emphasizes the actors playing quite different roles, as stage managers of themselves. Whether onstage or backstage or in the audience, the directors and actors and observers affirm a playful, free intelligence that takes positive delight in seeing problems solved with ingenuity. Moralized narrative is a secondary construct, a convenient framework, an occasion for theater.

Nothing so playful even glanced across Merwin's earlier work; this poetry would have declared its somber affinity with the tale of Noah. To measure how far we have come we need only compare "Dictum" with a predecessor, an unfinished poem begun in December 1949 entitled "Masque" (fig. 2). It also describes the occasion of a medieval mystery play, and like "Dictum" it opens before the production begins:

> There some faced
> Neighbors, and resurrected old-begun
> Arguments or, impatient, some
> Stamped the summer ground and stared
> Random direction.

Discord is resolved, however, as soon as the production is under way. This company performs the story of Jonah and the whale on a bare stage whose rude origins remain evident:

> An obscure corner, swaying, of that frame,
> Shadowed the fruitless, the improbable sea.
> The ranged idols of Ninevah
> To an odd song swallowed were,
> This we have seen, believing impartially.

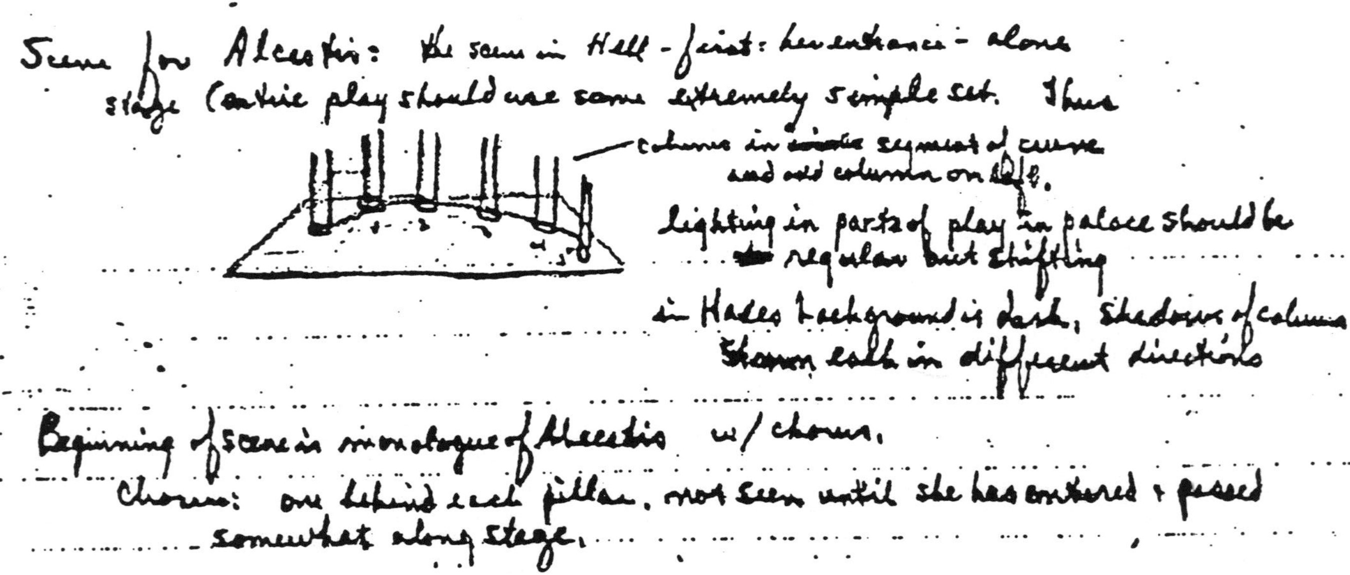

Figure 1. Enlarged sketch of stage setting and notes for "Shadows of Horses" (originally entitled "Alcestio"), a retelling of the Admetus and Alcestis tale from Notebook 09:1151, c. 1949–50. Merwin's notes and research for his plays were always extensive, sometimes in excess of any of his preparatory work for poetry.

MASQUE

Where we gathered the ~~Stream~~ river retraced
~~In wonderment, the~~ afternoon,
Lingered behind our whispers; there some faced
Neighbors, ~~and~~, resurrected old-begun
Argument, or, impatient, some
Stamped the summer ground and stared
Random directions; still a few became
As masks of quiet, their eyes turned, vacant, toward
The naked stage, the flimsy sheet
Hiding ~~the~~ other voices. Came
Tardily to that intenser light,
~~[illegible]~~s of humans, ~~the~~ ~~[illegible]~~ shadow, came
~~Strange~~ faces following ~~[illegible]~~
Prologue from the rough mask ~~singing~~ song
As ~~though~~ suspended from our time and ~~sight~~ eyes,
As ~~on~~ no ground or ear; others ~~then sang~~ began
Loud analects, postured and filed
Entrances; a gourd flower swung
Against the arras; its mystery entailed
The furtive prophet Jonas and his sign:
Three with one shape, one speech became
Leviathan, voice of many;
An ~~The~~ obscure corner, swaying, of that frame,
Shadowed the fruitless, the improbable sea.
The ranged idols of Ninevah
To an odd song swallowed were,
This we have seen, believing partially.
At our dispersion the late sky was fire
But darkness caught us privately
Before the shadow and its bone
Fed in the lighted house, reposed and dry,
~~We have dreamed~~ flowers whose untouchable sign
In that rainy, contagious place
The mind, a relic is, and quiet
As the evening's dead on whose decided face
Morning repeats the malice and the light.

~~[illegible]~~ or
Dreaming

Figure 2. Typescript of "Masque" (unpub. TS. 19:006/008a, c. Dec. 1949). An unusual explanatory note signed by Merwin on the holograph manuscript reads: "This is abandoned draft of a poem, written in December 1949. In April 1951 the poem was re-cast—'Dictum: For a Masque of Deluge'—but I had forgotten this earlier attempt—wrote *Dictum* almost at a sitting and found this later." The note may have been written for a display of his manuscripts sometime in the 1950s at the University of New York at Buffalo. Despite the note, "Masque" had not been left unread since December 1949; its two concluding lines were recast as the final two lines of "Variations on a Line by Emerson," the final draft of which is dated November 13, 1950 (and titled "Variations on a Line by Bryant" [TS. 19:6/014e]).

Merwin insists the production enchants, despite its rawness, transforming impatient crowd into enraptured audience. Art, in "Masque," is soothing; almost hypnotically, it quells disorder. By contrast, in "Dictum" the audience never forgets a performance is unfolding: art is a pleasure that all share by appreciating the details of production. Just the opposite of "Masque," "Dictum" turns a potentially passive audience into active stage managers, enjoying their glimpse behind the scenes.

Merwin indirectly alludes to the contrast between the story performed and the performing of the story, between a world of austere belief and a world of fictive delight. A late addition to the manuscript is a stanza describing the beasts left behind to perish in the Flood:

> the bull from the lotus flower,
> With wings at his shoulders; and a goat, winged;
> A serpent undulating in the air;
> A lion with wings like falling leaves;
> These are to wheel on a winged wheel above
> The sullen ark, while hare, swine, crocodile,
> Camel and mouse come; and the sole man, always,
> Lurches on childish limbs above the basket. . . . (FF, 39)

The contrast is telling. The fabulous winged creatures are first drafts doomed to be excised from the world's text. Those allowed to enter the "sullen ark" are not so impressive: they are tiny or ungainly, or crawl close to the ground. Man trails behind them "on childish limbs." After the Flood, the world is less diverse; the beasts that remain are less outrageous. A wonderful multiplicity has been lost after the intervention of the revisionary Creator.

That multiplicity returns again, however, in the pleasure and delight of theater and poetry. Merwin's opening moments are the most playful:

> There will be the cough before the silence, then
> Expectation; and the hush of portent
> Must be welcomed by a diffident music
> Lisping and dividing its renewals. (FF, 38)

As blank verse, this is sheer delight. The first line outrageously delays a strong beat all the way to the fifth word ("cough"), creating a rhythmic lapse that reproduces the silence out of which "cough" is heard. The "then" dangling at the line's end rapidly swerves into the crisply enunciated "Expectation"—which summarily halts. That pause leads into a series of hushed sounds that gradually disclose the "diffident music" that begins to flow. The sound of "i" trails through these last lines, in "diffident music" and "Lisping" and "dividing its," preparing to make the three disparate vowels in "renewals" sound gorgeously extravagant.

Merwin counteracts his deft beginning with a conclusion stunning in quite another way. Exiting the performance, we are brought up against this threatening scene:

> so now the dove
> Makes assignations with the olive tree,
> Slurs with her voice the gestures of the time:
> The day foundering, the dropping sun
> Heavy, the wind a low portent of rain. (FF, 40)

From the opening stanza, the word "portent" reappears, but while the earlier portent was all possibility and hope, this one is all darkening menace. Just as unnerving is the enjambment that stresses "the dropping sun / Heavy," for there has been nothing with weight in the production, from its paper rainbow to its ark-as-a-basket. The production was all light and air, a production of the mind in the service of art. The world as it exists beyond the stage contains forces not so amenable; the gathering storm is an authoritative presence that suddenly endows the play's story with a nasty verisimilitude.

"Dictum" is a revolutionary poem indeed. This is a new Merwin, but a Merwin looking back at himself as he had been a short time before, now seeing with a new generosity, surrounding the stiff narrative of Noah and the Flood with all the delightful details he had once been careful to purge from his own stiff narratives. Such a swerve, in which he rounds back upon his own previous work and recasts it from a wider perspective, is in keeping with that habit of mind, evident in his earlier work, that is sensitive to the changes that will occur with a new viewpoint. But it is also a pattern that recurs throughout his career, often in circumstances like those under which "Dictum" was composed: after completing a series of shorter poems that circle around a similar theme and review it from different angles, he will conceive a poem of some length, not to summarize the short poems that precede it but to reconsider them from a larger perspective.

The appearance of a singular work—a master-poem that overarches its predecessors—is no accident, but linked with writing habits Merwin has cultivated. He has taken steps that encourage him to be prolific. Rather than singling out an individual poem for intense concentration, turning its implications over until he produces a work of considerable polish whose nuances have been exhaustively explored, he completes poems quickly, one after another, taking each through a limited series of drafts. These poems usually appear as groups, clustered alongside each other in volumes. They are not quite integrated enough to be a long poem, or even a suite, yet they are not works that stand apart from one another. They are cycles, general explorations, like the "shadow" and "stone" poems scattered throughout *A Mask for Janus*. They convey Merwin's concerns at one point in time, concerns he is working out in this public fashion. The cycle may simply exhaust its own momentum—or it may yield to a master-poem, a work that radically recasts the material Merwin has been sifting over and over.

These master-poems tend to be landmarks of Merwin's career. "The Drunk in the Furnace" is such a master-poem, a final comment on the quality of exile implicit in the family-history poems of the last third of *The Drunk in the Furnace* (1960). But the true master-poem is not simply an end, it is also a beginning: it is a pivotal work, in transition between cycles, though the new direction it is disclosing is not yet apparent. Most notably, then, the master-poem represents Merwin's commitment to a poetry that remains unfinished, in process. The preeminent virtue of poetry is that it will go on for as long as one lives, one of the many stages in human growth. More precisely, for one cycle to end another must be ready to begin; the master-poem is the transitional work that signals the shift to a new perspective that now calls for its own exploration.

In its final darkening, "Dictum" recalls other early work by Merwin. It differs in its opening, its delight in the virtue of beginnings. But that delight plays through the whole poem, in its subtle celebration of the winged creatures excluded from salvation, in its implicit criticism of a paternal Creator who thought twice about his creations and pared down his initial effort into a more manageable species. The realization that art can be play—that poetry can be extravagant, sumptuous, self-delighting—signals a new beginning, to be lavishly on display in the love poetry of his next collection. The person to whom "Dictum" was first dedicated—Dido Milroy, herself an aspiring playwright and soon Merwin's wife—also receives the dedication in *The Dancing Bears.*

2

Appreciations of Innocence

MOST CRITICS, when bothering with Merwin's early work at all, have considered his first two books together.[1] But *The Dancing Bears* (1954) differs from its predecessor in several ways. Most notably, it is a collection of love poetry. Even in poems not demonstrative of love, the thought of love is never remote. A group of "Songs" resembles earlier verse (short-line quatrains in off rhyme) but there is a reason for the severity of these poems. Their speaker is terse because he has lost his love. The form does not reflect a sensibility reserved because of threatening circumstances but a distraught sensibility that has turned sullen because it is unable to love another.

Another feature of this collection is its trace of an organizing narrative. It begins in the tense, reserved mode of Merwin's first book. In its opening poem a voyager arrives at a dark land and is granted an unsettling vision of his head separated from his body. That image of the unnatural split between mind and body is the problem to be solved in this volume. Later, the "Songs" offer an explanation for this dissatisfaction: love has been frustrated. But after "East of the Sun and West of the Moon," everything swarms with change—the poet grapples with Proteus in "Proteus," and in "Colloquy at Peniel" Jacob confronts the angel with whom he wrestles. The contrast to the tight-lipped "Songs" is found in three long "Cansos"—"songs" in an elevated language. In these, song is recaptured in its essence because the poet can concentrate upon his love.

In the context of celebrating love, Merwin's title is an especially pertinent quotation from Flaubert (in Richard Howard's translation): "Human speech is like a cracked kettle where we bat out tunes for dancing bears when what we want to attain is the stars."[2] If human speech seems flawed, it is because our aspirations are so high, and those aspirations are linked to loving another.

Even Merwin's wonderfully cadenced language, which he offers in celebration of his love, is as inferior to love's beauty as a cracked kettle is to the music of the spheres. Merwin is consciously striving for an elevated discourse, inherently attractive; the subject to whom it is directed is herself so splendid that language can never be elevated enough. The allure of even the most sumptuous passage is as nothing—the clumsy lurching of a dancing bear—to the splendor of love's beauty.

Although these notions could be related to the medieval settings of *A Mask for Janus* through courtly love, a fascination with verse of the Middle Ages is never in the foreground.[3] Merwin is expanding in all directions, his excess permitted because it is as nothing compared to his love. This explains why, in the last two "Cansos," Merwin imitates Wallace Stevens in one, Dylan Thomas in the other. Rather than imitating them, he would contend with them on a field of honor. He would engage them as rivals, using their images and rhythms and diction, to insist that his own love grants him imaginative power in excess of theirs.[4]

The "Canso" that Merwin writes in his own voice, without contesting the voice of another, is the first of the three; in this poem, his presence is felt most directly in his use of a poetic line that is neither syllabic verse nor blank verse. If it were read according to blank verse norms, as alternating syllable-stress meter, it would violate more rules than it obeyed. But if read as emphasized below, it establishes its own rules:

> And that *stern evening, speak*ing of *snares,*
> Where the *hun*ter had *fal*len, where even the *wise* might *fall,*
> Or *speak*ing, in No*vem*ber, of *prim*roses,
> When *doubt* possessed me, and my *eyes fell,*
> To *stones,* half *trust*ing in *stones,* and my mind *fell*
> To a *mer*ciless *win*ter of bleak *words,* yet *you*
> Beyond *words,* be*lieved* me to be a *gen*tle
> *Sea*son, and *I,* as from *sleep* re*turn*ing
> Was *thence* the *sign* and green *wind* of *spring.* (FF, 108)

These lines diverge strikingly from blank verse norms. In blank verse the number of syllables per line is apt to remain constant; the number may drop to nine or rise to twelve, but further adjustments would be destabilizing. In Merwin's passage, the number of syllables varies from nine to fourteen. His lines can expand because their constant is the number of beats in each line; where those beats are distributed is irrelevant. Another violation of blank verse rules involves this distribution. The second foot in blank verse is the most metrically sensitive unit, because a substitution of an iamb at so early a point in the line jeopardizes the rhythmic base. In Merwin's passage, it is impossible to find an iamb in the equivalent of a second foot. The first three lines yield a trochee, a dactyl, and an anapest.

Yet Merwin's lines do not seem disheveled. His strong-stress meter depends on sounds to signal where a stress should fall. In the first line, the emphasis on *stern* is matched with an emphasis on *speaking* and *snares.* The accent is guided not by the alternation of stressed and unstressed syllables but by recurring sounds. One effect is to displace attention from the line as a unit toward the larger unit of the entire thought, carried through a series of lines. Pausing, shifting, digressing, the poem broadens its expanse, even as the impetus of recurring sounds keeps a steady pace. The passage lives by its own rules: alliteration ("winter / words," "Season / sleep," "sign / spring"), repetition ("fallen / fall / fell," "stones /stones"), and consonance and assonance ("half tru*st*ing in *st*ones," "S*ea*son, and I, as from sl*ee*p").

For the next several years, up until the free verse of *The Moving Target,* Merwin's poetry will follow this measure, as all-purpose for him as iambic pentameter was to his contemporaries. He now treads lightly, with an offhand grace remarkably different from the pinched severity of his first volume. The "thumping" that Richard Wilbur missed is not a serious absence because the lines bristle with activity. His achievement is a poetic surface with a sumptuous texture that is luminously attractive, a line ample, casual, and discursive at the same time as it is delicate, elegant, and alluring.

1

A note to the first edition of *The Dancing Bears* suggests a practical explanation for Merwin's new fluency: " 'East of the Sun and West of the Moon,' 'Fable,' and the three Cansos have been read on the BBC Third Programme."[5] Unlike other American poets in the 1950s, who rarely had the opportunity to hear how their poetry sounded off the page, Merwin was in a position to judge his writing for its performative features, not simply because of his occasional readings on the BBC (where it was usually spoken by professional actors) but also because of his commitment to play writing. The strong-stress meter that distinguished his poetry in the mid-1950s paralleled an interest in verse drama.

Drama in verse is a ticklish proposition: on the one hand, lineation encourages intensified language that can telegraph speech rapidly; on the other hand, a language that has been unnaturally heightened fails to sound conversational. Versification, to strike a delicate balance between these oppositions, has to be handled gingerly. Merwin's theater pieces divide dialogue into lines but avoid imposing a rigid rhythm on the cadences of speech. Regularly, the last word in a line is a key term in the character's speech. It benefits from the slight stress that falls on the end-word, as in this interchange from "The Wood of Women" (circa 1952–53):

MARTIN: Too much of the sweet wine for ladies
You've had, and the dancing's turned your head,
And I shouldn't have let you come with such
An enormous fan. A woman with a big fan
I've always heard, feels she must expand
Her capriciousness to match it. You're worse
Than usual tonight.
PILAR: (as a young man walks through)
I'm always worse
Than usual. I should hope so! Usual!
And I will be, too.
(flirting with the young man)
Now I'll leave you.[6]

This interchange has been deftly constructed: it does not sound versified, even as the speakers, lightly stressing the end-words, would emphasize important terms.

Although Merwin's work in the theater flourished between 1951 and 1956 when he was in England, the kind of drama he was writing had no precedent there. For Merwin, a commitment to the theater was a commitment to drama in verse, a form that attained its finest expression in the French classical drama of the seventeenth and eighteenth centuries. His earliest scholarly essay, a 1949 review of Martin Turnell's study of Corneille, Molière, and Racine, ended by announcing a void that neither the novel nor the poem could fill; only poetic drama, he concluded, offered the support of a rigorous form while allowing for a range of different voices.[7] Merwin stood behind this somewhat unfashionable position. Not only did he work unstintingly for five years to resurrect poetic drama, but the drama he set out to write usually took place in premodern times, and it presented personality types rather than individual characters. One of his earliest pieces was "Shadows of Horses," a version of the Greek tale of Admetus and Alcestis in a manner quite different from Euripides' tragicomedy. "The Wood of Women," set in sixteenth-century Seville, was a retelling of the Don Juan legend. "Darkling Child," which enjoyed a brief run on the London stage in early 1956, took place in the Puritan England of the seventeenth century. Only "The Monument" was a partial exception to Merwin's rules: it was a contemporary comedy about the goings-on of rambunctious Bohemian artists and eccentrics; even then, as a comedy, it restricted itself to types rather than realistic characters.[8]

The interest of such theater lies not in realistic portrayals; as in "Dictum," what the audience appreciates is not the story, which is apt to be familiar, but the pleasure of the stagecraft, the business the playwright has concocted to sustain the plot. This helps explain why Merwin borrows his stories from other sources and why he prefers types to characters. The audience is not to be held by the dialogue as though actual encounters were being witnessed; instead, the audience remains slightly apart, aware of the actuality of the performance, conscious of the pattern as it is unfolding. As in "Dictum," Merwin remains intent on leaving his audience alert to the fact that the artwork before them is never entirely engrossing; it is an approximation, a gesture toward an effect, not an object that commands total allegiance.

Merwin brought to his plays strong convictions about the virtue of the classical drama. The lengthiest comment in his 1949 essay is, in fact, a defense of Racine's *Phaedra* as a study of universal truths. Merwin quarrels with Turnell's insistence that the play is dominated by seventeenth-century doctrines of predestination and original sin; we can understand Phaedra's downfall, Turnell says, only if we appreciate the religious conventions held by Racine and his audience. But Merwin feels this jeopardizes the viability of classical drama by requiring us to bring historical knowledge to bear on the play. He offers an explanation hinging on the universalized term of "fate" rather than predestination; what is universal in the play is the "evidence of human helplessness to control the human process." Classical drama needs no historical context. Instead, it instills an awareness that "the nature of man is shown to be necessarily faulty and innocence is admittedly impossible."

He explores this notion in "The Wood of Women," his variation on the Don Juan legend. As in classical drama, the fundamentals of the story are already well known. What remains to be admired is the deftness with which the playwright arranges his material. The playwright's arrangements, moreover, are never out of mind because the Devil remains a central character who appears at conspicuous moments to comment upon the story. The Devil, however, does not precisely manipulate events: he merely sets them in motion by introducing characters to each other at critical times. The Devil cannot, and need not, shape matters because he knows that events have an impetus all their own. Once certain effects take place, they will lead inevitably to further occurrences; like the playwright, like the audience, the Devil is ultimately a spectator who can be no more than a witness to the human condition. He can comment upon what he sees, cynically or wittily, with a debonair attitude, but he is helpless to intervene.

The Devil looming over "The Wood of Women" lends the play its distinction precisely because he is not an omnipotent figure; he is, like all of us, condemned to remain in a world that is radically imperfect. How that imperfection is presented is central to Merwin's stagecraft. Don Juan, world-weary, bored with his conquests, complains that while he has everything, something yet seems to be missing. The Devil asks: "what / Have you ever wanted that you have not had / Without measure?" and then goes on to enumerate Don Juan's achievements:

The coins for all palms, the keys
To every door, the murmurs and words of persuasion
For all ears, pride unbounded and its
Satisfactions unbounded; a luck unbelievable
In the teeth of hazard and drawn swords; health
Without wavering, strength unwearied, appetite,
Which is the love of life, its secret soul
And very charity, all pleasures
And the limbs of all women—
JUAN: I owe none of these
To you.

DEVIL: —all these without debtorship, without
The burdens of compassion, without fatigue,
Without loss whatsoever, without conscience
Lingering, or entanglements,
Without mortal limitations and without
—To you—mortal consequences. You are,
In short, a monster.

The Devil's speech, after its interruption, crisply swerves to the other side of the ledger, suggesting the source of Don Juan's ennui: everything has fallen to him as a gift, exacting no payment of any kind. But the world, as the Devil knows, is not made that way.

When Don Juan expresses a longing to fall in love genuinely, the Devil is quick to arrange a meeting with the young widow Anna. She has been lamed by a fall from a horse, and her physical imperfection keeps him from viewing her as someone he is drawn to conquer. But her flaw prefigures the bitter truth the play unfolds: once Don Juan is in love, once he has discovered another he loves more than himself, then he has fallen into this broken world, where every gain is offset by a loss. Although the final act was never plotted to Merwin's satisfaction and the play remained unfinished, the conclusive event was to be the death of his heroine by her own hand, following an interlude in which she and Don Juan, having confessed their love, enjoy complete happiness. After her death, Don Juan, as he had earlier wished, will now experience fully what it means to be human, no longer a monster—the essence of which is to feel a loss so deep, so incommensurable, that it is beyond grieving. He is complete as a human being when he cannot escape his incompleteness.

This the Devil knows from the inside, for in Merwin's conception he is the figure who has lost more than any mortal. In one of the few passages written for the final act, the Devil was to lapse into this reminiscence:

The first star
Always like a tear in heaven. Listen, Juan:
Once when Paradise was a home I had

And earth was adolescent, a summer virgin
Lying among its groves—there were those of us
At the right hand of glory who on nights like this
Looked down, looked down from heaven
And saw, a little lower than the angels,
At country doorways the mortal girls
Between the starlight and the candlelight
Stretching indolent bodies: breasts lifted and fell
Sighing, hands for no reason played; we saw
Night forming as a gust to press their skirts
Against their thighs—oh women have been since those days
But a long falling off, believe me—we saw
How the days like garments fell from them utterly,
Not as with us; till their lips and eyes,
Their very imperfection came to seem
A maddening nakedness; till there were those
Who from watching with me, turned away their faces
In fear; till others among us
Could not contain ourselves till we had known
The brevity of those bodies and all the angel
Was trammeled in such mortality, till I
Too mindful of humanity, requited
But not appeased, locked in some woman, cried,
"The mind of heaven could not know itself
Till the mortal was its image." How it is now
With that music the stars once made among themselves
I do not know, and heaven may be height only
These days, for all I know. Hell, not a woman,
Even on nights like this was made to receive me,
And I for my pains am left too much my self.

In this unguarded moment, the Devil seems least monstrous, most innocent—recapturing his youth, bringing it closer and still closer, only to have the spell broken as the sound of his own voice speaks the words of unorthodoxy, and, as the vision fades, being suddenly weighted with the burdens of age. The passage, in brief, recapitulates the understanding developed in "The Wood of Women." We reach too far beyond ourselves, and we jeopardize all we have cherished, and make ourselves castaways in a broken world. Classical poetic drama, as Merwin conceives it, is not designed to present a harmonious resolution: quite the contrary, it is to articulate the paradox of the human condition with a clarity so sharp it stings.

2

In one respect, Merwin's light touch remains evident in his poetic dramas. His plays, usually set in a remote time and culture, unfold in patterns that ask to be appreciated for their generalized, universal truths. On the other hand, the distance Merwin achieves through artifice encourages him to deal with truths that are disconcertingly painful. Poetic drama, in his conception, would cultivate a certain strength of character in its audience. Not surprisingly, it also required a commitment quite unlike that of his poetry. His achievements as a poet were often attained with remarkable ease. Manuscripts show he rarely required more than two or three drafts to clear a poem from his desk (fig. 3). Beginning with a series of phrases, he often set out by sketching a conclusion. The next step was to explore openings, a procedure that led to false starts, some of which were salvaged for later in the poem. The whole business has the air of a confident, deliberate excursion, with little time spent on wasteful digressions. Once a poem was actually under way, Merwin followed through. The manuscripts of his plays present a considerably different picture; each gives rise to pages of notes, some of them scrawls on scraps of paper, others elaborate essays that wrestle with points of detail (fig. 4).

What is tragic in poetic drama, as types representative of our fate work out their destiny, may become, within the airy dimensions of poetry, essentially comic. Nothing better demonstrates the contrast between poetic drama and poetry in Merwin's early writing than "East of the Sun and West of the Moon." Merwin's version of a fairy tale does not simply stand against the dour vision of classical drama: it actually counters the conclusions he had been at pains to develop for the stage. Within the framework of the drama, innocence has no purchase; it cannot endure in a world of imperfection. In the fairy tale, innocence once lost can actually be regained, reconstituted in a different modality. In classical drama, imperfections dominate as matters change beyond the control or desire of the characters. In the fairy tale, change is to be celebrated as the very basis by which the world constantly refreshes itself.

That Merwin set out to reproduce a fairy tale, a narrative that would slip free of the restrictions of realistic storytelling, is evident in the text he chose to follow. One story he did not bear in mind was the Cupid and Psyche legend as told by Apuleius in *The Golden Ass.* (Critics link Merwin's poem with Apuleius not simply because the folktale of "East of the Sun" can be traced to the legend of Psyche, but also because they appreciate the connection between Apuleius and Robert Graves, whose children Merwin tutored for a short time and whose translation of *The Golden Ass* was published in 1951, the year "East of the Sun" was begun.[9]) Merwin's version, however, deliberately passes over the Roman tale of envy and jealousy and takes instead the version presented by George Webbe Dasent in his collection of Norwegian folktales, *East o' the Sun and West o' the Moon* (and retold by Andrew Lang in *The Blue Fairy Book).*[10] Merwin borrows not only specific details but even Dasent's narrative approach. For example, toward the end of the poem, after the poor man's daughter has found where her prince has been taken, she contrives to spend the night in the same

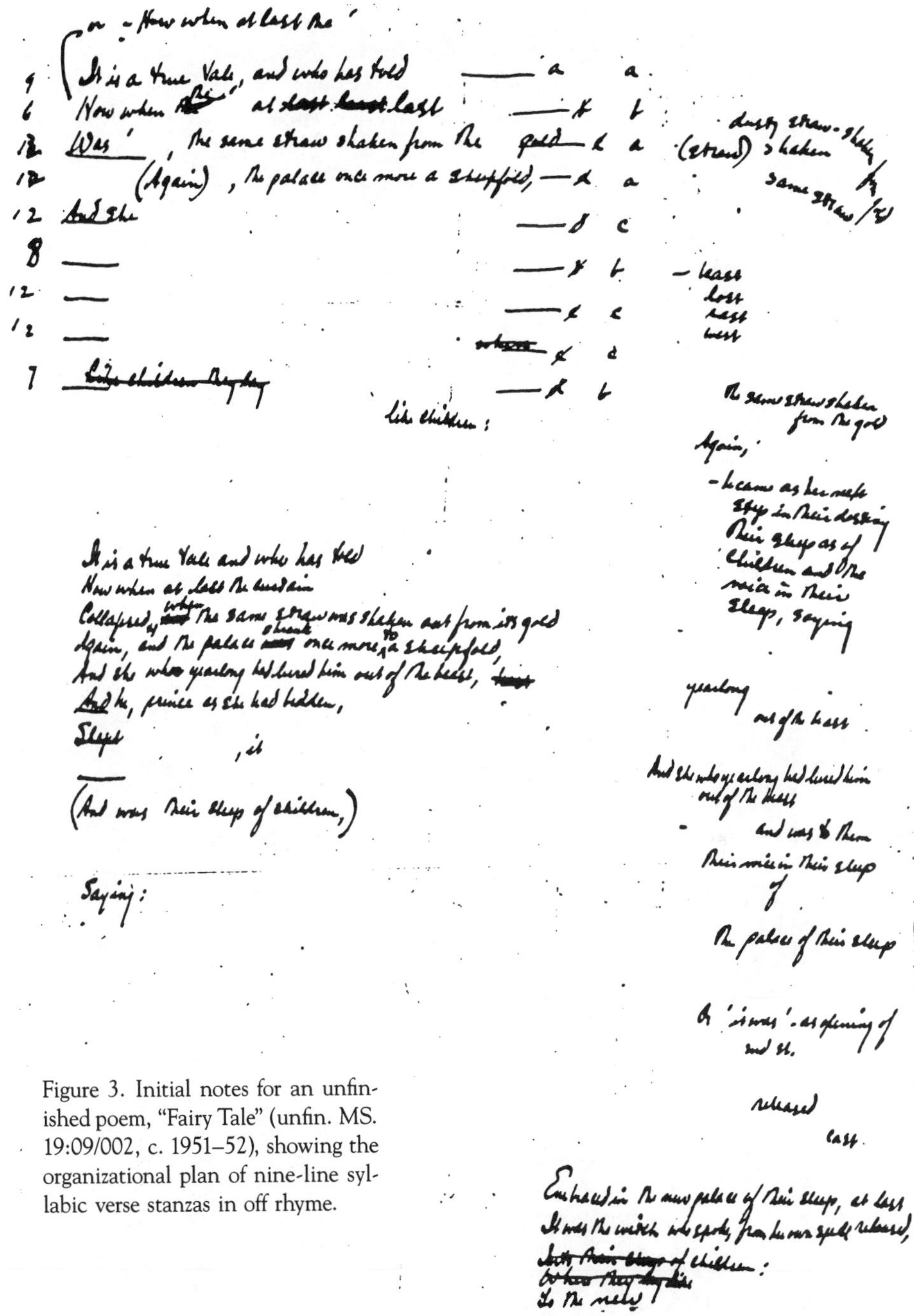

Figure 3. Initial notes for an unfinished poem, "Fairy Tale" (unfin. MS. 19:09/002, c. 1951–52), showing the organizational plan of nine-line syllabic verse stanzas in off rhyme.

Have something to do with why Juan has always had thing about sameness — thus connect with beggar?

The physical imperfection phobia in Juan was his refusal to recognize anything individual about women — anything but their simply being women: the sex whose mask was his mirror and whose ~~stuff~~ sex was the ~~[illegible]~~ gratification of his desire. Refusal to ~~[illegible]~~ have to accept, countenance, recognize inescapable individualities, which are the human condition. Refusal to consider death distorting life individually apart from himself. This refusal to recognize, accept, respond (& be responsible for) other individualities, identities, makes his own at last ~~[illegible]~~ indefinite — the very thing he uses women for, the ~~[illegible]~~ projection of his own identity, no longer works precisely because he uses it for just that

So play also about necessity to be human in sense of accepting humanity (individuality, individual imperfection in self and others, death) before love is possible — ~~recognizing~~ the human condition

All this must be worked back through the first half of play, with Daniel, Anna.

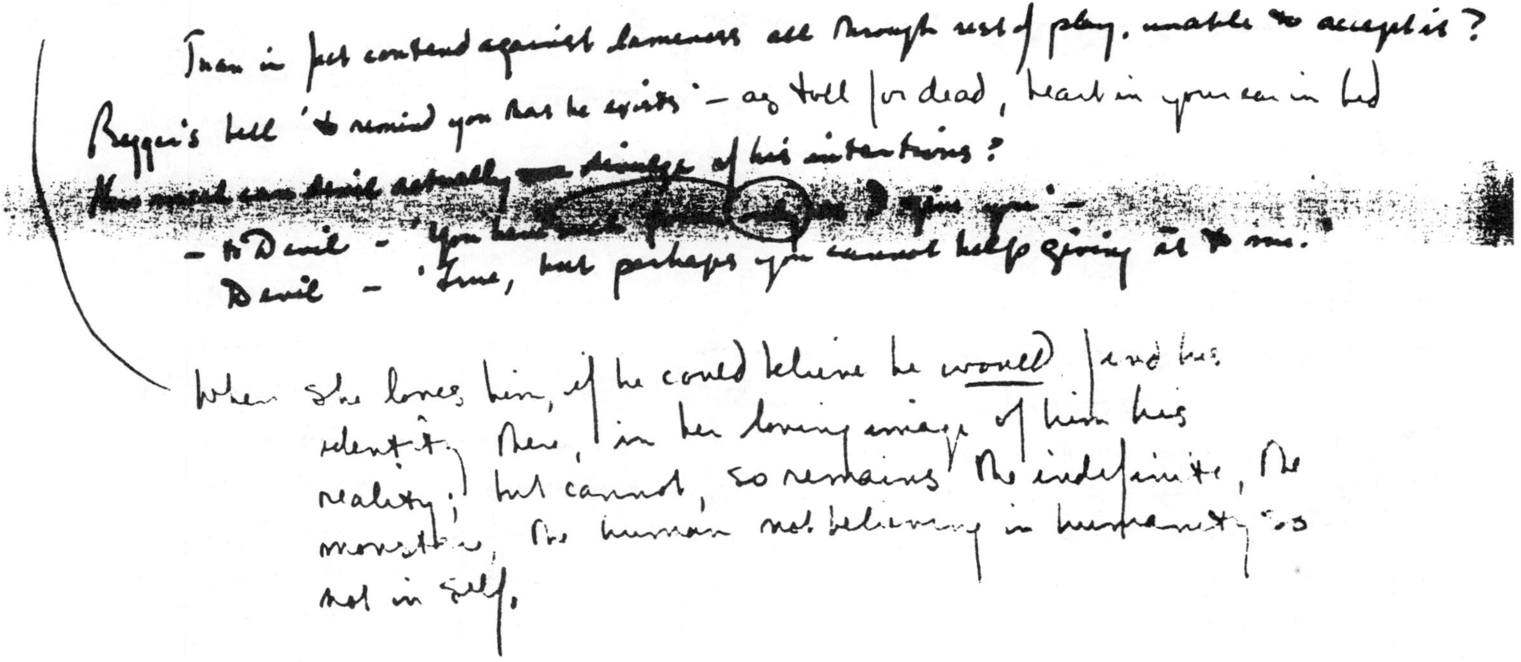

Figure 4. One of the sixty pages of handwritten notes (enlarged) accompanying the drafts and typescript of "The Wood of Women" (MS./TS. 09:1163, c. 1953). For his verse drama, Merwin always wrote such expositions, analyzing in some depth the significance of his characters. In other notes, he registers historical details, records snatches of dialogue, speculates about the direction of the plot, urges revisions that he goes on to justify, and pictures how the stage should look. The impression is of one who has become utterly immersed in every aspect of his play.

room with him, but twice her efforts at reunion are frustrated: the prince has been administered a sleeping potion by the evil stepdame, who plans on having him marry her daughter. Why, then, is she able to speak with him the third night?

> Suppose the requisite vigil. Say one lay
> Two nights awake beside the prince's room
> Heard crying there, as towards a vanishing spectre,
> Told the prince, and he, thus wise against potions
> The third night, sleepless, with wide arms received her. (FF, 97)

This "one," suddenly appearing, who "lay / Two nights awake" to hear crying would be disconcerting, were it not for the fact that this passage originates not with Merwin but with Dasent: "But now you must know there were some Christian folk who had been carried off thither, and as they sat in their room, which was next to the Prince, they had heard how a woman had been in there, and wept and prayed, and called to him two nights running, and they told that to the Prince." Merwin incorporates the *deus ex machina* of castle hostages who eavesdrop and tip off the Prince, but with an elegant sweep that preserves the sense of a lucky intervention without bogging us down in details. In Merwin's version, the emphasis falls simply on the fact of discovery. How the prince came to learn he was being drugged is passed over with no interest. Merwin's fidelity, though, to the shifts in the original reminds us that the compressed narrative of the fairy tale allows for such latitude, since it is more intent upon highlighting particular matters than upon telling a story with plausible detail.

Since Merwin follows Dasent with care, it is notable when he adds something of his own. Some of his elaborations are simple embellishments: there is a prologue, an epilogue that invents a dialogue between the sun and the moon (masculinity and femininity, reality and imagination), and a bird who croaks that all metaphor is magic. But one addition is striking because it changes what Bruno Bettelheim has identified as an important part of the story, and because it is unsanctioned by anything in Apuleius (or in Bulfinch, who also tells a Cupid and Psyche story).[11] To Bettelheim it seems unusual that the prince is a beast by day and a man by night, because this is a curious reversal: "The animal husband is an animal during the day to the world, but lovely to behold to his wife at night in bed." Along with this puzzle, Bettelheim notes that it is the daughter's mother who expresses shock when she learns of the sleeping arrangement. The daughter herself, at the time, felt no fear, and she wanted to visit her home simply because she missed her family. Her mother's reaction, however, is to cry in horror, "You are very likely sleeping with a troll!" Bettelheim concludes that the tale "subtly suggests that it is older women who give young girls the idea that males are beasts; that girls' sexual anxieties are the result not of their own experience, but of what others have told them." Sexual activity is perfectly enjoyable at the time it occurs, but that is at night in the dark; during the day, it becomes a problem as "the old anxieties and resentments, including the jealousy of one sex for another, reassert themselves." This happens "particularly when the world with its critical attitude toward sexual enjoyment (the mother's warning that it might be a troll) reasserts itself." Bettelheim's reading depends on the mother's intruding, an intrusion that parallels, in Apuleius, the meddling of Psyche's two envious sisters who plot against her because of their own unhappy marriages.

Merwin, however, redirects this drama. It is not the mother but the daughter who first questions the prince's story of his enchantment, and her desire to return home stems from her dissatisfaction with the artificial atmosphere of the castle interior. The interior is made up to resemble an out-of-doors scene, but its elaborate refinements can never satisfy: "pheasants amble in white glass, / Ducks strut ridiculous in stone, the streams / Slither nowhere in beryl." The immutability of this castle-museum vexes her. Merwin devotes two lavish stanzas to describing it, each line more daintily overwritten than the last. The daughter longs to return home not simply out of nostalgia for her family but also because she cannot endure the glittering perfection in which she must dwell: "Yet I sigh / For snips to whir and fall, for hawks to fall, / For one more mortal crimson that will fade."

In Merwin's version, even the intervention of the daughter's mother is subordinated to this theme of discontent with crystalline perfection. When the prince returns her to her family, his only warning is that she should not talk with her mother, who is, he says, "as wise as you." This warning goes unheeded but it is not the daughter's betrayal that Merwin emphasizes. Dominant even here, and carefully woven into the stanza, is the longing for change. Returning the poor man's daughter back to the castle, the prince (in the form of a bear) asks for a favor that can apparently be granted only through her volition; he cannot, on his own will, tarry in the natural world:

> "Shall we not ride a while in the mortal air
> Before we go," he asked, "for the love of fading?
> But wish, when you are weary, for the sound
> Of the silver bell, and we shall instantly
> Be home again. Did all happen as I said?"
> "Yes," she said, "how might it be otherwise?"
> "Did you, then, walk aside with your mother?" he asked;
> "Did you listen to your mother's advice?"
> "Oh no," she said. "Then all may yet be well."
> But she wished for the sound of the silver bell. (FF, 91)

The world that both long for, the "mortal air" experienced in a "love of fading," is forgotten as her evasions come forward. When she wishes herself back to the castle at once, the pure rhymes at the close signal an ominous finality.

The discontent the daughter feels with the immutable luxury of her new home is never emphasized in Dasent (where she is simply lonely), and in both Apuleius and Bulfinch, Psyche is utterly contented with the voluptuous pleasures of her golden palace, which seem to be a prelude to the delights of making love. Merwin, by contrast, stresses the obnoxious aspect of dazzling beauty because his particular theme is different: it is the beauty of simplicity or the virtue of innocence, and his central idea is that one must always love in the dark, without calculation or question or scrutiny. When the daughter follows her mother's advice and looks upon the prince she finds he is handsome—so handsome that he transforms the glittering jewels she has disdained. But having looked, she has lost. Physical beauty is nothing, empty as glass pheasants and stone ducks; only beauty known in darkness is genuine—an inner beauty, known out of the responsive chords of feeling that have no visual counterpart. To love in that way is to remain innocent, in accord with one's inmost feelings. The lovers in "Fable" (which, like "East of the Sun," was read on the BBC) arrived at a similar conclusion:

And most religiously they swore—
Pray for the word of folly—
That never they would look upon
The warm marvel that beat between,
Lest, should their eyes prove so familiar,
It take offense and die. (FF, 75)

Merwin's decision to narrate a fairy tale is itself an affirmation of an innocence; it is a refusal to scrutinize events with an eye toward realistic detail. If, at this crucial turning point, when the prince has been reduced to mere physical beauty, innocence has been lost, then it cannot be recovered. But the daughter can invoke that lost state by thrusting herself into situations that have no certain outcome, by following the advice of the three crones and the four winds. With little substantive change, these are taken over from Dasent, who offers no clue why the first crone should appear, or how the third crone should recall the first wind, or why the North Wind might know of the castle.[12] But a reason, Merwin knows, is not needed at this point: only a situation that seems hopeless, accompanied by failure after failure as each crone and each wind presents evidence that suggests her quest is futile. What is needed is a display of perseverance and patience, as well as a willingness to trust to the unknown. These qualities have been absent from the story for a long time, though they were the daughter's virtues at the start, when first taken by the bear into the night. These qualities, then, return us to the fresh viewpoint at the beginning of the tale. For the daughter to recover them is to demonstrate her superiority. Since she has regained her innocence, she is able to return to purity the white shirt that has been stained, a symbolic purification that also removes the drop of hot tallow spilled when she scrutinized the prince in the dark. She announces her achievement in a voice of pure innocence: "How should I not, since all pallor is mine?"

The innocence affirmed, lost, but then rediscovered and sustained by lovers explains in part why this volume has gone largely unrecognized as a collection of love poetry. These lovers do not act in the traditional fashion, withdrawing to their worlds of perfection. When they do withdraw, it is like a punishment. Merwin's lovers would prefer living in this imperfect world, reclaiming it, delighting in it. Moreover, they are notable not for their sensuality but for their innocence. "Non enium sciunt quid faciunt" (they don't even know what they do) is the tag line to stanzas in "The Passion," a poem that compares the public exposure of a love affair to the Crucifixion. The lovers are banished for their transgressions ("where we came / Hands were washed of our end") and left by others to suffer. But as long as they are together they cannot suffer. When they ultimately rise, they return to a world that is "Dividing infinitely," a world they share eternally with each other. The tag line, then, applies both to their prosecutors, whose attacks only solidify their love, and to the lovers themselves, whose innocence colors all they see.

Love, the twenty-six-year-old Merwin insists in *The Dancing Bears,* is the power that renews the world. Even darkness can be transformed, as in "East of the Sun," if one is ready to enter it wide-eyed, prepared for innocent acceptance. Yet even that is not quite the final point of the tale. Innocence by itself is not enough; it can only be lost. After that loss, what comes into play is nothing less than the strength of character displayed by the poor man's daughter, who keeps on moving, looking, searching—persevering through trials that restore her to an innocence like that with which she began.

3

"Physiologus"

IN TWO separate presentations in May and June of 1954, the BBC Third Programme broadcast "Physiologus," a nearly complete selection of the animal poems Merwin had been writing since early 1953. Part One comprised "Leviathan," "Blue Cockerel," "Two Horses" (three poems that would appear, in the same order, as the opening works of *Green with Beasts)*, "Hydra," "Toro," "Snail," "Cormorants," and "Mouse." Part Two was "Sow," "Spider," "Dog," "White Goat, White Ram" (these last two poems would complete the excerpts from the bestiary in *Green with Beasts)*, "Leopard," and "Camel." A fifteenth poem was excluded from the final script, perhaps because "Bear" would have exceeded the time limit. Neither performance was brief: all fifteen poems amounted to more than a thousand lines.[1]

Yet the entire work was in print for the briefest time. *Green with Beasts*, which British publisher Rupert Hart-Davis accepted in fall 1955, included seventeen bestiary poems ("Pigeon" and "Toad" had been written in March and September of 1955). Seeing this poetry in print, however, gave Merwin second thoughts, and from the galley proofs he excised all but five poems. These appeared under the subtitle "Physiologus: Chapters from a Bestiary." As this subtitle suggests, with its allusion to work in progress, he was not eliminating inferior poems but presenting an abridged version of a longer work. The work was not so much rejected as held in reserve.

But instead of adding further to his bestiary, Merwin decided to comment on its creatures. In 1956, he composed brief prose pieces for placement between each of the poems; together with a short prologue and epilogue, this mixture was retitled *The Ark of Silence*, recasting the cycle of poetry as a volume to stand on its own.[2] These additions, however, made his final product more, not less, diverse. The prose was a most oblique comment and it was often uncertain how it pertained to the poem it followed or preceded. The prose pieces lacked even a similar style. Some engaged in fantastic descriptions; some were as spare as proverbs, others as anecdotal as a notebook jotting or an excerpt from an autobiography. In recasting his bestiary, Merwin enhanced its unconventional features.

Judging from his other volumes, the disturbing element in Merwin's arrangement of *The Ark of Silence* was deliberate. When organizing his poems into books, Merwin is careful to make the final arrangement occupy some midpoint between a unified narrative and a miscellaneous collection. Both *The Moving Target* and *The Lice* generally present their poems in the order in which they were written. The text progresses through stages even as its development is nowhere stressed. Neither volume divides its poems into numbered groups, though they fall into distinct clusters—as when, two-thirds through *The Moving Target,* punctuation is dropped. Moreover, when a volume does conspicuously group its poems, the subdivisions raise further questions. *The Compass Flower* (1977) is the most dramatically unstable of all of Merwin's collections. Its four parts can be read as portraits of the poet as he appears against different backgrounds: as one drawn back to childhood scenes by the death of his parents, as an observer of the anonymous urban cityscape, as a swain whose affection for the country prepares him for loving another, and as a wanderer who will remain perpetually uprooted. Or the four-part grouping can represent a narrative sequence from death to resurrection as the poet passes through stages of mourning: losing himself in the anonymity of the city, returning to the healing calm of the countryside, where he is renewed by the love of another, brought back to a life that he embarks upon as a traveler, and voyaging freely from one place to another.

The Compass Flower, almost from poem to poem, inclines toward one approach, then the other. Merwin is prepared to accept this uncertainty: to order his work too heavily, whether it is a volume, a cycle of poetry, or a single poem, threatens to upset that balance between speaking and listening that is crucial to his writing and that he has identified as an essential component of all poetry. To hover in between, then, is by no means a mark of uncertainty, even in a volume as anguished as *The Compass Flower.* It is, instead, a sign that poetry is an interplay between order and disorder, a give-and-take between the one who is shaping and the one who is being shaped. Neither narrative nor miscellany qualifies as poetic—only the two together, as each actively disrupts the claims of the other.

In 1977, Merwin's stature was such that few editors would have been ready to deny him publication of any manuscript. Twenty years earlier, matters were different. Moreover, in 1957 poetry in America seemed to have reached a consensus about what it should be, as the anthology *New Poets of England and America* (which first appeared that year) indicated: aloof in approach, traditional in form, yet debonair in treating major cultural issues. This definition left no room for extended works that mixed prose with poetry, especially one whose extravagant prose took on features of the poetic and whose descriptive poetry appeared in long, lax lines that resembled prose. When Merwin submitted *The Ark of Silence* as a fourth volume of poetry to his current American publisher, Alfred A. Knopf, it was regretfully declined in November 1957.[3]

1

Exuberant enough in *The Dancing Bears,* Merwin intends, in his bestiary, to go further, to create a whole world of lavish delight. One sign of his new expansiveness is that strophic forms give way to stichic forms. Whereas the strophic arrangement by stanza supports concentration and density, the unbuttoned format of stichic organization encourages expansion. Lines continue until their thoughts play out.

Strophic form is for lyrics, stichic form for epics, and the bestiary is a miniature epic, at least with respect to breadth and scope. Its poems affirm the world as a place that becomes rich and strange when inhabited by a mind speculating with delight, speculating as though there should be no end to speculation. The extravagant, the exceptional, is positively encouraged. Again and again, poems approach ideas of order only to cast them away or soar beyond them. For example, repetition of color always promises to play an ordering role. "Green" reappears much like "shadow" and "stone" did earlier, mentioned twenty-seven times in nine poems. "White" vies with it, appearing thirty times in seven poems. Yet each recurrence differs from the last. No set of related attributes clusters about the reappearing color. In "Sow," violent sea water is a "green deep," but in "Dog" the glare of sunlight gives a "feeble / Green cast" to the creature's shadow, while in "Bear" the colors of dusk are a "yellowish green whiteness." Green as a concept to center the poems gives way to a diversity that only emphasizes its variety. In a similar way, whole phrases teasingly recur in individual works, as though they could be keys: "It seems to be summer" ("Blue Cockerel"), "You cannot know this place" ("The Hydra"), "By the fear of you or the desire of you" ("Camel"), "Fixed in unfurling" ("Snail"), and "The uncovenanted terror of becoming" ("White Goat, White Ram"). But each time, the words reassemble in a context so different from their first appearance that the context changes the meaning of the phrase rather than the phrase illuminating the context. These repetitions, rather than establishing stability, invite instability; the phrase acts like a point of reference around which the poem swirls, revealing its changing facets.

Merwin's bestiary is an expression of youthful exuberance: it transfers energy that, in his love poetry, had been directed toward one person and, as though it were too powerful to be restricted to just one other, extends it to the world. It also leads back to an even earlier love of his, the vernacular poetry of medieval

England. His bestiary lies deep in the origins of English literature. Its broadcast title, "Physiologus," is an allusion to the twelfth-century Middle English text known as "The Physiologus" (so called because it can be traced to a ninth-century dog-Latin translation of a Greek manuscript ascribed to a second-century Alexandrian with the name "Physiologus").[4] Moreover, early notes for the bestiary show Merwin planned to include the griffin, the phoenix, and the unicorn, fabulous creatures regularly featured in medieval bestiaries (fig. 5)—and primly excluded by the revisionary Creator (in "Dictum") who stage-managed Noah and the Flood.

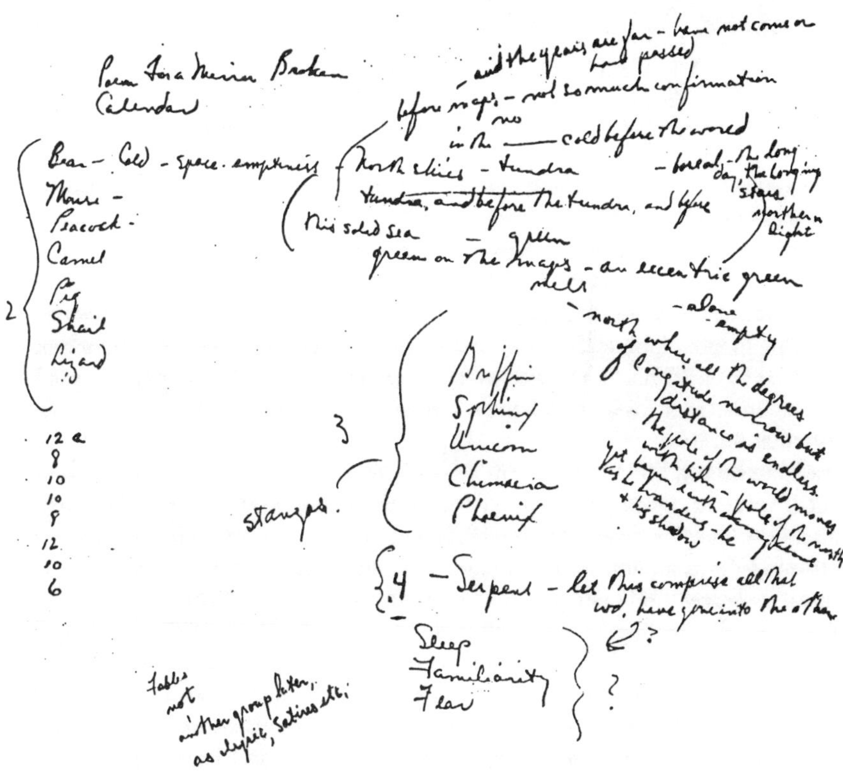

Figure 5. MS. 19:09/021, c. 1953. Plans for an ambitious four-part bestiary, with a third part on mythological creatures and a fourth part on attributes shared by humans and creatures. None of the later poems seems to have been written. The notes also include a draft of the concluding lines for "Bear."

Merwin's bestiary is an original series of meditations, not a translation of a previous text. Yet a bestiary is, by definition, a form open to contemporary emendation: a primitive encyclopedia, it has always been a group project. As knowledge about creatures accumulated over the centuries, each transcription of the bestiary text became an occasion for contributors to add their voices. Merwin's version preserves that medley of differing tones. Prone to unexpected shifts of focus as it encompasses its diverse subjects, the form places a premium on deftness and agility:

> I would speak now of the surpassing creature
> Leopard. He waits above the rocks
> In the shadowy branch, in the green light, patient
> Till prey come unwitting: his forepaws lie waiting
> Outstretched before him, claws sliding lazily
> Like the lids of his eyes. See how the curved
> Weight of his tail rests light as a long wave-top
> That has paused in its streaming and learned patience.

This opening to "Leopard" is a graceful update of the alliterated, strong-stress, four-beat meter of its Middle English predecessor. The movement of the poem is governed by nothing more than the next feature perceived, which may then require its own parenthetical aside. Byways, offshoots, and forking paths are enthusiastically explored. As intricate as the syntax may be, the line avoids by favoring monosyllables: "See how the curved / Weight of his tail rests light as a long wave-top / That has paused in its streaming." Monosyllables impart speed to the line, even as the elaborate syntax threatens to overwhelm us with information.

Quite simply, Merwin wants the freedom to wander about—to make a poem out of speculative roaming, doing no more than observing a creature from any number of perspectives. Yet he is careful to justify such extravagance by presenting it as an affirmation of curiosity. The wandering mind that investigates, compares, and draws conclusions that in turn lead to further rumination should be the distinguishing attribute of the human species. What too often occurs, however, is that the mind serves another function, employing its cleverness to manage, organize, and control its environment. Such a narrowing is indeed a characteristic of the medieval bestiary. Merwin's bestiary exposes the Middle English text as infected with a rage to order that is opposite to curiosity.

Richard Wilbur's translation of the medieval French of Philippe de Thaun (in his 1955 anthology *A Bestiary*) accurately depicts the managerial attitude of one twelfth-century text.[5] The opening lines, having suffered the least change over the centuries, still remain descriptive, closest to a naturalist's observations:

Pellicanus is the word
  For a certain breed of bird
Who truly is a crane;
  Egypt is his domain.
There are two kinds thereof;
  Near to the Nile they live.

A straightforward listing of facts, this aspires to objectivity. By the end, however, the facts have been "modernized" to conform to twelfth century belief:

Know that this Pelican
  Signifies Mary's Son;
The little birds are men
  Restored to life again
From death, by that dear blood
  Shed for us by our God.

Originating in curiosity and wonder, these texts close by submitting to orthodoxy, the features of the beast redrawn to conform to the outlines of Christian dogma. By contrast, Merwin seeks the original impulse, to restore innocence by proceeding as though creatures are objects of endless speculation that can never be resolved into simplifying categories. As a result, his versions establish vantage points from which we see that the efforts to tame or rationalize or categorize the creatures are doubly destructive: such categorization not only denies the mysterious nature of the creature but also suppresses the curiosity that is the distinguishing feature of human intelligence.

To counteract the managerial impulse of the medieval bestiary, Merwin did not have to go far. The compilation known as the Exeter Book, in which the scholar can find a version of "The Physiologus," also includes some ninety or so riddle-songs.[6] As an antidote to the intrusive hermeneutics of the medieval bestiary, the riddle-song could not be more appealing. The riddle-song maintains that if one describes a common object or event or creature without naming it beforehand, it becomes wonderfully strange even as it remains true to its characteristics:

Our world is lovely in different ways,
Hung with beauty and the works of hands.
I saw a strange machine, made
For motion, slide against the sand,
Shrieking as it went. It walked swiftly
On its only foot, this odd-shaped monster.
Travelled in an open country without
Seeing, without arms, or hands,
With many ribs and its mouth in its middle.

This opens a riddle-song that the translator titles "A Ship" (riddle-songs have no titles and the "answers" to some are still in dispute).[7] The power of the riddle-song rests not on its ability to create deception, but on its capacity to arouse wonder. Once the label is removed from a thing, it dissolves into its rich component parts, becoming utterly strange yet hauntingly familiar; the delight is to learn that so marvelous a description applies to so common a thing. Unlike the medieval bestiary, which describes its subjects in terms that make the beast easier to comprehend, the riddle-song keeps turning its subject about in so many ways that it escapes any clear category.

Merwin demonstrates a similar capacity: he values wandering on those margins where investigation must be exploratory—a point underscored in "Bear," the final poem in both early and late versions of the bestiary.[8] The white bear who was a prince in disguise in "East of the Sun and West of the Moon" reappears, this time as the poet in disguise. This creature receives the highest praise because he wanders through an uncharted realm "Beyond maps, before maps" about which nothing is known. This bear, like the poet whose writing always enters new territory, moves in "that place / That the maps make white for that they have not found it." But he is not lost in this emptiness; he delights in its freshness, the pleasure of being at the very tip of the world, where he is given the first glimpse of the new day:

> So that where there was nothing
> He breathes the air of origins, and under
> The boreal lights' shaking, and the stars' remote
> Aerie, the new mist is born floating, and beyond
> The mist the world may be. . . .
> Like the love
> Of heaven upon blankness musing, he slumps
> In slow circles, remote, conceiving, staring
> Upon the other side of light, into that cave and cradle
> Where, before separation, sound and silence,
> Shadow and the first filtering whiteness
> Sleep dreamless together and only in his stare
> Move toward their wakening: where, oh before
> All dawn and division, forever the world begins.

Emphasis on the moment "before / All dawn and division" reveals Merwin's concern with the innocent explorer whose sensibility guarantees that every option will be kept open, that territory will never be reduced to arrows on a chart.

One characteristic of Merwin's creatures is their lack of animality; his bear is less like a bear than a scholar poring over his books, lost in thought, working through the night. Breathing the air of origins is closer to what the young

Merwin would do, experiencing the rawness of language in *The Cid* (which he had been translating for the BBC in the previous year), than to the actuality of a polar bear foraging on the tundra. None of his creatures embody animality; they are always fading toward some margin where the scholar-poet meditates on their significance. But Merwin's point in these descriptions is to portray the creature not as it is but as it verges on the edge of understanding; if it can be kept there it becomes a presence to foster curiosity.

Just as "Bear" concludes two of the three versions of the bestiary, other poems remain stable units within Merwin's shifting arrangements. "The Hydra" followed by "Toro" is a sequence that occurs in the middle of both early and late versions of the bestiary. These two form a critical contrast prefigured in their titles which are unlike the all-purpose "Camel," "Mouse," "Pigeon," "Snail," or "Toad" that otherwise prevail.

"The Hydra" is the only poem to include the definite article in the title, as if this underwater creature were always generic, even in its individual manifestations. "Toro" is the only poem with a title that doubles as a contemptuous nickname, as if the ritual of the bullfight has permanently scarred the beast. The principle of diversity determines why one poem follows another. Sometimes "Toro" is followed by "Mouse," sometimes by "Snail," but in both cases, there is an evident contrast, if only of size. The gentle ruminations of "White Goat, White Ram" are always followed by the bold asseverations of "Leopard." The melodramatic legends of "Sow" always precede the elaborate conceits that unfold in "Spider." Merwin avoids arranging a hierarchy; if he cannot insist upon variety, his larger point is lost. It is true that he ends with the animal for which he feels the greatest affinity, the scholar-poet/explorer-bear, but that is orchestrated as a surprise. When "Leopard" precedes "Bear," there is every indication that the leopard is the ultimate creature, from the opening endorsement, offered with uncharacteristic bluntness ("I would speak now of the surpassing creature / Leopard") to the closing summation, presented in breathless admiration ("Oh he among beasts / Walks in his own story"). After this, what other creature could be held in higher admiration? The persistent bear, who meanders freely, breathing life into the moment before creation, remains closest to Merwin's values.

No juxtaposition is as striking as that between "The Hydra" and "Toro." The hydra is wholly identified with the watery world; self-contained, it propagates by division but never suffers the pangs of isolation:

> Patience belongs to it; and it waves
> No farewells but finds itself alone. Then may its motion
> Divide like music, tear, sunder utterly
> Into two, and each part keep patient
> And each be whole, whole.

Everything about it is alien, yet it is never forbidding: it is simply *other,* like the fluid boundaries of the sea. "You cannot know this place," the poem begins, "for if there are names for it / In the languages of other places they mean / Nothing here where names are not." Merwin conveys its apartness through negatives: in a fifty-one-line-poem, "not" occurs ten times, "no" seven, "nor" three, and "cannot" two. The hydra can only be known by the way it escapes our grasp. No sooner has Merwin proposed a description than he must modify it:

> it makes with its arms a motion but not
> Of music, but as though of hands meditating
> Across harp-strings that are not there, or as though
> There were a harp but no hands, and the strings, touched
> By no fingers, should have snapped slowly in the pellucid green,
> Lashed loose from the strains of sound.

"The Hydra" insists there can be recognition without knowledge. Always missing the exact word, as the creature is "Neither begging nor bewailing nor praying, though it uses / The gestures of all these," Merwin encompasses it by acknowledging its difference.

"Toro," by contrast, indicts men for using creatures for their own ends, instead of understanding them as representatives of what can never be known with surety. The men who have concocted the ritual in which the bull is ceremonially murdered say (in the only quoted lines in the cycle):

> "Now we are all together
> And seem brave in the light, let the challenging shadow
> Show itself among us; now, that we may shame it,
> Let there be dark."

Fear of the dark "that was there before the world was" is what drives men to this ceremony. The men who are "Performing with bright darts are toys merely, / Masquers playing with emblems"; they are "Those faces so small, so faint and far." Fear of the dark is real, but Merwin asserts that this stylized encounter never allows that fear to be met, only circumvented by ritualizing it into a brutal ceremony.

The evil in Merwin's bestiary is this order that imposes limits where there need be none. In the poem written last, "Toad," Merwin ponders why this harmless creature has been considered so loathsome:

> No logic for our loathing? The world is our image.
> What is there within us that we
> Deny, deny, yet tell tales of, yet shudder at,
> Yet cannot explain, yet invoke to excuse
> Errors and worse. . . .

The truth is that "There, in the dark aversions / Of our minds we feed it, and ourselves delight / In its fatness." If we could do otherwise, "in recognizing and naming it / Ours, might we see our veritable / Beauty there." Merwin can be unusually direct in these statements, because he addresses larger concerns through the form of this work, which most closely resembles a riddle-song. The name of the subject is left unmentioned, except in the title, and if we had to guess its identity, we might call it "darkness" or "night" or "shadow": "All day it sits / Just beyond the light, showing how shallow / The day is, and the undersides / Of the dazzling stones." The "jewel in its forehead"—another legend circulated about the toad—becomes a reference to the moon in the evening sky: "Though we say the stars sing where it goes, / They hide from its presence." Leaving the creature unnamed is in line with Merwin's contention that we thoroughly deny it; it is also an insistence that the darkness associate with the creature within us. By drawing us into a riddle-song in which we realize that the properties of the reviled toad are also the properties of the beloved evening, Merwin reminds us that the power of the mind never lies in its ability to deny but rests in its capacity to understand.

2

It is misleading, though, to single out themes in the bestiary, as though the poems aspired to an order. The uniqueness of the bestiary is that orderliness is constantly in dispute—so much in dispute, indeed, that at times the sequence verges on becoming a different set of poems entirely: a cycle in homage to the sea. Strictly speaking, only the creatures who appear in "Leviathan," "The Hydra," and "Cormorants" belong within or near the sea, yet the sea is a presence to which the poems compulsively return. Sometimes it happens to lie nearby, as in "White Goat, White Ram," in which a road winds along a shore. In "Camel" the creature's awkward gait reminds Merwin of a "wave-crest over / Far reef flung, its main strength still racing / For shore." "His back that bears us has a wave's shape / Drawn by a child." "Snail" digresses audaciously:

> And, like the sea's its live motion is,
> Self-effacing at a breath as the sea withdraws
> Its tides into itself to spread forth again;
> Or heaving and lurching like waves washing
> Far under the surface, whose working seems
> Irregular only because we cannot grasp,
> Living, the whole rhythm they are. And as
> The sea's flatness seen from far off, always
> Arriving, yet so slow in its sliding
> That you can scarcely say "It moves," so is the progress
> Of this shell's promise . . .

In "Sow" a sleeping sow and her litter are mistaken for islands in the sea:

> When
> The wind blows there is no white water
> Spills seething in over the outer reefs, though the sound
> Of the sea's edge plays all about there,
> But only from the tree-top the leaves' long sighing
> In the waving boughs lends to the silent
> Rocking shadow the rustling water-words
> That slide through the shallows of that island deep.

Although he knows his error ("there is no white water"), the speaker retains the comparison, playing details of the actual scene against details of the fictive scene, using both to jar each other.

Merwin sets out to describe a creature, not the sea, but the sea is a welcome presence because it remains impossible to fathom. Although it is familiar, we are unable to comprehend it. To delight in its mystery is a strength Merwin associates with describing creatures that escape his understanding. Even as it sets a limit to our knowledge, it compels us to imagine its infinity. In this double aspect, as a mark of the limit of our knowledge and as a sign of its own limitlessness, it is both an invitation and a demurral.

A primal sea-creature, "Leviathan," forms the opening poem in at least two arrangements of the bestiary. It has been much praised for its imitation of Anglo-Saxon alliterative strong-stress meter:

> This is the black sea-brute, bulling through wave-wrack,
> Ancient as ocean's shifting hills, who in sea-toils
> Travelling, who furrowing the salt acres
> Heavily, his wake hoary behind him. . . . (FF, 127)

This is wonderfully crude, its syntax a list of attributes, its diction a heap of neologisms, its rhythm held fast in a lurching alliteration. What has gone unnoted, however, is that by the end, these cumbersome devices—the list, the neologisms, the alliteration—have been thoroughly transformed:

> The sea curling,
> Star-climbed, wind-combed, cumbered with itself still
> As at first it was, is the hand not yet contented
> Of the Creator. And he waits for the world to begin. (FF, 128)

The attraction of the poem is its dazzling metamorphosis. In "Leviathan" what is archaic comes to seem very young. At the opening, the leviathan can only be glimpsed through the trappings of an archaic verse tradition, and he appears as a black brute, ungainly as a mountain, much like the poetic conventions that surround him. But just as those conventions are among the earliest efforts to comprehend the world, so the leviathan is only a beginning, a prototype. He is not crude, only incomplete, which is why Merwin can launch into the sweetness of saying: "Days there are, nonetheless, when he lies / Like an angel, although a lost angel / On the waste's unease." The ocean too remains incomplete, the mark of "the hand not yet contented / Of the Creator," still in the process of being shaped. As "Leviathan" deftly modulates from one perception to its opposite, inverting the terms with which it began, what we had once dismissed now appears, from a further perspective, as decidedly attractive. As an opening poem, this is a valuable demonstration: it promises other reversals to follow if only we can dissolve our customary ways of seeing.

For one arrangement of the bestiary, "Cormorants" is a rival to "Leviathan" for first place in the sequence. Its sea, however, in a vivid example of the instability Merwin cannot resist, is entirely uninviting: it stands as a barrier, supremely indifferent to whoever approaches it, an anarchic force that would obliterate all distinctions. "Leviathan" arched from darkness to dawn; "Cormorants" sinks from dusk to darkness, ending with:

The land-hills
Drain blue, grow indistinguishable between
The hills of the night sea and the darkening hill
Of heaven, until all fades into the image
Of the sea that, made in its own image, rolls
Like a ravenous eye between sun and moon.

Nothing escapes this indiscriminate leveling force. Just as the sea presses steadily on the land, so the cormorants intrude persistently, clustering "Between light and shadow, between air and sea, between / Earth and its resemblances; even the fish / Clutched in those ravenous beaks flash and slide / Between life and death." ("Between" appears nine times in this fifty-eight-line poem.) The birds' voracity is not passionate, just indiscriminate.

To Merwin's chagrin, any counteractive movement toward affirmation rapidly dwindles into a gesture. He notices the "one olive-tree" that lends its name to Dove-Rock, on which the cormorants perch "sagely." That tree, which is "hardly more than a branch,"

cranes out
Over the waste of water, watching
As it were for the end of a promise.
Shall there be no more, no more sea?

But the sea is endless—and its emblem is the cormorant, the in-between bird, all-devouring. If there were another Flood, this regressive creature "would bloat still and survive / Again as it did before, again and always / And raise its head at last under the olive branch."

Such indiscriminate leveling contrasts sharply with the care Merwin conspicuously displays throughout. He takes the trouble, in his opening, to establish a hierarchy: "High hawk and sea raven" that are "sailing in to the top trees," then "Swallows wheeling by the cliffside" and "raucous gulls swooping and homing," and finally cormorants "a bare foot above the sea." These careful distinctions return later when Merwin, craning like the olive tree, casts his eyes to the horizon, and discriminates precisely among the colors that flare in the distance:

> Light glints out at sea: gold,
> Blue, and the sky blue, and the farthest headlands
> Bronze and red in the late day, but here
> In the crag's splashed shadow it is already
> Cold and evening.

But the passage enacts the downfalls that the poem exemplifies. Lost at once in the gathering dusk is the subtlety of his careful measures, which distinguish "Blue" from "sky blue" and "gold" from "Bronze and red." The eye falls to the "splashed shadow" where there are only the abstract qualities of "cold and evening." No action is sufficient to fend off the leveling darkness. In the shortest sentence of the poem, Merwin summarizes the oblivion that surrounds him: "The birds stare and doze."

These rival versions of the sea—the alluring in "Leviathan" and the forbidding in "Cormorants"—establish the polarities Merwin must appreciate to write his bestiary. As the curious wanderer, he is eager to transform all he sees, but his loving investment is threatened by a brutal reality that will mock his affirmations as mere extravagant gestures. Most poems emphasize one extreme over the other, the sweetness of "The Hydra" or the brutality of "Toro." But which extreme will dominate is never clear from the outset. Essentially, the sensibility of the poet becomes an arena for disruptive confrontations. Writing poetry is a form of improvisation liable to draw out moments unexpected even to the poet. The scholar-poet, elated at wandering with no more destination in mind than a lumbering bear, is likely to wander into areas to which he is temperamentally unsuited. The extraordinary moments in this set of poems occur not when Merwin is thoughtfully describing a creature with whose innocence he feels an affinity or when he is exposing a fundamental brutality that victimizes a creature, but when he is drawn to the center of the poem and becomes like a creature himself, both innocent and victimized.

3

In "Physiologus," a sense of rich possibility entered the poem by way of extravagant digressions, lavish allusions involving comparisons or exotic points of reference. That was effective enough, given the elaborate frameworks Merwin had erected for his play of thought. But that play is limited almost entirely to dexterity with language. In the later, prose-and-poetry version of the bestiary, *The Ark of Silence,* Merwin would extend his sense of play but without depending on the music of his language. In this arrangement, diversity of language is supplanted by descriptions so rich in variety their language is best kept as transparent as possible.

The prose pieces are designed as a counterweight to the lavish elegance of the poetry. Although sparse and austere, they are never confined to a particular mode. They can be laconic epigrams, such as the one following the longest of the poems, "White Goat, White Ram": "There are those who are not looking for peace because it never dawned on them that they had it to lose." They can be as lengthy as the elaborate retelling of the experience of watching lake water at sundown gradually merge with the color of the dusk until air and water are indistinguishable. They can be fantastic, explaining the futility of expecting map-makers to be accurate about "St. Brendan's Islands," islands that do not exist but that keep appearing on maps.[9]

Most important, whatever commentary follows the poem must be unexpected. Its only obligation is to serve as a counterpoint. The prose may even take a poem as a springboard into an entirely different topic. The only link between "Leopard" and its prose commentary is a kitten:[10]

> Take a tame kitten of either sex, and record its most diminutive voice on a machine, then play the record very slowly. After all we have taught it, as you will see, the machine has never relinquished the jungle.
>
> Remark how time magnifies behind and before us, as though we were a lens. Which is why the outlines are more blurred, though more huge, the farther they are away from us.

When time is slowed mechanically, the "diminutive voice" of the kitten is magnified. It is, of course, an illusion: the machine can do no more than this clever trick, even "After all we have taught it." But that trick we are accustomed to play on ourselves, when we consider time past and time future. Events that have no immediate effect on us loom large, but only because they are remote; it is an illusion we offer to ourselves, an illusion we would dismiss as a trick if it occurred elsewhere.

Merwin's commentary may react to the poem with a fierce wit. In "Toro" he had pointed out with disgust that the fiercest and proudest of creatures had become the subject of a game that ended in its ritual murder. His disgust continues in the prose piece, where he comes upon a repulsive sight: racks of raw meat swinging from hooks. He proceeds to explain, in the gentlest of voices, that to the inhabitants of the land he is currently visiting, these chunks of meat are musical instruments. So sensitive are the natives to even the slightest vibration that "the waving of a hand is like a shout." The swinging meat, then, is a particularly common form of popular music, though he quietly adds that even the inhabitants might find it somewhat loud. But the association between the crudity of popular music and various national pastimes has been made.

Underlying the diversity of these pieces, however, is a theme that links this last version of the bestiary with the first: it is a virtue to proceed without fear or hesitation into unpredictable areas—areas inherently unstable or on the margins of the comprehensible. In the piece after "Bear," the speaker wakens into a "deep light, blunt but harsh" to which he grows accustomed as he recognizes the sound of a "struggling" that was either "crying or laughing or both." He finally identifies the source of these sounds as himself, and once that acceptance occurs, doubt and fear vanish and he enters a position of godlike creation: "I still do not know why, but when I knew that it made everything happen. I would never have known that it could be like that. First of all, the light fell apart from the water and was another thing. And I could see that it was good." One must accept that one cannot know "why" an event is happening. To try to know why only postpones the event. Once one knows that one cannot ever know, then everything that happens can be good. The contrast between the poem and the prose retains the counterpoint: in the poetry the bear is a wanderer who proceeds without a clear sense of direction, while the prose describes a frightening struggle. But in both cases, Merwin endorses the value of proceeding as though the outcome were always uncertain.

Merwin now substitutes extravagant situations for extravagant language. What he is seeking in his prose is a variant on the open delight expressed through the language of the first bestiary: he wants to involve us directly in seeing with an innocence he associates with the creatures. If we could view the world without the preconceptions we tend to bring to it, if we could view it with an open-eyed freshness, we would be closer to the animals without losing our humanity. The delight he would now create is not a matter of ecstatic wonder but a condition of open, steadfast curiosity. Equally important, he suggests that the plenitude achieved in his wandering digressions need not be reserved for special moments orchestrated through extraordinary language, but is available to anyone who simply opens his or her eyes and looks into the moment.

His most impressive pieces, like the one following "Cormorants," remain simple:

> In back of the church there is a little square with benches around the sides, and in the evening when the dusk has really settled, all the old women can be seen sitting on the bench along one side, and all the old men on the bench along the other. Even the ones with bony hands and skinny faces have stomachs that sag between their knees. But their shapes are concealed by the looseness of their clothes, which hang limp and seem empty if the wind touches them. The women have been in mourning for most of their lives, and the men wear black for other old reasons. As the night falls you can hardly see them.
>
> Up on the roofs of the chicken sheds and pig pens, wired away so that nothing can get at them, the figs are drying in the darkness.
>
> Sometimes you forget that the old people are still there. They cannot see the

> stars, but they can still taste what they ate years ago when they had their teeth.
>
> Later you hear noises that seem too near, and the only way you can tell whether it is their voices, or a breeze stirring the dry leaves on the hillside, is that the dry leaves sound like the sea a long way below.

This scene comes to life with the gentlest of motions. When "dusk has really settled" the old can be seen rigidly divided into two groups. All that seems left of them is their sagging stomachs, the mechanism that keeps them alive; they might as well not be there, for their clothes are so loose they even "seem empty if the wind touches them." Dressed in black, they are not just merged with the shadows, but are shadows themselves.

"As the night falls you can hardly see them," Merwin says, ending his first paragraph with a statement that threatens to appear redundant—except that the "you" that includes the reader in the scene invites a further regard. Having come this far and seen so much that only speaks of absence, what is there to experience now? The answer is the surprising richness that follows. You become aware of another kind of aging that transpires in this village, the figs that are "drying in the darkness"—like the elderly, except that these are guarded for their value. What is the value of the elderly? They have no sense of future, they cannot see the stars, but they have a memory, a sense of the past that is so deep that it is palpable, it is like a taste in their mouths. In this deepening darkness, which is now spreading in the way of memories, sounds become far more important than sights. Noises seem too near, and voices merge with the sound of dry leaves rustling on the hillside. That sound, which at first recalls only the whispers of the aged, wonderfully expands into a sound that is "like the sea a long way below," an eternal murmur that stretches into the night.

This description, which begins within the "little square" with the elderly in the last light of a day ending like their own lives, moves with simple directness toward its opposite: a night deep and rich with voices, with the ear discriminating among them keenly, aware of the sounds of the sea "a long way below" that had gone unheard up until this moment. This change is what happens if one recaptures an innocence, a way of taking in what is before one and letting it ripen as patiently as the figs in the darkness, establishing a pace that is its own. It reproduces in a deeper dimension the wayward curiosity that was the exclusive property of the poet in the original bestiary. It now unfolds within a scene available to anyone.

Merwin's prologue and epilogue recapture the delight of the original bestiary but in a different key. The epilogue concludes:

> Maybe everything that we cannot understand and cannot speak to is ourselves. Our delight and our shame and our necessity. They make us wonder. When we wonder and have no words we seem closer to them, and yet farther away. Because they know all that they need to know.

> But in the end, we say, they are not ourselves. They are everywhere. The world turns through their breath. You can hear them in your sleep. The night is full of their eyes.
>
> They never ask why.

Merwin would have us suspend that power of always asking why and supplant it with the strength to wonder. To wonder, as in these prose pieces, is to speculate without the prospect of an answer. When expectations are suspended, moments expand with a capaciousness in which the familiar becomes new. The meaning of the title *The Ark of Silence* is that this earth is an ark that we share with a host of creatures. Their eyes in the night haunt our sleep: they represent the endless, but often overlooked, abundance of the world. It is a world of silence because the animals are dumb: "There is nothing we can say to them that they will understand." But that means that we may try to say too much, that the real understanding we long for cannot be contained within words, though the right words may approach and momentarily encircle it.

4

Sea Poems

DAVID ASCHAM, the young poet who is the central character in "The Monument," a comedy in verse Merwin began in April 1954 but left unfinished halfway through the second of its three acts, finds himself at a turning point.[1] He has just been awarded the prestigious British Poets' Prize, and he has concluded that the next step in his career must be to get a job—his first job, any kind of job, as long as it is a regular job, with definite hours and routine obligations. His friends are scandalized. His mistress leaves him in a huff, denouncing his errant ways. The best-selling author whose travel chronicles Ascham has been ghostwriting is thrown into a panic. Even Ascham's mother arranges a hasty visit, certain her son has reached a true crisis in his life.

Only to his mother is Ascham able to confide the thinking behind his decision. The idea of submitting to the banality of honest labor, he explains, occurred to him after he had written "Lightbreak Hill," a poem recalling a scene from his childhood home:

> But in that poem I took the hill as the centre
> Of my own private vision; that, I suppose, was easy
> Compared to what I want to do, which is
> To take it as a symbol of the innocence
> That I believe is the reality
> Whose simplicity escapes us and escapes us
> Until it comes to seem more difficult
> To apprehend than anything else, but is,
> In fact, under all there is.
> MRS ASCHAM: Rather like Wordsworth's
> "Ode on Intimations of Immortality"?

DAVID: No,
Not romantic innocence, which was a thing
Not possible in the world, gone before or
Coming after, perhaps, but impossible in the real
World. But innocence as the thing that is real
Under all our complexities, a belief that
The more really real a thing is, the more
Innocent it is. Until you'd come
To God, who I could only feel as
The supreme reality, and believe, knowing all,
Is the supreme innocence. So a statement of faith, as
The romantics were a denial of faith.

From this, Ascham concludes he now should take an "ordinary job," not because it "will be getting any closer to reality," but because it will "force me to live / In the not utterly desirable ordinary / World." Since the play is unfinished, the working-out of this proposal remains lost. But Ascham's mother immediately sets in motion events that will reunite David with the father from whom he has been long estranged—an eccentric recluse who lives with his youthful wife in a villa in France. To his mother, Ascham's longing for innocence is, like the notion of innocence, beyond grasping; it must be translated into something less ineffable, a yearning for his lost childhood.

At this time, Merwin was a young prizewinning poet living in England—on the strength of *The Dancing Bears* he was awarded the 1954 Poetry Fellowship of the *Kenyon Review*—and as much preoccupied with the concept of innocence as, in his bestiary, he was drawn to images of the sea. Indeed, a poem written in August 1954, "To Brewster Ghiselin," linked both preoccupations.[2] This epistle-poem, which begins "Indeed, there is no such thing as the known sea," is a response prompted by the writings of the poet-critic addressed in the title. Toward the middle of the seventy-four-line poem, Merwin enunciated a cluster of ideas like Ascham's:

Stone or shell,
Kelp-strand or swimmer, each thing is
In its reality a mystery
Not to be known in terms of itself only,
Its simplicity watered over with shadows,
Their resemblances, telling it what it is,
Their realities, the names beneath which it lies.

No part of that water is gentle. I think
Of violence as part of the mystery,
And yet believe that all that is real, under
Its water-darks is innocent.

Leaning heavily upon the sustained parenthesis of the epistle-poem as a form that permits unguarded statements, Merwin allows himself this indulgence, this series of assertions that ask to be heard with sympathy. The poem is not antiphonic but homophonic: though we overhear only one side of a dialogue, we presume Ghiselin is eagerly nodding his own agreement. Why are poets drawn to the sea? The first line carries the answer that the rest of the poem unfolds: it cannot ever be known. And everything is in the sea, the whole world—it is as unrestricted as the potential subject matter of poetry. The poet appreciates this rich repository, this encyclopedic catalogue, that resists conventional forms of understanding. The form that can contain that uncontainable aspect of reality is the poem, for the poet is alert to the way objects in the sea escape fixity, blurring, shifting—their "simplicity watered over with shadows." The very medium of poetry is a watery flux in which words surrender their denotative properties. And so innocence is near, though just out of reach—an ultimate reality, a mystery, but one made palpable when one is submerged in the murky elision of the words of a poem.

Both Ascham's confession and Merwin's "reply" to Ghiselin emerge from a situation carefully authenticated as a truth-telling moment. We eavesdrop on the poet in the midst of an impassioned explanation of his mission, when he is pressed to divulge what it is he hopes to do. And to convey what is essentially a belief or code of values in this particular way, in a sudden moment in which speech is no longer guarded, is radically aligned with the convictions being proposed. The instant in which his convictions suddenly take shape as words is a fleeting one, not to be repeated with ease. So if the very words he relies upon, if "innocence" and "simplicity" (and "mystery" and "reality") seem to dissolve into the air almost as soon as they are heard, it is because Merwin's ear is attuned to that vanishing, that slipping out and away, which the terms are made not only to recount but to enact. The innocence he offers for consideration, then, is not a state of mind he hopes to attain: it is closer to a presence he is constantly pursuing, just out of reach. It is recognizable, indeed, only by its vanishing, at which point it is likely to expose the clumsiness and even the violence of our habits and assumptions, the mechanisms of thought we erect to conceive a practical order. In dissolving, it leaves not only a lingering memory but a vivid sense of all it is not.

1

Green with Beasts is the volume in which Merwin begins to work with subjects that require him to evoke peculiarly subtle discriminations; they are distinctions, however, that usually point up the falsity of trying to discriminate with total success. He is intent on catching the sense in which we must travel light because we only grasp a small part of that which comes to us. His subtlety lies in his ability to evoke not just what we cannot attain but our own realization of what we recognize as unattainable. His progress through the volume, moreover, places increasing demands on our willingness to accept how much lies beyond our control. Early on, it is primarily language that slips away from us, often for reasons easily understandable: the poems center on moments when we are confronted with extraordinary situations, when disorientation is the norm. The narrative situation itself is static, or made so by the inability of the poem's language to do other than circle helplessly about. In later poems, however, Merwin's language grows increasingly transparent, depicting situations that disclose facets that escape understanding. Ending the book with a sequence of sea poems (the last four of which were written in the month he assembled the volume) shifts attention to narrative lines, anecdotal incidents, descriptions of detail—all held in tension with the looming and potentially intrusive presence of the sea, which hovers throughout, always mocking the boundaries temporarily erected against its power.

Merwin set aside the standard poetic achievement of the 1950s—the dense production polished to perfection, encased within an elaborate framework—in favor of the light touch, the indirect approach. He wants his words to be heard as approximations. Only as language fails just before its occasion is it properly poetic. Consequently, his lines tend to deploy themselves along two contrary axes. Syntactically, they are extensive linkages, with phrases and clauses that proliferate and meander:

> Only on the rarest occasions, when the blue air,
> Though clear, is not too blinding (as, say,
> For a particular moment just at dusk in autumn)
> Or if the clouds should part suddenly
> Between freshets in spring, can one trace the rising
> Slopes high enough even to call them contours; and even
> More rarely see above the treeline. (FF, 154)

Tonally, however, as in this opening of "The Mountain," they are lavishly orchestrated, with sounds blending as effortlessly as passages of music, using internal rhyme ("rarest" and "air"), light alliteration ("blue" and "blinding," "call them contours"), and consonance and assonance (the interweavings of *t*, *m*, and *u* in "a particular moment just at dusk in autumn"). Merwin thinks like a scholar but listens like Ravel. The words and phrases he throws before him, like a lifeline strung out as he proceeds, preserve their air of provisionality, but that heady mix yields a persistent music that lends true support (fig. 6).

In 1954 and 1955, Merwin was working outside channels that regulated his contemporaries. Living in England, supporting himself with translations and drama for the BBC, he remained remote from the academic atmosphere American poets breathed in their university surroundings. In comparison to Richard Wilbur or Anthony Hecht or Howard Nemerov, he is positively disheveled, unbuttoned. His lines are startlingly close to prose:

> Of course to each of us
> Privately, its chief difference from its peers
> Rests not even in its centrality, but its
> Strangeness composed of our own intimacy
> With a part of it, our necessary
> Ignorance of its limits, and diurnal pretence
> That what we see of it is all. (FF, 155)

As in this passage, "The Mountain" simply describes a mountain from many perspectives, none of which is capable of grasping it completely. But like several of the bestiary poems that mention their subject by every possible name but the one that appears in the title, "The Mountain" invites comparison with other subjects, not the least of which is poetry itself. The elusiveness of the subject always requires one more statement, one more perspective, all of which point toward the mountain and none of which contains it. From one angle it is one thing, from another angle another, and the poem as a whole points toward this undefinable presence around which its words circle.

Merwin would evoke that which remains beyond his grasp, yet he would register that just-elusive presence. This delicate negotiation explains why *Green with Beasts* was, of all Merwin's collections, the most heavily selective. It retains only half his poems from early 1953 to the fall of 1955 and only a little more than two-thirds of the poems published in journals.[3] To be included, a poem had to do more than recognize that "the world is wide. / And how can we know even the place where we stand?" These lines from "Faces and Landscapes," an uncollected poem, state his theme but their straightforwardness fails to depict the unsettling effect of the perception. Poems that spoke with authority were set aside for those that enacted, through the exquisite disorientation of their language, the limits of understanding. Many of these omitted poems met high criteria: Karl Shapiro published "Corps de Ballet" in *Poetry,* Monroe Spears "Catching Leaves in Autumn" in the *Sewanee Review,* and John Crowe Ransom "The Nine Days of Creation" in the *Kenyon Review.*[4] Merwin reprinted none. Each ends in an adroit shift that curves back on the poem to encompass it. In "Corps de Ballet," he considers arguments that artists offer to explain why recognition has eluded them, but he ends by folding the rationalizations back into the pleasurable experience of watching dancers work against the expectations they arouse in their audience. The poem neatly collapses hesitations about the value of the artistic life into a sudden celebration of its graceful particulars. Hesitation and indecision, a constant awareness that one

Senility Cay — 18 A.

All the birds are dying on this beach

The birds are all dying on this beach

like a camp

No figures in sight. But see

Here ~~nothing~~ staring is the blank where a man will be.

gaunt gap

shape of man

Teeth dropped

falling

teeth, hair

skin

semi

palsied sea

manhood

moon

Gray grass twitching

in the green moony light

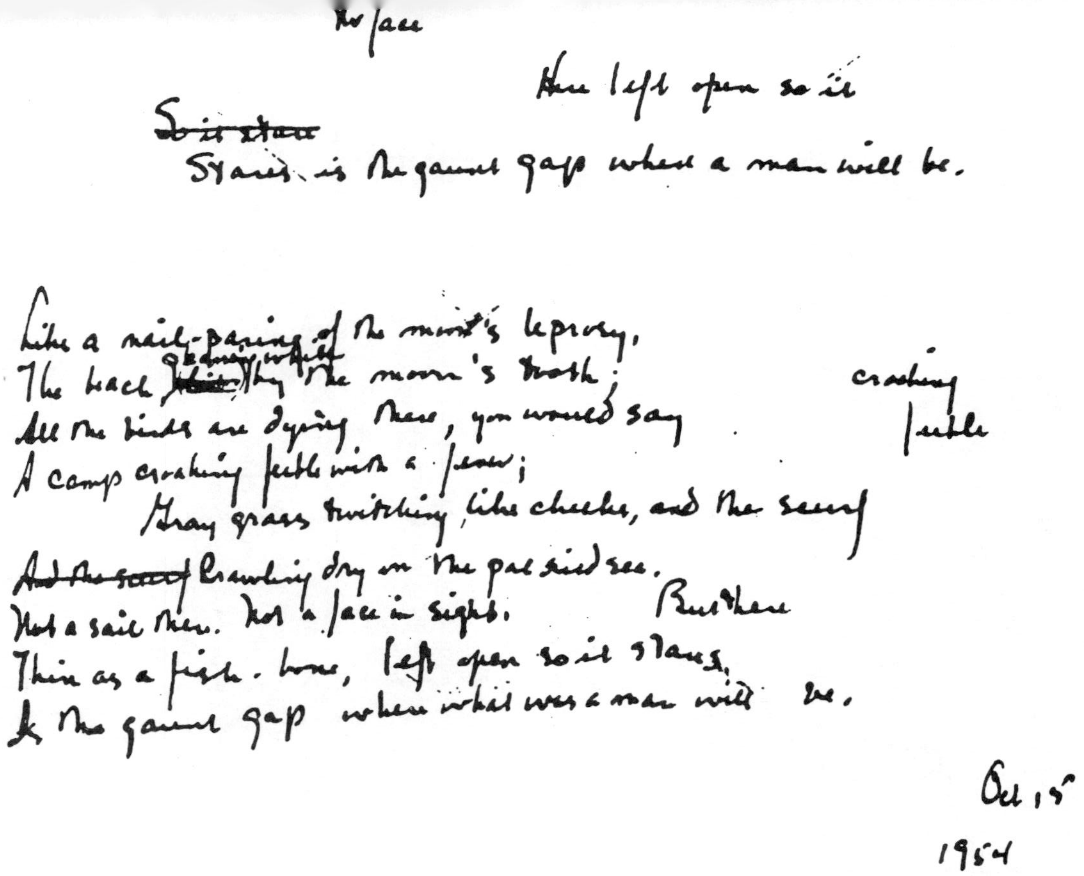

no face

Here left open so it

~~So it stares~~
Stares is the gaunt gap where a man will be.

Like a nail-paring of the mind's leprosy,
The beach, gleaming white by the moon's tooth;
All the birds are dying there, you would say
A camp croaking feeble with a fever;
Gray grass twitching, like cheeks, and the scurf
~~And the scurf~~ Crawling dry on the pale sick sea.
Not a sail there. Not a face in sight. But there
Thin as a fish-bone, left open so it stares,
Is the gaunt gap where what was a man will be.

croaking
feeble

Oct 15
1954

Figure 6. Notes and final draft of "Senility Cay" (MS. 19:12/040, d. Oct. 15, 1954), one of the sea poems from *Green with Beasts*. Merwin's notes suggest how rapidly he could work. He collects some key phrases, focuses on and perhaps rewrites a central passage, but soon proceeds to a finished version.

may be failing, are essential to the life of art—but the poem, in its conclusive twist, surmounts such uncertainty with a finale that makes the work all too self-contained.

By the fall of 1955, when Merwin was selecting the poems for *Green with Beasts,* his poetry no longer depended, as it had in "The Mountain," on examples of the untrustworthiness of language. Rather, the interplay between the known and the unknown is depicted in disarming moments for which there are no words. As a result, works of some length can be trimmed to one pivotal instant. "Backwater Pond: the Canoeists" excerpts only the last twelve lines of the eighty-five-line "Stump Pond."[5] About half of the omitted lines cluck their tongue over the brand of civilization summer inhabitants have brought to a lakeshore area:

> Those who come up to spend the summer
> In the cottages, dining on their porches, refer
> To the lake as "the wilds," because the lawns
> Are larger than their city gardens,
> There are no street sounds, but occasional crickets,
> And some must fetch their water in buckets.
> They have made shifts, though, against rustic discomforts:
> There are portable radios, a dancing pavilion,
> Lending library of detective fiction,
> Bridge clubs; so that, except for small
> Inconveniences, only the stump pond still
> Remains unfriendly: an eyesore, but
> Mercifully out of sight.

In this first version, the poem goes on to stress how little of the wilderness has survived these encroachments. Only the ugly backwater of the stump pond has resisted, and that is because it remains out of sight. Yet on Sundays, the tourists are drawn to explore this backwater, which humbles them with its imposing, alien, even intimidating presence. Something of the primordial innocence of nature remains and calls even to those who have apparently armed themselves against it with what they would call the comforts of civilization—and what Merwin would call the vapid emblems of a deracinated mass culture.

In the poem's later, revised version, published in *Green with Beasts* as "Backwater Pond: the Canoeists," Merwin downplays this heavy-handed contrast. His title immediately promotes the pond's visitors from tourists to canoeists, and in the twelve lines that remain, the power of the wilderness area is enhanced because experienced voyagers are struck dumb by it. "Stump Pond" had posed an aggressive question: Are the canoeists silenced because under their civilized veneer a respect for some pure, strange experience still exists, or is the devastated backwater a place whose ugliness they are intimately at home in? The later version shifts away from this issue, intent on bringing us in contact with an awesome presence that escapes our understanding. Lines describing the trappings tourists bring to a resort are no longer to the purpose.

In the early poems in part 2 of *Green with Beasts* Merwin fusses with ideas about the overall inadequacy of language itself, piling up parallel clauses and phrases, sliding from one approximation to the next. "The Prodigal Son" and "The Annunciation" are only two of several lengthy narratives completed at this time, all of which employ syntax in a way that offsets clarity. By contrast, the later poems in part 2 replace narrative with anecdote and feature an actual "I" speaking, a witness who lends credence to the unsettling shifts that make the poem. When creatures appear—the dog walked in "Thorn Leaves in March," or the sparrow sheltering under a column of the British Museum, or the birds on Primrose Hill associated with a pastoral apocalypse—they contribute to the poem but as accessories to the speaker's experience; they do not take the center of the work onto themselves, as they had in the bestiary. They are avenues toward that mystery Merwin would bring forward as the central experience of poetry. In a way that is quite unfashionable in the 1950s, this poetry is not intent upon extracting meanings or imposing connections, though it may, in passing, perform those functions. At bottom, its purpose is to dissolve certainties and blur boundaries. Indeed, it often serves to remind us how little we know.

"Burning the Cat" may have started as an eighteenth bestiary poem; "Cats" was its original title.[6] Unlike other bestiary poems, however, it evolved into three sections: "Cat with Bird," "Burning the Cat," and "Cats at Home." The first of these, a vignette straight out of the bestiary, describes an activity generic to the species:

> Without hate or haste, oblivious, needing neither.
> That moved gradual as alternate shadows on smooth water,
> Without haste or anything but the bird
> In its eyes; and its jaws' incontinent chattering
> Bespoke only a keyed fixity of pleasure
> In anticipation that was like admiring affection. . . .

Attention centers on the creature; the poet is not dramatically present as a witness. But Merwin chose to print only the second of the three, "Burning the Cat," the one in which he is not only witness but participant. He is even drawn up short by the conclusion at the end. In its offhand development, the poem hardly prepares for a profound conclusion; yet when Merwin realizes he should have simply buried the cat, he stands, for a moment, in awe before the completeness of death:

> for
> The earth is slow, but deep, and good for hiding;
> I would have used it if I had understood

> How nine lives can vanish in one flash of a dog's jaws,
> A car or a copperhead, and yet how one small
> Death, however reckoned, is hard to dispose of. (FF, 168)

If there is no trace of mourning here, it is because at the same time he is gratified to sense how distant he remains from that completeness. He misunderstood death, associating it with fire, not the earth. But fire is life, requiring more fuel, newspapers, sticks; it smears the woods with blackening smoke, mixing the rank odor of the charring corpse with the shining smell of dogwood. Fire brings things back to life, transforming them at once. It flashes, like the dog's jaws or the rapid car or the darting copperhead; it partakes of reckoning, as does Merwin at the close. But death is ponderous, inevitable, mute. Thus at the end, a startling gap, as profound as that between the earth and a fire, opens between death and life, with the poet poised above it, appreciating even the harried gestures that attended the building of the pyre—searching for newspapers, vowing to build the fire as high as the house, stoking the flames until his face is black with smoke—because that hasty activity confirms his remoteness from the solid, substantial, unyielding fact of death.

2

The sophistication new to *Green with Beasts* lies in Merwin's ability to set out with aims that are apparently modest—walking his dog, noting a sparrow on library steps, cleaning a garden, hearing the birds before dawn—only to be drawn into contact with powerful, even awesome forces that escape full understanding. The sea poems in part 3, along with a supplementary set written soon after (but not collected until 1960, in *The Drunk in the Furnace*), exemplify that brush with the unknown as it arises most unexpectedly and most distressingly.

In notes for a long poem entitled "Westfaring," planned in the early 1950s as a sequence detailing adventures of ancient and Renaissance voyagers, the nature of the sea's disruption is evident at once: the sea is where the known and unknown clash most dramatically. On the one hand, sea voyages require an investment in knowledge. They demand the most technologically advanced navigational instruments of the time. On the other hand, voyaging to new realms discloses how little we know of our world. "Westfaring" was to be packed with esoteric technical detail. "Check almanack for the time + months + work in astrological data," Merwin noted. "Get hold of 16th century manual of seamanship: *The Regiment of the North Star.*" He advised himself to make "Continual use of maps, cartography, image of world, earth, and of celestial globe—contemporary astronomy, aspects of stars." This elaborate machinery, however, will dissolve into useless gadgetry when mariners confront the unexpected. Merwin envisions an apparition that Columbus will encounter in mid-voyage. He sketches the appearance four times; a note that begins "How Gods change" develops it most fully: "recounting of apparition of Virgin—Christian deity, etc., patron of sailors, adequate to life of Spain, etc.—which had influenced voyage—on high sea, matrix waters, if he sees her it is as Great Mother, great mysterious She." Columbus may expect to identify the apparition as Santa Maria, patron of sailors, but that is inadequate on these "matrix waters." She becomes something else, less defined. "All human deities become distant and faint," he writes in another note. "They are among the great primordial forces that they have no names for, no adequate image for."

Merwin's sea poetry verges on becoming poetry about poetry, because poetry's value lies in the extent to which it reveals situations that escape confident understanding. That the sea, by the mid-1950s, had become identified for Merwin with poetry itself may explain why he was not quick to begin his own cycle of sea poems and why "Westfaring" was never begun. The standard for such writing would be very high. Indeed, when he finally began a cycle of sea poems in the summer of 1955, he was careful to downplay the dramatic aspects of voyaging. The sea, for his mariners, is just a dangerous, treacherous workplace. Yet he was no sooner done with this first cycle than a second was under way, and this second, which connects seafaring with poetry in a most indirect way, must be counted among his earliest unquestionable triumphs.

Altogether twenty-three sea poems were written, with eight collected in part 3 of *Green with Beasts* and twelve in the opening pages of *The Drunk in the Furnace.* But their publication in two distinct volumes is appropriate; they are related but separate sets of poetry.[7] The earlier set is a series of portraits or sketches about the sea, loosely arranged in a narrative; the later set consists of reports and narratives that recollect sea voyages. Initially, it seems the earlier set would be the commanding sequence. There, Merwin embarks, through his loose narrative, on a sea voyage. After a series of four miscellaneous poems that view the sea from the land, he locates himself on a fogbound ship that must turn away from home and sail for the open sea. The next poem recreates a shipwreck, including the terrible last moments in which the crew understand they will die. The following poem is written from the viewpoint of the drowned, who turn to a wide rhythm in which the hulls of ships overhead are as incomprehensible to them as the stars are to the living. The final poem is a carol about the dangers of voyaging. The narrative ends with our initiation into the fraternity of the mariners. It is a series of realistic encounters, by the close of which we move in harmony with the sailors whose lives are at risk.

The second set, by contrast, is a miscellany, unshaped by narrative. We now listen to dramatic monologues spoken by others in which they recollect their experience at sea. Instead of an actual voyage, we listen to anecdotes about voyaging. The shipwreck poem in the second set happens entirely offstage; no wreck is ever described, and the poem is only the recollection of one who was among the last to see the doomed vessel. The cast of characters broadens to include a sailor's wife. The setting broadens to include voyages to the Arctic. There is a portrait of a sailor ashore, far from the dangers of the ocean. Indeed, unlike the dangerous voyage of the first set, the poems of the second set take place on shore, or direct attention to details of the seascape, or relate tales by mariners. Yet insofar as these poems depict the habits of mind of those who have been brushed by the sea, they give us a sense of the sea's ominous uncertainty with a new forcefulness. With this sequence, Merwin keeps rediscovering situations in which the unknown is a constant presence: his voyagers are closer than anyone else to the conditions of authentic poetry. Like the poet, they must use what they know to speak in desperation of what they do not know.

These new poems rely on a language that is unadorned, modest, vernacular. Their achievement hinges on subtle details: parallelism and repeated phrases, the repetitions of which suggest the speaker is worrying about a problem whose scope is now expanding, now diminishing; a deft use of consonance, close to alliteration at key descriptive points, as though the speaker has hit upon a moment of firmness that needs to be sustained; and a sensitive attention to pace, fostered by the interplay between run-on and end-stopped lines. Each of these allows Merwin to write lines edged with nervous uncertainty. The words are as common as can be, yet they move in unexpected ways; they brush the familiar with the strange, until what is known and what is unknown become facets of each other. "Fog-Horn" points out the resemblance between the sound of the foghorn, meant to protect against danger, and the sound of a terror that stirs frightening depths. That sound is "not the thing / That men thought they were making, when they / Put it there, for their own necessities." As in "Bell Buoy," these "shaped tokens / Of our usage" disclose the dread they were fashioned to conceal. Their presence announces the marginal place, a point of intersection where certainty and uncertainty feel interchangeable.

The actual writing of the second set began with "Sailor Ashore," a poem that seems comic, even irreverent, when compared with the terror the first set associated with the ocean. Certainly it is an abrupt change from the dangers of voyaging: a drunken sailor, reeling on his feet, cries out, "The sea is everywhere." Lampposts are "Blinking and swaying above the wet cobbles" and darkness "yaws out and back." Yet the poem asserts there is no steady home to which to return, no end to voyaging; the sea is inescapable. It is not, then, that the sailor is a comic figure, unaccustomed to drink: he is unaccustomed to objects that are fixed, that lack the constant motion of the sea. When lamps blink and sway, when darkness yaws, he is at home because he might as well be at sea.

"The *Portland* Going Out," the shipwreck poem of the second set, uses an obsessive concern with homely details to evoke the nervous pressures of the sea. Its effect depends on a play between end-stopped and run-on lines, by which moments of rest are abruptly unsettled:

> By
> Five it was kicking up quite a bit,
> And the greasiest evening you ever saw,
> We had just come in, and were making fast,
> A few minutes to seven, when she went
> Down the harbor behind us, going out,
> Passing so close over our stern that we
> Caught the red glow of her port light for
> A moment on our faces. (FF, 209)

In a passage not governed by a steady meter, Merwin has considerable leeway as to where to break his line. But the line breaks have been used to such effectiveness the passage could appear no other way with the same impact. The first three lines are end-stopped, with the line break occurring naturally; everything is in its appropriate place, without drama. Indeed, for long stretches, things fall into place. But just the other side of this mundane orderliness is the sudden surprise, the abrupt turn, mimicked by the line break of "She went / Down the harbor behind us." The fearful words "went / Down" are both suppressed and emphasized, falling over the line break. Orderliness is temporarily restored in the following line, with the comfortable pause between "going out" and "Passing so close." But as the next lines scurry ahead, the ship's passing crowds forward: "So close over our stern that we / Caught the red glow of her port light / For a moment."

These disruptions in the line break are subtle, perhaps extremely so, but the point is not that terror lurks below the surface: the mind brushes up against fears, then swerves away by attending to detail ("A few minutes after seven"), minutiae that are protective but never quite adequate barriers. These poems are more than portraits of those who work with the sea; they reveal that we are all brushed by the unknown and that we all guard ourselves against a direct encounter with it by rehearsing details that deflect our attention. Merwin's sea tests our character because it so steadfastly retains its overwhelming perspective. And for that reason, the second set of sea poems naturally accommodates other intimidating presences, such as the South Pole in "The Frozen Waste" or the iceberg in "The Iceberg." Any presence so vast as to challenge our assumptions of control becomes the opportunity to recall that we live in a fragile, fleeting moment, and that even our most familiar possessions are not our own.

In this second set, Merwin is always aware of two clashing perspectives: the eternal, unyielding presence of the sea, a presence that touches all its points levelly and equally, dissolving space and time, and the fragile, temporary presence of the human, a presence that occupies a vulnerable space for an instant of time. This point is underscored in the most monumental of the sea poems, "The Bones": what is given with one hand is taken back with the other. In this poem, which could recall "The Idea of Order at Key West"—except that, pointedly enough, there is no woman, no song, and no order—shaping and wasting become indistinguishable.

At first the poem seems to affirm a distinction between human beings and the sea. The sea is a "tideless waste," casting detritus up on the shore, heedlessly mingling all in a "throaty / Rattle." By contrast, we walk by the sea and speculate and seem intent on making something of the tideless waste. Merwin recalls a man who once made a flute out of a bone, and he himself recognizes the now-shapeless hulk of a boat that was once capable of giving "weight to the winds." And the poem concludes in a way that appears to celebrate the powers of the human mind:

> a man's bones were framed
> For what? For knowing the sands are here
> And coming to hear them a long time; for giving
> Shapes to the sprawled sea, weight to its winds,
> And wrecks to plead for its sands. These things are not
> Limitless; we know there is somewhere
> An end to them, though every way you look
> They extend farther than a man can see. (FF, 217)

We are not limited by what our eyes fall upon. The mind ranges out endlessly, knowing somewhere there is a limit but never lighting upon it.

But also within the poem, at odds with this affirmative reading, is another that relentlessly undercuts any congratulatory tone. This other reading leads toward an austere appraisal of the endlessness of human effort, continually undone by the shapelessness of the sea. Merwin's effort to place distance between himself and the sea, between shaping and wasting, occurs early in the poem, but it ends painfully, in a line that strings itself out both hopefully and hopelessly. Just as he is beginning to develop an instructive and reassuring example that will illustrate how distinct the human is from the sea, he finds his example dissolving from beneath him:

> For years I had hardly
> Considered shells as being bones, maybe
> Because of the sounds they could still make, though
> I knew a man once who could raise a kind
> Of wailing tune out of a flute he had,
> Made from a fibula; it was much the same
> Register as the shells'; the tune did not
> Go on when his breath stopped, though you thought it would. (FF, 216)

Three complete thoughts compose this sentence. The first thought is most heartening, an instance of waste transformed, a tune created from a bone, life from death. But in the next thought that "wailing tune" is "much the same / Register as the shells'." The tune is like the wind blowing through the shells, and it is heard as peculiarly nonhuman. (The awkwardness of "shells'," with its odd but appropriate punctuation, helps to quell the poem's momentum.) The last thought recognizes that the tune had been identical with the man's breathing; when he stopped, the tune stopped. Though the tune emphatically "did not / Go on when his breath stopped" (the "not" at the end of the line receives an emphatic stress), the wish was that it would go on, that it would fill out the silence, much as this line goes on. This is the first recognition that what we make is ultimately as fragile as our breath and that we naturally desire to go on forever, yearning to transform and escape the waste and the silence—which are inescapable. Distance between the sea's wasting and human shaping collapses; our effort to give shape to the waste about us can only give rise to our awareness that the waste is endless.

How little control we have, even as we persist in our desire to make over things—that is the austere awareness developed in "The Bones." As the poem continues, Merwin shows that, while using his mind to make distinctions, he is at the same time swept up into the maelstrom he would shape himself against:

> The rest was bones, whatever
> Tunes they made. The bones of things; and of men too
> And of man's endeavors whose ribs he had set
> Between himself and the shapeless tides. Then
> I saw how the sand was shifting like water,
> That once could walk. Shells were to shut out the sea,
> The bones of birds were built for floating
> On air and water, and those of fish were devised
> For their feeding depths, while a man's bones were framed
> For what? (FF, 217)

The insights here are as ravaging and leveling as they are discriminating. This, the high point of the poem, a demonstration of our ability to pierce the surface and grasp connections, also turns upon an awareness that the most disparate things are identical. Once the dry sand appears as identical to water "that once could walk," the identity between things is as strong as their difference. Merwin's question "For what?" is answered in his concluding lines, but the enormous vista that opens there reveals not just the power of those who can see so far—"though every way you look / They extend farther than a man can see"—but also the endlessness of that task.

In the second set, what the voyagers display is not intelligence but character. The mariners are heroic in proportion to their modesty; they know, without ever stating it, that however they strive to give their world stability, at some point they must turn back to the open sea. The only genuine home is this aura of homelessness within which we all live. Yet what finally does distinguish humans from creatures is that humans feel things in their bones. Their bones are like dead shells not to "shut out the sea" but to come in contact with it, to invent a "wailing tune," to enter an uneasy pact with it. Apart from this wary receptivity, however, nothing is offered by way of guidance. To each of us, our tasks fall forward in a new way, or, as the mariners who have actually visited the treacherous waters at "Cape Dread" advise:

> But what we found
> You will find for yourselves, somewhere, for
> Yourselves. We have not gone there again,
> Nor ventured ever so far again. In
> The south corner of the cove there is
> An inlet flowing with sweet water,
> And there are fruits in abundance, small
> But delectable, at least at that season. (FF, 212)

The affirmation is a modest one, provisional, apt to be undone; but there is no alternative to making one's way carefully, cautiously, across an uncertain surface liable to give way at any moment.

5

His Bad Castle

"IN AUGUST 1956, the American poet and playwright W. S. Merwin flew home after seven years abroad": so appeared the prefatory note in *Paris Review* to "Flight Home," a journal Merwin kept of his last days in Europe. It is one of a number of public declarations of this time proclaiming his dual role as playwright and poet. References to play writing are scattered through his first interview, conducted by *Audience* magazine after his arrival in Boston in the fall of 1956. Does he prefer England to America? "The English put on my plays, and pay me for them." What advantage in play writing for the poet? "Dramatic verse tends to stress clarity, and in doing so, it occasions a certain immediacy and directness." Any plans for the future? "What I really want to do is sit home writing plays and not be around educated people. I find that a bit claustrophobic." Merwin intended to come off as a businesslike professional: given the opportunity to revise his replies, he did not soften them. Indeed, he modified the comment above to read: "Not around people who read my books, mostly. Or anybody's. Too many educated people around all the time—not that."[1]

He had every reason, in 1956, to claim the title of playwright. His return to America was made possible by a $3000 grant to work for a year with the Poets' Theater in Cambridge; he was one of a select number invited to apply for the fellowship. In February, "Darkling Child" (in collaboration with Dido Milroy) enjoyed a brief run on the London stage. Merwin the dramatist was a frequent contributor to the BBC Third Programme. Between 1950 and 1956, the network broadcast his original masque-play, "The Pageant of Cain"; his adaptation of *Huckleberry Finn* and Hawthorne's "Dr. Heidegger's Experiment"; and his translations of the medieval mystery play "Robert the Devil," de Vega's "The Dog in the Manger," de Rueda's "Eufemia," LeSage's "Turcaret" and "The Rival of his Master," and Marivaux's "False Confessions." For TV he adapted "Rumpelstiltskin." In 1956 a British radio audience might have been surprised to hear of his reputation as a poet. To them, his only nondramatic translation of length had been *The Poem of the Cid.*

But Merwin's two years in America, from 1956 to 1958, would ultimately shake his confidence in his ability to fulfill the expectations of a theater audience. He completed two new plays in America in 1957, but one was never produced, and the other was performed only in Coventry in 1961. In England, the BBC had been a benign if penurious patron; certainly its audience accepted projects—medieval mystery plays, eighteenth-century French comedies—for which no audience existed in America. Some years later, Merwin recalled his return home as though it had been a bad idea that he had been helpless to resist. In England, he remembered,

> I'd been living on very little money, but I'd been living on my own time, working on translations and poems. I could do that in Europe, but I couldn't do that in the States. There was no way I could afford it. On the other hand, I got very homesick. It wasn't a matter of approving what was happening at home, it was just a matter of hearing your own language. Lowell has a line in one of his poems, when *he* was living in England those last years, about one of his trips to New York. He said, "At least I don't have the feeling that I'm growing deaf," which is something I felt for several years.[2]

And yet the apprenticeship he had served in England would prove irrelevant to circumstances in America. As the bluff tone of his 1956 interview indicates, Merwin came to America thinking of himself as the no-nonsense playwright, the hardheaded professional who fled the company of the academic. The self-portrait was not entirely unjust: the play to be produced by the Poets' Theater was a documentary that broke from the tradition of verse drama he had been pursuing since 1949, and his second set of sea poems demonstrated that his idea of the poetic was entirely at home in the vernacular. What he was unprepared for, however, was the America that he found: a harsh and crude land whose inhabitants were hardened against each other. Instead of rediscovering the lost music of his native country, he found a discord unimaginable in England.

1

"Favor Island," the play for which Merwin received his yearlong fellowship in Boston, displays the gentility that guaranteed many aspects of American life would be a shock to Merwin's sensibility; however, it also shows a certain directness, a hardheaded toughness verging on the cynical that would form the basis for a new apprenticeship, one that would allow him to confront the brutality he saw in his homeland. The play, a documentary drama about an eighteenth century sea voyage from England to America, was written in 1955–56, contemporaneous with his sea poems.[3] As with some of his earlier plays, the plot was borrowed; a note for the playbill of the original production explains that it was

> drawn on accounts of an actual voyage of the ship Nottingham Galley from London in the year 1710, under Captain John Dean. The events of the voyage and the shipwreck caused a scandal and inquiry in London, as a result of which Captain Dean wrote "A Narrative of the Shipwreck of the Nottingham Galley." His account was disputed by the ship's mate, Christopher Langmann, who shortly after published "A True Account of the Voyage of the Nottingham Galley." Captain Dean defended himself so successfully at the inquiry that he was later appointed British Consul of the Port of Flanders.

Working with contradictory sources, Merwin steered a course between opposing viewpoints. His version, though, appeared on a scale larger than a court inquiry; he opposes the perspective of the sailors, which is set on matters of detail and fundamentally limited, to the perspective of the captain, arranging a distant conclusion that will be satisfactory to him alone. The conflict justifies the documentary approach. Vignettes feature conversations that touch upon the details of voyaging. But such conversation unfolds against an inexorable course of events, as the captain shapes a voyage he hopes to consummate with a carefully arranged disaster.

Searching for the right kind of disaster, the ship blunders onto the wrong kind: it runs aground off the coast of Maine in winter, its crew marooned on an island. Eventually the survivors are rescued but not until all, with the exception of Captain John Monk and First Mate Nicholas Short, have resorted to cannibalism. The remnants of the crew return to England, where Monk takes command of another vessel, presumably to continue his scheming. An onstage narrator speaks an epilogue that begins:

> Now go and say no answer came
> To the best question you could frame.
> Some die always, and some go lame,
> And some go begging, what a shame.
> (Fortune was always a heartless Dame)
> But most go on at the old game
> Some good, some lucky, and who's to blame
> If many things just stay the same?

This blunt summation links the documentary with the vision that underlies Merwin's conception of classical drama. What nice conclusion is an audience to draw from the play? The narrator dismisses the question as naive. The audience is abandoned to a harsh reality.

Yet that harsh reality is muted by the leisurely form with which the play unfolds. On the one hand, "Favor Island" aspires to the documentary mode—its two separate acts are a series of tableaux, with blackouts in between and an onstage narrator to distract from scenery shifting with transitional commentary. On the other hand, it resembles nothing less than the stylized interchanges of a medieval mystery play. As a secularized mystery play, the play attains a sort of bleak grandeur. The role of the mysterious, remote, capricious God is taken by the captain, who subjects his crew to a test of their character, which most fail. Anxiously, crew members go about their daily routine, gradually intuiting that they are in the inexorable grip of a disaster-in-the-making, but helpless to interrupt. They win our sympathy because they are victims of circumstances beyond their control. First Mate Nicholas Short emerges, if not as hero, at least with his dignity intact.

"Favor Island" as a mystery play subjects religious belief to a harsh critique. We expect some point to emerge, as though the form of the play was working toward some grand perception; but as the narrator insists, the point is the pointlessness of all we have seen. None of the crew members, it is true, invokes religion at any point in the play; but all take their place, more or less willingly, as ingredients in a scheme they cannot fathom. Like the mariners in the second set of sea poems, they cultivate habits of mind that guard against their constant brush with what escapes understanding. Playing God, Captain Monk comes to resemble nothing less than the sea itself, as Merwin evoked it in his poems. He is not so much malevolent as sublimely aloof, absolutely withdrawn; his disturbing presence recalls that the sea is simply impervious, empty of human traces except the ones we offer it.

The originality of "Favor Island" lies with this aloof personality both equivalent to the sea and reminiscent of God. Merwin deliberately moved his play in this direction, in revision eliminating material that would have afforded his captain a more conventional background. One late addition is a ship's boy, Charles, whose primary effect is to cast a mysterious shadow over events. In one odd moment he asks the ship's carpenter to fashion him a life-size wooden human head. When the carpenter asks why, the boy says: "Just to have. Just to watch it." This head survives the shipwreck to provide the first inkling that cannibalism might be necessary:

> CHARLES: There is nothing I would not eat. Is there anything
> you would not eat, Mr. Bracknell?
> BRACKNELL: No.
> CHARLES: You cannot eat my head.
> BRACKNELL: Your head!
> CHARLES: (laughing) My wooden one. The Carpenter's head. If it
> was a piece of meat you would eat it. If I would let you.
> If you found a dead horse on the rocks, would you eat it?

The significance of this wooden head remains purposely elusive. Its survivability mocks the frailty of the crew stranded on the island; it also recalls the captain's ability to endure as though not burdened with fleshly cares. But it remains an enigma—something sinister and irresolvable.

The original draft of "Favor Island" had neither ship's boy nor wooden head; instead, it carried a double plot that shed light on the captain as a character. The ship's boy in the final version speaks some of the dialogue first written for James Monk, the captain's younger brother, sailing to begin life over in Boston. James, a failure at all he has tried, is the opposite of his successful brother. Yet he is fully aware that his brother's success depends on criminal actions. The subplot offers James as a figure with heroic overtones; he would rather fail than emulate his brother. At the same time, he is divided. His older brother is a standard of worldly success, and his efforts to please him fail because he is incapable of his brother's supreme self-control. James succumbs to cannibalism, then in anguish reproaches his brother for his ability to remain aloof from human weakness.

"Favor Island" was conceived as a more conventional drama than it became in revision. The brother-to-brother quarrel renders the captain as a personality, not a brooding presence. Including the captain's brother among the crew introduces a level of explanation that vanishes when he is replaced by the errant, ominous ship's boy. Merwin's play takes on qualities of his poetry, incorporating deliberate black holes, textures of obscurity, even characters whose actions cannot be explained. It seems likely he made these changes in the winter of 1956–57, after his arrival in America (the prologue, completed in February 1957, was a last-minute addition), for similar disruptions radically alter his poetry of this time.

2

When he was still in England, Merwin had, responsibly enough, considered what his reaction to America would be. What would a young man feel, home again after seven years abroad? Perhaps affection as he rediscovered old familiar places, perhaps curiosity about his ancestors; perhaps, after the civilized landscape of Europe, surprise at a refreshing rawness or roughness in America. All these sensations are explored in poetry about America that he completed while still in England. In these poems, he actually depicted himself as already having returned to America, and no reader could have guessed these poems were written while their author was still an expatriate. Merwin invites us to surmise, in one poem after another, that he is reporting his immediate impressions of an American landscape in which he stands.

Of these poems, the most persuasive is "Luzerne Street Looking West," completed in February of 1956, six months before his return.[4] Even its title openly proclaims its speaker to be reporting from within a particular American setting. It begins with a streetcar ride to the end of town, the kind of ride any visitor might take, observing

> A marsh, on the left hand, too small
> To be called a swamp, and a weedy tract
> Of shale and cinders, on the right,
> Too indefinite to be called a field,
> And that is all. The car tracks end,
> The paving dips under a railroad bridge
> And stops. Direction abandons
> Any pretense of a plan and frankly
> Returns to being whatever
> You make of it, on any side, through
> A prospect of unrelieved waste,
> Of so much that no one had known to save.

Syntactically, the writing strives for balance, with its "on the left hand" and "on the right," its things "too small" and things "Too indefinite." But the line breaks play havoc with the balancing act. At the close of one line, the car tracks "end," but then in midline, paving "stops" with a period. The poem goes on as the momentum of the ride stops, for the landscape continues to sprawl in its dissolution. We do not halt but peter out with a line that conveys its inertia: "Of so much that no one had known to save." Introducing one-syllable words that slow the pace, the line depicts the dissipated clutter too submerged in the gray area between town and country to bear notice.

Though the passage appears to be offhand, it artfully deploys syntax against line break to convey an emotionally accurate response to a specific place. The poem continues in this reportorial vein. The eye travels to the most distinctive feature in the landscape—the culms, man-made heaps of slag next to collieries, outlined against a backdrop of mountains. They are dismissed at first as pseudomountains whose ugliness affronts nature. But such a dismissal only encourages a turn beyond it, a gesture in accord with the spirit of reclamation the culms engender:

> It seems
> It is, above all, the unacknowledged,
> The unreclaimed, the entirely
> Useless, that will not be forgotten or
> Disowned, but follow us to spread
> Their variety at the edge
> Of all we have made, and give us
> No peace. But at least may it never be
> With anyone I ever knew
> As it is with this unexcusable
> Unavoidable place that once

I knew as well as any friendly mind;
I never missed it when I went,
And never knew I loved it until now.

The poem surprisingly reverses itself through a change in perspective, enacting an authentic reclamation in contrast to the spurious mountains of culm, which remain disconcerting examples of human intrusion. The issue has changed from aesthetics to ethics, with the words "the unacknowledged, / the unreclaimed, the entirely / Useless" applying to human relations. Merwin warns himself not to reject the inhabitants as slickly as he turns from the culms. What helps prevent this admonishment from appearing moralistic is the sense of surprise that overtakes him, as though he has opened realms in his memory he thought closed off entirely. The surprising word "love" conveys the helplessness into which he has fallen. No wonder, then, that the landscape resists yielding to the poet's eye yearning to give it orderly shape: the sprawl is identical to the indiscriminate embrace of loving, which takes in what is before it without judgment.

The excellence of "Luzerne Street" explains why Merwin would take this situation as prototypical, employing it in other poems about his American ancestors. As he conceives it, the American landscape will have a disarming effect, opening him to emotions that are familiar yet new. In "After Some Years" (written three months before leaving Europe)[5] he explains he wants to leave

before the speech here has become
Natural to me, even more so
Than the tongue I was born to, before these
Sights cease to be foreign and are more familiar
Than any I can recall.

His apprehension, however, is expressed in unconventional terms, for the poem reverses usual fears about loss of identity. Here, unease is generated by the prospect of finding an identity—he wants sights that will remain "foreign," but the natives have pleasantly received him "among them as one of themselves." Beginning to blend in, losing a sense of disproportion—that is what causes him hesitation, and he hopes to leave "while I / Can still clearly remember that at home too the world / Is made up of strangers." To be among the unknown, as an eye seeing with freshness, becomes of utmost importance.

Not all of Merwin's American poems written abroad eagerly anticipated homecoming. An exception is "Oh, Susannah!," an unpublished poem written in March 1956.[6] But his doubts are resolutely buried almost as soon as they are expressed. The speaker of the poem, though unidentified, resembles the figure of Merwin's grandfather as he appears in later poems, as a wanderer notorious for his vagabond ways. If that grandfather is addressing a woman who is his wife, his words also invite consideration as Merwin's remarks to his homeland. Divided from the start, the poem begins, "Well, I will come back to you, you black bitch," and then ponders this decision:

> I have been warned that it will be
> No use, that both of us have changed,
> That no man can live with you; and look how nice
> Life is away from you; and yet I will
> Come back. Nobody is more astonished
> Than I am; but maybe this is why
> You never cried when I went away.
>   And who
> All this time, would ever have suspected
> That I care whether you lived or died, except
> That maybe I denied it too fiercely.

The reference to denying with ferocity what one is drawn to by love links this with "Luzerne Street," and the notion resurfaces in the "Flight Home" journal Merwin kept of his last days in Europe. There he records that Europeans lack the "same sort of passion for home" as Americans because in Europe generations have "worked out a way of regarding the place." The calm beauty of the European landscape has "taught them where to fix the feeling, what to see and how to communicate it." But Americans cannot gently and gracefully love their land; they declared themselves Americans by uprooting themselves from their first home, as if they had been unable to master or bear the European art of loving. So they "began as a loveless people": "Our fathers began by caring little enough about Europe so that they could leave it. We've used the place, wasted it. It has made us prodigal, restless. And we are attached to it in still-raw ways that we aren't aware of, most often. We ought to know that we can't hate it as fiercely as we do sometimes without there being something honest in our attachment to it. But there is always the sense of surprise, of inarticulate awkwardness, at discovering the name for what you feel is love."[7] Merwin resorts to the word "love" frequently in these meditations on America produced in England. Love is a word he uses when he is disarmed—helpless but delighted—as in this entry where the emotion is associated with a "sense of surprise" and "inarticulate awkwardness." As new vistas open before him, he enjoys a sense of pleasant disorientation.

It is not surprising, then, that Merwin portrays himself, in the earliest of these poems written in Europe about his ancestors in America, as an onlooker baffled yet enchanted by the mysteries before him. In "John Otto" (written four months before his departure) he ponders an ancestor who remains inscrutable, a "Latin scholar, / Settler of the Cumberland Valley, / Schoolmaster" who met his death at the age of ninety-six, leaving his home on foot to climb beyond a mountain. Though the geographical details of Otto's final journey can be presented with confidence ("the house near Blain, in Perry County" and "the road out of the valley, up the hill, / Over the south mountain, to Carlisle"), the details that would explain how Otto felt or why he took this late journey remain unknown. But that lack of knowledge becomes Merwin's means of entry into the poem, as a voice pursuing questions. Why did he leave his home?

> To ask some question, tell some secret,
> Or beg some pardon before too late?
> Or was it to look once again
> On another valley green in the sun
> Almost as in the beginning, to remind
> Your eyes of a promise in the land? (FF, 245)

To write about a subject that remains out of reach, with a mystery at its heart, brings Merwin back to familiar ground. To the questions he poses there are no answers, only the mystery it is the business of poetry to engender. "Uncle Hess" (written in May 1956) ends in a similar confession: "whatever / You were was unmistakable, but never / Could be explained." Yet the setting in which Merwin locates his uncle is capacious enough to accept all unanswered questions: a large house overlooks a river "Before it twists toward Ohio around the bend / As though there were no questions and no end."

As Merwin's leave-taking draws near, doubts or hesitations about returning begin to dissolve entirely, absorbed in the expanse of an American landscape increasingly mysterious, even beautiful. In these last-minute poems, America is no longer encroached upon by urbanization or industrial waste, neither scarred by culms nor dotted with ruins. Merwin looks backward to a preindustrial, pastoral setting whose ample spaces welcome meditation. The uncollected "Rimer, Penna." (written in June 1956)[8] again positions him back home, "By the broad river, among the foothills / Of yellow Allegheny clay." Enamored of the beauty of the spot, he is held because he cannot explain why his family stopped here instead of pressing westward. Moreover, he knows the mystery will remain, for those who might offer reasons were reticent and untalkative even when they were alive:

> It is quiet here, and their fields
> Still rich, and most things could come by river
> But not answers, however long
> I stand here looking down at their houses.
>
> For not in the country the answer lay
> Why they went no further, but in the men,
> Who might have been the last to say,
> And the land keeps their silence without their reasons
>
> Up on the hill where they still stay
> Above the trains that roar north to Erie,
> And the river sliding the other way,
> Mindless and old, to its destinations.

Mystery itself suffuses the landscape, with a calming effect like the ancient river, "Mindless and old." The "trains that roar north to Erie" seem a touch that only set in relief the river's eternal wandering. Merwin's ancestors, too, recede to distant points, dots on a hillside, perhaps a cemetery, as this gentle poem yields to the slow meandering of the waters. Whatever anxiety had once attended his leave-taking is, at this late stage, in complete remission. As he stands on the edge of his repatriation, he positions himself as one who is ready to be folded lovingly into a pleasant, bucolic landscape.

3

With its passing reference to ancestors who keep their silence "Up on the hill where they still stay," "Rimer, Penna." may qualify as an elegy in a graveyard, a meditation in the family cemetery as the poet ponders questions that, because they can never be answered, open endlessly before him until he too becomes one more in a long line of ancestors. After arriving in America, one of Merwin's inevitable destinations had to be the family plot near Rimerton (once Rimer), to pay homage to those of whom he had written with such care. The result of his visit, however, was a poem that would remain unfinished. "The Cemetery at Widnoon" is the first hint that he has been rapidly overtaken by a sense of genuine dislocation.[9] Evidently planned as an elegy, the poem maintains a gentle enough stance toward his ancestors. A late draft begins:

> There will be children for a while yet climbing
> The mud lane to the bell and the drafty building
> Up there by itself that still serves as a school
>   And sometimes as a chapel.
>
> For a while yet the cracked boards will shelter
> The droned words for what happens, mumbled, over and over,
> Of little use, and heads bowed to receive them, aware
>   Of no good reasons.
>
> And vacant glances, like flies, will rise and float
> Out the window to the leaning graves, and be caught
> In the names and retain some without curiosity
>   Or comprehension.
>
> All one kin: Jacob, died eighteen sixty-two
> Was Old Jake, shot by someone they never knew,
> On his way home one night with some coffee
>   In a pillowslip.

Notes for two other stanzas suggested the poem would take form as Merwin spoke a few words over the headstones of each family member. A draft for his grandfather's stanza reads:

> John D. was the pilot, who was never
> Very far from either drink or the river.

> Dewey his youngest, was named for the admiral
> But died, aged four years.

Yet "The Cemetery at Widnoon" is, unlike any of the European poems, stark and austere, alert to the impoverished air of a country graveyard. It is not on a hill above the wandering river of "Rimer, Penna.," with a prospect that allows his ancestors a vista as expansive as the years; it is adjacent to a "drafty building," and gravestones are wedged next to one another as implacably as the stanzas dole out information relevant to each ancestor. The gaunt phrasings recall the bleakness of a cemetery that has been without visitors or tending for some time. It is difficult, moreover, to find anything to say in a setting where forgetfulness seems to hold dominion. "Vacant glances, like flies" pass over the headstones, and some names must be viewed "without curiosity / Or comprehension." Forgetfulness is emphasized in a draft for what might have been the concluding stanza:

> But what a creature can neither keep nor understand
> He may carefully bury till he can use it, and
> What a man buries will be forgotten, only
> It may yet take a while.

Creatures bury their valuables with care, eventually to unearth them, but men bury only to forget. The decrepit state of the cemetery seems deliberate; that so much has remained after the passage of years is due to little more than accident.

"The Cemetery at Widnoon" was not entirely abandoned. Its form—treating family members one by one in separate stanzas—reappears in "Nothing New," the first of the family poems to be fully completed in America (in January 1957).[10] But the poet in the graveyard, musing quietly over headstones sinking into oblivion, is now replaced by Merwin speaking in a voice whose acid rancor startles. It begins:

> You were always a stray and grating
> Stiff-necked lot, I am sure of it; graceless
> And nothing loose about your hands.
>
> Great ones at vanishing, some all the time,
> Bearing little but grudges; though some
> Relieved by violence; each one lost in the end
>
> Without maps, in the niggard unlovely
> Waste he had found for himself, sick of it,
> Wondering where else there was to go.

A statement like "I am sure of it" would have been unthinkable a few months earlier, such certainty out-of-place in Merwin's poetry. The reversal is unnerving. Every instance that in Europe would have been taken as an example of his family's mysterious, restless nature is here subsumed into a general pattern in which all have sought to escape from each other, "lost in the end / Without maps."

Why should Merwin have turned against his ancestors so vehemently? One answer is rooted in the kind of poetry he had schooled himself to write in England. Poetry evoked awe and wonder, recovering a state of mind that could be described, somewhat inadequately, as "innocent." But the thrust of poetic experience was to expose the limits of knowledge, to depict realms in which conventional ways of understanding simply lacked a purchase. Thus when Merwin, in England, questioned his ancestors, he had no idea what answers he would receive if they had been able to reply. That was fine—poetry introduced questions into situations that might previously have been constituted as all answers. But soon after Merwin was back in America he set about finding information that would in fact produce nothing but answers. Less than six weeks after his arrival he jotted a note to Arthur Mizener, citing "One sample of the family junk I've been digging up in Pa., never knew before—the story of my great grandfather's murder. I never even knew I *had* a great-grandfather, for God's sake!"[11] To dig up "family junk" is to be burdened with knowledge. Inquiry is over; in "The Cemetery at Widnoon," each stanza can maintain its own set of definitive facts. The angry tone with which Merwin talks back to his ancestors, then, is justified in one sense: once they have defined themselves, he has been robbed of his approach, which had been to write of them interrogatively. He is now encumbered with knowledge.

Yet the extremity of Merwin's response merits further consideration. He could not have been entirely surprised about some of the information his research uncovered. Inevitably, his investigations were bound to uncover surprises; indeed, that was what he had planned for in Europe: a shock that would disorient him. The shock is evident. But he flinches as though he has been burned by fire. His extreme reaction may have a source in deeper aspirations, such as those confessed in "After Some Years," a poem that, on its surface, fretted over whether the poet was losing an ear for American language. That poem's speaker expresses a longing to live without an explicit identity, as a wanderer to whom events will appear with a freshness and an oddness that keeps them forever strange. Merwin may react so negatively to his homecoming, then, not simply because knowledge about his ancestors prevents him from conceiving of them as mysterious entities who can live as questions in poetry, but also because such knowledge threatens to provide him with an identity—an identity, moreover, that explicitly relates him to individuals who have consigned themselves to an existence that is deliberately narrow, conventional, and mean. In this respect, homecoming is nothing short of a nightmare, an upsurge of fears that he had hardly recognized within himself.

Lending credence to this surmise is the way Merwin treats the figure of his grandfather. His grandfather is the family member about whom he (and all others in his family) know the least, a shadowy mask; stories and legends circulate about him, now reporting his legendary skill as a river pilot, now relating his prowess as a drinker. The only certain fact is that he was, for years, a wanderer, leaving behind his wife and children, only returning home at uncertain intervals. He is, in short, the single ancestor who lacks a clear identity. When Merwin wrote of him in Europe, in "Grandfather in the Old Men's Home" (April 1956), he approved his air of mystery. The poem fixes on the inscrutable smile he wore into old age; in the old men's home he

> still smiled kindly in
> His sleep beside the other clean old men
> To see Grandmother, every night the same,
> Huge in her age, with her thumbed-down mouth, come
> Hating the river, filling with her stare
> His gliding dream, while he turned to water. (FF, 247)

Is he smiling at his own escape to freedom or at his wife's distress, or at some combination? The crucial point is that "he turned to water," fleeing downriver as well as dissolving from anyone's grasp.

But Merwin in America finds it difficult to summon his grandfather's presence. His grandfather is included among the list of relatives castigated in "Nothing New," but there he has the reprieve of appearing pseudonymously, as it were, not as Merwin's grandfather but under his given name: "Scary John D., the clean drunk river man / With delicate fingers, who had nine lives elsewhere, / And the scheming drone he bred to abhor him." As judgmental as these lines appear to be, doubts still play around them: Are "delicate fingers" a sign of sensitivity or a mark of fastidiousness? Is a "clean drunk" responsible or evasive? But the spirit of questioning is banished by the remarkable slinking ugliness of the final line.

The "scheming drone" whose appearance so disturbs this stanza—John D.'s wife, Merwin's grandmother—holds center stage in the poems written in America. In the American poems, personalities known for their rigidity assert a powerful role, taking over from those who have resisted such fixity. Indeed, there could not be a more striking contrast between the European and American poems than that between "Grandmother Watching at Her Window" (written in Europe in August 1956) and "Grandmother Dying" (written in America in January 1957). The former is a sympathetic portrait, spoken by Merwin's grandmother as she poses a series of questions to herself, questions that recover memories of her childhood and reveal how traumas suffered then offer an explanation for her stern ethic. The appeal of the poem lies in the way the voice of the grandmother slips in and out of simple, childlike phrasings, as though an important part of her self remained locked in her childhood. By contrast, "Grandmother Dying" not only portrays her at the end of her life but views her through the eyes of those who have committed themselves to care for her, to whom she is a burden. Drastically foreshortened, the poem witnesses the external features of a personality in its last stages of decay. Grandmother is intent upon clinging to life even though, in her advanced old age, she is no longer truly living, and when her soul finally departs her body, the ground shakes as though a steam engine from hell itself has passed through.

The American poems are so remarkably different from their predecessors as virtually to constitute a new, almost unrelated cycle of poetry. In three of the four poems in which Merwin's grandmother figures, the needle's eye is invoked as emblematic. It first appears in the European "Grandfather in the Old Men's Home," where it is no more than a passing reference, perhaps an allusion to the biblical injunction that a wealthy man is as unlikely to enter the kingdom of Heaven as a camel is to pass through a needle's eye: his grandmother went about "raising her family / Through the needle's eye," supporting herself by sewing, by living frugally. In a later, but still-European poem, "Grandmother Watching at the Window," the image continues as an inoffensive descriptive detail: "I brought the children up clean / With my needle." But in "Grandmother Dying," written in America, the image is not only linked with "the strait gate," but its biblical meaning has become patently distorted. The saying suggests that the kingdom of heaven is all about us and enormous, and its endless riches exceed the paltry wealth of a rich man as much as a camel exceeds the eye of a needle. But Merwin depicts his grandmother as dwelling not upon the magnitude of heaven but on the minuscule pinpoint that is the needle's eye. She

> believed you could get
> Through the strait gate and the needle's eye if
> You made up your mind straight and narrow, kept
> The thread tight and, dead both to left and right
> To the sly music beyond the ditches, beat
> Time on the book as you went. (FF, 249)

The task of remaining virtuous is what grandmother fixes on with a "mind straight and narrow," a task as arduous as keeping a needle's thread tight; everything else—all the richness that exists in this world—is consigned to the ditches.

The difference between the two sets of poems is not confined to matters of detail. The actual cast of characters and their backdrop change. The European poems present men outdoors; the American poems focus on women indoors. Men are outside, in an expansive realm that opens out before them, inviting their wandering; women are inside, surrounded by objects, encircled by things of their own choosing. In European poems like "Grandfather in the Old Men's Home" Merwin traces his grandfather's life from beginning to end. Similarly,

John Otto at ninety-six dies on his long walk, at the top of a mountain, and his Uncle Hess is addressed "under your trees, / By your big house that watches the river still / Turning the cranky wheels of your mill" (FF, 246). In an uncollected poem written in Europe, "Uncle Cal,"[12] Calvin Jones, a minister, is recalled as an "Old stumper and thumper, rough on sin / As ever your namesake; heavy father, / Lover of food, cigars, and beer." And of course Merwin's grandfather is always slipping away, "Down the green river, finding directions for boats."

But to Merwin, now in America, that spaciousness is inconceivable. The opportunity to wander freely, to drift through a spacious expanse, evoked in a poetry that graciously disorients, is beyond reach. Every poem depicts an environment that is lightless and airless. Consequently, in "Grandmother Dying" all the scenes are fixed within a series of interiors; moreover, her daughter "lived and dusted / A nice brick home a block away," rehearsing what she will say when she learns of her mother's death. That house is described again, in an uncollected poem, "Aunt Alma": "Only / The eye of God ever got past the drawn / Blinds and belted drapes at her locked window."[13] "Grandmother and Grandson" is set indoors, the grandmother "stuck standing / In her corner like a lady clock long / Silent," while her grandson lures her into an attic room and locks her in. Being inside, furthermore, associates these women with other negative portraits, such as the inhabitants of "Pool Room in the Lions' Club" with their "spidery hands, stalking and cautious / Round and round the airless light."

The blunt reality of actual family history, with its ancestors who could not be accommodated to Merwin's agenda for poetry, interrupted his plans to create a poetry cycle that would chronicle the repatriate's rediscovery of his ancestral home. If his European poems are any indication, that cycle would have been a production with considerable appeal. Uniformly, the European poems attractively portray the poet quizzically pondering his roots while all the time depicting the mysterious grandeur of the American landscape. But back in America he falls into a different role, engaging in quarrels, resurrecting memories that are painful, talking angrily back to his ancestors instead of evoking them as gentle ghostly presences.

4

Perhaps it was inevitable that Merwin's family poems, collected in 1960 for *The Drunk in the Furnace,* would be regarded as imitations of Robert Lowell's *Life Studies,* published in 1959. Although the poets who first reviewed Merwin's book failed to notice the influence, critics writing since have tended to take it for granted.[14] Yet perhaps the most striking difference between the two sequences is that in contrast to the strong narrative line that can be traced in Lowell's openly autobiographical sequence, which explores the relationship between the child and the adult, Merwin has no such narrative and no such open exploration of his own relationship to his father and mother. His final arrangement of the poems seems designed to be more silent than communicative, even when we know the order in which the poems were written and appreciate the startling change in Merwin's attitude.

Knowing as we do that sharp disruption, it might appear that his grouping represents nothing more than a salvage operation. Able to compose neither a family history nor an accurate record of his negative response to America, his arrangement is simply an effort to retrieve what he can from the ruins of his project. The final text excludes, for example, works at both ends of the emotional scale: the ultranegative "Nothing New" and "Aunt Alma" are omitted, as are the pleasant, lyrical "Rimer, Penna." and "Luzerne Street Looking West." Furthermore, two poems openly critical of provincial Pennsylvania town life, "The Gleaners" and "Pool Room at the Lions' Club," are placed at the opening of the set, where their dark pronouncements can seem blurred, as though they offered only a preparatory sketch of the setting, a background against which individuals might emerge. Finally, toward the end of the text as arranged, Merwin includes a series of poems about local legends, an inclusion that directs attention away from family members.

This swerve toward the legendary can appear to be an outright evasion. As arranged in *The Drunk in the Furnace,* the sequence begins in the early nineteenth century and moves to the twentieth, following chronology up to its closing pages, in which, abruptly, we enter a realm of legend, tall tale, and local color. The historical record dissolves at the moment we expect it to be most complete. But the legends Merwin relates are more informative than they at first appear to be. These stories direct attention to episodes of forgetfulness, episodes in which any long-term sense of the past is ignored or overlooked. As we read the cycle, we expect that the past will be related to the present, that the narrative of Merwin's ancestors will be carried forward into contemporary times. What these local tales instruct us in, however, is the folly of that belief. The link to the past is broken, as legends displace information. In this land, there are no long-range perspectives, no deep historical connections that lead back to the past; we may want to recall the disarray in the country cemetery at Widnoon. Would we be best off, then, if we abandoned hope of an emerging narrative? Should we merely enjoy the eccentric tale of the drunk in the furnace as a bit of picturesque local color?

But Merwin has also made it impossible to heed such advice. For one thing, the poem about the drunk in the furnace is itself notably marred with an obscurity that prevents it from being resolved into a set of amusing anecdotes. And how can we adopt a dismissive attitude when the story we are to dismiss is about someone who has been dismissed but who insists on persisting (and whose persistence only serves to raise further questions about him, all of which the poem steadfastly refuses to answer)? "The Drunk in the Furnace" is the master-poem that supersedes, but as it does so also subverts, the poems that precede it; it is Merwin's gesture of rage and despair at not having access to his family history, so much of which has been forgotten or warped into tall tale by the utter diffidence of his own ancestors who cared so little for the past; and it is even his portrait of the poet in America—of where the poet is placed and of how the poet is regarded by those who live at the center of the town.

The subgroup of legend poems within the family cycle is, then, sinister and subversive, not a simple diversion. The final poems to be written, they represent Merwin's furthest efforts to transform his disrupted project into a set of poems that offer an insight into America by way of his experience with his family—the authentic product of confronting his homeland. The legend poems are not divorced from the family poems; rather, they carry the family history one step further, and Merwin indicates as much by including a family poem, "Grandmother and Grandson" (dated January 2, 1958), within the subgroup. This work not only draws a comparison between Merwin and his grandfather but links that comparison with his family's unwillingness to remember the past. Since the past is unremembered, it is apt to repeat itself, which is why events in the poem fall into a pattern. The work describes a perverse game played by the grandson against his grandmother, but it begins with the grandmother displaying her grandson to visitors and asking, "Now who, / Who does he remind you of?" Yet no one sees a proper resemblance. When the guests have gone, the grandson deliberately wanders off, and the grandmother searches for him until she is led to the "Dust-coop, trunk- and junk-room at the top / Of the stairs," where he slips out, locking her in:

In the unwashed light,
Lost, she turns among the sheeted mounds
Fingering hems and murmuring, "Where, where
Does it remind me of?" Till someone comes. (FF, 257)

Who is the "someone" who comes? Any rescuer—or is it that person whose face she could discern in her grandson's, though no one else could see it, that someone she had been trying to visualize as her gaze grew "more and more / Absent, as though watching for someone through / A frosted window"?

In a deeply indirect way, "Grandmother and Grandson" acknowledges Merwin's identity with his grandfather. Yet the oddity of the poem is that it begins with the words "As I hear it," as though this story were a legend, recalled by family members but unremembered by Merwin. This emphasizes Merwin's anomalous position within the family: the grandson appears to resemble no one else in the family, but in fact that is only because the person he resembles, his outcast grandfather, is unknown to others in the family, and half-forgotten by his grandmother. Both grandfather and grandson have been endowed with a family identity that withholds the possibility they can have an identity. Alone with his grandmother, then, the grandson acts out the role he has been cast into by pretending to be lost or missing; the outcome of the game reveals the truth, which is not that he is lost but that his grandmother dwells behind a locked door that protects these secrets. At the edge of "Grandmother and Grandson" is the sequence of poems Merwin would have written about his grandfather, which might have led him closer to an understanding of his own years of wandering; but the information that would have opened that door was withheld earlier and continues to be withheld even now.

The truth Merwin falls back on after the disappointing reality of his American experience is that the sheer indifference of his ancestors has closed off the past to him. The point he stresses is not that persons suppress the past—for such suppression would depend on an active awareness of the past—but that they are simply indifferent, and their suppression is as innocent as ignorance. In this respect, the legend poems are more than simply tales of the grotesque: when events of the past become tall tales, we have abandoned our connection to history. The tall tales themselves that Merwin singles out enforce this perception. Although the local residents in "The Hotel-Keepers" believe that the landlord regularly murders itinerant strangers who stay at his provincial hotel, when he dies the local people accept his wife wholeheartedly, ignoring the legends they themselves had been quick to disseminate. Deliberately retelling a tale that has ancient roots, Merwin reserves his surprise ending to emphasize that for Americans the past is utterly blank. It is not forgotten; it cannot be forgotten because it is nonexistent.

The pertinence of the legend in "Burning Mountain" is that it, too, reveals the American fund of indifference. The poem was written much earlier, in February 1957, but it belongs among these late works because it reports a trail of dismissals. "Unnatural, but no mystery" is how the burning mountain is dismissed, set afire by a miner who was "The worrying kind, whose old-womanish / Precautions had been a joke for years." But the truth is that most Americans don't worry, and our lack of care for the environment that surrounds us is expressed in the tiny time scale we are capable of comprehending. Merwin notes that the coal burning underground "consumes itself, but so slowly it will outlast / Our time and our grandchildren's, curious / But not unique." This passage returns hauntingly in the final lines, with their offhand allusion (which may be all we deserve) to our pathetic sense of scale, especially in contrast to natural forces that, whether we may acknowledge them or not, surround us with a grandeur we neglect:

> Not a good day's walk above it
> The meteors burn out in the air to fall
> Harmless in empty fields, if at all.

Before long it practically seemed normal,
With its farms on it, and wells of good water,
Still cold, that should last us, and our grandchildren. (FF, 252)

Practiced as we are at distinguishing the unnatural from the mysterious, the curious from the unique, we neglect the falling stars, turning them into meteors that "burn out in the air to fall / Harmless in empty fields." The empty fields are what is left, it may be said, of our imagination. If we were capable of sensing a vast time scale, we might enliven the night sky, turning empty fields into rich ones.

These legend poems form a prelude to the final poem in the collected text, "The Drunk in the Furnace." Aggressively, self-consciously, defiantly, it reasserts themes in a new key chosen for its excruciating dissonance. The derelict who has "established / His bad castle" in an abandoned furnace never appears, but his residency can be deduced from "a twist of smoke" and "other tokens," and he becomes the subject of local sermons, though he draws the fascinated attention of the children who "flock like piped rats" as he bangs out a grotesque music of "Hammer-and-anvilling," "jugged bellowings," and "groaning clangs" bumping against the walls that confine him but that he will not leave. Mingling despair and anger, Merwin, like his derelict, refuses to go away, even as he realizes that he must go underground to survive—that the atmosphere is poison to him.[15]

The poem actively subverts the pattern otherwise stamped on the family poems, that rigid division of interior and exterior. Being inside a furnace that has been discarded outside blurs any clear-cut distinction, and the poem poses two irreconcilable questions: Is the drunk's cloddishness all that the community deserves, his relegation to the edge of town revealing the narrowness of people who tidy up their environment by creating junkpiles at the edge of town for those they cannot comprehend? Or is the persistence of the drunk, minding his own business and making his harmless music as he wills, distilling his spirits into a clanking all his own, a lesson in individuality, in perseverance, through his recycling of what others would discard by reshaping it to an individual purpose that blithely ignores what others conventionally expect (as Merwin has managed to recycle the refuse of his family poems)? As these two irreconcilables clash, neither resolved, it is clear that Merwin has found a way, in anger and in anguish, to express his own reaction to being a poet in his own homeland. And yet who is the drunk in the furnace if not his grandfather, an invisible outsider, as Merwin the child knew him, consigned to his marginal role, innocent and oblivious of his stature as a rebel and iconoclast, an example for children to follow. The lesson they learn, quite different from the preacher's text on stoke-holes that are "sated never," is that one must leave this confined community, going further than the junkpile at the edge of town.

Often admired as a work that prophesied an impending change in Merwin's style, "The Drunk in the Furnace" establishes a complex vantage point from which Merwin can survey the wreckage of his family cycle. The poem is, like its central figure, both defiant and circumspect: it secretes stories, none of which are allowed to emerge. But in the context of the entire cycle, especially in the light of its reconstructed development, it is lucid enough. Merwin's homecoming revealed a ruined landscape inhabited by figures sullen, secretive, and withdrawn, and a cycle of poetry that had begun expansively hardened into an abrasive pattern. This unexpected turn ultimately led to a wider understanding of the America into which he had fallen. In the cycle as arranged for final publication, his homeland is the place in which the habit of forgetfulness has become thoroughly ingrained. What he understands is the fact of his own exclusion, and by the close he has found the only home available to him: the margins of the community, where he will dwell as an exile.

PART TWO

Open Forms

6

Lost Voices

WHEN MERWIN was asked, in interviews in 1980 and 1982, how he had managed to transform himself from the merely promising poet (and playwright) of 1956 into the startlingly original writer of *The Moving Target* (1963), he replied abruptly: "Having come to feel dissatisfied with a way of writing, you don't simply say, 'I'm going to give up A, because I would prefer B.' At the point when you're making this decision, B doesn't exist, or at least you don't know what B is."[1] The distress of a painful period lingers in the touchiness of this remark. He had left England in August 1956, having achieved recognition at the age of twenty-nine that other poets might expect in a lifetime. His conquests rivaled the accomplishments the Devil listed for Don Juan: publication in the Yale Younger Poets series, a *Kenyon Review* Fellowship, and a Poetry Book Society recommendation, plus a first play on the London stage, numerous appearances on the BBC, and book reviews and essays. Less than two years later, when he returned to England in March 1958, his prospects had altered dramatically. His cycle of family poems had taken a disconcerting turn. *The Ark of Silence* had failed to find a publisher. His two new plays aroused no interest among producers.

The America Merwin had found was not what he expected to see. Its coarse and brutal features dominate the legend poems that close *The Drunk in the Furnace,* with their collapsing shacks, junkpiles, hotels on the edge of civilization, and burning mountains. His surprise and disgust surface in an unpublished sketch, probably written in 1957, describing the Sunday afternoon crowds in the Boston Common who listen to speakers harangue each other. Despite the high level of invective, everyone is remarkably polite because, Merwin concludes, as he glances at the lingering spectators, no one expects to change their convictions: "They sit there thinking of nothing, knowing that nothing has been resolved this Sunday either, and that nothing is going to be. They never expected conclusions—just an airing."[2] Americans exchange ideas freely, with intense energy, only because no one expects things will really change. In Merwin's two plays of 1957, the central characters turn down the chance to make a bold change, settling instead for the propriety of stale custom and the illusion of stability, even as their compromise draws them into self-deception.

Yet on occasion Merwin could see another side. All through the two plays, his characters verge on taking that radical step for change. If the crowds in the Boston Common expect nothing to alter, that does not prevent them from listening with seriousness to their favorite speakers. Political discourse is capable of animating others, and a police escort is regularly required for the right-wing bigot Father Feeney, who once brought the crowd to the point of riot. Underneath the hand-me-down structures, the makeshift homes, the bad castles, there are errant individuals who persevere, eccentrics who have made a place for themselves on the margin.

More precisely, Merwin returned to England with a sharpened awareness of the social context of writing. His American plays are quick to shift focus to the cultural background that determines how persons will act. One of the projects he proposed for the BBC was "Hangman's Helicon," a reading of verses from the Renaissance onward by prisoners condemned to death.[3] When he arranged *The Drunk in the Furnace* in 1959, he included a swatch of poetry between the sea poem cycle and the family poem cycle that was aggressively unlyrical—snatches of narrative, fragmentary episodes, anecdotes, and illustrations. These shifted the reader's attention away from the poet's depiction as a delight in itself, to consider instead the consequences implied by the work.

Back in England, Merwin did not recoil from the America he had discovered; he seemed to recognize that his American experience had broadened his sense of what writing should do. And that led him to react against the person he had been before returning to America: the poet of decorum who had cultivated a promising career, the playwright intent upon reviving verse drama for the English stage. What he may have failed to anticipate, however, was the tenacity with which his old self would hang on. The story of his conversion to free verse in open forms is not told simply; it is complicated by a series of divided loyalties. Like the characters in his two plays of this time, he is capable of bold action, but he continually postpones it. His struggle in 1958 and 1959 yields no conspicuous breakthrough. If he recognized the need to be implicated in the life of his times, he could not approach it through what was closest to him, his poetry. As a result, he found himself unable to write for months at a stretch. The British Merwin, who had been capable of rapidly processing a poem on any number of subjects, could not easily yield to the American Merwin, apt to be held by contradictions that escaped resolution because they opened onto social and cultural dilemmas. The American Merwin could speak freely in the book review pages of the *Nation,* where, after 1958, he found urgent topics in even the most unlikely of places. A review of two coffee-table books, *The Warblers of America* and *Wild Paradise,* turns into a discourse on ecology; considerations of the short stories of Camus recall the Algerian question; and the prison writings of Brendan Behan turn on involvement with the IRA.[4] But no similar social awareness appears in his 1958 poems. The British Merwin continued to write elliptic poem-parables that at best alluded darkly to features of their own constraint.

Given the contradictions in his situation—an American who had achieved more prominence in England than in his homeland, a poet fascinated by the theater, a translator of medieval epics who participated in the first Aldermaston-to-London nuclear disarmament march of 1958—it is not surprising that when, at last, he began in the winter and spring of 1960 to write a poetry that satisfied him, verse in brief, gnomic fragments one to six lines long, it resembled not a breakthrough but a breakdown (fig. 7). He did not resolve the contradictions riddling his life but submitted to them, often with an undercurrent of despair, as in "Star": "All my light having left me / I threw myself after it / And I fall through darkness like a heart."[5] After every option has been exhausted, until all that is left is a gesture of helplessness, that gesture is suddenly redeemed, though with an ironic twist. Now one's feelings are exposed as never before, the heart open even as it falls. As somber as these considerations are, they are somehow proposed with a curious blitheness, as though a great weight has been lifted. Disparities are united with a sweep verging on the dismissive, even as they register a disarming vulnerability, like an expiring sigh. This is called "Arrival": "Hope has set. We can still see enough. / The ruin at the end of emptiness. / What a view it must have had before it fell!"[6] Even as hope departs, a glimmer remains, a spark from which the last hopeful line, which brings together both the vista and its loss, can be rekindled, just long enough to be extinguished. In earlier drafts, Merwin settled first on "History," then on "Love" as what has set, not "Hope." But "History" too pointedly recalls current events (the American Merwin with his commentaries in the *Nation*), while "Love" too indirectly alludes to the particulars of his increasingly awkward marriage (the British Merwin with his sideways communications). "Hope" covers both realms, the public and the private, the historical prospect and the personal condition. It is neither American nor British but rather the poetry of an exile, of someone who owes allegiance to nothing except the bitterness of unavoidable, contradictory truths.

1

Is it possible to trace the steps by which Merwin moved, as he said so unhelpfully, "from A to B," from a condition of dissatisfaction to a site of

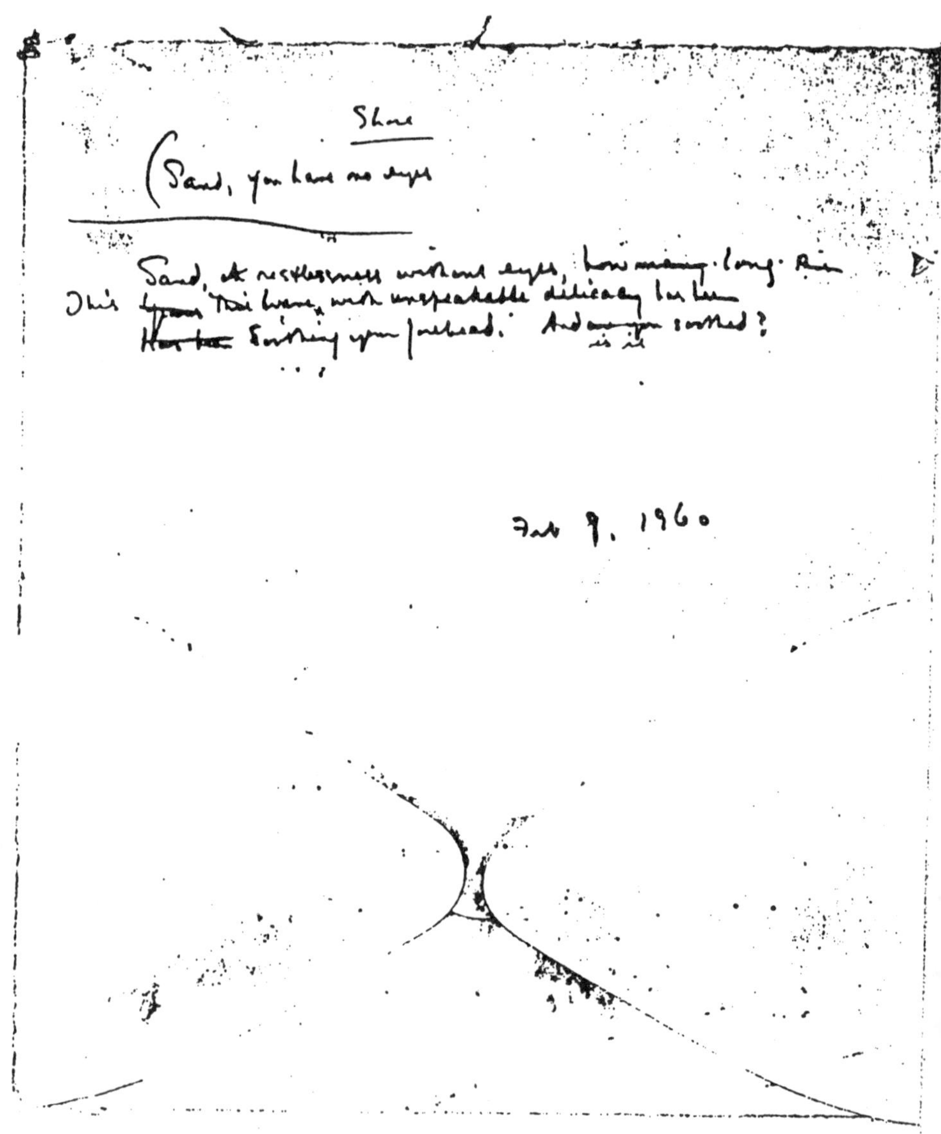

Figure 7. Final draft of "Shore" (uncol. MS. 20:06/003b, d. Feb. 10, 1960), one of the numerous brief poems written in the winter and spring of 1960.

renewal? It is not too early to look for signs of impending change in the two plays he wrote in 1957. At first they seem more commercial than anything in his previous drama; neither was conceived as verse, neither was the least experimental. (Two other plays promised to take risks with theatrical conventions, but they were not pursued.) Both took America for a setting and dealt with explicitly American themes. In the first one completed, "A Peacock at the Door," the sober tranquility of an 1832 provincial Pennsylvania household is disrupted when a handsome young Latin appears at the door with a fantastic tale about robbers who set upon him while he was on his way to visit a wealthy ancestor; the lady of the house encourages her seduction, then plots her husband's demise. "The Gilded West" features Buffalo Bill in 1910, an aged man, trying to hold together the remnants of his Wild West show. This American hero no longer battles Indians but creditors, the onslaught of old age, and a lawyer who offers him a handsome settlement if he will only testify in court against a woman with whom he once had a passionate affair.[7]

Despite their provocative plots, neither play won an audience. "A Peacock at the Door" was never produced; "The Gilded West" was performed, but far from America and the London stage, in Coventry, England, in 1960. As different as they are, both plays ultimately end as critiques of American culture; they depict Americans as eager to compromise, quick to embrace conventionality, enslaved by the pressures of custom.

To be sure, all custom appears swept away in the opening scenes of "A Peacock at the Door," as the woman of the house enters into a clandestine love affair with a Latin lover. Lino (short for Carolino Amalio Estradas de Espos y Mina) seems nothing if not exotic, and his unprovincial manners reveal to Lucretia ("a handsome woman in her early forties") the drabness of daily life. But Lino's tales of his background not only strain credibility, they seem improvised according to whoever happens to be listening. Yet Lucretia eagerly yields to even his most transparent ploys. It is uncertain who is seducing whom. She feels she deserves more from life than marriage to a bland schoolmaster. But if Lucretia and Lino are kindred souls, they disagree over how to express their love. Lino is a low-grade Don Juan, and after becoming Lucretia's lover, he seduces her sixteen-year-old daughter. Lucretia's next step is to poison her husband. Lino expects to broaden his freedom, while Lucretia expects to legitimate her love. Lino advances to his next conquest, while Lucretia clears the way toward widowhood and a second marriage. Neither central character is admirable, because each acts not boldly but circumspectly.

While the play echoes the divided relations between men and women of Merwin's family poems—men want to leave home, women want to make a home—the question the play poses is, How can someone with the intelligence of Lucretia be drawn into a love affair with a fatuous charlatan? The answer is not that she has a propensity for deluding herself, nor is it quite that the routine of provincial life fosters a taste for the exotic. The answer is delivered slowly, with a ruthless finality, through the course of the play: No one acts with spontaneity, and so every event is muddled with compromise.

Halfhearted indecision taints every moment in a play that ostensibly deals with rebellion. Just as the encyclopedia peddled in an early scene only runs from "A to Ipswich" ("The other two volumes are in preparation still"), just as Ellen the maidservant decides to leave the corrupt household in act 1 but is still around in act 3 ("I'm not returned here for regular, for good, just come in to give a hand for a bit"), just as Mr. Chapman suspects his wife's infidelity but fails to speak out, turning to overeating and heavy drinking to compensate, just as Lino converses throughout in an annoyingly childlike pidgin English that sounds neither convincingly foreign nor patently artificial ("Is not how to talk. Is bad. I try to be nice."), things throughout are done halfway, with second thoughts, indecisions, and waverings. Merwin's affection for that which is still in process, for events that remain incomplete, tentative, hesitant, is mocked and traduced by this clutter of half-thoughts and convictions held only to be suspended. No rule is ever broken boldly, just slightly bent. Though protocol weighs against Lucretia and Lino traveling alone to Philadelphia, they do so anyway, as an exception to the customary, because Lucretia must visit an old friend. Though Lucretia's husband sets a limit on how much money to advance to Lino, he is persuaded to loan more. Though Lucretia insists Lino should not purchase a shawl for her daughter (it figures in her eventual seduction), she finally relents. And, as Lino recalls, Lucretia was cautious about purchasing arsenic herself; she asked Lino to do it, coaching him to say it was for taxidermy.

Instead of genuine standards, American culture offers only stale customs, in which no one quite entirely believes, vulnerable as they are to endless adjustments, minor modifications. Yet the customs are so vague, so bland, it is impossible to counteract them. Inch by inch, excruciatingly, Merwin shows his characters selling themselves out. He was to have made a similar point in a play he outlined in late 1957. As a child, Merwin had met his grandfather only once, on the day when his father and uncle, after much family deliberation, instructed his grandfather they were transporting him to the old folks' home, uprooting him from the cottage at the edge of town where he had been living in peaceful seclusion. The plot of his play involves a similar scheme hatched by his grandfather's wife, with Merwin's role as witness taken by Merwin's mother, who would be a young bride meeting her husband's family for the first time. In his outline Merwin explains that the grandmother and grandfather

> have been separated for twenty years, and she has not softened toward him in the slightest. Rather, if anything, she has built him into a monster and made sure the children remember him that way. . . .

> The action of the play . . . begins when the youngest son of the family, who has bluffed, wheedled and charmed his way through several small religious schools in succession, into the ministry and an assistant pastorate at a large church in Pittsburgh, brings his new bride to meet the family. They have been wanting to put the old man in the Old Men's Home. . . . The development of the action consists of the working out of their decision; at the end of the play the old man's entrance into the institution has been arranged, he has agreed to it. All this has been kept from the young bride; she has met the old man once, by accident, and by the close of the play she is the only one (apart from the two husbands, who are careful to have no opinions) who has doubts about the old man's absolute villainy. But even she, it is plain, will soon be won around by the others, to doubt her own experience and think of him as a monster.[8]

Although the young bride, as an outsider, has the perspective to see freshly, without the bias of the family, she will succumb to the accepted view. The authority of other people's convictions is enough to undermine even the strongest counterimpression; indeed, their weight is enough that the bride will come "to doubt her own experience."

For Merwin, the most honorable are, like this young bride, next to silent, or they come to be silenced. Volubility is to be distrusted; anyone who speaks at length, with ease, is likely to be enmeshed in scheming, or will soon be compromised. Lucretia's daughter, the most innocent character in "A Peacock at the Door," is afflicted with a saving stammer that consigns her to the sidelines. (It vanishes after her seduction: having lost her innocence she enters the fallen world of the articulate.) The honorable character in "The Gilded West" is the young doctor who quietly administers enough medicine to the aging "Buffalo Bill" Cody to keep him out of pain. The doctor's restraint is an exception, however, to the torrents of rhetoric that spill through this play (fig. 8). Honorable characters are reluctant or unable to speak because speech so rapidly declines into self-deceiving rhetoric. As in "A Peacock at the Door," what happens in "The Gilded West" is that, after much complication, no one succeeds in making a change.

In 1910, Buffalo Bill, with an entourage of old friends, still contrives to be star of a Wild West show, though most of his feats of daring are show-business illusions, and each performance threatens his health. The plot begins when he is asked to testify against Caroline, a flamboyant ex-mistress who had left him several years back when his fame began to fade. She went on to marry an aristocrat who now seeks to divorce her without a settlement; the handsome bribe his lawyers offer for Cody's testimony would support the expenses of the Wild West show for years and deliver Cody from the hands of greedy promoters. But Cody spurns the bribe, and Caroline wins her settlement, afterwards offering him nothing but a hurried thank-you.

Cody's refusal to compromise, as Merwin points out, is based on convictions who die suddenly after drinking cold water have been habitually addicted to the free use of ardent spirits. Excite a man by this fluid and he is at once bad enough for anything. Oh, my young friend, your heart may be the seat of every virtue but ardent spirits will strip it of all and convert you to a demon. Statistics prove that if drunkness increases in the next twenty years at the same rate as in the last twenty, one-third of our voters would be drunkards, and half of the remainder somewhat intemperate. It has deprived one-third of the crazy wretches of our land of their reason. A woman eighty years of age who had drunk nothing but ardent spirit for several years, sitting by a candle in her elbow chair, her maid found her on fire and gave the alarm, and buckets of water were flung on her body in abundance yet the fire became ever more violent and would not be extinguished till the whole body was consumed. And need I depict a drunkard's family?

(The Kid gets up, moves to another chair and starts to read "The Stock-Grazer". The Doc comes in, in a rain-coat, and stands looking around.)

The very hair of a drunkard's head has a crispness which renders it less valuable to wig-makers than the hair of sober people.

(Burke points to The Kid and addresses Doc.)

This guilty wretched creature had an immortal mind like us, once. Our brother, destined to the same eternity.

(To The Kid, behind "The Stock-Grazer".)

Rise thee, ye young hope of your country and the world, exhibit one general combination of moral courage, intelligence, and purity. Happy, thrice happy ye who may thus have the honor of dashing away forever the cup of drunkeness --

(The Kid, without dropping the paper, joins in, and Burke's demeanor becomes more and more disheartened to the end of the speech.)

BURKE & THE KID: -- and like the rainbow above the retiring cloud, reflect from one end of the earth to the other the glories of a millenial sun.

KID: (Putting down "The Stock-Grazer") Your deal.

(Weavley enters, in a raincoat.)

WEAVLEY: (To Doc.) You're just the man I've been looking for.

DOC: As a matter of fact, I wanted to see --

Figure 8. Excerpt from the final typescript of act 2 of "The Gilded West" (unpub. TS. 08:1144, c. summer-fall 1957). We are listening to the last bits of an authentic nineteenth-century temperance lecture that Cody's publicity agent, Burke (who is losing at cards), has launched into. Beyond the humor of this bit of stage business, the speech also recalls not only the ease with which rhetoric clouds reality but also the willingness of others to accept such rhetoric as common.

that are thoroughly compromised: he cannot relinquish his image as larger-than-life hero. To testify against Caroline would be to indict himself: "I'm a name to conjure with. I'm somebody. They all know I'm genuine, that's what I stand for. That's respectable, that's got dignity." As Cody says, "Buffalo Bill" is a symbol of the genuine, a symbol that must be preserved, even if that requires an inauthentic role. Caroline, an actress who understands the attractions of the stage, elaborates: "Nobody remembers the *real* west any more, it's all gone. Nobody believes in it, really. There's nothing left of it but make-believe. But the make-believe West must go on. Maybe that's what they always wanted after all, maybe that's what they always really came to see, the make-believe West. . . . You've become a figure, like Santa Claus, that's supposed to come around every year, just the same, whether or not they pretend to believe in you." Reality gives way to an illusion of reality that leads persons to play out roles in which they observe with approval persons they know to be playing a role.

"The Gilded West" is not simply a satire on American promotion, although Merwin continually reminds us that Cody was invented, as a cultural hero, by hack writers. Rather, Merwin would have us ponder the fact that everyone—even Cody, perhaps even Cody's audience—knows Buffalo Bill is an illusion, yet it is perfectly acceptable to allow that illusion to persist. Everyone sees through Buffalo Bill, but instead of dismissing him as a fraud, they join together to perpetuate the fiction. "The make-believe West must go on," as Caroline says. Even the audience for "The Gilded West" is implicated, watching a play about actors who debate the roles they play before their audience. The action occurs entirely in Cody's dressing room, where at several times objects are swept away and the room rearranged as though stagehands were assembling a new set of props. Caroline's first entrance is accompanied by a bevy of gifts, each of which is placed on display. The compromises that infected "A Peacock at the Door" have been transformed into deceptions that seem harmless because everyone agrees to accept them as deceptions. And Merwin gave the ending of "A Peacock at the Door" a nasty twist that foreshadows "The Gilded West": Lucretia and her daughter will be rescued from an angry mob by a theatrical promoter if Lucretia accepts the offer to be on display, as a notorious woman, in a series of *tableaux vivants*.

2

To be a silent character on the sidelines of a drama where everyone is mouthing rhetoric is one thing; for the writer to fall silent is another. After returning to England, Merwin found himself able to complete, in eighteen months, less than a dozen poems—a remarkable change from his ordinary productivity. In these poems, moreover, his attitude toward silence is quite different from what it would become over the next ten years. Ultimately, silence would be, especially in the poems in the latter half of *The Lice*, not simply a necessary companion of the poet but a presence within the finest of Merwin's poems. It is related to the "innocence" and the "mystery" that he had sought to evoke a few years earlier, except that it is more extreme, deferring even the possibility of finding a word to describe it. Silence is opposite to the empty prattle of a civilization bent on reordering reality—a reality Merwin will identify with silence not because it is inert but because we cannot have words for its immensity. We cannot have words for it, but it is a high achievement indeed to use words to acknowledge the inarticulatable aspect of existence. Silence is associated with awe and respect, as well as with the poet's recognition of a humility that he must accept; silence commands us to listen, to realize what surrounds us. But it is not only what lies beyond words: it is what words ceaselessly, helplessly attempt to capture. Without the presence of that silence, there is, in fact, no poetry, only the vain babble of human speech.

But to Merwin in 1958, silence was a harbinger of failure, not a feature of poetry. His poetry of this time, much of which remains uncollected, recreates the silence into which he feared he had fallen, but it does so in writing that swarms with sound. Consider "Lost Voices," written in June 1958:

i.

Far from willow-home and flow of fountains,
Silent, the water-lark
Hearkens in awe to the yellow
Fear-fox and snake of sorrow.

ii.

In this shell a bell called across water
Once. I will wait for it
Till I am shrivelled like some dried
Mud-flat waiting for the tide.

iii.

Many silences besides do not return
Any more than the stars
That fell before we were born.[9]

The poem is not incomplete without a final line: the very absence of a final line is its necessary closure. (Up to its final draft, the third stanza had ended with a twelfth line: "under the silent spheres.") Absence, rendered palpable, is chilling; silence dominates so completely it can only be rendered in this dramatic fashion.

Merwin's previous work revealed an unusual sensitivity to sound. Indeed, in his previous work, denial of silence was so pervasive that even visual images soundless in themselves were rendered with an aural component. In the dream poem "The Sapphire" (March 1954), the vision of the blue crystal stone coincides with "a trumpet's thin sweet highest note" and the crystal forms only "as the trumpet pierced through the silence." In "The Annunciation" (January 1954), silence is surrounded by its own noise: "It is like a humming, but it is not a sound / But the edges of the silence whirring / To tell you how deep the silence is" (FF, 147). Silence might seem unavoidable in "Learning a Dead Language" (March 1954), but the trick of understanding a language unspoken for centuries is "to hear what never / Has fallen silent."[10]

But when the poet is literally unable to write, silence is no metaphor but a state to be feared. Yet the striking feature of "Lost Voices" is the extent to which it reveals its predicament by denying it; rather than exploring silence for its source, Merwin overwhelms silence with noise. Notes for the poem show he decided from the start to jam this work with internal rhyme and alliteration far beyond the ordinary. This poem about loss is crowded with words that so echo each other they almost turn into sheer sound ("willow," "flow," "yellow," "sorrow"; "water lark / Hearkens in awe"; "shell," "bell," "till," "shrivelled"; "water once. I will wait"). A posture of listening dominates the first two stanzas, but such keen listening, it seems, only amplifies language as sound: there is nothing to be extracted. Alliteration runs rampant and consonance is out of control. His response to incipient silence is to fill it with sound until, the poet having exhausted himself, silence descends in the widening scope of the dread-filled last lines. Beyond sound there is only silence; to hear it is to accept blankness. The reference to a falling star alludes to hopes or dreams that died long ago. This shattering awareness concedes everything. Eliminating the final line of earlier drafts becomes an admission of defeat, a yielding to a silence identified with sorrow and loss.

"Lost Voices" is not the only poem of this time in which silence is a nemesis to be desperately countered. "On a Sacrifice of Darkness" (July 1958) is especially revealing because it was commissioned for an anthology of responses to photographs of Aztec sculpture. Imposed upon by a subject about which he had no choice, Merwin writes a poem that reacts with repugnance to its subject. Having accepted his task, he figuratively refuses it, and his revolt takes shape as a reaction against the silence of the figurine:

> Say you know it is not so, say
> Over and over this is not the world,
> No, it is no day ever known, say
> He lies all the time, that grey god with
> His white mouth wide open giving rise
> To silence, with nothing in his face
> For eyes . . . .[11]

A torrent of speech meets the dreadfully imposing figure—and Merwin urgently cries for more speech: "Say" and "say / Over and over" and "say" again. Merwin completes his assignment with integrity by drawing upon his dread of silence. Despite the clamor in this work, however, it suggests that the poet is the one who has fallen silent; he depends on an outside assignment to provide an occasion for using his voice. Again, silence as terror is left unexplored; it is generalized, associated with a despicable civilization. But the shrillness of Merwin's invective points to an anxiety that is his own.

3

Merwin's fear of silence was well founded. When he was assembling *The Drunk in the Furnace* in December 1959, he wrote to Arthur Mizener that "the new book of poems still awaits a piece or two, I think." Then he added laconically: "It's been awaiting them since April."[12] Not only did he complete less than a dozen poems in 1958 and 1959, he did little else. Drama had preoccupied him since his undergraduate days, exerting an attraction at least as powerful as poetry, and yet in July 1958 he had confessed to Mizener: "I've not mucked around with plays since last November, and I am in no hurry to set about it again—it has occurred to me at last that perhaps I am not a playwright."[13] He was questioning not simply his vocation as a poet but his entire career as a writer.

That questioning both continues and finds an answer in early 1959, when he translates the satires of Persius, a work that not only offers him a model for a poetry engaged with cultural concerns but that provides an example of a writer actively yielding to divisions in his thought. Up to 1959, Merwin's translations had been commissioned by the BBC, and they were usually dramatic works from the Romance Languages he had studied in Princeton. His decision, then, in 1959 to fulfill a commission to translate Persius was uncharacteristic: for one thing, Latin, as he was to explain in his foreword to *Selected Translations 1948–1968*, was a language he had long ago forgotten. As a result, the project required an unusual investment of time. The translation was patched together "with the help of every previous translation I could find, and whatever line-by-line notes I could lay hands on, and was then gone over by a scholar."[14] Translating would replace play writing, in the next decade, as a second career, but in 1959 Merwin's real compensation may have been to recognize the affinity between Persius's situation and his own.

Persius requires Merwin to sustain a notably individual voice. By contrast, his other translations—*The Cid,* the anonymous epic-fragments of *Spanish Ballads,* plus two other projects completed in 1960 and 1961, *Lazarillo de Tormes* and *The Song of Roland*—are written in a general mode, not a particular voice, in keeping with the anonymous cultural epic that aspires to be a recording device for history. The language of these translations is positively unadorned, at times crude. No distinctive personality shapes the writing, and Merwin remains true, in his translations, to language in its collective mode, worn smooth after centuries of retelling. *The Song of Roland,* he insisted, was rendered best in prose, not verse.[15] His Persius, however, is translated as though he were the Roman version of a New York intellectual—brash, perceptive, needling—and his style is rife with idiosyncrasies, startling perceptions, swipes at rivals. It is vividly explosive:

> Locked in, we get down to it—verse, prose, something
> Grand, making uncommon demands on the breath.
> And in due course you'll favor the crowd with it, out of
> A raised chair, in a new white robe, groomed to a hair,
> Your throat loosened with syrup, a birthday sardonyx
> Large in your gestures, and your eye, and every so often,
> Letting them in on it. Then, as the deft phrases
> Find the way to their loins and stroke them within there,
> You'll see the hefty sons of Rome's best families roused
> Not in a nice way: quivering, and their words not edifying.

Every word is colored by convictions and shaded by quarrels barely concealed. This ancient is more modern than his medieval successors.

Merwin's version of Persius is not only a superb rendering of the colloquial energies of the Latin verse, but it also defends Persius from the severe qualifications proposed by W. S. Anderson, the classical scholar who introduces the text. Anderson is distressed by Persius' disdainful tone. In the brashness of his youth, Persius fails to persuade his audience, and Anderson, contrasting him to Seneca, calls him a "lost child": "Seneca's letters abound in scenes closely observed, filled with exact details noted down by the writer in person; Persius' Satires reflect no such minute observation."[16] Merwin's version turns such dismissals into scholarly quibbles. His Persius is not youthfully brash but arrogantly intellectual, instructed to high standards in a notoriously decadent time, and his uniqueness lies in his excess. By always overstating, Persius reveals how much pressure he must exert to overcome the lures that he would condemn; fascinated by what he has been tutored to reject, he must be actively derisive to sustain his distance. Intent on asserting his superiority to the corruptions of the city, the market, the political forum, Merwin's Persius never feels secure. The vehemence of his excoriation is necessary because it alone breathes life into his ideals, which are familiar as concepts but unrealizable except through this constant, abrasive negating. Anderson notes that scholars have disagreed over whether Satire Three is an internal discussion between opposing parts of the self or a dialogue between two distinct characters. In Merwin's version the question never arises: his Persius is self-divided, torn between ideals he keeps vitally alive by finding examples, which he can disdain, of the absence of those ideals. For Merwin, Persius' claim to greatness is that he can transform the confusion of his own position into the pain and anger of poetry distinctively overwrought, excessive, extreme.

As a model, however, Persius is closer to Merwin's previous verse in strong-stress meter—casual, prolix, discursive—than to the startling images and unsettling rhythms of *The Moving Target.* While Merwin's versions of Persius can assure him that compelling poetry can emerge from a divided self, it is not until he translates Pablo Neruda that he has a glimpse of the direction he will follow. Persius is youthful, conspicuously brilliant, flaring with disdain for his enemies, but if he answers that aspect of Merwin which values the energetic and the defiant, he fails to account for that aspect steeped in sorrow and despair. But the inward Neruda of *Residencia en la Tierra,* for example, who employs an imagery that seems to be "surrealistic" because it is the only way to convey his *angustia indirecta* ("oblique anxiety"), is a model for a self in touch with inmost feelings. In Merwin's versions of Neruda inklings of the free verse of *The Moving Target* first appear.[17] Neruda's "Widower's Tango"—

> I have gone back again to single bedrooms,
> to cold lunches in restaurants, and I
> drop my pants and shirt on the floor as I used to,
> there are no hangers in my room, and nobody's pictures are on the walls.

—looks ahead to the litany of sorrow in Merwin's "Home for Thanksgiving":

> I bring myself back from the streets that open like long
> Silent laughs, and the others
> Spilled into in the way of rivers breaking up, littered with words,
> Crossed by cats and that sort of thing,
> From the knowing wires and the aimed windows,
> Well this is nice, on the third floor, in back of the bill-board
> Which says Now Improved and I know what they mean,
> I thread my way in and I sew myself in like money. (MT, 2)

Neruda's "Ode with a Lament"—

> What a pity that I have nothing to give you except
> The nails of my fingers, or eyelashes, or pianos melted by love,
> or dreams which poured from my heart in torrents,
> dreams covered with dust . . .

—is echoed in Merwin's "Letter from a Distance" (revised as "The Nails"):

> I gave you sorrow to hang on your wall
> Like a calendar.
> I wear a torn place on my sleeve. (FF, 18)[18]

The qualities Merwin values in Neruda can be isolated by setting his translation of Neruda's "Walking Around" against Robert Bly's. Anthony Libby, speculating on the origins of Merwin's new writing style, compared their quite different versions of Neruda's opening stanzas:

Sucede que me canso de ser hombre
Sucede que entro en las sastrerías y en los cines
marchito, impenetrable, como un cisne de fieltro
navegando en un agua de origen y ceniza.

Merwin:

As it happens, I am tired of being a man.
As it happens I go into tailors' shops and movies
all shrivelled up, impenetrable, like a felt swan
navigating on a water of origin and ash.

Bly:

It so happens I am sick of being a man.
And it happens that I walk into tailorshops and movie houses
dried up, waterproof, like a swan made of felt,
steering my way in a water of wombs and ashes.

Bly's version, Libby says, "improvising rather freely with individual words, catches more of the energy of the original."[19] Though he concedes Bly's vocabulary is free—his "sick" is an unusual rendering of *canso,* his "waterproof" places considerable spin on *impenetrable,* and his "wombs" only relates tangentially to *origen*—Libby finds Merwin's versions lacking in gusto. He concludes that Merwin, in 1959, was unaccustomed to a poetry of such energy: "Closer in spirit to Neruda from the beginning, Bly feels less hesitant to release his own characteristic tone. Merwin, whose poetry in 1959 sounded nothing like this, listened more carefully to the surface of the poem, like one learning a new language."

But Merwin's ear is attuned to another aspect of Neruda. Bly emphasizes an involvement so intense as to seem compulsory, as though images were straining to fuse wide-ranging opposites (so that the speaker is cosmically "steering my way in a water of wombs and ashes"). Merwin hears a nervous edge in the speaker's voice, an anxiety that barely masks a troubled desire to withdraw (so that his speaker is fastidiously "navigating on a water of origin and ash"). Bly's "It so happens I am sick of being a man" is spoken with an underlying gusto, as if the speaker is fed up and ready to break loose; Merwin's "As it happens I am tired of being a man" is spoken with genuine weariness. By translating *Sucede que* as "It so happens that," Bly presents a speaker about to take charge, on the brink of revolutionary changes he will initiate; Merwin's "As it happens" reproduces a speaker acted upon by events that bewilder. In Bly's version nothing is alien to Neruda's forceful presence; his Neruda is brother to Whitman. Merwin's Neruda is sensitive, even overly sensitive, to the way even the most benign objects, encountered in casual moments, can take on a threateningly blank gaze, as though they were fundamentally alien. Merwin hears in Neruda an unusual mixture of the aggressive and the uncertain, the defiant and the apprehensive. Neruda's protagonist speaks out of his own frustration and paralysis, alienated from a way of expressing his feelings. As a result, every action is magnified and distorted, either a thoroughly new beginning or an ending of total finality: "origin and ash."

Carefully reproducing the anxious disturbance in the original, Merwin presents no continuous or coherent surface; it is broken by the errant shiftings of the speaker whose attention is drawn in haphazard directions, from tailors' shops to cinemas. Neruda's example offers Merwin a poetry that manages a broken surface with immense skill. He proceeds nervously, shifting precariously from one point to the next, as though circumventing the gaps in his own thought. To convey conflict and doubt, one need not write verse that stalls and hesitates—quite the contrary, one can speed up lines as though the alternative to collapse were to work the mind as rapidly as possible.

4

Neruda's example prepared Merwin for an ambitious project. In 1959 he set out to write an autobiographical poem, entitled "Congé," designed to clear the air, a confessional epic in which he would, Persius-like, reveal his contempt for England and the English. If nothing else, the length of this piece revealed his determination to break from his year-and-a-half-long silence. But the work was unusual not just for its length but also for its candor: it was to be a frank appraisal of his upbringing, his poetry, his expatriation, and even his marriage. Neruda set no limits when he wrote; anything was likely to appear. Whether Merwin could be as candid was open to question; while sketching "Congé," he was also applying for grants that would support the writing of a project opposite in every way: an epic verse-narrative of the Washington, D.C., march in 1893 by Jacob Coxey's army of the unemployed. If his nerve failed at the first project, the other was ready, it seemed, to take its place. Yet the similarities between the two are more striking than their differences: the verse-narrative of social history was to be related by a participant bewildered by events, and the personal poem about the life of a bewildered poet was to include a public gesture, a defiant break with the past that would actually unfold in the midst of the poem.

Of the two projects, there is less to know about the piece on Coxey's Army.[20] Unlike "Congé," it never earned more than a generic title; in grant applications of 1959, as in letters confirming its progress (or lack thereof) from 1960 to 1967, it remained "the Coxey" or only "the long poem." But its narrative was outlined in grant and fellowship applications, and what these documents reveal is how closely it resembled a play, that form which Merwin had been so uncertain about continuing. It was to be in three parts, with the first simply introducing Coxey, his family, and Coxey's "chief assistant, Brown," who was to be "the hero of the poem." The second part presents the march itself, with its failings intact—"Coxey's family difficulties which prevented his daughter from appearing at the start as the Goddess of Liberty," as well as "Brown's behavior, his loss of rank and reinstatement." The third part, set in the camp at Washington, presents Coxey's arrest against a background of the historic panoramas the demonstrators conceived for the public, "including Brown's performance as the Goddess of Liberty." Merwin's interest in drama keeps surfacing throughout, not simply in the demonstrators' spectacles (presumably depicted with accuracy) but in the conflict between Brown and Coxey. To focus on Brown shifts the center of the piece from Coxey's assurance to Brown's hesitancy. "I want the poem, first of all, to tell the story," Merwin says; this remark is an afterthought to his explanation that Brown's presence will give not only "a distorted perspective upon the conditions and ideas of the period" but "a distorted analogue to the action and what I take to be its meaning."

That distortion remains the most intriguing feature of the outline. Merwin, it seems, would interject Brown as a necessary point of weakness. In a more general sketch supplied when Merwin applied for support from the Ford Foundation, he explained that regarding the march from an "ironic view" would only emphasize its tragic elements: "I use the word 'tragedy' here not because the march was, on the face of it, a failure, but because I see the story as a parable of man, whose normal condition is one of bewilderment, finding himself in the struggle to follow his conscience whatever it may lead him against, and whatever suffering it may lead him through." Whatever confusion or misunderstanding Merwin associates with the march, either with Coxey or with Brown, he suggests it may be our own. "The theme of the poem," he wrote, "is a dramatization of the protest of the individual conscience faced with a society hung between old and new values, old and new problems of size, balance, justice, old frontiers closed and new ones not understood." Certainly Merwin's ambitions proved a major obstacle to the writing; he admits to being "not yet sure how far I want to depart from the historical events and characters" and says that he "will not be able to decide this until advanced further with the reading and the organization of the poem." Rather than simply reproducing a historical narrative, the piece will explore what avenues are open to the individual who must act according to his conscience but who is confused about how to express himself.

Merwin's sympathy with the bewilderment of Brown, rather than the assurance of Coxey, is understandable in the light of his other project. While work on the Coxey's army piece was to stall almost before it was under way and then linger persistently for the next several years, the project entitled "Congé" proceeded at an extraordinary pace.[21] He had no need to research his own life. Yet "Congé" stalled over a problem that resembled the question preoccupying

Brown: How were feelings of dissatisfaction to be expressed? Over a hundred pages of notes were prepared for this work, whose title is defined as: "1. Authoritative leave to depart; passport. 2. Ceremonious dismissal and leave-taking. 3. A bow; originally at taking one's leave. 4. Dismissal without ceremony. 5. Permission (for any act)" (shorter *OED*). Internal evidence suggests note taking began in the summer of 1959 and continued through that winter in England perhaps to the spring of 1960, when Merwin took up residence in rural France. What is clear is that the poem, planned as an extensive work, possibly in multiple sections, never came together on the scale envisaged. Yet its notes became the genesis for specific poems in *The Moving Target* and its themes would reappear, much transformed, in the long poem in that volume, "For Now."

Notes for "Congé" multiplied because the very idea of the poem encouraged Merwin to let himself be pulled in opposing directions. In its earliest stages, "Congé" promises to be a long poem of self-analysis, with a confessional element. His 1956–58 family poems escaped the influence of *Life Studies,* but "Congé" seems drawn to Lowell's orbit, and one note refers to "the confessional part of 'Congé' ":

> It was said I was precocious / but I matured late
> It is only now gradually I have learned / that you
>   must rush in your fate

Some passages suggest the work will be staged as autobiography:

> In disc. of beginning of love
>   —even / loved London for a week or two—
>   (disc. of it in autumn)
>   and then depar. for Spain

This autobiographical impulse is complicated, however, because the writing of this very poem will be the occasion for a deliberate break with the past and the impetus for beginning a new future. But analysis of the past cannot proceed until that future direction is set, and that direction depends on an analysis of the past. Many passages in the notes cancel themselves as they unfold. Merwin reminds himself that there needs to be "Somewhere an analysis of emotions of departures—from person, from place, from self." And he castigates himself for an unwillingness to take the risks he is now entertaining: "I have been false to self / compromise / death of spirit." But no sooner is he resolved to depart than he regrets his decision. His leave-taking, he recognizes, will be sorrowful, but he makes that admission in French: "Partir c'est mourir un peu" and "Suis-je trop vieux mon coeur pour faire ce voyage mystérieux." As intent as he is on a departure, he remains only certain about his uncertainty:

I am as hung between as a clothesline
as a nail between 2 pieces of wood
as vacuum jars w/horses pulling
as a string on an instrument (I make same note at both ends)
as a bridge
(Ben Jonson in bedevilled voice
    "Let me be what I am"—

"Let me be what I am" is the cry of this occasion, yet the statement emerges from Ben Jonson. "I hesitate like a week in spring," he notes in one place, and adds on the same page: "Up + down like a diving board / elevator / fucking sailor / fire siren."

Merwin wants to break into decisive action, but he is pulled in opposing directions. Sometimes he attaches blame to another person: "The gods we serve are not even friendly w/ each other" and "My gods are different fr. yours." Then again he admits that he may be at fault, that he has lost his youthfulness: "To youth—poets now bid it farewell before starting to write (since Eliot) like girls—their hair when take the vow. I have known friends of my youth who never had any youth of their own (describe) and I would rather be young than good." (This echoes a fragment on another page: "Knowing even now more than what I know now / I wd. rather be twenty than good.")

Change is sometimes embraced, sometimes questioned. A passage of detailed confession takes shape only to lapse into generalization. Autobiographical fragments recur, but it remains uncertain whether Merwin addresses himself to the muse or to a muse, whether his farewell is to a personalized vocation or to an actual person, whether the love that he would define is a love for a profession or a love for a person. What is unquestionable is that pessimism clouds almost every passage; youth is remote, misspent, lost: "I still believe in fate, fatalist, but believe you can miss your destiny like a plane (always the last one) and after that the weather breaks."

In 1960, Merwin could translate only these negative elements into finished verse. The poem would be reincarnated, in a much diminished form, in 1962 as "For Now" in *The Moving Target.* But by then he has understood that this work must be a reciting of everything he wishes to place behind him (including such evasive teeterings as are on display in "Congé"). In 1960, he lacks that confidence, and absolute pessimism dominates "Words for Departure" (dated January 27, 1960), whose earliest drafts bear the title of "Congé."[22] In six nine-line rhymed stanzas, he writes with a chilling disdain, deliberately skirting the edge of mere doggerel, encouraging rhymes that blatantly clash, as though this were how he would display his distaste for the occasion. In his conclusion, he develops a metaphor so distressingly inane it can only serve as a mark of his contempt:

God knows your hopes were nothing hot
But you nursed a few modest expectations.
However, they leave, and as they depart
Mortification milks the heart.

The milk is good for snacks, for kitty,
You can serve it to your friends
Till they let on with more [illegible] than pity
That they've got it in their own kitchens.
I've seen it waiting like long teeth
On every doorstep in the city.
Babies are given it like the titty,
And any mother's son will tell you
It makes a man (or woman) of you.

This sour and sullen outburst is his ambitious long poem withered by his inability to deal with the changes called for with such urgency. Yet it is with that sense of an overwhelming failure—rather than the dramatic transformation urged by "Congé"—that Merwin is able to begin *The Moving Target.*

5

Not the opening poem but the opening three poems of *The Moving Target*— "Home for Thanksgiving," "A Letter from Gussie," and "Lemuel's Blessing"— are the crossroads upon which converge the oppositions Merwin has been divided among for the past two years. Two poems precede the likely choice for an opening work, "Lemuel's Blessing," because their dissatisfied voices represent all that the poems to follow would move away from. They stand as surrogates of the poems uncollected or unpublished over which he had stalled in the years just before. He would introduce his frustration economically, just long enough to initiate a recoiling movement, to gain the energy to turn toward the willful rebirth of "Lemuel's Blessing."

Yet the first poem, "Home for Thanksgiving," reveals a new appreciation of why one might be unable to change one's life. Instead of earnestly pursuing the contradictory strains in his autobiography, Merwin presents another person who deludes himself into enduring his own contradictions. This sudden broadening of his view is a key to the appearance of the new free verse: rather than attempting to change his life, as he had so helplessly in "Congé," he focuses on the mind's operations as they frustrate change. Merwin's breakthrough into free verse is accompanied by his awareness of what prevents a breakthrough from occurring, and when the need to be active is replaced with analysis of the reasons for inactivity, that signals a new beginning. Merwin achieves a blend of detachment and understanding that allows him to present his protagonist's divided mind with keen sympathy.

Why does the sailor persist in the misery of exile? One answer is he has no choice: wherever he lands he still remains homeless. The poem begins with one long sentence that, as it degenerates into run-on sentences, confounds steady progress; the only difference between the streets "littered with words" and the third-floor room "in back of the bill-board / Which says Now Improved" is that the room allows a respite in which the scattered words of the street take shape as a slogan. But there is no fundamental shift, only a hoarding of what might otherwise be scattered, and that action is tainted with a miserliness that reflects a narrowed perspective.

Yet "Home for Thanksgiving" is not a simple portrait of the man so alienated from himself he cannot discern when he has left off voyaging. The poem breaks into two halves, Saturday night and Sunday morning, and the speaker's afterthoughts on Sunday morning help explain why he cannot break the pattern of homeless Saturday nights. In the earliest draft (originally entitled "The Sourdough Feeling Better About It"), Merwin summarized the work as follows: "The sourdough's hesitations about the wives he would have had if he hadn't spent his life in Alaska, how he'd have been miserable with them and left them and felt guilty and gone to Alaska and thought of other wives he could have had."[23] More important than its sketch of the plot are the linkages in its sentence that portray the mind rounding back until one decision cancels another.

The Sunday-morning half of the poem enacts this cancellation. The exile sets out "with my ears wiped and my collar buttoned," "all the way out and back on / A street car" like a boy entrusted to undertake a journey by himself. The model he bears within him is emphasized in the repeated phrase "I bring myself back." He must always bring himself back from his journey, because the safe return, the port at the end, is valued, not his adventures on the way. During his streetcar jaunt, when he is safely enclosed (repeating a journey with origins in his childhood), he ponders a question that has occurred before: whether he "should have stayed making some of those good women / Happy, for a while at least." To remain, though, conflicts with the idea of the successful return, for the return will be judged a success if nothing has happened. (That is why "New Improved," apart from its sidelong swipe at the way advertising debases language, can echo so ironically.) To stay, he would have to shed his childlike attitude toward these maternal women who pamper him with offerings and and distractions: "Vera with the eau-de-cologne and the small fat dog named Joy, / Gladys with her earrings, cooking and watery arms." Even as he speculates, they begin to impose adultlike demands on him, drawing him toward other adults and obligations: "they would have / Produced families their own and our own."

When the sailor says "I bring myself / Back like a mother cat transferring her only kitten," he is identifying his role—the adult who protects the child within. This adult can play no other role, which is why other adults can seem threatening. To interact with adults is to lose touch with the child, and for the sailor, what it means to be an adult is to protect the child within, even though that responsibility will nurture a sober child with "ears wiped" and "collar buttoned," capable of taking a jaunt by himself. The sailor is condemned to relive a childhood voyage in which he was enjoined to act as an adult and bring himself back safely, a voyage that has become the model for his later life. That safe return echoes in the last line of the poem, "I did the right thing after all," which sounds like a child hearing an adult praise him for acting properly, though he has no clear idea why.

Not the least of the extraordinary things about this poem is that it captures the division within the sailor, the tough adult who walks the streets like "long / Silent laughs" and the frightened child, the boy who knows enough not to open the door to the wind. The adult's role is to be tough to protect the tender child within; the child within remains fearful of the adult role that requires such toughness. Ultimately, the poem is a fierce attack on the destructive consequences of propriety, as imposed upon a child at an early age urged to be careful to bring himself back safely. The sailor cannot grow up because even as a child he acted as an adult. And he cannot be an adult because the adult only exists to protect the child within. Anything else—the demands of others, the opportunity to grow through a new and unexpected occurrence, a genuine voyage with no decision made at the start to bring oneself back safely—appears as a terrifying threat. The sailor never wants to remove that "good grade suit of longies" better suited for a child than an adult, though they make him miserable.

What has condemned the sailor to his wandering is his inability to escape his ingrained idea of what it is proper. Like the protagonists in Merwin's 1957 plays, both of whom fall into the very position of compromise that each could have escaped, he ultimately shrinks from the bold gesture that could release him from bondage. The weight imposed by conventional propriety—a weight Merwin understands to be self-imposed—is not a new theme. Indeed, the crisscrossed drafts of "Congé" are a chronicle of the damage inflicted on the sensibility that persistently yields to convention. That such a yielding may issue in frustration and anger is evident in "A Letter from Gussie," a poem that, with "Home for Thanksgiving," forms a coda to *The Drunk in the Furnace* in that both recall the division in the family poems, in which men became itinerant wanderers, incapable of giving their lives a necessary focus, and women remained at home to care for the family heritage, steeping in a dark bitterness. "Don't you think I'd have liked / To get away also?" asks Gussie, emphasizing the options that limit both her and the sailor. One is either at home or has got away.

Other poems written in 1960 could have appeared in these opening pages, such as "Words for Departure" or "Wishes for Old Age," a predecessor of "Lemuel's Blessing" that begins:

Senility, if you're waiting for me
    Like a Wise Virgin,
Unexceptionable, holding the ring,
    Let me make plain
Now in sound mind my hope never in your
    Obscene embrace to soften
Like an orange, and succumb to an alien
    Wisdom. Always it has been
One or other of your sisters with dark lanterns
    Whom my passion
Has followed blindly like the shadows. Missing them all,
    Rather than set my hand
To a different blindness, may I stumble to the end
    Strong in my own. . . .[24]

But if this resembles certain passages in "Lemuel's Blessing" ("Let fatigue, weather, habitation, the old bones, finally, / Be nothing to me, / Let all lights but yours be nothing to me"), its difference in attitude is striking. In "Wishes" Merwin looks ahead with little confidence to a test that, even in his poem, he turns away from confronting, veering instead toward a balanced recounting of what he has aspired to be. But the spirit addressed in "Lemuel's Blessing" has avoided the lairs of civilization, and it actively enters the texture of the poem in lines that dart erratically, turning against expectations. What is killing, as Merwin now understands, is to be unable to escape responsibilities; they are self-imposed prohibitions that are intimately a part of the individual. The deeper form of the poem, then, has little to do with literary predecessors like *Leaves of Grass* or Christopher Smart's "Jubilate Agnato"; rather, the enumeration of those elements that conspire to constrain the individual conforms precisely to the course Merwin has been following over the last few years. Only when every alternative has been tested and found wanting has one earned the right to address this spirit that lies beyond definition or constraint not because it is an outlaw but because it has found the way to follow its own laws. "You that know the way, / Spirit," Merwin begins, as he starts his search for the laws he can follow.

7

The Good Voyage

ACCUSTOMED AS we are to considering *The Moving Target* a seminal work of contemporary poetry, it is startling to find how poorly it fared with its original reviewers. Even the blurb from James Dickey, conspicuously posted on the back cover of second and subsequent editions (". . . images and poems that have the handprint of necessity upon them"), had a different orientation when it first appeared in the *New York Times Book Review:* "One hopes that Mr. Merwin will now find a way to make his images less fortuitous, that he will eschew the use of dilettantish shock-metaphor, and opt for the images and poems that have the handprint of necessity upon them instead of the quickly tarnished sheen of the merely novel, the fetchingly precious, the *different.*" Other reviews were even less complimentary. Joseph Bennett (who had deplored *Life Studies* in a recent review) found passages to appreciate but never for long: "One cannot find five ordinary lines without coming on something extraordinary; but it is all dispersed, nothing connects; all the good stuff is scattered there impartially, inexplicably." Ralph J. Mills was upset by a "willful and cryptic privacy" and complained "the book creates a general feeling of sameness, of monotony, which is quite unrelieved." David Galler began his review with a gloomy portrait of an audience for poetry that had grown "shock-prone," "nihilistic"; he suggested Merwin's work contrived to ingratiate itself with that audience, one perversely delighted with examples of "Accident."[1]

From qualified acceptance to outright bafflement—so ranged first responses to *The Moving Target.* One sign of Merwin's collapse, according to reviewers, was his new allegiance to a long-discredited tradition of European surrealism. Mills and Galler note resemblances to Eluard, Lorca, and Breton, darkly suggesting this verse lapses into a mode exhausted thirty years ago. It seems common knowledge among these reviewers that other young poets—Bly, Wright, Kinnell—are drawn to that tradition, but that is regarded as an alarming state, a situation that threatens standards and invites chaos.

It is useful to know how uncertain Merwin's steps must have been in the early 1960s. The reviewers assume the poet's role is inherently responsible: it is to be a cultural leader. The poet renews or erects standards, shaping a future for the culture by continuing to organize words intelligently, compellingly, reminding us of a noble heritage. This was a legacy of the 1950s, a period when values were assumed to be stable. Where Merwin's new work falls open to criticism, then, is in its acknowledgment that standards have fallen or changed. Interestingly, Merwin's reviewers feel free to take note of such a crisis, and virtually all of them allude to it, but they declare it an area off limits for poetry. Only R. K. Meiners suggests that the crisis in the poetry might be an effort to break down habits of thought and redraw lines of connection. "In a sense," Meiners writes, adopting a tone of speculation rather than a voice of authority, "the poems cannot be called private; they cultivate a radically public inwardness. 'Here I am once again with my dry mouth / At the fountain of thistles / Preparing to sing,' Merwin announces in 'Invocation,' and we are invited to identify with the scanty lot of the poet."[2] Meiners's thoughtful review considers the contradictions others recoil against. Rather than offering wealth and riches, this poetry invites us to consider our "scanty lot"—that what we hold to be wealth is poverty, that what we think stable is groundless.

Merwin's reply to his reviewers is already implicit in *The Moving Target.* The role of cultural leader in these times falls to the one with the courage to follow through on his intuitions, even when they place him beyond the pale. Indeed, the most disturbing idea in the book is that a sense of despair may not originate as a psychic problem, a failure on the level of the individual, but could emerge from an insightful assessment of cultural circumstances. Such a turnaround occurs to Merwin in the course of *The Moving Target.* One reason reviewers were blocked from appreciation was their inclination to view the book as an example of one new style. But as the arrangement of poems indicates, with the omission of punctuation two-thirds of the way through, this work remains under way, in a process of evolution. That process is especially evident in Merwin's arduous efforts to assemble the volume—to break from silence, to examine himself, and to find himself speaking as a critic of his culture. But the process is evident in the final text, which, with some exclusions, reproduces the stages in that struggle.

The Moving Target, as finally assembled, is about its own creation. It represents an extraordinary pilgrimage. In its opening poems, it appears to Merwin that the contradictions over which he stalls are of his own making, the result of his inability to voice his desires in time, or to break free of the kennels and halters that reduce him to servility. By the end of the book, his perspective has changed radically. The divisions he sees are not internal but external, the symptoms of a culture that fails to comprehend its own contradictions. The malaise is not his individual flaw, and it cannot be addressed by analyzing one's upbringing or lamenting one's fate. The malaise is real and widespread, and it is only to be addressed in poetry that analyzes the cultural circumstances that allow it to persist. The problems Merwin had associated with himself alone originate with no one and belong to everyone; they are the very source of poetry crying out to be written.

1

A most dramatic indication that change is under way appears in Merwin's worksheets. The enduring legacy of "Congé" was its revolutionary effect on his habits of composition. Before "Congé," Merwin shaped his work steadily toward its finish. Heading his notes with a tentative title, he began by seeking an overall form. The poem first emerged as a key passage, followed by further whole passages from which a beginning or conclusion could be selected (fig. 9). The next step was to compose the secondary passages linking the primary ones. Often this led to a complete draft. Only minor adjustments in wording or lineation were needed, and then a fair copy was produced.

With "Congé," however, Merwin's process resisted such handy streamlining because his topic was the network of personal relationships in which he was enmeshed. Instead of beginning by establishing boundaries—those key passages that mark a beginning and an ending—and then filling in the movement from one point to another, he found that all boundaries had become alarmingly fluid. Thus he began his notes for "Congé" in the usual fashion, jotting down key phrases, anticipating that they would crystallize into key passages and in turn function as markers, the start and finish of his exploration. But markers kept eluding him: to set even one required that he act decisively toward matters in his own life about which he was still unsettled. One recurring idea in "Congé" is that the poem itself will break with the poet's past—except that this task burdens the work with its impossible complexity: if the poem is to explore his indecision, it must keep postponing its breakaway in another direction, its new beginning.

"Congé" certainly succeeds as postponement: on page after page, notes proliferate. More notably, when a passage emerges that might be central, Merwin isolates it, extruding it from "Congé" by assigning it to another work, one to be written outside this long poem (fig. 10). Because it is a key passage, it must be distinguished from "Congé" because the scale of the long poem is so large that no single passage could possibly be central; such passages are reserved for shorter poems. "Congé," then, remains perpetually in process, waiting for a break from the indecision central to the poem. But for such a break to occur Merwin would have to reconceive the work as a poem in which these

Sea Monster

We were not even out of sight of land
That afternoon when we saw it. Not one of us
Would have disagreed as to where we were
Or mistaken the brown cliffs or the town
On top.

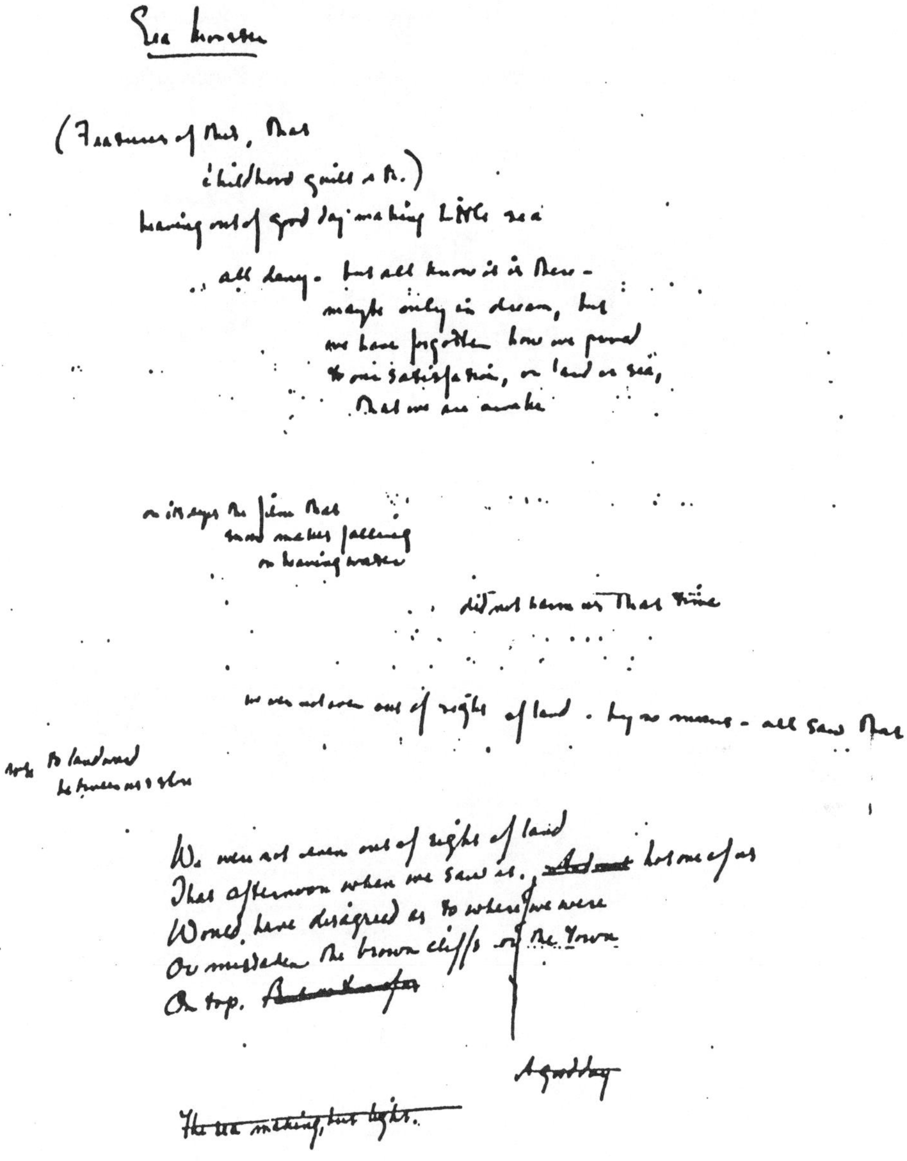

Figure 9. Initial notes for "Sea Monster" (MS. 19:12/053, d. Oct. 23, 1955). The poem begins as a sketch of the overall situation, which leads into two fragmentary passages. Both were used in the final poem, and the second of them formed the poem's beginning.

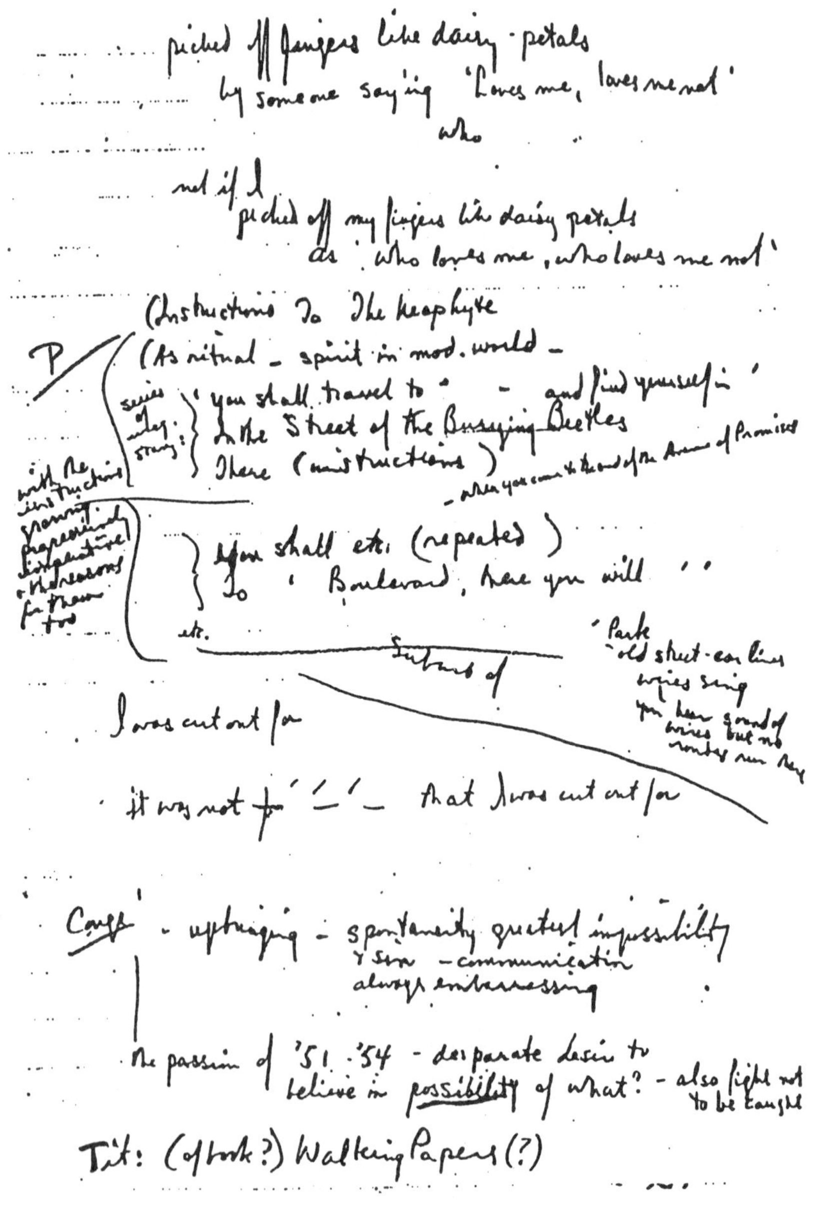

picked off fingers like daisy-petals
by someone saying 'Loves me, loves me not'
who

not if I
picked off my fingers like daisy petals
as 'who loves me, who loves me not'

Instructions To The Neophyte
P (As ritual – spirit in mod. world –
'you shall travel to – and find yourself in'
In the Street of the Buzzing Beetles
There (instructions) – when you come to the end of the Avenue of Promises

You shall etc. (repeated)
To Boulevard, here you will
etc.

Park
old street-car lines

I was cut out for

it was not for '–' that I was cut out for

Congé – upbringing – spontaneity quested impossibility
& sin – communication
always embarrassing

the passion of '51–'54 – desperate desire to
believe in possibility of what? – also fight not
to be caught

Tit: (of book?) Walking Papers (?)

Figure 10. Notes for "Congé" (unfin. MS. 20:05/001, c. 1959–60), showing a cluster of notes being detached and identified as the subject of a separate poem. The upper half of the page becomes the seed of "Route with No Number" (MT, 25–27), tentatively titled "Instructions to the Neophyte" and marked with a "P" to its left.

disturbing fragments no longer cancel each other out. The note taking will never end.

Merwin finally escapes this loop by embracing it as a working method. The notes for "Congé" covered so wide a spectrum that they were always a record of Merwin thinking, casting up insights and notions as they occurred; these notes veered about, sometimes expanding a thought, sometimes opposing it. He begins, then, to encourage this process by writing down simply what occurs to him, however odd or trivial or obscure it seems. From snatches of phrasing, sometimes as small as a word or two, sometimes as complete as an elliptical image, Merwin gathers fragments, expanding them into key passages that can set a poem in motion (fig. 11).

Merwin's procedure for shaping a final draft remains unchanged: it is still crucial to link central passages. But the core of the poem, those central passages, now has an intimate source. Instead of erecting an individual poem out of some observation, employing the title as a sort of balancing-point, Merwin now insists that his poetry must be found within his sensibility as it reveals itself, in an unguarded fashion, in this free-association process. The method, then, quite deliberately seeks access to ways of thinking, eccentric attitudes, indirect observations, that are within the poet but not obviously apparent. He is now literally writing his own life, the poetry an intensified record that carries forward and emphasizes feelings that might not ordinarily find expression. They are too elusive, too fleeting, to endure for long; many appear at first as unconventional turns of thought that lack affinity with ordinary linguistic constructions; but caught on the wing, as instants in this list, they become available for meditation and exploration. They can be coaxed into a life of their own, while still maintaining deep attachments to Merwin's inner life.

2

Merwin's changing methods of composition stand behind the three stages through which *The Moving Target* passes. Each stage is distinctive enough to warrant its own section in the volume, except that such categorizing would appear at odds with the exploratory spirit that the poems hope to sustain. Nonetheless, Merwin presents his poems, with few exceptions, in the order in which they were written, inviting the collection to be read not as a miscellany of impressions but as a chronicle of growth. The volume commences with poetry written in England from January to March in 1960, after a nine-month silence during which Merwin had worked only on translations and the notes for "Congé."[3] But it is something of a false start. After writing the three poems that open the volume, he settled into jotting brief epigrams, from one to six lines in length. These are short because the truths they state are so bitter. "Unforgiveables" simply lists those things its title defines: "The wise bird who

~~Something~~ is harder to give up what ~~something~~ you never had

I can't get it out of my mind

Vamp: fat / fag

Mary: they're always washed in company

didn't
Know he'd been born

congregation of coughs – the sea's congregation of coughs

Thunder coughing

banged in the high mouth (crucifix) — and their working [illegible] all [illegible]

/ is gone, and no question

Ignorance is a double thing:
nothing behind it, everything before it.

gave himself away

hold the summer in shell (walnut) – all that's left of it
· walnut. here is the small brain of one extinct summer
and already it remembers nothing

carried by the rats · mementos

to [illegible] steeps in a little at a time · logging, weighting

no cares – but the empty spaces waiting
where they would be – balloons in space

There were no rooms but
the emptiness was already waiting
there in the air

The chairs meditate on their ——

I have arrived too late I will come again

The animals came then and confessed that
they had known about death all along

They told of it:
(what does that do to/man's position in
the universe)

he ask them why they continue then. Their
answer

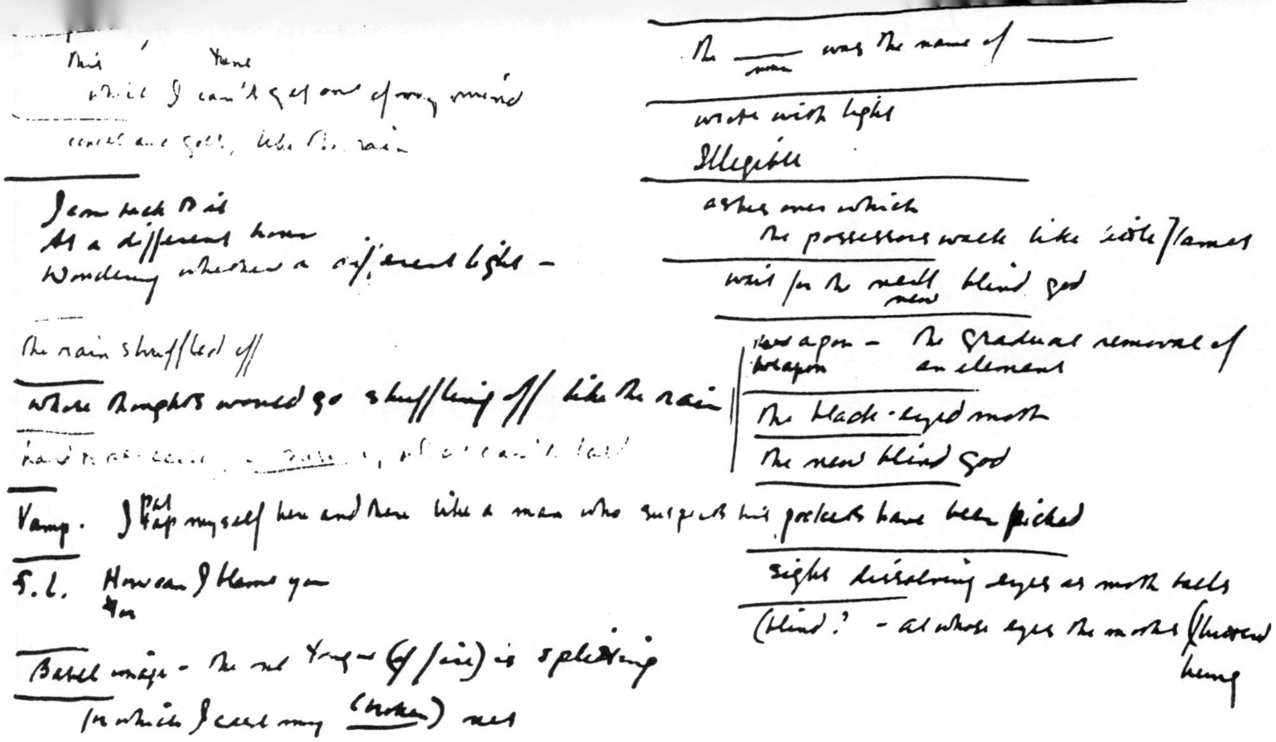

Figure 11. List of notes, c. 1960, among which can be found (halfway down the page) the concluding lines of "Now and Again" (MT, 31–32): "hold the summer in shell (walnut)—all that's left of it / walnut—here is the small brain of our extinct summer / and already it remembers nothing." Also, there are three references to a vampire poem (preceded by the notation "Vamp.")—first inklings of "The Indigestion of the Vampire" (MT, 45–46). Notes in pencil scattered between notes in ink suggest these original notes prompted a second set of annotations at a later time.

told somebody else. / Youth. The Wise Virgins. Independence."[4] These starkly impersonal poems stopped once Merwin settled in France, where he continued to write fluently through the summer and fall of 1960.

From this mass of poetry so rapidly produced between January and October 1960 (at one point he thought he might have accumulated enough for a volume), Merwin chose to reprint primarily the longer pieces completed in France. They reveal a profoundly divided nature. They depict someone who has decided to break with his past, who regards with a sardonic eye relationships he once revered. But he never stands fully behind his cutting phrases, as a master of ironic deflation: he preserves a sense of his own confusion even as he would erect defenses against it. This poetry, as a result, is both immensely defiant and almost impossibly tender. Its double edge, its mixture of barbarous behavior with exquisite vulnerability, makes it emotionally exhausting.

Consider the new spirit he would invoke in "Finally," a spirit both fierce and shy, wild and gentle. To succeed, the poet must speak with strength and courage, but with a gentleness that will convince the spirit of the poet's worth. It begins with an assertion that can only be expressed coaxingly. On the one hand, the poet's "dread" and "ignorance" (which are identical to his "self") resemble a wild creature within: "Your imminence / Prowls the palms of my hands like sweat." On the other hand, that creature can be frightened away: "Do not now, if I rise to welcome you, / Make off like roads into the deep night." To invite such a spirit, wild and unfamiliar, his tone veers between the flippant and the solemn: "The dogs are dead at last, the locks toothless, / The habits out of reach. / I will not be false to you tonight." One must sever oneself from all habits and customary bonds, an aggressive act, while at the same time displaying a care and sensitivity that are unimaginably gentle. The ending of the poem is absolutely right:

> Come. As a man who hears a sound at the gate
> Opens the window and puts out the light
> The better to see out into the dark,
> Look, I put it out. (MT, 22)

When the light is extinguished, the gate ceases to protect or mark a boundary; to sustain the possession of his own territory, the speaker offers himself in trust. The dark evoked here is by no means a blackness: it promises that the eyes will grow accustomed to it, exactly to the extent that one trusts to willing receptivity.

Merwin remains acutely aware of the gulf that separates his own gentleness and even fragility from the strong will needed to embark on a new beginning. The vagabond sailor in "Home for Thanksgiving" can only circle back to his initial position because the relation within him between tough adult and fragile child is hopelessly locked in a set format; these later poems unlock the tense relation between the two and emerge from the interplay that opens between them. As first written, some struck Merwin as too openly vulnerable. "Lemuel's Blessing," first completed in England in January 1960, was revised in France in April 1960; originally, it built slowly toward a climactic plea, but the final version starts the poem abruptly, without time spent beseeching (fig. 12). "The Ships Are Made Ready in Silence," its typescript dated March 5–6, 1960, but revised later, first appears as a most reluctant leave-taking; a later version excises personal allusions ("a dead leaf of yours scrapes the deck asking / Whether I remember the house / In the plum orchard, the meanings of 'we' . . ."). By eliminating the imploring voice of his love, he strengthens his resolve. But even when lines snap forward aggressively, wielding slang and cliche, mixing metaphors with abandon, they are apt to turn suddenly toward a statement that reveals the helplessness of the speaker. "Route with No Number," whose form recalls the puzzle-book mazes of childhood with their cartoon menaces, adeptly displays these sudden switchings. A collection of wisecracks sets us off balance as the voice cracks instead, revealing the speaker plunged in melancholy, fragile as an eggshell:

> There's not even a little privacy: you can see
> Eyes lined up to ripen on the sills
> And once here you're better than I am
> If you can find your way back again.
> However, I have visited the Day of the Dog,
> But it was not yet open and I passed on.
> Tell Mrs. H. just the same,
> Who said I'd never get anywhere. (FF, 25)

The reason for the smart remarks is that the speaker cannot approach for long his true condition, for to near it at all is to risk collapsing entirely.

How can the child and the adult benefit each other? How to reconcile one's gentle nature with the strength needed for action? Merwin identifies the dilemma without resolving it. He stubbornly refuses to yield to either, as emotionally exhausting as it is to endure the two together. The speaker in "The Saint of the Uplands" has been misunderstood: speaking after his own death, he recalls his efforts among those whose "faces were hard crusts like their farms / And the eyes empty." He aspired, in his lifetime, to fill those empty eyes:

> I took a single twig from the tree of my ignorance
> And divined the living streams under
> Their very houses. I showed them
> The same tree growing in their dooryards. (MT, 17)

But at his death, they offer him the honors he had rejected in his life: "over / My dry bones they build their churches, like wells." Their response to

LEMUEL'S BLESSING

Let Lemuel bless with the Wolf, which is a
~~dog~~ dog without a master, but the Lord hears
his cries and feeds him in the ~~desert~~ desert.

Christopher Smart: Jubilate Agno

~~You that made me,~~
You that know the way,
~~Spirit,~~
~~I bless your ears. Let me approach.~~
I bless your nails which are like dice in command of their
own combinations.
Let me not be lost.
I bless your eyes for which I know no comparison.
~~Run with me like the horizon, let me~~
~~Do nothing which would forfeit me your presence, for~~ ~~Without you~~
I am ~~no more than a dog~~ lost and hungry,
Ill-natured, untrustworthy, useless.

~~All~~ My bones ~~together~~ bless you like an orchestra of flutes.
~~Let the weapons of the settlements fall exhausted a long way~~
~~from me,~~
~~And their dogs the same. My laugh blesses you.~~
~~Whereas~~ A dog is shameless and wears ~~his~~ servility / in his tail
Like a banner;
Let me wear the opprobrium of ~~the~~ possessed and ~~the~~ possessors
As a thick tail properly used
To warm my worst and my best ~~my~~ parts. My tail blesses you.

Deliver me from the ~~coyotes,~~ dingoes, foxes, jackals, hyenas,
Which deny your very existance.
~~Let me approach distress, when I have to, as a good dust to~~
~~roll in,~~
Discouraging pests of my own.
~~My pelt~~ blesses you. Let it never be owned or walked on.

~~But Deliver~~ me ~~from~~ the error ~~which hangs around~~ at the fork of
hesitation,
~~And has many arms and endless patience, knowing~~
~~Its moment and the sequel,~~
~~For~~ It can go before and wait, or follow and be there, ~~crossing~~
~~The heavens like a goat, jumping from star to star, even~~
~~In the daytime when the stars are invisible.~~
~~Let me not be made the sport of the deadly truths~~
~~Every one of which is more intelligent and knowledgable than I am:~~
~~Deliver me~~

Figure 12. Opening of the revised final draft of "Lemuel's Blessing" (TS. 20:12/011, d. Apr. 21, 1960). The typescript under revision is identical to a typescript dated January 24–25, 1960.

his absence is to commemorate him in stone, when what he had sought to bestow on them were the delicate changes of the living moment. Their prayers are vexing; they "still swarm on me like lost bees" looking for a home. Instead of praying, he would have them realize at last that "In the high barrens / The light loved us," insisting that even those born with nothing may have everything that matters: "I taught them to gather the dew of their nights / Into mirrors. I hung them / Between heavens." When empty eyes soften with tears, the tears are like a dew that become a mirror in which all see they share a common fate, the realization of which is the closest one gets to heaven. Yet such an achievement is precarious, temporary at best; at the death of the Saint, it is lost, and the voice of the poem mingles regret with anger, sorrow with impatience. The high point of the work is the line "Over my feet they waste their few tears"—which harshly dismisses their mourning as a waste of their time, even as it immediately understands how rare and precious is their weeping. Always in between—that is the drama that the poems must acknowledge as they emerge, appearing from between the opposites formed by the impenetrability of the barren stone and the ineffability of the loving light.

Such irreconcilable oppositions mark these early poems and justify their unstable discourse. Their "surrealism" has been much misunderstood: their bizarre images often appear to be brusque, like tough poses taken to deflect emotions that might otherwise overwhelm the speaker. "To My Brother Hanson" revisits the situation in "Home for Thanksgiving," with the relation between the child and the adult now openly dramatized to an unbearable breaking point. Addressing his elder brother who died after living less than a day, Merwin's complaints center on the responsibilities he must bear in the brother's absence: "with / My eyes still shut I remember to turn the thorn / In the breast of the bird of darkness." The poem hinges on a "witty" reversal, that the elder brother remains, in his death, always a child, requiring the younger to play the role of the adult. But the wit is a transparent cloak, allowing Merwin to confess his weariness without succumbing to self-pity. In "Sire" the grandfather who might be capable of offering guidance is himself a mixture of impossible contradictions, his wanderings impossible to reconcile: "Wearing boots, on crutches, barefoot, they could never / Get together on any door-sill or destination." Such diametric opposites cannot be reconciled, and Merwin's achievement remains his anguished awareness of the contradictions that end with no clear direction emerging from the work. On a grand scale, everywhere he looks, division is rampant. What is needed, it seems, is not a reconciliation of opposites but a position from which their inherent duality can be seen as dynamic, not destructive.

3

The poems in the middle third of *The Moving Target,* written in New York and France in 1961 and 1962, differ pointedly from those in the first third.

They feature an unsettling, wild, bitter humor, which often has the effect of goading the poet out of his self-pity and despair.[5] They take a perverse vitality from the erratic activity of their urban settings. The modern city can, at different times, serve to recapitulate the poet's confusion as well as jostle him out of his self-absorption by quickening his observations.

"Departure's Girl-friend," the first of these consciously urban poems, is a breakthrough of considerable magnitude: though he begins his second cycle as he had his first, with a dramatic monologue spoken by another, the situation has markedly changed. The poem has a swiftness of purpose, an intent focus, missing from its predecessors. It begins with a purposive gesture; instead of avoiding loneliness by suppressing it, the speaker takes it as an occasion to act, and that decision transforms her surroundings, so that "The night / Was mine but everyone's, like a birthday." The "bon voyage" wreath she has concocted for delivery to her boat even feels responsive; its leaves were "holding my hands," and "the rest waved good-bye." But there is no delivery to be made, no boat at the wharf—and though the speaker insists that the wreath she hugs to herself grants her the right to expect her boat, the truth is delivered bluntly by a sailor: "He said, this is the stone wharf, lady, / You don't own anything here." But from this dismissal emerges a vision of the city in sharp focus:

> and there I was
> In the other and hated city
> Where I was born, where nothing is moored, where
> The lights crawl over the stones like flies, spelling now,
> Now, and the same fat chances roll
> Their many eyes; and I step once more
> Through a hoop of tears and walk on, holding this
> Buoy of flowers in front of my beauty,
> Wishing myself the good voyage. (MT, 36)

Those who would be so foolish, in the city, as to expect events to conform to their wishes will always be disappointed, for "nothing is moored," and the bottom continually drops out. But just as the city places the protagonist, the protagonist finds the strength to place the city. That "other and hated city" is by no means portrayed as devouring the speaker: its blazing lights are reduced to crawling flies, its opportunistic offerings to the "same fat chances." Understanding the city's energetic aimlessness, the speaker can now comprehend herself, in a way that is ironic yet not self-lacerating. The wry tone into which she falls is, in fact, her triumph. At the very end, she has the strength to see herself against the city, a new version of the mirror she had so conspicuously avoided at the start.

The urban backdrop is a fractured mirror, a testing-ground upon which one learns survival. It tests the wreaths one weaves around oneself like protective amulets; it may expose their inadequacy even as it reveals they are needed all the more. The wreath in which the speaker invested so much, which hovered perilously close to being a funeral wreath, becomes a "buoy," both a guide and a life jacket, once it becomes an individual gesture, not a gift that one pretends is for another. In a similar way, what a poem is must be reconceived: if it is supposed to be a present for others, an offering made as a self-sacrifice, it can only be rejected by the men at work on the stone wharf, who are quite certain who owns what, and for whom nothing else matters; the poem must be acknowledged by its poet, above all, not as a gift but as a personal impulse, as frail as a wreath, woven with affection, but of use primarily to its maker.

In his city poems, Merwin values the odd, quirky gestures he makes through them, accepting the helplessness of their gestures, but insisting on their rightness. Unlike the poems in the first third of the book, where the poet is constantly stymied, always trying to clarify a point, to niggle over a detail, to begin again to justify himself, these urban poems are full of declarations, insistences. In 1960, when expanding one of his short poems into "The Nails," his strategy was to add a refrain that undercut his previous words: "It isn't as simple as that." By contrast, in 1961, these city poems cut against such irresolution; he declares himself having arrived home, even as the essential rootlessness of the modern city reaffirms itself.

Even this impulse, however, was stalled at first. Living in New York between January and July 1961, he divided his time between acting as poetry editor of the *Nation* and working on the narrative poem about Coxey's Army. He resumed writing poetry only after he returned to rural France in July. Although the poetry in the middle third of the volume was composed in a rural setting, it was written in response to his time in New York. It remained not only urban, but decidedly distinct from the work completed in France the year before—as he quickly learned when he began to revise poems written then (and in some cases, published in journals).[6] These revisions, in fact, proved unsatisfactory and were excluded from the final collection; he had traveled too far, in one year, to return. Looking at them now, one sees his new impatience with his old hesitations. Consider the two versions of "Foreign Summer," first written in France on August 28–29, 1960, the revision made in 1961 (fig. 13). In 1960, the poet is surrounded by fog, unable to see; in 1961, the fog lifts, and he can see. The previous imagery of blindness must be eliminated—the fog withdraws as a cataract from an eye; the sightless coin is held before one as a useless lantern. That haze of misunderstanding no longer surrounds him. Originally, the lines dragged, weighed down with burdens; now, they dart abruptly, disjoined from each other by unexpected twists. The revision eradicates that underlying sorrow that he bore reluctantly, replacing it with a keen sense of paradox that employs a cutting sarcasm.[7]

The features of the urban cityscape imposing upon the poet disrupt his

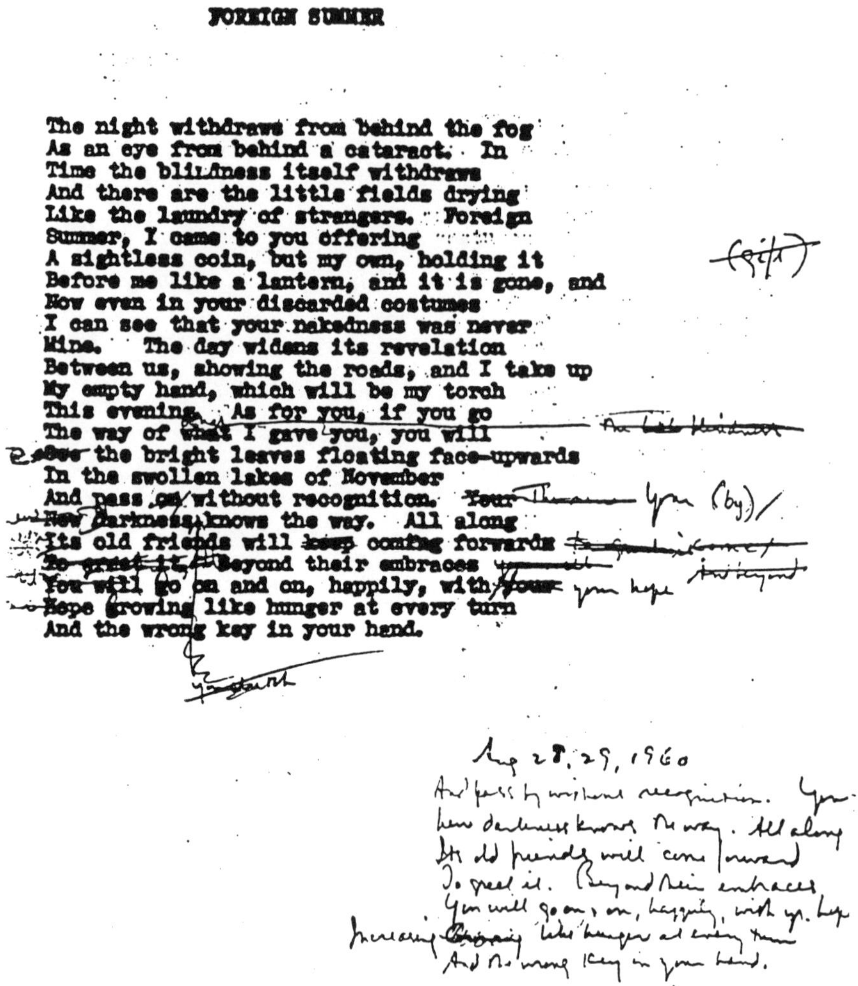

FOREIGN SUMMER

The night withdraws from behind the fog
As an eye from behind a cataract. In
Time the blindness itself withdraws
And there are the little fields drying
Like the laundry of strangers. Foreign
Summer, I came to you offering
A sightless coin, but my own, holding it
Before me like a lantern, and it is gone, and
Now even in your discarded costumes
I can see that your nakedness was never
Mine. The day widens its revelation
Between us, showing the roads, and I take up
My empty hand, which will be my torch
This evening. As for you, if you go
The way of what I gave you, you will
See the bright leaves floating face-upwards
In the swollen lakes of November
And pass on without recognition. Your
New darkness knows the way. All along
Its old friends will keep coming forwards
To greet it. Beyond their embraces
You will go on and on, happily, with your
Hope growing like hunger at every turn
And the wrong key in your hand.

Aug 28, 29, 1960
And pass by without recognition. Your
new darkness knows the way. All along
Its old friends will come forward
To greet it. Beyond their embraces
You will go on, & on, happily, with yr. hope
Increasing like hunger at every turn
And the wrong key in your hand.

Figure 13. On the left, revised final draft of a variant of "Foreign Summer" (uncol. variant TS. 20:12/003, d. Aug. 28–29, 1960); this was submitted for publication but never accepted. On the right, revised final draft of final version of "Foreign Summer" (uncol. TS. 20:10/004a, c. summer-fall 1961); this was published in *Poetry* 99 (Jan. 1962): 209.

FOREIGN SUMMER

Night goes, the fog lifts, there
Are the little fields
Drying like the laundry of strangers.
Foreign summer,

~~Nor~~ Even ~~in~~ your discarded costumes
~~I can see~~ that your nakedness
Was never mine.

The day widens its revelation
~~Between us~~, showing the roads
And I take up my empty hand
Which will be my torch this evening.

You yourself
~~Of~~ Will go the way of everything I gave you.
You will notice the ~~golden leaves floating~~
~~Face upwards on~~ the ~~swollen~~
~~Lakes of November~~
And you will pass by without recognition.

All up the road
The trees will miss you
When you have climbed their shadows.
Far from their embraces you will go on.
You will be happy.
Hope will have thought of you at every turn.
You will have the wrong key in your hand.

tendency to brood; he has not cast off his self-absorbed melancholy, but the forces within the city—loose, confused, animated, brusque—dilute his morbid concentration. They disperse his focus, then call out for attention of their own. The poetry plays in, out, among them. No one would deem such writing playful, but self-cancellation is no longer so agonizing when events outside the window casually cancel each other. "The Present" opens:

> The walls join hands and
> It is tomorrow:
> The birds clucking to the horses, the horses
> Doing the numbers for the hell of it,
> The numbers playing the calendars,
> The saints marching in,
> It seems only yesterday . . . (MT, 51)

"Tomorrow" comes with rapidity, in a series of events barely related to each other, so jumbled are they in a way designed to be overwhelming, until tomorrow has turned into yesterday. The jumble is, however, rather benign, like walls that meet in greeting: the language simply gets out of hand, one thing leading to another. Against that noise and activity, Merwin sets himself as someone trying to make over his life: "Take a leaf from the fire, open / Your hand, see / Where you are going. . . ." He is looking for "the stars at noon, // While the light worships its blind god." He associates with natural images—the leaf, the fire, the hand—as though seeking a firm path, but the unnatural clashings in the city—from numbers to calendars to saints—are no distraction to his quest but a texture out of which a search could emerge.

If nothing else, the driving force of the city demands that one live or die. In "Walk-up" the poet is threatened by the "inspector of stairs" paying an unexpected visit; it is as though once again one's personal life will be intruded upon by the impersonality of the city. But in this poem Merwin says:

> No
> The sky's at home in these windows, and the maps
> Of themselves on these walls,
> And your letter is enough improvement
> For anywhere, lying open
> On my table, my
> Love
> I won't close a thing (MT, 59)

Merwin's rejections are never negative: they are substitutions, made with an air of discovery. Much that might have struck reviewers in 1963 as contrived, deliberately bizarre or mysterious, is often a rendering of straightforward detail, with Merwin claiming a new distinction for his own gestures, for personal objects, for private instances. But so little holds him together—the will to consider the moment, to hope for the future: to believe that some relief will arrive, though in this moment he is incapable of even imagining what form it will take.

4

The singular achievement of *The Moving Target* is not, however, these restless, urban poems at the center of the book; they might best be considered a point of transition, an escape from the self-destruction that threatened to overwhelm Merwin at the outset of his volume. The urban poetry of 1961 splurges its cockeyed energies, lighting up surfaces that jostle against each other. What it downplays, though, is the ominous side of the city: energy as meaningless commotion, the gaps and voids that lie between its swirling motions. It is true there are constant allusions to those vacancies, but Merwin overrides them by adopting a tone, as in "Air," both determined and jaunty:

> This way the dust, that way the dust.
> I listen to both sides
> But I keep right on.
> I remember the leaves sitting in judgment
> And then winter. (MT, 50)

He accepts that "I am going my way / Which has a strange sound." What keeps him moving along is his memory that fall passes into winter, that the judgment of the leaves is left behind by the sheer progress of events, as though there were a sense of momentum one needed to identify with, a deliberate light touch that had to be maintained. On the one hand he remembers examples of the passage of time; on the other hand he says: "I forget tomorrow, the blind man." It is an act of will, a foray that remains consistent with the speaker's decision in "Departure's Girl-friend" to think of a better thing to do than suppressing the loneliness that darts from the mirrors.

Merwin's third and final turn coincides with his willingness to question most rigorously the facade of the city. This decision helps explain why he would shift, in 1962, to unpunctuated verse, for the immediate effect of such a shift is to slow the poem's pace.[8] Punctuation helps marshal words energetically. It drives the work by collecting phrases into jostling groups, one spinning out of the next; muscling over the line break, punctuation guarantees swiftness of pace, as in "The Continuo":

> What can you do with this
> Wind, you can't
> Reason with it, entertain it, send
> It back, live on it or with it, fold it
> Away and forget it. . . . (MT, 56)

The wind as errant rebel, "Turning day and night into / Back yards / Where it knows the way," is a natural emblem of the emphatic momentum of the city, which seems to have no apparent direction but which is inescapable.

When Merwin eliminates punctuation, he forsakes that momentum. He isolates images, opens his tone of voice to questioning, and begins to allude to vacant depths beneath the activities of the urban setting, as in "The Way to the River":

> In a parked cab by the sealed wall hats are playing
> Sort of poker with somebody's
> Old snapshots game I don't understand they lose
> The rivers one
> After the other I begin to know where I am
> I am home (MT, 76)

The unpunctuated verse marks the difference between writing of a place as though one were a visitor or tourist, delighting in its apparent display of strange energy, and writing of a place that is one's home, in which what is alien needs to be understood. In "The Way to the River" the other side of energetic momentum is revealed to be meaningless activity, out of which temporary gestures emerge to vanish ("game I don't understand"). Now, one no longer views the city as a place of opportunity but as an enemy at odds with what one cherishes:

> To the city of wires I have brought home a handful
> Of water I walk slowly
> In front of me they are building the empty
> Ages I see them reflected not for long
> Be here I am no longer ashamed of time it is too brief its hands
> Have no names
> I have passed it I know
>
> *Oh Necessity you with the face you with*
> *All the faces*
>
> This is written on the back of everything
>
> But we
> Will read it together (MT, 77)

The ending of "The Way to the River" unfolds in a series of extraordinary turns. The dark meaning in its title—that one who would kill himself seeks the way to the river—lightens: there may be a way to the river of life-giving waters. But this transformation occurs only if one discovers how deeply one is enmeshed in the death around one. In this city of wires, a handful of water can electrocute: its life-giving properties are mischanneled. Indeed, the city is building "empty / Ages" that will be "reflected not for long." If ever there was energy here, it is now viewed as a meaningless kind. Yet the sense of brevity creates a focus on what is necessary, on discovering the essence that lies "written on the back of everything." Merwin insists that such a reality depends on sharing it with another. This work was dedicated to his wife, and the refrain "Be here" is addressed to her. But the triumph of the poem is to see past the beguiling energy of the city into its empty depths, then to return with a renewed sense of conviction, longing to make contact with "Necessity." That necessity resides in the face of another, not in the collection of "somebody's / Old snapshots" that the hats deal out in a "sort of poker" game in which the rivers are lost "one / After the other."

Although the last phase of *The Moving Target* begins an unmistakable drift toward love poetry, with the reconciliation that was impossible in "Congé" seeming now within reach and desirable, the revolutionary product of this third stage is a group of poems that are political in nature. While these clearly reflect Merwin's growing political concerns (at the time he was reporting on the "Everyman" incident, an attempt by a group of activists to interrupt a nuclear test scheduled in the Pacific) they are unlike other political poetry.[9] Using figures of speech that should be accessible, the poems distort them ominously, as though fundamental understandings had grown hopelessly obscure. "My Friends" is an especially striking example; clearly written about peace activists, the poem veers between describing their activity in simple and straightforward terms and depicting them as dense and obscure and difficult: "My friends with names like gloves set out / Bare handed as they have lived / And nobody knows them." In these poems, failure to be understood takes on a particularly disturbing force. For from one perspective, Merwin's writing is as lucid as can be. Yet these common images and accessible concepts appear awry, deeply obscure, baffling, alien. It is a measure of how ingrained a perverse complexity has become; Merwin's approach is deliberately conditioned to make civilization seem burdened and overwrought, its occupants so enmeshed in meaningless intricacy they have lost sight of fundamental particulars. From one angle, what the poem describes is monstrous; from another angle, it is an absolutely clear portrayal of a situation of pointless complexity exposed through a series of simple images that may appear baffling because we have lost touch with ourselves.

"The Students of Justice," which may stem from witnessing the court proceedings in San Francisco that affirmed the government's right to conduct tests of nuclear power in the Pacific Ocean (as described in "Act of Conscience"), opens with:

> All night I hear the hammers
> Of the blind men in the next building
> Repairing their broken doors
>
> When it is silent it is
> That they are gone
> Before the sun lights the way for
> The young thieves (MT, 86)

Individuals in authority are preoccupied with a task they set about to do unthinkingly; hence their blindness. But their work is notable for its crudity. Silence does not signal a pause for reconsideration; it just means they have left. When they have left, their jerry-built operations will be undone. In the daytime, they are further preoccupied with "Coloring a rough book," not creating a new vision but crudely filling in rough outlines, patching temporarily. That "rough book," which is "a long story,"—another excuse for meaningless preoccupation—is too important to be merely colored. For one thing, the book reveals "our blood" being borne away by "caravans of bugs." This disturbing vision prompts a cry that is both alarmed and tinged with despair.

The poem implies a crisis exists, but those in power attempt to disguise it, continuing as though it could be successfully avoided:

> They take their hammers to the lesson
>
> The last words so they promise me
> Will be thank you and they will know why
>
> And that night they will be allowed to move
> Every day
> They leave me their keys which they never use (MT, 86)

The blind persist in believing the problem will be solved through patchwork; they expect the work to be done eventually, so they can leave, escaping the situation. Meanwhile, the poet stands outside all this, as he has from the start, with an awareness of another way of working with doors—keys, which may also evoke the sense of countersymbols or legends that are simply unknown to the crude workmen. Those other keys, which expose the crudity of these workers, allude to a counterexperience suggested by its absence throughout: using delicacy and consideration in place of patchwork performed crudely. The blind men keep forgetting "under their white hair," in contrast to "The young thieves" whose way is lighted by the sun; and there is also a suggestion that the aged, in the dark, are blind to the youth in the sun, considering them the cause of the broken doors in need of repair each night. In fact, the poet, entrusted with the keys to the doors, may pass through the doors at will, as though the old were so intently preoccupied with repairing their doors, the rooms beyond them were never used.

Nothing in this poem is inherently obscure; what makes it difficult is its distorted situation. Essential to the work is its air of complete misconception: what the blind men think of as a sturdy and trustworthy tool is perceived by the poet as hopelessly crude. The men's preoccupation with coloring in a book, a meaningful task to them, is viewed as a pathetic failure, and the words they uphold as talismans of hope—"Thank You" and "We will Know Why"—are as empty as their gestures. Misunderstanding is so complete there is not even a point of discussion over which there is disagreement: it has become a conglomerate reality with its own tangibility.

5

Merwin's worksheets for the closing poems of *The Moving Target* display how thoroughly he is engaged in a process of renovation and renewal. Having reached the understanding that the malaise with which he has been burdened originates without rather than within, in the network of convictions and beliefs that the culture blankly propagates, he is able to return to his earlier work and see it in a new light, not as an expression of his disaffected personality but as the bewildered record of distortions caused by a deeply flawed culture. "For Now" confirms this insight; it reaches back to the very origin of *The Moving Target* in the pages of notes for "Congé. At an early stage of "Congé," Merwin's notes described the work as a poetry of departure, with a "goodbye" refrain to unify its separate parts. That refrain dominates "For Now," broken by two secondary patterns, a "Tell me" refrain that starts in the middle and an "I know" refrain that completes the poem. From speaking farewells to listening to others to understanding what matters: as the poem moves to widen its own vista it replicates the arc of Merwin's struggle since 1959.

But the very form of "For Now" preserves that sense of an electrifying discovery that Merwin must have experienced as he repositioned himself. Like "Dictum: For a Masque of Deluge" or "The Bones" or "The Drunk in the Furnace," "For Now" is another master-poem, a work whose significance rests in its ability to encompass previously explored material by reconceiving it and recasting it from within a perspective immensely wider and deeper. "For Now," however, differs from its predecessors by being a master-poem of master-poems. Its appearance recognizes and sanctions the concept of the master-poem: Not only does it cast its net further than any of its precursors, reaching back to encompass not a single cycle of poetry but numerous cycles of poetry representing years of work, it explicitly embodies that very act of reconceiving and recasting. It is what the poem performs as it unfolds.

One of Merwin's achievements in "For Now" is to conjure intimate moments from his past, fragments of memory that he has been carrying like excess weight, and to view them as burdens to jettison:

> Goodbye faces in stains churches
> In echoes dusters at windows
> Schools without floors envelopes full of smoke
> Goodbye hands of those days I keep the fossils
> Goodbye iron Bible containing my name in rust
> Cock Robin and
> The date
> Goodbye Cock Robin I never saw you (MT, 91)

The "faces in stains churches / In echoes" will be described in greater detail in the chapter entitled "The Skyline" in his 1983 memoirs *Unframed Originals,* just as "dusters at windows" looks to the chapter in which he writes of his father's sister Mary. The Cock Robin story he first mulled over in his earliest notes for "Congé." For now, though, it is enough to set these matters aside not because they are trivial but because what he knows now, in the "I know" refrain of the poem, lures him into the present and the future:

> My scars will answer to no one but me
> I know the planet that lights up the rings in the hems
> I know the stars in the door
>
> I know the martyrs sleeping in almonds
> I know the gloves of the hours I know Pilate the fly
> I know the enemy's brother (MT, 94)

Especially after the jagged gait of so many poems in *The Moving Target,* the cadences of "For Now" are wonderfully free. The poem rocks along, gathering impetus by pushing off from passages in which rhythms falter. It stumbles and hesitates over instants from the past, then breaks from them in triumph.

At its simplest, "For Now" takes shape as a catalogue of distinctions that grow increasingly assured as Merwin progresses, which is why the poem's triumphant ending can insist there is a difference "between death's republic and his kingdom"—a difference between the compromises we lead ourselves into making and the necessities we can only accept. The ability to draw such distinctions is what the poem cultivates, beginning with its listing of erroneous necessities, all now rendered obsolete. But the poem also affirms the necessity of continuing to draw distinctions, to take the measure of every moment against these two contending opposites. As it continues, passages within the poem enact this winnowing process:

> Goodbye to the dew my master
>
> And you masters with feathers on your key rings
> Wardens of empty scales
> When I find where I am goodbye (MT, 94)

Merwin will recognize dew as his master, for it only lasts long enough to refresh what it touches. He rejects others who would be his master, who disguise their instruments of repression (key rings) with decorative feathers; those false masters will be left with "empty scales" because the poet eludes all captors. Why is he successful? His wry comment at the end is a clue. He will say a goodbye that can be heard by the master of keys only when the poet finds where he himself is, and that will be never.

Merwin's procedure is delicately judicious rather than presumptuous because not every goodbye in "For Now" is a departure that has been willed; some he must recognize as beyond his control, and to which he can only accede:

> I kiss
> The light to those who love it it is brief
>
> Goodbye before it is taken away
> I have been with it the season could sign for me

That he is insistent upon sharp distinctions, however, cannot be forgotten because he is never prepared wholly to include the reader as an equal; the knife edge of distinction on which he moves between contending opposites, discriminating as carefully as possible, carries into the strategy of his language in which he hovers between bold affirmations and ironic explanations. "To those who love it" the light is brief, and that qualifying clause suggests that not everyone will understand why he would cherish the light; if there is doubt about whether he has loved the light, he notes that the "season could sign for me." These asides are more than witty exchanges; they acknowledge Merwin's isolation even as they invite us to break through it, as the poet challenges us to extend our own understanding to his. "Tell me what you see vanishing and I / Will tell you who you are," he says at the midpoint of the poem.

"For Now" confirms the authoritative vantage point the poet has attained, from which he is able to distinguish between what is inevitable and what is imposed, between the necessities that are unavoidable and so must be embraced and those that were invented by his culture and his upbringing and that would impose shackles. Against the clutter of lines and images on the page, which appear to be fragmentary and distraught, the voice of the poet, strikingly clear, surprisingly lucid, rings out. The clutter follows him and will continue to surround him but he understands how to move within it, when to approach and when to withdraw, when to hang on and when to let go.

8

In a Clearing

THE POETRY written at the end of time turns out to be remarkably similar to the poetry written at the beginning of time. This is the unexpected discovery Merwin makes in the course of *The Lice* (1967). If his language is, on the one hand, disintegrating into proselike fragments that mirror a culture collapsing under its own weight, it is, on the other hand, just beginning to turn with a grace like the purity of a medieval air. In *The Lice,* after less than a dozen poems, Merwin withdraws from the urban setting of *The Moving Target* and exiles himself to rural France. But he cannot leave behind the poisonous atmosphere of New York; if anything, his conviction that these may be the last days only deepens. Yet the poetry he writes in France—which in his own mind comprises perhaps the last lines of poetry to be written, and which may seem formless and fragmented—bears a startling resemblance to a poetry that promises recomposure. Its uncertain hovering is strange and discomforting. But its very formlessness allows for turns of phrase that startle with their lyrical grace: "The heavy limbs climb into the moonlight bearing feathers" (L, 43). Inadvertently, Merwin rediscovers the timeless element in experience once he writes from the conviction that the end of time is near.

When *The Lice* was first published, "and for some years thereafter," Merwin recalled in a 1982 interview, "it was spoken of by some people as a book that was so bleak and black and pessimistic that it was practically intolerable. That on the one hand. And on the other, that it was so obscure nobody could understand it. . . . There was one teacher in a university in those years who said she didn't understand this poem but she was frightened. I said, 'Why are you frightened if you don't understand it? I mean, you must understand something to respond to it. Why don't you pay attention to your response?'" He added that his intent as a writer had been neither to obscure nor to intimidate but to correct and to help: "I really thought I was trying to write more directly and simply in that book at a time when there was a wind of desperation and a feeling that too much was being written in a society in which writing was of decreasing importance."[1]

This exchange touches on the two fundamental opposites that form the experience of reading *The Lice:* Merwin's revulsion toward and withdrawal from a culture that has lost respect for evidence delivered by the senses because it prefers the technical, the preordained, and the managerial, and his insistence on countering that disrespect through simple and direct writing. What complicates this opposition is that the very idea of the simple and direct may be precisely what we are no longer prepared to recognize. In the epigraph from Heraclitus that introduces the book, children puzzle Homer by posing a riddle, the answer to which is the book's title: "What we have caught and what we have killed we have left behind, but what has escaped us we bring with us." In other words, what the mind already understands can be forgotten without harm but what eludes the understanding should remain a presence we always seek.[2]

This epigraph might also stand at the outset of an essay of Merwin's published in 1966, "Notes for a Preface," which could in turn serve as an introduction for *The Lice.* The essay analyzes the limitations of contemporary culture even as it explores the connection between a cultural crisis and the rediscovery of the essentially poetic. For the distinctive quality of *The Lice* lies in its unexpected renewals, and in "Notes for a Preface" the predominant feature of poetry is that its appearance is unpredictable: "The encouragement of poetry is a labor and a privilege like that of living. It requires, I imagine, among other startlingly simple things, a love of poetry, and possibly a recurring despair of finding it again, an indelible awareness of its parentage with that biblical waif, ill at ease in time, the spirit. No one has any claims on it, no one deserves it, no one knows where it goes" (RM, 295). The essential independence of poetry has never been more distinctive or more threatened: "It is a tongue that is loosed in the service of immediate recognitions, and that in itself would make it foreign in our period. For it conveys something of the unsoundable quality of experience and the hearing of it is a private matter, in an age in which the person and his senses are being lost in the consumer, who does not know what he sees, hears, wants, or is afraid of, until the voice of the institution has told him" (RM, 294). "Notes for a Preface" argues a historical theory of the poetic at a time when the end of history seems imminent. When all experience is managed, when senses are manipulated by the institution (and Merwin defines the institution broadly: "all injunctions that do not proceed from the biblical waif ventriloquize for the institution"), the very idea that experience could have an "unsoundable" aspect will be literally inconceivable.

More pointedly, Merwin suggests the poetic will endure; what will vanish is our ability to recognize it. For the poetic is, at bottom, life as it appears spontaneously, without contrivance. But even now, publishers commission commentary like "Notes for a Preface" that encourage us to read about poetry rather than read poetry. Perhaps art is always atavistic, a throwback but a way of recognizing a lineage with the past "with the nonhuman world entering always into the definition." The "nonhuman world" resists understanding; indeed, its negative function, what it does not do, is crucial: "It does not necessarily entail going along with all possible activities of an emergent and epidemic species which scorns all life except its own withering existence, and is busily relegating the senses its predecessors were given to apprehend their world, and the creatures with which they were privileged to share it" (RM, 297).

What Merwin conceives as the poetic is unlikely to meet our expectations. And even if recognized, it may deliver a message not easily assimilated. It is doubly strange; alien to our anticipations and alien even when acknowledged. It might be, for example, this event, noted in "A Glimpse of the Ice":

> I am sure now
> A light under the skin coming nearer
> Bringing snow
> Then at nightfall a moth has thawed out and is
> Dripping against the glass
> I wonder if death will be silent after all
> Or a cry frozen in another age (L, 46)

The poetic arises without forewarning. "I am sure now," he says, anticipating snow. Instead, the body of a moth, frozen at the onset of winter, begins to thaw and drip against his window, bringing thoughts of his mortality. It prompts a further meditation, an "I wonder" emphasizing that, of the various ways to die, none can be foreknown. The poem gives him the opportunity to look back, from out of the future as it were, on his own death, wondering whether his presence will be felt, as the moth's presence is felt again, or whether there will only be silence, the blankness of falling snow.

"A Glimpse of the Ice" is only one of a series of poems at the center of *The Lice* that may appear to be listless fragments, annotations of despair, but that widen under repeated readings until they disclose an enormous vista, connecting our own lives to dimensions that surround us but that elude our understanding. The poem is simultaneously inherently strange and immediately identifiable. That we can conceive of it at all, that we can apprehend the dimension of our own death and imagine alternatives, is the affirmative aspect of the poem, qualified at once by the realization of our mortality and the unpredictability of the future.

So strange is this perspective that Merwin discovers, writing out of his despair and startled by the vistas that open before him, that it is not surprising that *The Lice* has been most honored but least understood of all his work. The conditions under which the spirit appears are so often unpropitious. Least understood, perhaps, is the importance of the book as a sequence, though that must be tempered by evidence that it became a sequence only at its midpoint, beginning with a suite of poems among which "A Glimpse of Ice" can be found. Jarold Ramsey glanced at such an arrangement when he noted the volume followed a seasonal rhythm.[3] More specifically, the composition of the book parallels Merwin's decision in April 1963 to withdraw from New York City (where he had been living through most of 1962) to rural France. The Cuban Missile Crisis of October 1962 provided the occasion: "The thing that came out of [the crisis]," he explained in a 1980 interview, "was the very end of *The Moving Target* and then a good bit of *The Lice.*"[4] But what began as a withdrawal in disgust from human affairs became a withdrawal from his own disgust. The narrative of *The Lice* is not a movement away from the public realm into the private, but one from the public to the private, then toward tentative reintegration with a human community. Least strange, perhaps, is his discovery that if he is to speak at all, he must speak for others. By himself he has no voice, and when he tries to speak for himself, as in the early pages of the book, he churns out dazzling, bizarre images that lead him nowhere. But in the final pages, when he speaks from the viewpoint of the Asian peasant or with a sardonic voice that imagines the extinction of a species, he no longer stammers but writes with a bristling, eloquent, angry clarity that does not simply vent rage but exposes roots of stupidity and malice.

Essentially, renewal in *The Lice* is uncertain; but it hinges on a definite concept, one depending on a redefinition of the strength of human intelligence. In this respect, *The Lice* displays an affinity with the bestiary poems of 1953–54. Intelligence is presently being misused as a managerial skill, to organize the world so that the uncertainties of the future will no longer exist; when the Asian peasant says, "I am bringing up my children to be like you," he perceives exactly the message sent by those Westerners who would colonize the future. He has understood the message delivered by his conquerors, as Merwin notes in horror. The proper use of the intelligence recognizes that the ability to project the future can be a way of imagining alternatives that still can be avoided. The apocalyptic future evoked in the course of the book stands to be a self-negating prophecy, but only if the strength of the intelligence is used to check its own powers.

1

No such confidence in the saving power of the mind is evident in the first eleven poems of *The Lice,* completed in New York between February and April 1963. "I Live Up Here" sketches a longing to manage life so as to avoid accidents:

I live up here
And a little bit to the left
And I go down only

For the accidents and then
Never a moment too soon

Just the same it's a life it's plenty (L, 8–9)

This is not a voice Merwin would accept for himself. But he would acknowledge how cultural circumstances accustom all of us to become observers who are helpless and passive. In "Caesar" the speaker cannot escape his task of wheeling the president past the banks of flowers. Though he can insist that "Yet this is still my country" (L, 19), he feels powerless within it.

The impact of these poems resides in their deadpan tone. The news that Merwin would bring is, it appears, no longer news. The first poem to be written for *The Lice,* "The Last One," unfolds with an opening refrain that suggests we are beyond surprise. "Well they'd made up their minds to be everywhere because why not." "Well they cut everything because why not." "Well the others ran" (L, 10). The woodchoppers approach the last tree with boredom, long past the point of asking questions. In "Some Last Questions" Merwin lines up queries about essential parts of the body; but the disruptive effect of the poem is that its answers are so uninventive. The tone remains weary, exhausted, like last questions indeed:

What is the head
A. Ash

What are the eyes
A. The wells have fallen in and have Inhabitants (L, 6)

In these opening works language is not just distorted—it is distorted in a deliberately vacuous way. "The judges have chains in their sleeves," he writes in "Bread at Midnight." "To get where they are they have / Studied many flies" (L, 18). These lines arrive already worn and weary; Merwin's negative characterizations are obviously staged.

"Unfinished Book of Kings" is written in a way that should be obtuse but remains alarmingly clear. When we read that "The fingers of the prophets fell but were not visible because they wore no rings," we can process this rapidly enough: symbols of ostentatious wealth count for more than the gestures of those concerned for the welfare of the community. It is not just that language has been debased by events: we have grown accustomed to horrors, and language that should be disconcerting has turned commonplace. In contrast to the early political poetry in *The Moving Target,* where simple images lost their conviction through distortion, here distorted images seem uncannily self-evident, unnervingly appropriate.[5]

At one point, Merwin identifies this weariness with his immediate environment, his life in New York City. Thus withdrawal to France promises a respite, as in the uncollected poem "As the Dark Snow Continues to Fall":

> Summer will be there because I can
>
> Remember it coming again to the hollow stones full of water
> That regard it from among the sheep tracks
>
> And I said For whom have I been mistaken[6]

Here in winter, he can look ahead to a summer elsewhere, a summer that leads to the image of "hollow stones full of water." If he hovers uncertainly between the life-giving properties of water and the tomblike qualities of hollow stones, in the next turn of phrase the stones of water validate the existence of summer as they "regard it from among the sheep tracks." Temporarily, the image is strong enough to allow for a recoil against this winter of dark snow.

Merwin may have returned to rural France believing he could escape that position he had taken in *The Moving Target,* at the center of the culture, directly impinged upon by crises. If so, problems arise at once in the first poem he writes, the enigmatic "Pieces for Other Lives." A door returns at the end of each of the three sections of this poem, the first opening onto "not darkness but / Nothing," the second "not shown // But which anyway is standing open," and the third waking the speaker as it slams under the pressure of the "old wind" that "vanished and vanished but was still there." The door is an escape from two mazes: the dark labyrinth in which the miners crawl, "extending the darkness," and the map of the route of the blood through the body, "its comical story." If so, its final appearance is disheartening: the door closes but the wind remains, and "everyone but the cold was gone for good." He has left behind his political friends, who remind him of the miners of his youth, submerged in their labyrinth from which they cannot escape. He has also left behind those who remain apart from politics, reducing their own life-stories to comical tales, though it involves their very lifeline. But he cannot escape the wind and cold he has brought with him. The summer he envisaged earlier is not a true salvation.

Merwin's American homeland is no anomaly; it is only ahead of other places on earth. A tone of sorrow permeates these first poems written in France; the poet acknowledges a despair that, in New York, could vent itself in the anger of "Unfinished Book of Kings." Wrath, turning inward, becomes sorrow. Hank Lazer has described *The Lice* as a "planetary elegy," a farewell to a world that men have destroyed through their carelessness, an elegy interrupted by quiet moments that celebrate silence as more appealing than one might have imagined.[7] But as "The Widow" indicates, only our vanity makes us suspect we might be eliminating the earth; in truth, we are eliminating ourselves, and the earth remains indifferent. We believe we erect lasting monuments, but in our short-sightedness we resemble the "ripe grain" that "Leaves the husk / At the simple turning of the planet" (L. 34). Merwin refers to the earth as "The Widow" not because she mourns us (that would be arrogant) but because the earth is accustomed to the weight of the seasons through which all must pass and, eventually, pass away. Humans should weep; after all, "The Widow does not / Hear you and your cry is numberless." The earth will abide but "there is no season / That requires us."

"The Widow" is one of three elegies that question the survival of the human species. In "The Gods" it is

> the fighting in the valley
> The blows falling as rice and
> With what cause
> After these centuries gone (L, 30)

that lead him to doubt the species will continue: "What is man that he should be infinite." But the second elegy, "The River of Bees," is just different enough to count; in it, the memory of a house by a courtyard in which a blind man "stood singing / Of what was older" pains Merwin because it emphasizes his own remoteness from recollections of mysterious perfection: "I took my eyes / A long way to the calendars / Room after room asking how shall I live" (L, 32). Although he would identify with the blind man, urging himself to live, the best he can produce is: "Once once and once / In the same city I was born / Asking what shall I say." The blind man, who has somehow overcome his own grief and found contact with "what was older," stands apart, while Merwin knows only his own misery.

Yet Merwin's despair is not complete, even at this point in his volume. Lines twist and the poem shifts: "Men think they are better than grass // I return to his voice rising like a forkful of hay." Two voices contend for Merwin's allegiance in these two lines. The prophet's voice of the first line is dismissive and disdainful, castigating humans for their unforgivable arrogance, suggesting it is appropriate they cannot transcend their condition. But the voice of the second line, which hears the blind man's singing, chastens the first. It recalls that we can rise above our misery, that we do not pass away like numberless blades but inexplicably endure, that we can transcend our condition. This thought, however, is a torment, not a solace, because it poses an essential contrast: "But we were not born to survive / Only to live." To live, one would need to be like the blind man capable of singing; to survive is a lesser ambition, leading to the mistaken belief that "nothing is real," which virtually guarantees that humans will not survive.

The confusion and despair and misery here arise from Merwin's struggle to believe that the species is worthy of consideration. Worksheets for "April" show it began with doubts about a future in which the poet's words will matter. In one passage he conceives his present voice heard by us as emerging from the past. But then he mocks the idea that there can be any connection between the two:

> Days to come
> In which no stars are hidden
>
> Who will know anything
>
> Here in the past let us pretend

In a further draft, this last stanza sputters out: "Let us pretend there will be / Someone let us." Additional stanzas turn bitter: "A tongue is knowledge of its teeth / Full of sadness and without authority." But from all these options, Merwin shaped this final poem:

> When we have gone the stone will stop singing
>
> April April
> Sinks through the sand of names
>
> Days to come
> With no stars hidden in them
>
> You that can wait being there
>
> You that lose nothing
> Know nothing (L, 29)

From what has become the past, Merwin speaks to us in our present, his future. What we have no knowledge of, we cannot lose; if we never know the hidden stars, we can never miss them, and so we appear to Merwin as knowing nothing. But the new addition absent from worksheets is the opening line that focuses on Merwin in his present. The stones will stop singing, and the lovely name of "April April" will sink down through the endless sand of names and be lost—if those like Merwin, in the present that will be our past, fail to write of the hidden stars or the names like April. While the poem remains suffused with despair, what has been added is Merwin's own edge of responsibility, his impetus to transmit his immediate recognitions to us. The worksheets, that is, are dominated by the voice of despair, which says, "Men think they are better than grass," and prophesies doom; but the poem is animated when the second voice contends with the first by recalling the singing and passing it on, though such a feat may be useless. Even in this elegiac section, then, Merwin is alluding to some form of necessary action, some purifying change, that he would move toward despite its unlikelihood.

2

The purification begins at the midpoint of the volume, in a cluster of nine short poems from four to twelve lines in length, which unfold a chronology of discovery. Although brief, the poems take shape from each other, as a growing process. If their language is sparse, it is not the gaunt and barren discourse of the three elegies. Distraught imagery is in abeyance or, when introduced, is less startling. Unlike Merwin's earlier poetry, stitched together from disparate impressions, these poems like others to follow were often drafted at one sitting, with only minor revisions (fig. 14). Many lines are clear and straightforward and simple. Rather than dealing with abstractions, Merwin is observing. This distinct cluster inaugurates a group of spring and summer poems, similar in brevity and simplicity. Together, the two groups constitute a significant change of direction.

These brief poems tend to shift abruptly, even turning against themselves in midcourse. Merwin is no longer turned inward as passive recorder of his own sensations but looking outward as active observer. In "The Room" he admits that "I think this is all somewhere in myself" and goes on to describe a bird trapped in a room in the stillness before dawn: "the sounds of a small bird trying / From time to time to fly a few beats in the dark / You would say it was dying it is immortal" (L, 48). The note of defiance is a deliberate affirmation, a denial of what could be perceived as failure. Instead of negatively twisting experience that might be positive, as in "In Autumn," he affirms as positive an image that might seem negative. (Imagine "In Autumn" ending with such a strong statement as this: "Those are cities / Where I intend to live.") Merwin's acceptance that the room is within himself allows him to intervene at the end.

As small as it is, such an intervention is crucial. In several short works, events unfold that resist conforming to the poet's predetermined sense of bleakness: real crows gather and quarrel, magpies are kept awake by the moon, a moth flies against the glass. It is relevant that the cycle begins in November and proceeds through winter, for to someone in Merwin's state of mind, the onslaught of winter would be anticipated with dread; what actually happens, as the poems record, is that this winter has its own life, which is by no means equivalent to the wintry expectations within Merwin. Yet the extent to which Merwin regains activity is modest; these poems shift about in minimal space with the smallest of gestures. But they are beginnings, stirrings from within a hopeless condition. They suggest that the modest gesture may also be exact and appropriate. An affirmation not intended to be all-encompassing or powerful is also a denial of the virtues of sweeping authority. "The Cold Before the Moonrise" ends with a simple hope: "If there is a place where this is the language may / It be my country" (L, 46). Although the poet is tempted to lament that he "was born far from home," he notes the animating edge of "frost

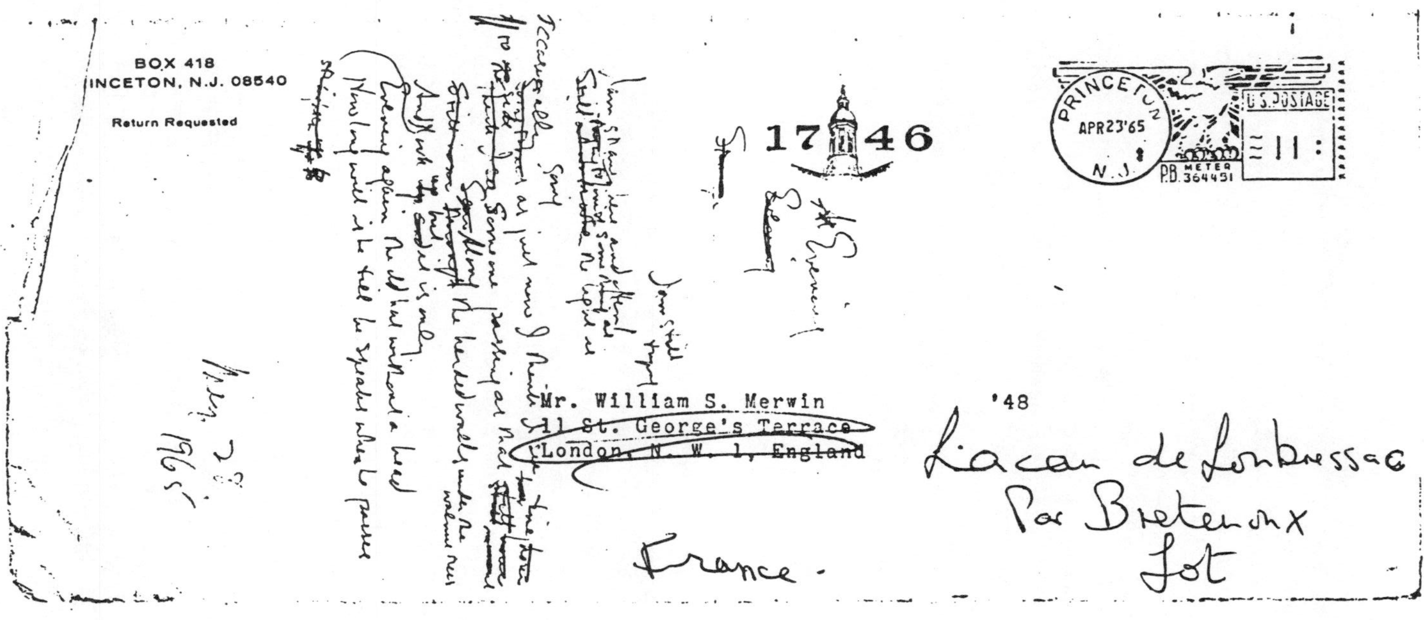

Figure 14. Initial and revised final draft of "Evening" (MS. 21:02/021, d. May 28, 1965).

stirring among its / Stars like an animal sleep" and emphasizes a sound where there could have been a silence. A similar counterstatement governs "In January." The unknown aspect of the new year could have elicited dread; instead, Merwin uses the new year's arrival to expose "hiding places" that reveal us as "a stranger to nothing." Rather than intimidating us, the new year becomes exemplary. Although "it is hard for us to be sure that it is here," uncertainty is preferable to the surety of "hiding places."

These are modest turns, but their very modesty is to be valued. If this delicacy goes unappreciated, then all that Merwin prophesied in alarm may be true. To move outside a sheltered area is important to him, in retreat in his shelter in France. "December Among the Vanished" (originally entitled "Shelter Among the Vanished") inaugurates the increasingly defiant counterstatements of the works that follow. Rueful as it may be to remain in this shelter that is no shelter, it is an appropriate midpoint between the brutality of winter, "that lipless man" who can only roar as a wind, incapable of forming clear syllables, and the helplessness of creatures that "hide in knitted walls" (L, 45). "December Among the Vanished" supersedes positions displayed earlier in this cluster in which the poet had longed for invulnerability. "The water flows through its / Own fingers without end," he sees in "December Night" (L, 43), longing to let go, to be entirely renewed; it is like the ending of "New Moon in November," where the darkness is transformed at once into a mythic journey: "By the dim road that the wind will take / And the cold / And the note of the trumpet" (L, 42). If one could break entirely from the human world, with its insufferable aspiration to take control of events, its managerial attitude toward the future, then one might be able to sense the stark joy of the seasons turning. But Merwin cannot make that shift; even when he is so inclined, he keeps intruding with a commentary. He ends "December Night" with a sullen mutter: "Tonight once more / I find a single prayer and it is not for men" (L, 45). He cannot be at one with the "heavy limbs" that "climb into the moonlight bearing feathers," or let go as "the water flows through its / Own fingers without end."

A complication in these poems, then, is that as pure homages to nature they are unsuccessful. Merwin's awareness of his humanity intrudes upon them, at first bitterly, then with a grudging acceptance, ultimately taking the form of his defiant counterstatements. Such intrusions are necessary if he would emerge from his withdrawal. The idea of paying homage to nature would be no different from a disgusted dismissal of the affairs of our species. But he understands he cannot retreat, that he belongs with the dead shepherd in the line of broken huts.

In this respect, the most important poem in the group may be "Dusk in Winter," which carefully distinguishes what Merwin hears, as one who knows anguish and loss, from what happens in nature, which is free from emotion:

> The sun sets in the cold without friends
> Without reproaches after all it has done for us
> It goes down believing in nothing
> When it has gone I hear the stream running after it
> It has brought its flute it is a long way (L, 49)

If the sun were human it would complain bitterly at its own extinction, but instead it sets as a titan, "believing in nothing." To the listener left behind in darkness, hearing the sound of the stream "running after it," the admission that "it is a long way" recognizes not the gulf between the sun and the stream but that between the listener, attentive in the darkness and made inescapably aware of his feelings of loss, and the natural world wheeling in oblivion through its cyclical continuity. The human condition is to feel left behind, apart from the immensity of nature; it is to identify with the stream, which sounds with its lonely urgency, rather than with the aloof and oblivious sun. On the one hand, the poem leaves us in the dark, longing for the sun's strength. The isolation is so intense that it explains why we would model ourselves on the sun rather than on the stream. On the other hand, the poem celebrates the delicacy with which the moment is rescued, our attentiveness to the soft sounds of the running water. Instead of being isolated, we tend to identify with all that surrounds us, both sun and stream, balancing between them. If we are out of sync with nature, we are nonetheless sensitive to its nuances. Although we feel left behind, listening in the dark to what escapes us, the truth is that we encompass the whole, not only the power of the sun but also the delicacy of the stream: "it has brought its flute."

3

One difference between the opening set of poems written in New York in the winter of 1963 and this midpoint cluster written in France in 1964 and 1965 is that the wintriness of the opening set is a state of mind possessed by Merwin, while the cold of the later group is a physical condition that generates its surprising oppositions. An even more dramatic difference separates the two: real deaths are under consideration in the final group, while the only death acknowledged in the opening set is metaphorical.[8]

In the closing group, death is an occurrence that links us with others. This realistic acknowledgment of death can appear with the old abstract concept in the same poem; it is one reason why the ending of "The Asians Dying" is so powerful. In the middle of the poem, Merwin uses "the dead" to speak of persons who were once alive: "Rain falls into the open eyes of the dead / Again again with its pointless sound / When the moon finds them they are the color of everything" (L, 70). Their "open eyes" also proclaim their status as individuals, not generic categories. Like the animals who would "look carefully" and return the glance of the poet in "The Animals," perhaps even speaking back to him, these too would look back accusingly if they could. But at the end of the poem, the old abstract, categorical idea of death emerges again, as "the possessors moved everywhere under Death their star." For the possessors, death is as remote as a star, an emblem calling them forward in their rapacious progress; it is a concept, having nothing to do with individuals. The two versions of death radically distinguish Asians from Americans, a distinction underscored with irony: the death the Asians experience leaves them with their eyes open; the death star under which the possessors march leaves them as blind as ever.

Merwin's insistence on death as an actuality explains why he finds it important to write simple and clear poems of mourning, like "The Dry Stone Mason," whose directness makes it seem out of place, except that such directness is needed if Merwin is to rejoin the community from which he has excluded himself. The poem enacts such a recovery of a community:

> The neighbors found where he kept his suit
> A man with no family they sat with him
> When he was carried through them they stood by their own dead
> And they have buried him among the graves of the stones (L, 65)

Standing among their ancestors, "by their own dead," the mourners include the stone mason within their community. Merwin now understands what seemed impossible earlier: the actions of an individual may outlast his life. The stones the mason erected into walls not only endure—"What he made of his years crosses the slopes without wavering / Upright but nameless"—but are individualized: "And stones drip where his hands left them / Leaning slightly inwards." The memory of "the gentle drunk" continues in these stones that lean "slightly inwards," and the stones, as they drip, even recall the communal act of mourning.

Two other apparently simple poems, "Death of a Favorite Bird" and "Fly," which might otherwise be judged inconsequential, take on great importance as acts of mourning. Throughout the volume, flying creatures of all kinds, beginning with the quarreling crows in the November trees, have appeared as images of redemption, but a crucial twist is given with these two confessions: to return to the community, one cannot stand apart, and Merwin must acknowledge he is not immune from the failings he ascribes to others. These confessions, with their sweep of understanding and self-acceptance, permit Merwin to accept a community that is essentially flawed, just as he is.

Another brief poem, "The Mourner," introduces an even more personal theme. (The original title of the volume, *The Glass Towers,* comes from a phrase in this poem.)[9] The passage of "a small old woman an aunt in the world / Without nephews or nieces" interrupts the placid satisfaction of the speaker working in the fields "in the cool of the morning." Everything about her is strikingly unnatural. In a preceding poem, "The Dragonfly," Merwin established working in the bean fields as an image of satisfying unity with the earth. Echoing Thoreau's occupation in *Walden,* the speaker's modest crop recalled the plenitude of wheat; his profound satisfaction was conveyed in the way he incorporated himself into the landscape—"these feet on it / My own"—and in the hoe's falling within his shadow. But the woman who passes in "The Mourner" intrudes as a whole constellation of inorganic images:

> Her black hat shining like water
> Floats back and forth climbing
> Along the glass walls of the terraces
> Bearing its purple wax rose (L, 57)

For whom, then, is she mourning? This is the unspoken question of the poem, the disturbance that intrudes on the speaker; but the larger intrusion is that this small old woman is the first other person to appear in *The Lice,* the individual who breaks in upon a solitude strictly maintained since the volume's opening pages. It is significant that this first person is a mourner who has no one for whom to mourn, because Merwin's return to a community will hinge upon his understanding that if one can learn to mourn oneself, one can begin to mourn for others.

Merwin's own act of mourning himself occurs in "For the Anniversary of My Death," a work that opens in the realm of immense abstractions, with Merwin positing that "every year without knowing it I have passed the day / When the last fires will wave to me." Like the enormity of the sun, this cosmic view is appalling in its undeniability and in its emptiness, but here it gives rise to its opposite, an urgent wish to embrace the earth, a longing to honor even the smallest of moments as though they were utterly significant: "As today writing after three days of rain / Hearing the wren sing and the falling cease / And bowing not knowing to what." The renewal as rainfall ends is magnified, transforming the wren's song into a celebration both modest and all-embracing. The rest of *The Lice* flowers out of this grief-stricken understanding that no reference to death can be allowed that does not in some way include one's own loss of all that is beloved. Moreover, what is truly beloved is yet to be discovered: what one honors, at this moment, is unknown—one bows "not knowing to what."

"For the Anniversary of My Death" is one of a number of poems that hold out an opportunity to reverse the course of events. Sometimes that opportunity is dismissed as unlikely: in "When the War is Over" Merwin insists that "we will all enlist again," having learned nothing at all. In "The Finding of Reasons" and "For a Coming Extinction" he writes with certainty of a future that holds out no promise at all. But in "Come Back" he imagines a reunion—only he confesses that he had held back, as one paralyzed, "until you were gone." The gift of renewal is sought out now that it may be too late. Merwin cannot shake off this constant awareness that it may be too late, even as this future that is "dead / And our own" is offered so it may not come about.

The Lice is finally so impressive not because of Merwin's righteous anger at the imperfections of the human world but because of his tenderness toward those imperfections. Writing fiercely of alienation and despair in the opening pages of the book, then writing delicately of the natural world and its purity in the central pages, Merwin combines all he has learned in "Avoiding News by the River." Before the sky "fills with blood," before humans awake, the world exists in intricate concord. Stars hide while warblers hunt and trout rise as light flows—events not directly related to one another even as they effortlessly harmonize. When humans awake, all turns problematic:

> In an hour it will be summer
> I dreamed that the heavens were eating the earth
> Waking it is not so
> Not the heavens (L, 68)

The future tense appears in this stanza, distinguishing us, who mark off time in segments and give names to seasons and conceive a direction for the future, from the creatures. Our intelligence sets us apart from other species, but our responsibilities increase proportionately. We should expect to know what we are doing.

That demand complicates the second stanza, dissolving the harmonies present before dawn. Our intelligence should lead us to recognize that it is not the heavens eating the earth, not some natural catastrophe over which there can be no control: that is only a dream from which we must awaken. And awakened, we stand further distinguished from creatures essentially innocent: the murders of the wren and the dinners of the badger are no cause for shame, for creatures act as they must, without awareness beyond the moment. Our problem is that we do not distinguish ourselves enough, as the phrase "worldly good" suggests. For the wren and badger, their motive is survival. For us, gifted with intelligence, living should be more than survival—it should be burdened with responsibility, with care for others, which is why we are given to feel a shame absent from the natural world turning in its self-sufficient unity. Yet the thrust of the poem, with the convoluted syntax of the last line—two negatives from which we must deduce a positive—points to how heavy a burden that intelligence can be. The burden of intelligence is anguish, a division from the wholeness of nature—as the logic of the "if-then" of the final line weighs ponderously on the entire work, grinding it to a dead stop.

Intelligence, as Merwin conceives it, must not become power because its strength is too enormous; our distance from other creatures is simply too great. The check on that power is nothing less than our shame, which is the state into which we fall when our awareness singles us out as the interloper with enormous powers. To endure that sudden arrest of our inherent authority is the problem Merwin comes to appreciate in the course of *The Lice.* On the one hand, it is natural for us to overstep our bounds, to press beyond our limits. That is the elemental use of the intelligence, especially when placed in the service of technical feats. On the other hand, what is harder to realize, because it contravenes our techniques for managing matters, is that the intelligence can also measure its limits—that the ability to imagine the future is given to prevent us from yielding thoughtlessly to our power. To conceive of an apocalyptic future can become a self-negating prophecy; the conception affirms the mind as it serves in its own preservation, using its strength to know when to limit its power.

9

The Day for Carrying Loads

THE PARADOX of Sebastien Chamfort's aphorisms is that even as they display contempt for the compromises of the social world, they return obsessively to the terms of that world. Chamfort is not so much the misanthrope icily detached from human affairs as he is the outcast who looks lingeringly in the window, with so much to tell the shadowy figures inside. Introducing *Products of the Perfected Civilization,* which he was translating in 1966–67, Merwin remarks that Chamfort is constantly justifying his "taste for retirement": "The most interesting thing about the justification is that as its argument recurs in letters, aphorisms, and essays, it seems to be addressed to a person who is essentially a figure of the society that is being shunned—and there are other occasions when the figure appears to be an aspect of Chamfort himself" (PPC, 44).[1] Merwin notes that "his withdrawal from society and literature did not prevent him from presenting himself three times, between the years 1777 and 1780, for membership in the Académie Française—without counting a fourth application in the latter year" (PPC, 66).

Chamfort's attachment to a society he had been situated to despise, not entirely through his own choice, vitiates so many of his aphorisms, which simply have no sting: "In renouncing the world and fortune, I have found happiness, tranquility, health, even wealth; and whatever the proverb says, I conclude that he who leaves the game wins it" (PPC, 166). Chamfort invites rebuttal; he softens his conclusion by recalling, just before it, a proverb his audience would have known, opening a space for a counterargument. Never absolute pronouncements or summary judgments, his aphorisms resemble the gambits of animated conversation: "It is almost impossible for a philosopher or poet not to be misanthropic, (1) because his taste and his talent lead him to observe society, a study which is an endless torment to the heart; (2) because his talent is almost never rewarded by society (in fact he is lucky if he is not punished for it) and this saddening fact merely redoubles his tendency to melancholy" (PPC, 184). The philosopher-poet is not bitter but regretful. He even digresses into a personal allusion, "(in fact he is lucky if he is not punished . . .)," as though inviting us to ask for more specific details. Typically, he begins with a tentative frame ("It is almost impossible"); he avoids the defiant pronouncement, cultivates the arguable point. He drops clues suggesting he is not as he appears: "In order to view things correctly, one must give words the opposite sense to the one the world gives them. Misanthrope, for instance, means philanthrope; bad Frenchman means good citizen, which implies certain monstrous abuses; philosopher means, 'a simple man, who knows that two and two make four, etc.'" (PPC, 153). And social outcast can mean engaged participant.

Like other translations Merwin initiated on his own in the late 1960s (in contrast to the version of Lorca's "Yerma" that Lincoln Center commissioned in 1966), Chamfort's writing has an indirect bearing on Merwin's original work. What may have consigned Chamfort to relative obscurity among his contemporaries is precisely what makes him an attractive figure to Merwin: his reluctance to dissociate himself from the society about which he was able to write (in Merwin's edition) almost two hundred pages of observation and commentary. Much as Chamfort fails to make a clean slice in his aphorisms, Merwin cannot at first speak directly in *The Carrier of Ladders,* a collection that must undergo a dramatic reversal before the poet can escape from a network of self-canceling cross-purposes. Like Chamfort, he is unable to leave behind what he would scourge.

1

The Carrier of Ladders (1970) offers instruction, by example, in active listening. The cryptic epigraph that furnishes its title turns out, on inspection, to introduce not only the double context of these poems but also the way to understand that doubling:

> The bearer of the dead
> Says to the carrier of ladders,
> It is the day for carrying loads,
> It is the day of troubles.

Two views inhabit the poems, and one could be a corrective to the other. But the corrective view, as in the epigraph, will go unvoiced in any direct manner. The words announce the dark impressions of the bearer of the dead, yet as overwhelming as these are, they need not be the last words, for they are addressed to one who is the carrier of ladders. The bearer of the dead, who is only used to thinking of burdens, may benefit from the carrier of ladders, who is burdened lightly—indeed, he carries a device that lifts him above the earth and introduces a wider horizon. It is true the carrier of ladders does not reply; it is the task of the volume, however, to elicit that reply, an alternate perspective that would conceive a horizon beyond this day of troubles. Yet the question is whether this reply can be elicited: Is there still a carrier of ladders who can see beyond the despair of the moment? Merwin is uncertain, but that reply is tantalizingly evoked throughout the volume, in lines that could be taken as one-sided, simple expressions of despair.

These poems make an unusual demand on the reader. They are not supported by timely references to current events, as in *The Lice.* Their subtlety is twofold: not only do they require that we attend to the language as though each word were an assertion simultaneously placed in question, but anything like satisfactory closure is withheld. Poems stop without resolutions, but at the end, Merwin invites a decision, and even announces a need for action. The poem may be completed, that is, by a next step that we may take but that Merwin is not yet prepared to commit himself to, though his deliberate evocation of it is a form of commitment.

That Merwin is aware of this double edge is evident not only in the epigraph to his volume but also in "Envoy from d'Aubigné," a poem that at one time carried the following explanatory note:

> Agrippe d'Aubigné, French Protestant poet, 1550–1630, soldier and courtier from the age of 18, served Henri IV with devotion and candor even after the latter bitterly disappointed him by abjuring the Protestant faith. d'Aubigné's great poem, *Les Tragiques,* on the subject of the wars of religion in France, was written when he was no longer a soldier, and when the cause of Protestantism in France seemed lost. This defeat, and what it implied to him, was the "prison" of the latter part of his life.
>
> In the title, I intend the ambiguities in the word "from." I am in no sense trying to lend my own words to d'Aubigné's historical circumstances or character. Certain passages and phrases from the preface to *Les Tragiques,* together with his sense of being a witness to the degradation of his country, recurred to me, as suggestions, over several years.

Merwin's final draft bears the dates "December 1964 / April 25, 1967," but its note came later, at the behest of Howard Moss, poetry editor for the *New Yorker,* who needed background explanation.[2] The note explains that the poem, like d'Aubigné's poetry, arose from a moment of defeat, and it praises the character of one who remained loyal to a cause despite its impossibility. Just as important, it inserts a reference to personal loyalty, to underscore that political feelings are rendered complex by individuals whose allegiances may shift. Bitter disappointment need not lead to silence. Merwin also acknowledges his unwillingness to intrude into the "historical circumstances or character" of d'Aubigné; indeed, he calls attention to himself as one who prefers to remain in the background. This contradiction, in which he appears to note his own invisibility, dissolves if his intention is to emphasize the importance of listening to words both alien and familiar. Hearing d'Aubigné's words across the centuries is the crucial event of the poem.

One passage in "Envoy" could stand as a summary of Merwin's intentions for his poetry of this time:

> Go without ornament
> without showy garment
> if there is in you any
> joy
> may the good find it
>
> for the others be
> a glass broken in their mouths (CL, 35)

The poems will bewilder, for they will proceed "without showy garment" in an air of austerity. But to those who are "the good," able to recognize joy, the poetry will repay them in kind. For the others, there will be only pain and suffering returned, the agony that always was their own. For this to happen, Merwin's text must reward careful reading, and that is one reason why lack of punctuation in this volume often disrupts syntax. The line break is a point where treacherous changes may occur if one is reading too rapidly or simply. The line break often springs a trap around which the reader must maneuver with care, sorting out the true from the false, the pure crystal from the broken glass:

> if they ask you why
> you do not boast of me
> tell them as they
> have forgotten
> truth habitually
> gives birth in private (CL, 34)

This passage taunts as though truth itself has gotten muddled. The lines read double, with the reader left to determine a preference. "Truth," as it happens, is not simply part of an independent clause, but can also be the subject of the sentence; truth can emerge actively to guide the syntax, or it can be set aside as a passing reference.

"Envoy from d'Aubigné" is an indirect manifesto. The message is lost on one group, while another group extracts a positive insight. In most of these poems, Merwin would fuse those two experiences, as though the bearer of the dead and the carrier of ladders inhabited one person. It would be, then, an error to see poems of *The Carrier of Ladders* as optimistic or pessimistic: they are pinned agonizingly between denial and affirmation. But their virtue is they always sense how an affirmation may emerge from a denial, whether or not one actually occurs. With their misleading line breaks, the poems are designed to thrust us into listening with a subtlety we had not believed available.[3]

The most disarming poems read in two divergent ways simultaneously, like "February," which begins:

> Dawn that cares for nobody
> comes home
> to the glass cliffs
> an expression
> needing no face (CL, 51)

If the negatives that dominate this opening ("nobody," "no face") stress the bleakness of winter dawn, it is no less true that the independence noted here may be a virtue and a model. Coming home to "glass cliffs" is not inevitably a cause for withdrawal; it may be a reason to remain open. As cold as the winter dawn may be, the products of civilization are more chilling:

> night
> lives on in the uniforms
> in the silence of the headlines
> in the promises of triumph
> in the colors of the flag (CL, 51)

These are false, misleading, deadly obligations, associated with modern civilization (its standing armies, its media productions, its publicity relations, its nationalism). Dawn, which cares for no one, is true to itself in a way the uniforms and headlines and flags can never be, since each demands its special allegiance. Knowing all this, however, Merwin remains in between, awed by the pure but aloof brilliance of the independent dawn and appalled by the night of blindness that has been instituted as everyday routine.

As a choice, the distinction between dawn and darkness seems obvious; but Merwin's achievement is not simply to identify the good and the evil. His poems end as challenges; the choices have been identified, the fears have been acknowledged, and we are led up to the decisive moment:

> while the ends and the beginnings
> are still guarded
> by lines of doors
> hand in hand
> the dead guarding the invisible
> each presenting its message
> *I know nothing*
> *learn of me*

The poem either twists shut or breaks open on its paradox, depending on how we have heard it. What is it precisely, then, to "know nothing / learn of me"? We can read these lines as though they put glass in our mouths, as though they were the essence of the bleakness of deepest winter, where the dead stand watch and bar the living; or we can choose to recognize the examples of independence that offer strength throughout the poem, so that we are prepared for the joy of learning. More dramatically, the choice is ours, since it is we who are brought up against the guardians at the close. They turn to us, presenting the same message that cannot be avoided, a message that is a pure contradiction, the distillation of the dilemmas upon which the poem is tautly strung.

Whether it is possible to effect a resolution that answers the oppositions strung out through the poem may be a useless speculation. To force one position to displace the other is not, it would seem, within the province of the work; instead, the poem leads up to a moment before choosing, at which point it halts, the choice not yet taken. A syntactic formula that recurs in several poems suggests that Merwin's true intent is not to press through to a choice but to wake us to the magnitude of whatever choice we decide to make. The formula, unique to this volume, is the persistence of an interruptive clause, a feature that if punctuated would call for the grammar of a dash: "still guarded / by lines of doors / —hand in hand— / the dead guarding the invisible." These disturbances occur throughout the poems: "with my fear by the hand / by the hand / and no father" ("The Hulk"); "watching us out of the stars / ancestor // and the black fields" ("Night Wind"); "some of us will meet once more / even here / like our own statues" ("Now It Is Clear"); "what hearts are moving toward their garments here / their days / what troubles beating between arms" ("The Night of the Shirts"). The interruption appears to add little or nothing to, or even to detract from, poems of such brevity, in which every word is supposed to count. But the interruption is not simply a hesitation; it expands meaning and, as it does, disturbs any forward motion. It undermines the poem's process, suggesting a meaning that may be a burden, an added responsibility, a dimension unaccounted for until now. The interruption looms with implications that, in such brief poetry, are almost too much to bear. As much as the interruption opens the work, it threatens to overwhelm it; as the work touches on a vastly larger dimension than had been anticipated, it stops as it opens. Moments contend with each other in these poems. If Merwin identifies a direction, he also draws back from it. D'Aubigné's formula persists on a level that remains tantalizingly ideal: the poet does not always escape with his own mouth free of broken glass.

A related feature is a series of terms repeated from poem to poem. Notable for their simplicity, they are not intended to be restrictive but are employed for their transparency. They are so immediately recognizable that they concede the governing of the poem to other elements of poetic discourse. As the authority of individual words declines, elements usually considered supplemental take an increasingly active role. The last eight lines of the eighteen-line "Lark" are remarkable for each containing a key word from Merwin's prized lexicon:

> In the hour that has no friends
> above it
> you become yourself
> voice
> black
> star burning in cold heaven
> speaking well of it
> as it falls from you
> upward
>
> Fire
> by day
> with no country
> where and at what height
> can it begin
> I the shadow
> singing I
> the light (CL, 38)

This brevity is deceptive. The second stanza may be a cry of awe at the renewal held out to the speaker as he realizes his own connection to the song of the lark, though at the same time (as so often in this volume) it is an opportunity offered rather than a condition attained. It emerges from his question "can it begin," which is also a statement that establishes both his connection to and distance from what he would achieve. In the first stanza that song appeared "in the hour that has no friends," like a "star burning in cold heaven / speaking well of it." The second stanza is an assent to the renewal of this song, with each word transforming the poem into a slightly different key as it progresses. That song is "fire," organic, lively, warming, which appears "by day," distinctive even in the setting of the bright air, and it is "with no country," free of artificial constraints, a wanderer. There can be no answer to the question that follows, "where and at what height / can it begin," because the very point of grasping this song is that it launches one into questions that dissolve any chance to pinpoint matters clearly. The question duplicates the soaring of the lark's song by lifting us into heights. With "I the shadow / singing I / the light," Merwin brings together, in a lilting fashion, the poet and the lark, the shadow and the light, relying on the line break as an obstacle that is integrated into the poem at the end, used as a virtual springboard into a positive rhythm.

Merwin's form has been chosen for its airy formlessness, and it is not apparent from one moment to the next what his words will be. At the same time, it is gaunt; if this is a lyrical statement, it is one that is pinched to severity, painfully minimal. From one perspective, Merwin is barely able to speak at all, and his gesture of admiration for the song of the lark is made from a remote distance; the emptiness surrounding the brief lines stands for the darkness of which he is so aware. From another perspective, Merwin must make a support for himself as he moves along, through subtle variations; he slowly unfolds the first five lines of the second stanza, beginning with the compression of "fire" and ending with the expansiveness of his question. But from still another perspective, what sustains the work is its generalized diction, words so vast their appearance demands that we read slowly, savoring all their endless suggestions, even as their vastness is not overwhelming because they all appear to be linked to one another in a definite way. "Fire," "day," "no country," "height," "begin," "shadow," "singing," "light": these are each progressively associated with the others. At the same time, they always threaten to break that linkage, and the writing seems on the edge of stopping entirely.

Yet Merwin is never entirely mute, and if his gestures of affirmation are, at this point, radically reduced, they nonetheless still emerge. A twist in the penultimate line is almost inaudible but, like the faint notes of the lark, undeniably present. The word "fire" alone in one line establishes a rhythm of one strong stress per line, with the key word in each receiving emphasis. But in "singing I," the emphasis falls first on "singing," next on "I," sounding as two stresses rather than one. Apart from reinforcing the lilt in the line urged by the strategic placement of the line break, the surprising and unexpected second beat not only expands the duration of the line but also places a vigorous emphasis on the "I." Leading into the final line, then, "the light" must be heard with a very strong emphasis, at least equal to that in the preceding line. This subtle rhythmic movement establishes the poet as one who is in relation to that light, a transformation of the "fire" that began the stanza.

2

With hesitation, Merwin cultivates opposing viewpoints that still progress toward a point at which change should occur. But the change is held out, evoked as a possibility rather than proffered as a certainty. Especially in the first two-thirds of the book, poems are about preparations for action, not journeys but stages before a journey. This volume is notable for sequences that never get under way or that flourish only to be dropped; some end prematurely, others are resumed at a later point.[4] Eight of its first nine poems are addressed to another person, whose absence explains the poet's anguish. This set culminates in "Words for a Totem Animal," a searching account of the poet's uncertainty. After four miscellaneous poems, another set takes shape as autobiographical reminiscence, but only yields four poems, after which follow six miscellaneous poems and "The Black Plateau." One poem later another cycle is under way, centered on the Pennsylvania landscapes of Merwin's youth, beginning with "The Wheels of the Trains." Just how this group develops, where it ends, and where it branches into a new set remain impossible to determine with finality.[5] After a personal memory, "Lackawanna," five poems follow—but each is about the settlement of the West. Then come seven poems that waver between personal reminiscence ("Huckleberry Woman"), political commentary ("Presidents"), and lyrical praise ("Little Horse"), culminating in "The Removal," a suite that recalls both the uprooting of the American Indian and displaced refugees in Europe. "The Old Room," the next work, not only returns to autobiography but initiates a group of four poems that mount a critique of the culture. Teasingly, fitfully, up to just past the midpoint of the book, Merwin leads us in and out of sets of poetry that begin and end abruptly, or swerve into another cycle. As loosely arranged as Merwin's previous cycles were, they were performances that were sustained, but these die well before they mature. Moreover, at intervals throughout these broken cycles, Merwin makes continual references to childhood in general and his own childhood in particular, as though underlying these groups were one master-cycle, an early but unsuccessful beginning to his autobiographical writings.

At its simplest, the idea of childhood can be associated with receptivity, first steps, moments in which one is ready to learn. Childhood could become a metaphor for renewal, as in the second poem of the book, "Teachers." Midway through it, attempting to escape his despair, Merwin turns away from brooding:

> but I say to myself you are not a child now
> if the night is long remember your unimportance
> sleep
>
> then toward morning I dream of the first words
> of books of voyages
> sure tellings that did not start by justifying
>
> Yet at one time it seems
> had taught me (CL, 4)

Instead of renewal, he experiences further defeat. While he sees that his earlier advice to himself, "You are not a child now," was an error, and that he needs to be more rather than less childlike, needs to reawaken memories of "the first words / of books of voyages," he dissolves that memory soon enough. Lecturing to himself, he extracts a very adult moral from his dream: those adventure-filled beginnings of his youth were "sure tellings," never the weak justifications in which he has been indulging. The end of the poem, then, is particularly shattering: he has recovered a memory of childhood, only to transform it into a lesson. He seems more hopelessly adult than ever; and his poem, far from catching fire as a "sure telling," looks back to days of childhood that seem wistfully remote.

For Merwin childhood is a lost joy, not a source of renewal, and his distance from it is a burden under which he labors. Notes are sounded frequently, if in passing, that confirm this. In "The Black Plateau," commenting on a landscape of ruins, he says that "things grow old where nothing was ever a child," and the bleakness of the French countryside seems to be his psychic double. Poems that specifically allude to his own childhood uncover disabling memories. Listening to the song of birds in "The Birds on the Morning of Going," he says:

> a life opens it opens it is
> breaking
> does it find occasions for
> every grief of its childhood
> before it will have
> done
>
> oh my love here even the night turns back (CL, 33)

Although he glimpses the joy of welcoming bird song with unalloyed delight, the adult intervenes, and the night rounds back to engulf him. At the end of an autobiographical sequence, in "The Church," he returns to the site in New Jersey where his father had once been pastor; nothing remains there now. However, the nothing that remains is eerily identical to a nothing that had been there before: "only I am still standing / on the weedy rock in the wind." Where the altar once stood he sees "the eyes I left / as a child there."

The discovery that he has no childhood to which he can return for helpful guidance is a fugitive subtext of these broken cycles. "Lackawanna" recalls the Pennsylvania river of his past, a river he had, as a child, obediently refrained from stepping into; now he enters it as the "Jordan," to be reborn—except that the poems that follow substitute for his own history the story of the settling of the American West. That westward journey is shown as a passage into ever-widening circles of emptiness. Grief and loss are particular to the one poem that carries an explicit recollection from childhood, "Huckleberry Woman": he remembers waking to her weeping when her basket of carefully gathered huckleberries fell. That loss unites the child with the exiled immigrant:

> and I am borne with you on its
> black stream
> oh loss loss the grieving
> feels its way upward
> through daggers of stone
> to stone
> we let it go it
> stays we share it (CL, 52)

When the immigrant woman weeps, it is not surprising that she would grieve momentously, for her grieving must have roots deep in her own past. That Merwin as a child joins her so readily is unexpected, as though the fund of his own grief were as immense as hers, needing only to be touched to be released. More disturbing is an ambiguity fostered by the framework of the reminiscence: the speaking "I" is both child and adult. Merwin the adult still identifies with the anguish of Merwin the child, just as Merwin the child identifies with the anguish of the immigrant woman. In the nightmarelike "The Old Room," a work that heavily draws on autobiographical detail, he has become a child again, only to finds his actions circumvented by adults who speak for him. His call "*It is not me,*" which is at best a negative act of identification, not only goes unheard but sets in motion opposite results:

> What if I note *It is not me* will they revive
> I go in my father has voted for me
> I say no I will vote in my own name
> I vote and the number leaps again on the wall (CL, 64)

In three poems scattered through the volume Merwin vainly attempts a meaningful journey across water; he is always too late. In "The Lake" he is a child who rises at dawn ("no father in the house at least") to discover an Indian village he imagines sunk beneath the waters. It never discloses itself, and the opening question of the poem—"Did you exist / ever"—sounds like the adult Merwin asking if the child had ever existed. In "The Port" he is of no determinate age but arrives at a fishing village late, with all the boats departed but one, "full of water / with my rotted sea-clothes lashed to a piling / at the head." He had wanted to deliver a message of salvation, "but the whole town has gone to sea without a word / taking my voice" (CL, 56) With no one to hear it, his urgent message goes undelivered. In "The Hulk" he is again at a dock, this time as "the small child the small child / alone with the huge ship at last." He is free to do as he wishes, but he finds his boat is a hulk, "a name rusted out / in an unknown / unknown language." Such complete dereliction gives rise to fear: "no one will come / to call me by any name." Although he is entirely free—"I can sail if we sail / I can wander / through the rusting passages forever"—he remains, once again, unable to act, held in that moment "with my fear by the hand" (CL, 82).

Thoughts of childhood and the figure of the child are appropriate to new beginnings. Yet in these poems the child is portrayed as a helpless victim, never a confident beginner. As a result, the child's appearance halts the journey rather than setting it in motion; he is unprepared, too hesitant, or genuinely fearful. What might have been, then, an opportunity for recovering a fresh perspective by drawing upon those "sure tellings" from one's youth turns into something else. The poet remains very close to the fearful child, his journey still standing before him as a vague, intimidating presence.

3

Near the midpoint of Merwin's two preceding volumes, the work underwent a purifying change, a significant reversal in which old attitudes were suddenly reconsidered from a new perspective. The final text of *The Carrier of Ladders* also reflects such a change, but at one time, in the spring of 1968, Merwin believed his volume was ready as it was, without that rejuvenating turn. He had every reason, in that spring, to believe his poems were ready for collection. Since December 1966 he had completed over sixty poems, and in April 1968 he added two new poems to his American sequence ("Other Travellers to the River" and "The Gardens of the Zuni"), and supplemented "Footprints on the Glacier" with three poems on a seasonal theme ("Midnight in Early Spring," "Night Wind," and "Full Moonlight in Spring"). On April 11, 1968, he wrote to George Kirstein that his next volume of poetry was almost complete, and by April 20, all the poems in the first seventy-seven pages of the Atheneum text (up through "As Though I Was Waiting for That") had been written.[6]

In fact, the final poem to be included in *The Carrier of Ladders* would not be written until almost a year later, in March 1969. The new cycle of poetry that would expand the collection by one-third may have been prompted by Merwin's review of his own work.[7] When he had assembled *Green with Beasts* in the autumn of 1955, he had almost immediately embarked on his second set of sea poems, and his thoughts had returned to his much-delayed Coxey's Army project in 1963 and 1967, after he had assembled *The Moving Target* and *The Lice*. But this new poetry was explicitly linked to its predecessors; indeed, it was the deliberate next step beyond the poetry of hesitation that otherwise marks *The Carrier of Ladders*.

In the poetry written before this decisive step, Merwin insisted that every choice had to be an either/or: either truth was ground up like broken glass or it rang with a crystal purity; either he remained among the silent stars of the night or he sang like the lark at dawn; either he recovered the innocence of youth or he remained locked in the burden of age. Beginning with a series of poems written in June 1968, he views this dilemma in an entirely different way: from either/or he shifts to both/and. Instead of weighing his oppositions as finely as possible, he actively embraces them as necessary contradictions that he must accept. Two distinct cycles of poetry appear in the last third of the volume, one initiating this new stance, the other consolidating it; the poems in between test how things look from within this new capaciousness.

The first cycle is a group of three poems, "Fear," "Pilate," and "Shore," written in rapid succession in June 1968. Each work is a break from the intensity that had previously held his lines clenched in a taut reserve. From the outset, he recognized the newness of this work. In his notes for "Fear," the first of the three to be written, he inquires, "new mode? this run-on explosion of logic connecting phrases."[8] Fear spills forth illogically, in run-on lines that imply no order when they break. Fear destroys the shape of the poem, stretching without end, linking with everything. But the explosion is contained in the final statement, "it is me," the center of these openly incompatible perceptions.

As completed, "Fear" resembles automatic writing, with free associations spilling in any number of directions:

> I'm here today this is New York I'm more
> than any one person or two persons
> can stand fear the way down in everything
> the way up is the same fear the next place
> the next I said fear come on you it's you
> I'm addressing get into line you're going
> never fear there is a hair hanging by
> everything it is the edges of things (CL, 83)

Not just a chain of free associations, the poem serves as a mechanism of release. The piece begins: "Fear / there is / fear in fear the name. . . ." If the name of fear itself is fearful, then the poem is a ritual of exorcism, diminishing the power of fear by pronouncing its name with such frequency it loses its talismanic power, merged as it is into the grainy clutter of the poem, until Merwin even indulges in a rare foray into flippancy: "I mean / you again fear it's a strange name not / for a stranger ma'am he said lying." On the other hand, fear retains fearfulness by remaining something that can only be approached indirectly. Only through an unexpected swerve can fear be named, and then it is rapidly incorporated into a new train of thought. The poem ends when Merwin is able to say that "there is fear in everything and it is / me and always was in everything it / is me." This moment is simultaneously a yielding and a mastery, a moment repeated as a definite assertion that withstands the unbounded spillage of the poem.

"Fear" is Merwin's decisive effort to exorcise his own fears, to step past the hesitancies that marked his previous poems. The hanging-back that lingered as a spell over his earlier work is broken: fear, at one point, seemed like "a ring a ring a ring" encircling the poet, but in this poem the ring becomes as fragile as "a bit of grass green swan's down." Other works in this "new mode" also shatter what had once seemed firm. "Pilate" is a meditation in a time of anxious change and crisis. The empire is passing, but "lo empire itself / is not visible," and its trappings persist even when it has lost its authority. There is

> the call
> the call that hangs in the banners until
> it falls as shall the banners fall
> from the walls the walls (CL, 88)

The authoritative call remains, but only because it is instituted in banners: it is no longer voiced, and these banners will eventually fall. "Could I change myself," he wonders, speaking from within a time of change that nonetheless remains cluttered with false signs. The answer comes when he insists that the false signs of the empire can have no hold over him ("lo myself / is not visible to these"), and the poem ends with an image of soldiers clustered around a campfire fading into the darkness—the empire depicted as a frail vestige of itself.

The third poem, "Shore," depicts a powerful vessel heading inland at dawn toward an eager crowd awaiting its arrival. What that arrival portends is not enunciated in the poem, but in his second cycle, in four psalms that follow, Merwin adopts an entirely new form, one that encourages absolute inclusiveness. Nothing about these poems is either/or; everything is both/and. None of the four is hesitant about the way it unfolds; each is designed as an occasion for embracing opposites and contradictions. The first, "Psalm: Our Fathers," written directly after "Shore," is not only the most capacious, but also sweeps insistently forward. Its very form flirts with a breakdown. It is always in two parts ("I am the son of . . . but . . .") and the second term always radically qualifies the first. However, the point of "Our Fathers" is that the crinkle in the syntax, the "but" that might stall the forward momentum, is always overtopped by Merwin's embracing of the second term. It is the sweep over and beyond the "but" that brings the two opposing terms into an unlikely but definite relation.

It hardly matters, then, that the relation between the two terms fails to remain uniform. At the outset, the first term tends toward a positive statement that the second term undermines: "I am the son of joy but does he know me / I am the son of hope but he ascends into heaven / I am the son of peace but I was put out to nurse" (CL, 92). Initially, the poem is fashioned as an expression of loss, so that whatever had been given as a general inheritance is withdrawn in its specific instance. But the psalm is not under way for long before this arrangement reverses itself: now the first term, what has been inherited, becomes negative, so that the undermining performed by the second term bodies forth an affirmation: "I am the son of blindness but I watch the light stretch one wing." "I am the son of untruth but I have seen the children in Paradise walking in pairs each hand in hand with himself." "I am the son of ghosts clutching the world like roads but tomorrow I will go a new way."

Many lines could be recast as aphorisms, like those Merwin had translated a year earlier in Antonio Porchia's *Voices.* "I am the son of blindness but I watch the light stretch one wing" could be rewritten aphoristically as "Those who are blind can still watch the light stretch one wing"—except that the change would smooth out the bump in the line, the signature of the "but" over which Merwin twists to embrace the destiny that is his. On the level of its essential formula, "Psalm: Our Fathers" continually insists that we are our own progenitors, our own fathers, and that we create ourselves by embracing the contradictions that might otherwise threaten us.

This decisive, all-embracing act is a marked step beyond the agonizingly careful positioning that dominated the preceding poems. The three remaining psalms follow a similar format: a mysterious but authoritative initial statement is disruptively modified with information that increases the contradictions the poet can bear.[9] Although each formula is unique, each poem presents itself as a vessel for inclusion. The last one, "Fourth Psalm: The Cerements," adds a further comment: Do not believe, it warns, that when all the contradictions are summarized, you will have a three-dimensional portrait of the speaker. The speaker's vanishing is entirely appropriate; the contradictions he recognizes and embraces mean that he cannot be held in any way, by traps either elegant or cunning.

The four psalms are not the only sign of Merwin's renewal. Absent now is the mischievously disruptive line break. If a line breaks awkwardly, it is rapidly reintegrated at its next turn:

> The leaves turn black when they have learned how to fly
> so does the day
> but in the wind of the first hours of darkness
> sudden joy sent
> from an unknown tree
> I have not deserved you (CL, 110)

Lines stand firm, without a disarming surprise lurking in their future. The opening of "Now It Is Clear" fulfills the promise of its title:

> Now it is clear to me that no leaves are mine
> no roots are mine
> that wherever I go I will be a spine of smoke in the forest
> and the forest will know it
> we will both know it (CL, 109)

Each line gathers a subject and verb to make a point building upon a previous point without hesitation.

At times when Merwin verges on his old despair, he may summon the strength to reject it. "Signs" groups brief lines together; most pieces are two lines long and less than seven words. Merwin's producing meaningful observations in so small a space would have been unthinkable earlier. Even more revealing, however, is his elimination from his original manuscript certain pieces that conformed to his standards of brevity but curved darkly toward confusion: "you draw back from it / it follows," "whatever it is / is a reminder," "you love too much / what you have been / and you didn't love it then," "leave something / for chairs for the scholars / they will explain why we suffered."

When he does experience, as in "The Web," the old sensation of being trapped and held—"the old scars waking opening / in the form of a web"—his very description of the web is designed to evade its entrapment; even as he tells how thoroughly the web surrounds him, he is subtly expanding the field of his poem until the web is already dissolving:

o web

over the sand you are woven
over the water you are woven
over the snow you are woven
over the grass you are woven (CL, 126)

And onward, for six more lines in parallel phrasing that generate their own momentum, the web expanding until the speaker has slipped free of it:

but I remember also the ringing spaces
where I have crossed you like a hand on a harp
and even now
in the echoless sky birds pursue our music

hoping to hear it again. (CL, 126)

This complex of images weaves the hand of the poet into a relationship with the birds that cross the sky: the "ringing spaces" are "our music," points spread across a widened sky that both poet and birds conspicuously share. Unlike "Lark," where the poet was left to listen for a sound that seemed just beyond his hearing, here the poet confidently recalls moments whose recollection affirms continuity.

Insistent gestures toward rejuvenation, like the claim that ends "The Web," recur throughout these closing poems, all written between June 1968 and March 1969. Unlike the problematic delineations with which the volume opened, leading us painstakingly through a net of conflicting perceptions, drawing us to a point of decision only to break off, these works intend that the poet will resolutely and dramatically enter the scene of his poem, take hold of matters and enact his decisive revival. And as these pieces promise, Merwin is in fact on the brink of a period of extraordinary creativity. In a cycle of prose pieces composed rapidly, usually at the rate of one a day, between April and July 1969, he will discover a range and a freedom of movement that would have seemed unimaginable to the poet of the opening pages of *The Carrier of Ladders*.

10

A Guide to This World

The *Miner's Pale Children* (1970) opens decisively; its first piece, "The Dwelling," charts the speaker's growing certainty. "Once when I looked at myself there was nothing," it commences, but then "one morning when I woke up I saw my shape." Later, "one day I was sure who I was." Finally, ". . . I could see what I was. I was alone. I was waiting. I had a shadow outside me." What explains this rejuvenation? The speaker has conquered his fears; or more accurately, he has embraced them. He cannot escape his fears, but he can accept them.

Conquering fear by embracing it links "The Dwelling" to the major turn in *The Carrier of Ladders.* But what is new in the prose pieces is Merwin's sense of a definite expanse opening before him, as he emerges from nothing to the climactic moment of "a terrible tremor" when "all of my fear came out of the cliff and joined me, leaving only a ghost of itself in the old place." As this promises, the prose pieces will be very much outside and overlooking the world; Merwin will now step away from his shelter. And as much as he alluded to political and social events in his poetry, he often approached those concerns from the side, as a concerned spectator, deploring them wistfully, in the spirit of the one who had arrived too late at the dock. This new work will be engaged with concerns heretofore only noted indirectly.

Helen Vendler thought the title gave away the second-class status of the pieces: these were the poet's stunted offspring, pale because prose lacked the vigor of poetry.[1] But it would be out of character for Merwin to be so arch with his titling. These works bring to light what had been formerly cloaked in darkness, but more than that, they ask us to reverse our thinking, they expose our assumptions and question the extent to which our apprehensions have distorted what we see. The title not only touches on bringing the underground to light, it initiates the first of a series of challenges to conventional expectations: Who would have thought the miner had children? At once, the title clashes with usual attitudes toward this all-male occupation, with which tenderness is not usually associated.

Although *The Miner's Pale Children* was published concurrently with *The Carrier of Ladders,* it is not a parallel text but a step beyond the poetry, an extension of Merwin's eagerness to seize the both/and rather than fret over the either/or.[2] His appetite for working with material not entangled with his own hesitancy and doubt is satisfied in this prose, able to go anywhere, do anything. When the pieces first began to emerge, somewhat unexpectedly, they were often vehicles for satire. The earliest are variations on a theme of dystopia; they employ irony and sarcasm to shame their audience into recognizing the extent to which it has grown comfortable with a civilization that aspires to manage every aspect of existence. This satiric approach soon loses its appeal, but the strongest of the pieces remain closely linked to critical analysis of habits and customs. As Merwin grows accustomed to the spaciousness of the form, the prose pieces take advantage of their lack of any tendency to settle into a perspective. From their far-ranging vantage points, they are able to reveal and to question assumptions so embedded they escape our notice. Prose, with its uncentered perspective, can make visible what would otherwise be invisible. Like the free verse in *Writings to an Unfinished Accompaniment,* to which they are a prelude and their own unfinished accompaniment, the prose poems both reveal the limits of the customary and seek to lift us to a perspective that encompasses those limits and stretches beyond them.

1

Merwin's approach of exposing assumptions otherwise taken for granted is already at work in his earliest prose. Off and on, since the late forties, he had turned to prose on occasion, but never with extended success. Among his earliest works are four tales from the late forties and early fifties, which reveal a theme that would resurface years later: the force exerted, invisibly but powerfully, by the conventions that persons adopt for themselves and apply to each other.[3] In the most effective, "A Friend of Bill's," a downtrodden, menacing derelict named Jake (the name, incidentally, of Merwin's outcast grandfather) appears on the doorstep of Walter and Ethel's small-town Pennsylvania home. He claims to be a close friend of Bill, Ethel's minister brother (Merwin's minister father was named Bill), but the anecdotes he tells to win Walter and Ethel's confidence never ring true. Many refer to counseling inmates at a prison, and Jake seems capable of adjusting the tenor of any anecdote as he proceeds:

> "Well you know that kid Jimmy Loftis," the man went on; "Bill went and seen him a couple of times and he gave the kid a little book and all. You see that little book I got?" He fished down into his overcoat pocket again and then drew his hand out without the book. "Well it was just like that little book I got," he said. "He got that kid going straight you know. That's how I seen Jimmy, out on parole in Allentown. He told me a lot, you know, an awful lot. Yeah, if only Bill was around, he'd see I got fixed up."
>
> He looked carefully at Walter. "You ain't changed your mind about letting me stick around overnight, have you?" he asked.

Merwin's achievement is to present moments in which uncertainty holds sway, as when Jake offers a book in evidence yet fails to produce it. Walter and Ethel govern their lives by certain firm conventions; as Jake manipulates them, Merwin is exposing how fragile their deeply held beliefs are. Inevitably, Walter becomes Jake's victim. After Jake wheedles his way into staying, Walter is awakened in the night, and when he steps out on his porch to investigate a strange noise, he is shot by the police who have surrounded his house in pursuit of Jake.

People are governed by beliefs that are, on the one hand, utterly inflexible, and, on the other hand, less substantial than air. The irony of the tale is that the more secure and substantial persons are in their beliefs, the more susceptible they are to manipulation. It is not simply that Walter and Ethel are naive provincials who can be duped by a con artist: they are, in Merwin's telling, unprepared to acknowledge a world that might be distinctively different from their own. Everyone insists, in these early tales, on maintaining a viewpoint that is only personally true. Although the violence of "A Friend of Bill's" is absent from the other tales, Merwin never swerves from the conviction that persons shape their worlds to see things according to their own light. "Thaw" is the monologue of a man describing his town to a stranger; to the outsider, the town appears remarkably desolate, but the narrator sees it through his own eyes and its ugliness is invisible to him. Merwin, it seems, was remarkably sensitive toward the fixed attitudes held by members of his family and his neighbors; it is not surprising, then, that even his earliest poetry constantly yearns for new perspectives, viewpoints that radically displace those previously in place.

In the first in a series of unfinished tales about Gussie (completed at last in the "Laurie" chapter of *Unframed Originals),* who is convinced her brother is withholding her royalty checks on an oil well, the story is told from the distorted view of Gussie herself, who carries on a polite, detailed conversation with the royalties agent, T. Shetland De Vyne, who is a figment of her imagination. In a later version of the same story, "The Parrot" (probably written in 1956), Merwin slips into her viewpoint:[4]

> And she would get up sometimes when the calendar light bowed in a certain way toward the stone tub where the washing hung, when it bowed and showed her the cans all empty on the floor, and when down under the curve of buttonless sweaters pulled to raveling scallops, and ends of frilled shirt-waist like papers piled on a rainy street, and bits of grime-shiny taffeta, when under it all there was Gussie's stomach, a growling hunger-dog twitched and whined and reminded. Up she would get then out of the rocker, making the sunbeams swirl indignantly, startling the gray-green smell of mould that was the dream her limp washing was dreaming. And would find the money and the spectacles, and not need to put on her green hat because it was there already, loose and to one side, pushed by the rocker-back, but it would not fall off because it was pinned with pearls to make it part of the auburn wig that rose like two birds' nests on top of her white wide head.

Everything is askew. At the same time, from Gussie's perspective, everything is in place as always—familiar, carefully planned (her hat "would not fall off because it was pinned with pearls to make it part of the auburn wig").

Merwin is impressed by the extent to which people invent their world, then imprison themselves in it. In these early pieces the prose writer's role is not so much to invent stories or to create characters as it is to expose the ways in which characters drawn from real life create stories they have invented for themselves (fig. 15). As a result, details are not the only things set in eccentric orbits. Conversations, like those in "A Friend of Bill's," fly past each other as each speaker probes how far he or she can safely penetrate the protective circles with which characters surround themselves.

"The Barn," for example, written in April 1956, is a coming-of-age story.[5] Vacationing with his family on a lake, Walter (perhaps as young as ten or as old as thirteen), the outsider, strikes up a friendship with Freddie, the insider, whose family has for years spent its summers at the lake. Freddie has an intuition of when to approach and when to retreat from activities that are dangerous, activities of which adults would disapprove. Walter, a neophyte, must quickly grasp the rules of conduct that Freddie has internalized, and the first half of the story, which seems no more than an aimless record of games played by the two boys, is a series of tests Walter must pass. He must move in harmony with the world Freddie has created if he would be accepted by him. In the original opening of the story, the point is made at once: "Freddie called it a pier." To Walter, Freddie's pier looks like "a sort of long shallow box as long as a room and only a couple of feet wide turned upside down on barrels." Walter sees what is there, but Freddie has a name for what he sees. And if Walter is to keep up, he must recognize whose territory he is inhabiting. Overcoming misgivings, Walter walks out on the rickety contraption as though it were as firm as a pier. "The Barn" extends this rite of initiation as far as it can. The story ends

It was hard to say when " was a ' and when she was a ' . She came down the

Stories. Mrs. Pecot. – Nancy, brother & the real & step father. – Lee
Tom Mickle – suicide

Scratch a Kitten

Alan
The Monroes
Tess Wilson
Jon Price
Eddie Phelps on the canal
Dan & his family – & Jenny & her father
Uncle Sam
Gussie – & oil shares & parrot
June Geiss – Biddy Wyatt etc.
Uncle Cal ——— at Shadow Lake holding forth?
Sunny Shot's sisters
Mr. Barnard – [illegible] painter – gambler?
The Deans
Martha Lawrence dying
Claudia & Mary

Gussie – Orville & Wilbur –
– selling her candy & dishrags – for Sunday School
for hymn book
brother royalties sister
vine growing in window
– will brother come when she dead – & what we going to do w/ this thing

Going up with father to buy sugar during war scare

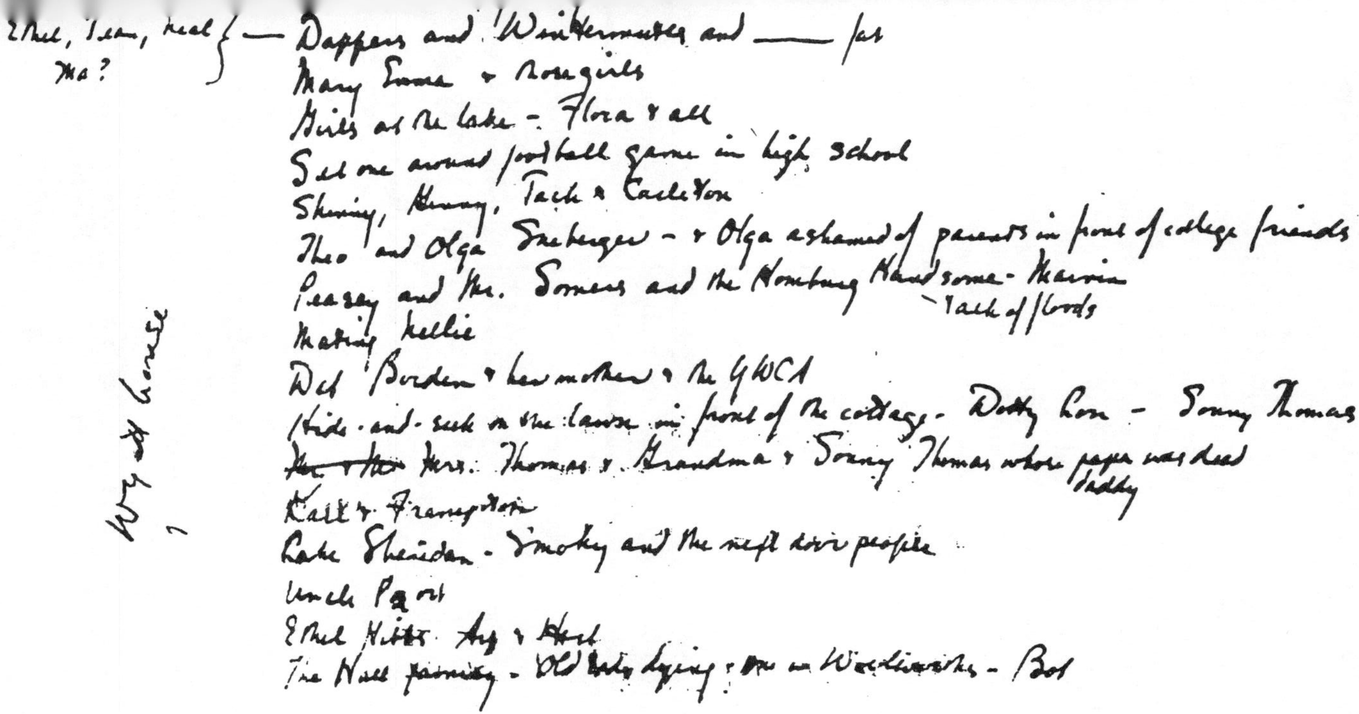

Figure 15. "Notes for stories" (MS. 11:1211, c. 1955–56), showing Merwin's interest in topics drawn from his childhood. He developed the ninth entry in the list (with a line drawn to its right) in his unfinished story "The Parrot." The note lists incidents that appear in the story: "Gussie + oil shares + parrot," then "selling her candy and dishrags for Sunday School." The listing just below the line ("brother royalties sister vine growing in window") is in pencil, not ink, suggesting Merwin returned to this note at a later time. "Uncle Cal" (the eleventh entry) figured in a poem by the same name (uncol. MS. 19:12/072, c. 1956), published in the *Nation* 184 (Mar. 2, 1957): 190.

when the two boys, exploring a remote barn, come upon two naked adults, evidently making love. In trying to describe and identify what they have seen, neither boy has the words for it. Although Walter has spent the day carefully extending his knowledge, this information is too powerful to be processed.

What remains unchanged between the 1949–1952 and the 1956 stories is the way characters set their boundaries by creating a world they accustom themselves to inhabiting. It is surprising how much dead weight we bring with us, but Merwin believes that such weight can be gradually lifted. At least he so demonstrates in a later round of stories in which he as author and participant submits to reversals and inversions and transformations like those he has withheld from his characters. In 1963 and 1964 he published three unconventional short stories, "Return to the Mountains," "The Museum," and "The Church of Sounds," each a first-person narrative in the guise of a memoir.[6] Each story exposes expectations the narrator had been unconsciously employing to hold fast to events; as the story unfolds, the widening disparity between the narrator's line of thinking and the wayward course of actuality leads up to the crisis with which each tale ends.

"The Museum," the most sophisticated of the three, looks furthest ahead. Stopped unexpectedly at a provincial border town (it might be in Mexico) after his luggage temporarily goes astray, the unnamed speaker amuses himself by setting out to visit a museum recommended by the local people. By mistake he stops at a mansion at the outskirts of the village, where he is granted an extensive tour of the grounds because the caretaker mistakes him for a prospective buyer. Redirected to the proper site, an unmuseumlike peasant dwelling, he is led into catacombs in the basement, only to find that the exhibit—ancestral bones—has been removed and replaced by a menagerie of stuffed animals. The keeper bitterly explains that the local aristocrats, whose house had been mistakenly visited earlier, long ago arranged to transport the contents of the museum to the capital for safe preservation, thereby dissolving the collection and bankrupting the museum. All that remains are yellowing photographs, displayed at the end of the tale.

"The Museum," from one perspective, is a parable about the destruction of an indigenous culture: local aristocrats ship their ancestors to the capital and pillage their own heritage. Their actions duplicate, on a local level and a small scale, the attitude of America and Europe toward Third World countries. But Merwin is more interested in exposing the assumptions that persons bring to situations—a point first developed in a passage that seems otherwise irrelevant. When he believes he has found the museum in a well-tended mansion on the outskirts of town, his presence is accommodated by servants who show him about, believing he is planning to buy the mansion. Everyone carries a baggage of assumptions as they attempt to bring order to their world. The story focuses, then, on the strength of the museum-keeper, whose livelihood has been destroyed once the artifacts have been taken from his museum and relocated elsewhere. He has used his ingenuity to assemble a counterfeit museum out of stuffed animals and such materials as were on hand. If his efforts seem at first pathetic, they ultimately represent the hardiness and inventiveness of the peasant who will fiercely cling to what he believes to be his own and who will keep alive a distinct relationship to the past; in contrast to the prim decorum of a central museum, the peasant's museum is a variation on folk art. "The Museum," then, is only tangentially about exploitation: it is primarily a celebration of peasant ingenuity, and the museum reveals the need to fill an aching void, the peasant's desire to possess a past that remains continuous and unbroken.

The most effective of the prose pieces take this extra step: not only do they expose the assumptions that people bring to situations, but they also convey how situations appear when those assumptions give way to eccentric orders that are less defensive, closer to a less accessible truth. An inability to yield to that eccentricity is what mars three tales completed around 1967 or 1968, "The Academy," "Campbell," and "The Flyover."[7] In every case, Merwin or the narrator either is as distant as a bemused observer or only registers impressions of a child too young to comprehend. The interest of these tales lies in the way events have been skewed, but Merwin is unwilling to yield his own remote perspective. When he allows himself to be drawn in, when he must shift out from under his own assumptions, then he has entered the uncertain and unbounded world of his short prose pieces.

2

Merwin is not entirely comfortable with his new form at first, despite his strong assertions in "The Dwelling." The prose pieces appeared abruptly, among the jottings and notes for poetry in a notebook that includes fragmentary beginnings for poems in the later pages of *The Carrier of Ladders*.[8] The first entry for a prose piece began as a note for a poem ("What happens in the drawers at night when [illegible]"), but then a beginning phrase is crossed through and marked "Prose P." Thereafter, ideas for prose poems flow rapidly, sometimes several to a page, always prefaced with a "PP" to distinguish them from ideas for poems:

> PP of endless bar w/apparitional
> each section same—but
> different
>
> PP Cliff dwelling—build out
> Then our self off tr. Cliff w/
> + 7 wall + free—sailing
> in wind
> Like the chamber of heart

PP—Unchopping a Tree
and everything is going
to have to be put back

the shoelace (freedom, terror
as it is approaching chance—
now something calls once
—gone—the terror—
alone—goes slowly and
down the first
bend of a long journey

Typically, these notes for "The Bar," "The Dwelling," "Unchopping a Tree," and "Ends" are short sentences that barely outline a concept. Writing rapidly from May to July 1969, Merwin would develop at least one of these virtually every day, sometimes two a day, producing a first draft that received only minor revisions.

Spontaneity is important to the pieces; without it, they might return to a level of satire that hobbled the first of them. The tone of the earliest pieces owes a great deal to "A New Right Arm," a satirical essay in the manner of Swift, composed shortly after the Cuban Missile Crisis of 1962.[9] What sharply distinguishes this from Merwin's other occasional prose is its focus on the misuse of language. The distortions language suffers here reveal how easily it can be corrupted as a medium for genuine information. The thesis of "A New Right Arm" is that concern about mutations caused by fallout from nuclear testing has been overstated. Mutants can be utilized to perform various tasks heretofore deemed too odious for human beings; or, as the narrator avers, in words that fester beneath their veneer of tact and discretion: "The consideration of mutant persons not in terms of their handicaps but in terms of their possible usefulness as soldiers would permit the government to extend to them medical benefits and compensatory training such as would scarcely be possible, or could not be administered with the same liberality, if the defectives were simply left to their civilian fate and the hazards of individual resources" (RM, 256). The syntax is just intricate enough that the central idea is buried, touched upon in passing: "their possible usefulness as soldiers." The piece suggests that a lexicon is at hand for an outrageous proposal; none of the words seems strained—indeed, they articulate their proposals so smoothly it is easy to lose sight of their ideas.

The target of some of the first pieces in *The Miner's Pale Children* is language debased in this way. Rarely will Merwin speak in a voice that is his own. Adopting ways of speaking that we deem to be proper, he reveals how those ways have blinded and deafened us. "Within the Wardrobes" is a report on "the life in the clothing drawers," the secret life that unfolds once those drawers are shut, except that the piece reports that nothing has been discovered. Efforts to measure the inner life of the clothing drawers have been vain. Cameras with flashbulbs timed to go off at intervals only disclose "still more eerie vistas of inert recumbency." A tape recorder has only presented the machine as "registering its own unrewarded vigil." In each case, of course, the machine or measuring device has been substituted for the human perspective, but Merwin's point is not simply that relying on machines to extend the senses only distorts our perception; it is also that the absence of any finding must be presented as a finding. The genre of the report, which must produce a conclusion because it sets out to find one, is unswerving and therefore blind. The emptiness reported parallels the blindness of the genre.

Yet Merwin never ridicules the idea that there may be another order of things, a life that unfolds in the absence of the human; what he ridicules is the effort of "scholars" to approach that life using instruments of measurement. That other life cannot be measured, yet it is a life that we—even scholars—suspect continues without us. Composed in a fussy, pedantic prose that unwinds with a restrained earnestness, "Within the Wardrobes" is not the satire of "A New Right Arm." Merwin's primary concern is to consider there may be other realms of existence that our habits preclude us from noticing. What is right about this piece is the idea of searching for that other life's point of view; what is wrong about it is that the search is so thoroughly constrained by its very approach. It is a contrast touched upon in the last two sentences: "The witnesses suggest that their own order of things, its darkness, its anticipation in which time plays no part, its community without sound, its dances, its dances, whatever they may be, are part of an order that is older than the cupboards and will survive them. They also infer quite calmly that the world of uses, for which they were fashioned and in which they are worn, knows almost nothing of reality" (MPC, 9). Just as the cupboards come later, surrounding an order of reality that has always existed, so the format of the report jackets that other order and therefore discloses only blindness and deafness. Merwin's success is to evoke that other order, that essentially timeless realm ("its dances, its dances, whatever they may be" suddenly emerges as a wonderful evocation of the scholar's search for a truth still unknown), through revealing the limits of the report.

Not only how we have deceived ourselves but also what we have forgotten and can rediscover is a major theme in these pieces. But Merwin's position is not that we are weak, lapsing into jargon and systematic modes because we lack the energy to shape our world. Quite the opposite, the position he develops is that the mind too easily oversteps its bounds, imposing its powerful perceptions on a fabric of reality that, in its essential neutrality, is vulnerable to manipulation and management. The power of our minds to bend reality to fit our human needs is both our greatest strength and our most terrible weakness. In "Knives" Merwin asserts that "a curtain of rain" that we cannot touch surrounds us, and even though "it wears us away," "we believe we would be nothing without it. . . . We look out and see nothing, through the curtain, but uses." Looking out upon knives, he claims that "we see only the service we ask of them—separation, separation, and pain." The message he would bring is that knives have the meekest of faces: "They who eat nothing, who do not even defend themselves against the dew, against rust, against any of the bearers of loss, and who make no sound, except an occasional clear note like the calling of a bird, when they have been struck, or abraded with a stone. They who will obey any guide" (MPC, 185). Objects unminded are neutral, blameless, and innocent; they are submerged in a multifaceted reality that extends endlessly out in every direction. We tend to extract the objects from that flux and to transform them into a pointed use that makes them the same no matter what the context. "Knives" suggests a contrast between using words as though they could never be more than jargon and respecting words for the mysterious reality that seems to surround them when they appear in poetry.

These prose pieces escape easy satire because Merwin indicts us as powerful beings who misuse our strength. The mind is a powerful force that keeps finding support for its every action. "Unchopping a Tree" both celebrates and deplores our ingenuity. At a late stage in the elaborate repair of the tree, the chips and the sawdust must be returned to their former positions, a task requiring an almost incomprehensible delicacy:

> Weathering makes it harder to identify the smaller fragments. Bark sawdust in particular the earth lays claim to very quickly. You must find your own ways of coping with this problem. There is a certain beauty, you will notice at moments, in the pattern of the chips as they are fitted back into place. You will wonder to what extent it should be described as natural, to what extent man-made. It will lead you on to speculations about the parentage of beauty itself, to which you will return (MPC, 87).

The genre of the instruction manual itself sends mixed signals. Compared to the inexhaustible intricacy of the natural, with its complex harmonic system, its infinite checks and balances, the manual sounds inept and cumbersome; with its fussy and prim sense of detail, its attempt to take note of every contingency ("the fixative for this part is not the same as the one for the outer layers and bark, and if either of these is involved in the splintered section they must receive applications of the appropriate adhesives"), the language points up, dramatically enough, how awkward and crude is the highest technology compared to a tree.

Yet the overall intent is not to expose us to our crudeness but to evoke an intricacy beyond us. The piece is not a parody of an instruction manual but near to a celebration of the virtue of close attention to detail; the instruction manual, which aspires to be neutral before its task, devotedly turns outward toward what it would reconstruct. This paradox exposes our vanity: we find it natural enough to rise to the challenge of unchopping the tree, but unnatural to resist that chopping in the first place. Even so, by reminding us of our limits ("We do not have the spider's weaving equipment. nor any substitute for the leaf's living bond with its point of attachment"), the writing makes contact with qualities we most need: humility, attention to detail, reverence for the intricate interdependence of our surroundings. The prose of the manual, insofar as it stands aside to undertake an impossible task with deftness and regard for detail, becomes an exemplary virtue: its modesty, its willingness to serve, and its honesty before its own limitations testify to what we can become.

3

Many pieces in *The Miner's Pale Children* reprise the following scenario: something of value has been lost or stolen or taken away. It is irreplaceable, yet we search for a way to assuage our grief. A substitute is sought out. The substitute may lead to further deprivations ("Memory," "In a Dark Square"), or to a stalwart avowal that this world is composed of imperfections, none of which produces what one desires ("The Bandage," "The First Time"), or to a realization of the superiority of the substitute because it shifts an attitude or changes a perspective that would not otherwise have been adjusted ("The Fragments," "The Dwelling"). "Unchopping a Tree" is remarkable because it blends all three possibilities: the recomposed tree will never be as fully alive as the original, but it will be a major reconstruction based on a series of intricate compromises, the understanding of which both deepens appreciation of the original and emphasizes the virtues of care.

What appears as eccentric in Merwin's prose pieces can often be traced to his tendency to make this third turn, to insist that what might from one perspective be conceived as a boundary may become, from another perspective (the attainment of which demands a thorough reorientation), a threshold. Indeed, it is only when the two opposites are conceived as one, as both barrier and entrance, boundary and threshold, that Merwin is close to his goal. In "The Songs of the Icebergs" we cannot hear the songs completely, since "the water, and the habits of our own ears, distort the sound so that what usually reaches men seems to be nothing but a series of creakings, splinterings, gnashings, occasional screams—emanations to which the hearer, with the familiar door-shutting movement to which he believes he owes his very identity, hastens to deny any vestige of intention, plan, form, spirit." But whales, "imprisoned in no such rigid refusal," catch occasional chords and echo them in "their rich and happy music," just as porpoises shape "delicate carols" from "still fainter refrains." But the reason we turn away from these sounds is that they echo our condition. The tragic story of the icebergs, reflected in their songs, is that they could have remained silent. Brought up in silence,

> they might have remained there in perfect peace until they died. But there was a flaw in the whiteness. It was in love with the light. And with unspeakable pain it set out to reach the sun, forsaking everything else forever. However the planet turned it continued its journey, gathering to itself a few ghosts, a few bones, a few echoes of bones, a few curses, a voice. Crossed by a few white creatures. Unconsolable. Breaking. That is in the songs (MPC, 125).

"That is in the songs": it is an admission that these characteristics are immediately understandable to us. It is all known, the love of the light that draws the icebergs out of the silence where they had been content, their journey toward the sun in unspeakable pain, with only their singing to console them. And the singing, which is in any case "unconsolable," is avoided by those who could understand it best. To respond to those songs would be to stop forever, which is why, understandably, we populate icebergs with legends of mermaids and sirens, "their hands extended in gestures out of the dreams of men."

Yet if we could stop and listen, would it not be less painful, whatever the outcome, than our agonized gestures of avoidance? Some of Merwin's strangest pieces resemble riddles in that they describe a situation that resists understanding until we deduce the precise angle from which they were written. When we have shifted our own habits of thought enough to understand them, we have at once slipped away from the staleness of convention.

"The Animal Who Eats Numbers" returns to the source where conventions are nurtured, the grade-school classroom, to remind us that the daydreams we experienced there were already suggesting an alternative to bland regimentation. It is ominous that it is the animal who is disappearing, as Merwin notes in his final paragraph, because the animal's function is to intervene as a daydream intervenes. Numbers, we are taught, are supposed to be just as they are, without character or personality, but when the animal eats them, they lose their impersonality and take on the distraction of the child inventing stories about them. The unusual device of writing about numbers as though they had a character all their own—"Two is a little girl in a starched muslin dress," "Three is a bigger boy without much to say for himself"—is a way of evoking the organizational tidiness of the classroom. Gradually, a teacher emerges who herself is never devoured by the animal but who comments disapprovingly when the animal devours another. Each number is distracted in a different way:

> Four is eaten a lot. Very often she looks as though it's dark beyond her. You can hardly see her. Even when she's out she must be thinking.
>
> Five is overweight. He laughs. The teacher doesn't like him much but he's funny and kind. He gets eaten all the time. He says he doesn't care. His clothes are all old anyway. He says he'd rather get eaten than do homework any day. He says he sits and plays cards with the animal as though he were at the firehouse (MPC, 80).

The context is the aspirations toward neatness of the classroom, so that the thoughtfulness of Four is as much at odds with the classroom as is the slovenliness of Five, who encourages daydreams because they are preferable to homework.

The ambiguity of what it means for a number to be eaten by an animal is never resolved: what Merwin evokes in this story is the dusty air of conventionalizing order that everyone remembers from grade-school classrooms—its offerings of explanatory stories that even the teacher seems to realize are inadequate compromises but that are regarded as necessary steps toward cultivating good study habits. Those numbers who are "good," like Six, the older sister of Two, hate being eaten: "She thinks about going to college all the time. She thinks you don't get eaten there. . . . When she gets eaten sometimes nobody notices, but if they do they're just quiet for a minute because they don't know what to say, and then they forget." Six is the very portrait of the model student whose attention is only rarely distracted, and not the least of the attractions of this piece is its re-creation of the attitude toward the world fostered by the grade-school environment, in which adults appear as "a quiet man in old clothes" or "a cheerful nice lady in a flowered dress who seems to know everybody."

"The Animal Who Eats Numbers" evokes an experience so familiar it would appear to be beyond evocation; it accomplishes its feat because of its unique perspective, one that is, as it turns out, entirely apt. In the best of the prose pieces, Merwin himself achieves what he otherwise upholds as an ideal—the form of the piece is not just unconventional but true to its own freedom as it reveals a weight of custom that might have been forgotten or gone unnoticed. Yet his aim is never to isolate that custom as though it were reprehensible: quite the contrary, he weaves the custom back into the world so that it has become visible within its invisibility. It has been turned into something that can be grasped, even as it retains its uniqueness.

If the world is devoid of meaning except what we discover there, then all value rests upon our own character. The world is a vast arena in which we are all isolated from one another, conceiving our own limits, habituated to our customs, at the same time as it is about to reveal itself as more wonderfully and intricately interrelated than we had conceived.

That is the doubleness touched upon in "The Moles." On the one hand there are the ants, all regimen and order; on the other, the moles, all uncertainty and question. The contrast also underscores both Merwin's reaction against the organizational aptitude of the mind, which imposes structures that enforce predictability and essentially eliminates the concept of a future, and his endorsement of the mind as an instrument that poses questions and discloses resemblances. Merwin maintains his contrast, though, by differentiating between each creature's response to our death. The ants conceive of an architecture that is "at once a portrait of their minds and a model of the universe with its conflicts in harmony": "When they bury us it is with a utilitarian coldness and finality which put those qualities in ourselves to shame. The blood, the brains, the organs they pile above the spot, after changing them back to red earth. They use only the veins, gradually improving everything beyond recognition" (MPC, 118). They transform the world as it is given into their world, improving it according to their customs, just as one facet of the mind is to reorganize what it has been given. By contrast, the moles commemorate our deaths over and over:

> Each time that we are led at last to lie down in green pastures they raise near us their little mounds that are models of our graves. Is this dust yours, they say? Confronted with silence they raise another one, a lost city in the twilight. Is This Yours, is its name. Is this the one you will return to? Is this the one you were made of? Is this you—the rest of you, which you left behind? If this had been taken up in the same hand, and the breath of life had breathed into it the same command, and it had come with you, would you be whole now, would you be at peace? The stars come out. New hills rise around us. More lost mothers. Once again we become part of the darkness. It is not too late. The moles, propelled by a small model of the forgotten sea, with eyes for nothing but their labors, urge their black bones forward in our endless quest (MPC, 119).

It is one of the loveliest and most hopeful of passages in all Merwin's prose, for it comprehends most fully the pain of incompleteness and folds it back into a series of responsive questions, each miniature resurrections. As the stars emerge and more hills rise and lost mothers appear, we fall back into the silence again, yet feel it may not be too late. The next question may be the one that will bring an answer.

Merwin transforms an emblem of death—the mound of earth that is our inevitable end—into a celebration of endless change, "a small model of the forgotten sea." The ants, in their brilliant organization, patiently waiting their turn, are ingredients that do no more than grind away; like the sun or the stars, they are utterly remote, detached, invincible: "Pain for them is a lantern signaling at a distance." Within the profound reaches of an empty universe, it is all too easy to withdraw into a blank silence like that of the ants. But the example of the moles—to quest blindly, raising modest inquiries that lift themselves up, even though they will rise only to fall, like the crest of the ocean wave that lifts itself up only to fall into its own trough—becomes the way that denies that emptiness even as it acknowledges it, seeking "tirelessly for new places."

11

The Debt to Anonymous

MERWIN HAS twice collected a sampling of his translations—*Selected Translations 1948–1968* and *Selected Translations 1968–1978*—and it is no accident that the year dividing them is 1968. Up to then, he limited his translating to the Romance languages in which he was fluent, and his first collection draws heavily upon Spanish and French poetry in the Middle Ages and in modern times. Many were commissioned, and in his introduction to *Selected Translations 1948–1968*, he curtly distinguishes the piecework of translating from his original poetry: "I have not come to use translation as a way of touching off writing that then became deliberately, specially, or ostentatiously my own. On the contrary, I have felt impelled to keep translation and my own writing more and more sharply separate" (STa, viii). Always in danger of distorting the translation by applying his own standards, the translator must remain "wary of any skill coming to shadow and doctor the source, any deftness usurping the authority it was reared to serve" (STa, vii). Just as one loses one's identity in love, so the translator must hope to lose his poetic identity when translating, setting aside his own predilections for the sake of the poem to be translated.

After 1968, though, Merwin's position changed: half the translations in *Selected Translations 1968–1978* are anonymous writings from unfamiliar languages and cultures; many require a collaborator. In 1968, Merwin's selections were arranged along a historical continuum proceeding from Egypt in the twentieth century B.C. to Joseph Brodsky (born 1940). In 1978, the selections are in two parts. The first half, beginning with Julianus (fifth century A.D.) and ending with Lars Noren (born 1944), is arranged chronologically; the second half is composed of anonymous translations from various oral traditions. That division invites the anonymous writings to present themselves as a parallel order standing over and against the more familiar tradition of compositions with an author.

Like the communally produced anonymous writings, translation is now a collaborative task. Before, the translator effaced himself; now, he is involved from the start. In his 1978 introduction, Merwin wants "the translation to present, with as much life as possible, some aspect, some quality of the poem which made the translator think it was worth translating in the first place" (STb, xi). The translator is now a discerning judge who appreciates "some aspect, some quality" and seeks to carry it forward into other words. So translations are apt to resemble the poet-translator's original work. Conveying that certain quality, Merwin says, is "both a hazard and an opportunity," because "a poet-translator cannot write with any authority using someone else's way of hearing" (STb, xi). Though he is responding to someone else's way of hearing, his appreciation must respect his own way of hearing. These remarks form a prelude to the admission that he has reversed his thinking:

> For several years I tried to maintain illogical barriers between what I translated and "my own" writing, and I think the insistence on the distinction was better than indulging in a view of everything being the (presumably inspired) same. . . . Whatever is done, translation included, obviously has some effect on what is written afterwards. Except in a very few cases it would be hard for me to trace, in subsequent writings of my own, the influence of particular translations that I have made, but I know the influences were and are there. The work of translation did teach, in the sense of forming, and making available, ways of hearing (STb, xi–xii).

This suggests why a poet could benefit from translating: it teaches "ways of hearing" distinct from one's own. And if Merwin would use translation to invite experience distinct from his own yet ample enough to encourage his collaboration, then the most useful translations would be drawn from the oral literature of a variety of different cultures, remote in time and place from his own: Incan, Mayan, Eskimo, Indian, Persian, and Urdu, as well as American Indian. Merwin's translations after 1968 indeed begin to resemble his own writing, but they do so because his writing now actively invites different ways of hearing to inhabit it.

1

In 1981, asked to name those poets with whom he felt the closest affinity, Merwin singled out Villon and Dante, then went on: "I have a debt, as I think everyone does whether they know it or not, to Anonymous; to oral literature as the best one can work toward. That's the real matrix of possibilities that's always there."[1] More pointedly, he then explained that the virtue of "a great deal of anonymous oral literature" was by no means associated with simplicity.

Rather than considering it as reductive, he viewed it as "endlessly suggestive, not as something to be imitated, crudely and directly, but as a reminder that the possibilities open to us at any moment are not as limited as we might suppose. The world is not as simple and as codified and conventional as you thought it was." When an event is repeated, when parallel situations recur, the repetition is a signal that infinite possibilities are being evoked. For Merwin, the primary convention of oral literature is this "form" that asserts the impossibility of encasing events in a specific form.

The great advantage of escaping from a focus on technique is that when a poet has no given approach he has before him a vast unknown that is itself a provocation and a denial of the limitations offered by a technical civilization. Merwin writes in "On Open Form" that "to recur in its purest forms . . . poetry seems to have to keep reverting to its naked condition, where it touches on all that is unrealized" (RM, 299–300). It is not simplicity that is discovered in nakedness but an expanding sense of possibility, of "all that is unrealized." Such expansiveness itself goes against the noxious features of the age, which can be summarized as "the illusion that we have realized a great deal." As Merwin dryly comments: "The agitation serves chiefly to obscure what we have forgotten" (RM, 300). When we step aside or apart from the claims of our own age, we discover not a simpler alternative but a vast range of other alternatives. The ideal of "transparent form" is not simple or single but manifold and plural; what Merwin advocates is a ground from which possibilities will expand.

In 1973, the year in which *Writings to an Unfinished Accompaniment* was published, Merwin also published *(Asian Figures)*, a work that occupies an anomalous position in his own writings.[2] Though listed among his translations, the work is both collaborative and creative, produced by working with literal renderings of Asian language ideograms along with accompanying notes. Rather than translations, *(Asian Figures)* are better understood as "adaptations," which is how Merwin refers to them, as work that emerges from some middle ground, not quite original writing but not quite a direct representation of an explicit set of ideograms. To what extent they are poems or epigrams or aphorisms or riddles is precisely the question he would pose, with the idea of erasing the distinctions between these various forms and ultimately erasing the difference between what is literary and what is worldly.

The final, and perhaps most enduring, attraction of oral poetry is that it is about what matters: it is never frivolous, marginal, or negligible—though it can assert why the apparently frivolous is necessary, and it can take marginal things as its topic, and it can appropriate the tone of common speech. Its wisdom depends on perceiving events from an unexpected angle, which is why its questioning of genres is by no means mischievous. *(Asian Figures)* aspires to offer insightful advice. Even when the reconstructed ideogram seems alien to us, as though it could apply only to the culture from which it originated, it serves to reveal indirectly assumptions we carry with us. But the most important aspect of the adaptations in *(Asian Figures)* is that they continually turn corners, providing new approaches not just from within themselves as a two- or three-line unit but in relation to one another. Consider this grouping from the *Selected Translations 1968–1978* selection of "Japanese Figures":

Better than the
holiday
is the day before

Departs once
is forgotten day
after day

Spits straight up
learns something (STb, 97)

To mull over the relationship between these is to move adeptly and freely through changing perspectives. But the form itself deserves praise, for it is more challenging than it first appears. What is demanded in each is a turn of some kind, almost a reversal; anything less would not repay the slowing-down the form demands. The best of them begin casually, as a mere notation, then swerve about to end as a full-blown maxim, as though light-years had been traveled in a dramatic leap. That unexpected switch over the line break creates the illusion of massive movement, an illusion exaggerated by the brevity of the form. When a number of these are placed together in series, the effect underscores the magical aptness of the movement from opening to close, because the juxtaposed units allude to one another in a glancing fashion. On the one hand, these unaccountable and ultimately disorderly perspectival shifts can be a delight in themselves, but they are finally nothing more than a show of suspense; for on the other hand, the meaningless movement from unit to unit only emphasizes the marvelous agility of the meaningful movement from first line to second (or third) line.

On a superficial level, *(Asian Figures)* could be seen as a mere curiosity, a group of maxims that, assembled, offer a portrait of other cultures. Merwin indeed passes judgment on cultures through the ideograms he chooses to reconstruct. For example, the "Japanese Figures" are notable for their delicate comparisons with creatures: "Autumn / the deer's / own color," "Loves even / the crow on her roof," "Bell cricket / caged for singing" (AF, 35, 36, 41). The "Chinese Figures" are often realistic and practical: "Before you beat a dog / find out whose he is," "See three days ahead / be rich for a thousand years," "Can't put out a fire / from a distance" (AF, 66, 84, 82). The "Korean Figures" are especially wary and prone to voice complaints: "Get rid of one wart / end up with two," "Dress sword / and no pants," "Even honey / tastes like medicine / when it's medicine" (AF, 17, 21, 23). The "Malayan Figures" are conspicuously erotic: "I would die / of your fingers / if I could be buried in your palm," "Stepping on a long thorn / to me the sight of her hair," "I thought my soul was dead / and you found it was a box of sweet basil" (AF, 75, 73). The "Lao Figures," shortest of all the groups, are moody and baneful: "Outside the ways of the old / the ghosts," "The more you want to own / the more you die," "Close to death / you see how tender / the grass is" (AF, 93).

But to view the lines as revealing some elusive cultural unity is an incomplete response. The deeper pleasure of the adaptations is not the insights they offer into alien cultures, nor is it the delight of recognizing a statement's wisdom. What gives special pleasure is the grace and ease with which the mind leaps toward satisfying connections even when they yield unexpected viewpoints. It is a movement replicated within two- or three-line units, savored over and over as its absence hovers in the spaces between individual units, which sometimes echo, sometimes contradict, one another. Certainly the plain statements here, with their one breathtaking turn over the line break, resemble the "transparent form" Merwin spoke of in "On Open Form," where he closed his piece by citing two proverbs. At their best, they are deeply resonant and utterly plain. They scrupulously avoid the literary, the vaunting display or ornate divagation; they always aspire to wisdom. And the way in which they most closely resemble Merwin's own writing at this time is the continual change of viewpoint that occurs from moment to moment. That flexibility, which is the "matrix of possibilities" in the act of being recognized, is what he would carry over into his own writing.

2

Not surprisingly, *Writings to an Unfinished Accompaniment,* the volume Merwin published in 1973, the same year as *(Asian Figures),* most clearly resembles anonymous oral literature. As the volume's title indicates, these works are to be approached as writings, not poems. They recite fables or offer specific instructions ("Surf-casting," "Exercise," "Division"), or echo proverbs or pose riddles ("Ballade of Sayings," "Ship"), or seem to be versions of oral poetry ("Song of Man Chipping Arrowhead," "Nomad Songs,") or, most frequently, offer advice on how to live ("The Day," "Clear Skies," "Spring," "The Place of Backs," "Old Flag," "Habits"). In short, this volume is almost entirely a homage to the oral literature that Merwin was translating at this time.[3]

Work modeled on oral literature, as Merwin conceives it, follows quite specific guidelines. Such poetry should not be set within a formal pattern but should make its own pattern as it proceeds. The language should echo a spoken idiom, never anything consciously elevated; if one word will do, two words must be unnecessary. If the individual words in any line are familiar, the sum of them together should not be. Emphasis falls away from the texture and surface of the line, to center instead on a new angle of vision, an insight from a new perspective. The aim is to step beyond current habits or prejudices by exposing them. But mere novelty is never the standard: the new angle should awaken a sense of possibility that had been absent before. Though the poem never loses contact with the weight of custom, with the inertial drag of the culture in which we stand, it aspires to enough momentum to escape that inertia by conceiving of possibilities beyond it.

These are high standards indeed, but they emerge almost spontaneously if the poet agrees that his work must turn on a moment of rigorous self-examination. The essence of oral literature, in Merwin's view, is not that it purveys traditional or customary ways of seeing, but just the opposite: it captures a moment when the assumptions we customarily inhabit fall away, and the world seems fresh and strange. Just how that new world appears is, in fact, of less consequence than the ability to undergo the renewing turn.

Several poems in the volume take that necessary turn as their subject. For example, four poems with the same title, "A Door," have been carefully arranged into a small suite. These four note a recurring theme: any one thing, if it is honored, will not have its meaning exhausted quickly. A door should be a threshold but often is not, and returning to that perception from different perspectives recalls Merwin's statement that parallelism in oral poetry is not mere repetition but a sign of infinite expansiveness (fig. 16).

The idea that a door can fail to be a threshold, is, in fact, the starting point of the fourth poem:

> What is dying all over the world
> is a door
>
> you will say That
> is a dead thing
>
> and you will be talking about the entry
> to a chamber of your heart
>
> you will say of the door
> It is a thing
>
> and you will be speaking of your heart (WUA, 34)

To reject a door that opens onto strangeness, or beckons toward a future, is to close your heart and to deny yourself. Yet such is our current inclination, fostered by the paraphernalia of our culture. The list that follows enforces Merwin's perception until, as it reaches a pitch of intensity, there is sudden relief: "and still someone touching / a silence / an opening / may hear all around us the endless home." If we could understand and live as though doors were able to open before us, as chambers of the heart, each door a threshold, then we would find ourselves in the endless home. The noise that "turns high as it approaches" is created by our self-imposed deafness. To discover the endless home depends on the way we conceive the doors: any opening that one touches creates a "silence / an opening"—in contrast to noise that simply fills space repetitively. Silence is both a relief from meaningless noise and an unknown opening, a threshold. What makes a door a dead thing is our refusal to touch it; if touched, it is transformed. One is, in fact, always at home if all doors open to one.

The climax of this four-poem sequence is the envisioning of a door as an entrance or threshold identical to a chamber of the human heart. The first poem submits that you are always carrying "on your shoulders / a glass door / to some house that's not been found." That door, though, is useless as a door: "there's no handle." It is a concentration of all the concerns, habits, assumptions in our lives, none of which we believe we can do without, that we carry about with us. The fear is that if the door were dropped, "you'd drown like water / in the pieces." The simile is pointed, for if the fear is to drown "like water," then the fear is not of drowning but of becoming lost in a fluid element, like that perceived in distorted fashion on the other side of the door beyond which "skies are marching / like water down the inside of a bell." Urgently, on that other side, just a turn away but impossibly remote as long as you "walk with your hands frozen / to your glass wings," there is this other world:

> those skies are looking for you
> they've left everything
> they want you to remember them
>
> they want to write some last phrase
> on you
> you
>
> but they keep washing off
> they need your ears
> you can't hear them (WUA, 29)

What does it mean for skies to be "looking for you," wanting to "write some last phrase / on you"? Merwin's statements threaten at the same time as they beckon, an ambiguity not to be resolved as long as ears and eyes and feet are all on the other side of the door, a useless glass wing. Separated from those skies that call but that keep "washing off" because they need your ears to be heard, you cannot understand the "dark birds" sent in search of you, "each one the last," individual and precious and never to be repeated, each one "like shadows of doors calling calling / sailing / the other way // so it sounds like good-bye." The cry may sound like good-bye, but who knows how it really sounds on the other side? The answer is left to us. Whether in fact it will happen is still open; Merwin would make us aware of just how close we are to new possibilities—possibilities that will remain infinitely remote as long as we stay on one side only.

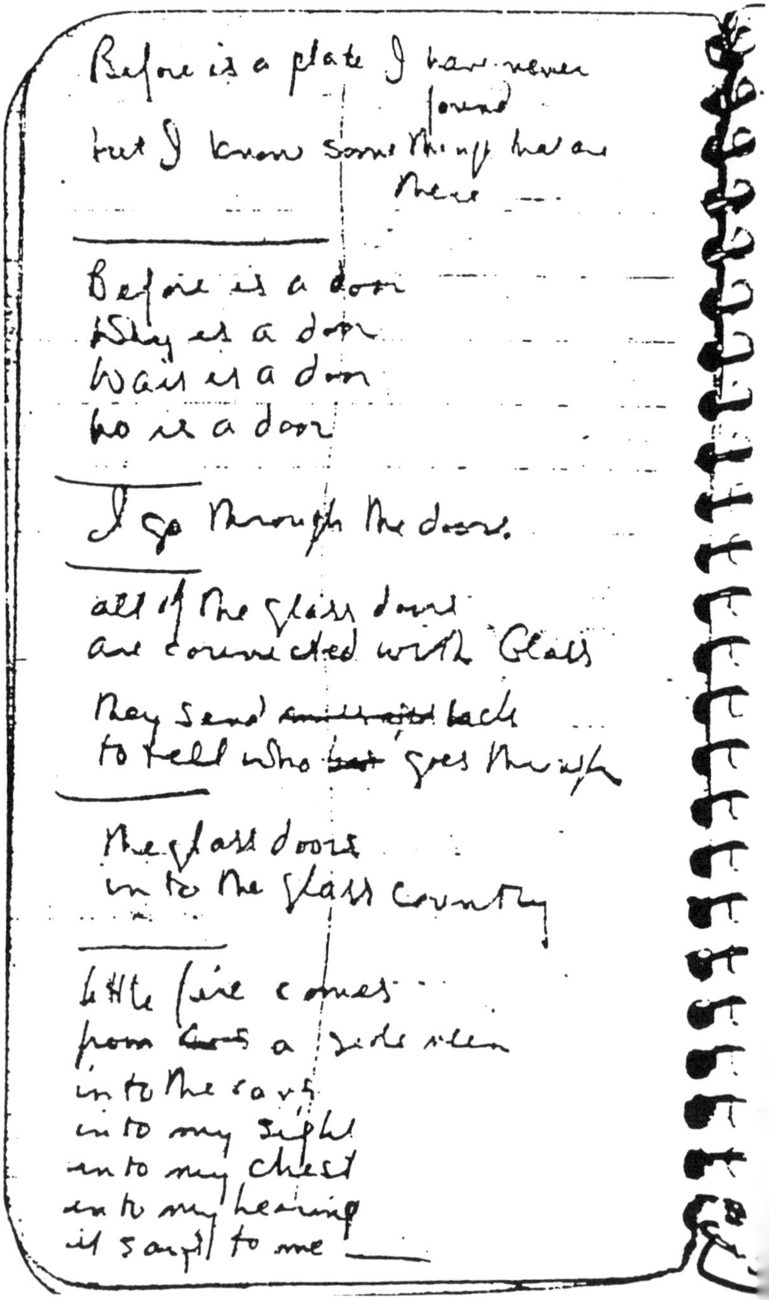

Before is a plate I have never
found
but I know something that are
there ---

Before is a door
Sky is a door
Wait is a door
Go is a door

I go through the doors.

all of the glass doors
are connected with Glass
They send ~~[illegible]~~ back
to tell who ~~but~~ goes through

The glass doors
into the glass country

Little fire comes
from ~~[illegible]~~ a side seen
into the ears
into my sight
into my chest
into my hearing
it sayd to me ___

Figure 16. Excerpt (enlarged) from a 1970–71 Notebook (20:18/001, c. 1970–71), with variations improvised on the theme of a door. The last entry on the right-hand page is the first appearance of the opening lines of "Eyes of Summer."

7 (tells/me what is outside
in the country of what part
of my body —

---

my fingers swim ahead of me
calling ~~in the~~ w/the unheard
voices
of the mating of fish

The Route — collection of myths of the
~~mouth~~

~~Once darkness~~
The darkness is a door
Once it was a door

---

darkness was taken out of us a long
time ago and hung far away from
us
we keep — (feeling the amputation)

but the light ~~still~~ is still going from
us all the time
~~to sta~~ toward the sun

---

all the stones
were once us
and will be again

A similar lure toward possibility is the focus of the third poem, which begins: "This is a place where a door might be / here where I am standing / in the light outside all the walls." Where the speaker is standing is not yet visible; a door might be there but its existence remains uncertain. What else could be there? A shadow and a door into that shadow "where now there is me," as this poem extends and further defines itself. The poem appears, at this point, to be drifting toward darkness and obscurity. But if someone came and knocked on "this air / long after I have gone"—long after the poet has finished his work—then "there in front of me a life / would open." If someone entered the poem, turning the flatness or finality of each statement into a gesture requiring a response, then the person's life would open. It is not simply that the poet's life would open; Merwin is careful to say "in front of me a life / would open," as though the ones entering the poem would then become as open to Merwin as Merwin is to them. When an active decision is made, it does not lead one into a forbidding realm; rather, one enters a community of openness.

The second of these four poems now takes its place among the sequence. Here the door is beaten and kicked yet refuses to open, but "later it opened" effortlessly, only to reveal "nothing / starlight / snowing," an empty throne, and an unspecified "instrument" that has failed to aid in communication. This second poem is, at least in its yearning, near to being an elegy for a lost love, a confession of the poet's real fears at moving through his own doors because of his past failures. By the time the door opens with understanding he has delayed too long, and he now relives another scene, another room that he once entered to move past dancers to reach the one he desired. In that room, too, he "came in late," and now, stunned by a sense of what he failed to do earlier, aware the door has opened too late and onto a scene of loss, he finds himself unable to move, his focus on an empty chair:

> thin
> in an empty bell
> lighting that chair
>
> could I turn at all
>
> now should I kneel
>
> and no door anywhere (WUA, 32)

It is like a desolate inner chamber, perhaps of the heart, in which one should kneel with the hope of asking forgiveness, except that it is too late even for that.

As a small suite, these four poems move from discovery through doubt toward understanding and affirmation. In the first, Merwin understands the weight of his own habits, which are invisible as glass, yet which prevent him from hearing what is calling to him, all that goes unseen or unheard or misunderstood because it needs his eyes and ears to complete it. In the second, he draws back fearfully, recalling the pain of taking a step too late; the anguish in this work transforms the emblem of the door into a personal image. In the third, he recognizes a true invitation now, in the present, which can create a life, but it necessarily involves the action of another who is willing to create a threshold where at first there appears only a voice standing alone. Finally, the fourth is a direct address, asserting that the activity of touching creates its own value, a value with the strength to deny all that is rigid in a civilization grown increasingly certain that only its own ways are correct.

3

The final turn in the fourth "A Door" is crucial. If in the first poem the poet spoke only from a viewpoint that stressed how limited we are, bearing this fragile door on our backs as we walk on, then by the end of the group he has superseded that limitation, viewing the door as an analog to a chamber of the heart that will open if we understand how it may be touched. So many poems in this volume seem at first obscure, then become clear once it is understood that the very poem is enacting the transformation that is at once the subject of the poem. The poetry embodies the moment of reconception, that reabsorption from another perspective. We would understand all, he says in "The Cry,"

> so you would know
> if you were to stand in that doorway
> if you were to open the door
> if you were to find it (WUA, 85)

The poetry is clarified once we actively inhabit it; just the opposite is true if we refuse to participate: "if you were to see that window / from the outside / you would see nothing." Merwin's images are rarely esoteric, though his approach to them is always eccentric. The terms he proposes for his verse are available to all—that is the universalizing aspect of these poems—but their presentation depends precisely on the involvement of others, an involvement the poems continuously invite.

In this volume, Merwin keeps to a restricted lexicon of images because he values their accessibility. The simplicity to which he had aspired in *The Lice,* as an antidote to technical virtuosity of various kinds, asserts itself in poems that direct how they should be read. As a window is less inviting than a door because it allows only observing instead of participating, so a wall is less inviting than a window because it is opaque. "A Purgatory," which describes "a wrong moment" when the eye fails "to cast again / the light in which that landscape / was a prospect of heaven," speaks of "the house in which every word / faces a wall." When Merwin gives his "Instructions to Four Walls," he saves the wall that has a doorway in it for last, and while he has recommendations to make to the other three walls, he has none for this one except the following:

and one of you
stay still just as you are
with your door
be yesterday
be tomorrow
be today (WUA, 72)

General images like that of the door recur throughout the volume; they are not so much points of stability as they are thresholds over which we may pass into a wider understanding.

Although the collection constantly risks turning into an anthology of helpful maxims, it never quite does so because Merwin's struggle to escape from the blockage of his own assumptions is never-ending. In "To the Hand" he states that the eye "wakes to . . . a dream of sight" but that

in the dream
for every real lock
there is only one real key
and it's in some other dream
now invisible

it's the key to the one real door
it opens the water and the sky both at once
it's already in the downward river
with my hand on it
my real hand

and I am saying to the hand
turn

open the river (WUA, 66)

That advice to the hand is wrong yet inevitable. Merwin wants to convey that aspect of experience in which events never completely mesh, that sense of incompleteness that he fully understands is a fundamental limitation he must acknowledge. As the poem explains, nothing is ever quite unified. The "real hand" may be grasping "the key to the one real door" but it is turning the key in the river, as though the river could open. The phrase "and I am saying" also suggests that he repeats his advice over and over, helplessly and to no avail, sensing it is not right but unable to act otherwise. What might be the proper advice? The poem alludes to that, though only suggestively: it may be to open the hand and drop the key; with the key gone but the hand open the "one real door" may also open.

"To the Hand" is one of a number of poems in which the hand and the eye figure together as unlikely partners whose movement in tandem creates a superior tactile vision. After "The Initiate," for example, has stepped out under the stars and begun to weep, he catches his tears and juggles them:

> he sees the stars swimming up
> in his tears
> and he feels in his hands his tears
> fly trembling through the night (WUA, 105)

When the night is over, the initiate has lost his fear; he needs to take nothing "into the day," "into the light." Vision without feeling is, as in "The Cry," like observing events through a window: one is liable to see nothing. There may be, for Merwin, no higher accolade at this point than to be perennially the initiate; to be the master is to suggest a fixity and strength of purpose that is liable to be too protective.

In "Folk Art" a similar lesson occurs, but it comes home more smartly:

> Sunday the fighting-cock
> loses an eye
> a red hand-print is plastered to its face
> with a hole in it
> and it sees what the palms see from the cross
> one palm (WUA, 67)

Once again, hand and eye figure together, but this time in a context peculiar to the violence of the fighting-cock. What is remarkable about the poem is the way in which it turns inside out; it begins in arbitrary violence, which it dwells upon painfully, then suddenly transforms itself into a startlingly unified vision, the "one palm" that is the way the palms "see from the cross," as open and vulnerable, inviting yet violated. Folk art carries a truth within it but usually in a raw form that the action of this poem evokes. If we are able to see past the rawness of the violence, what we discover is not what we expect: not a one-dimensionality or the crudeness of a flattened vision as though folk art were a kind of blindness or a sign of maiming, but rather a remarkable unity that reveals an intuitive awareness. "One palm" has a finality about it. At first it seems to be only a blunt simplification and a form of blindness; but it becomes a sign of the tactility of vision, asserting that we can only truly see if we accept our vulnerability.

4

Merwin values folk art not only because of his experience as a translator of anonymous oral literature but also because of the folktales he invents for himself. From 1969 to 1972, he moves adroitly between prose and verse, completing either a handful of poems or a group of prose pieces. Under the influence of his verse, his prose begins to take on characteristics of folktales, which in turn shape qualities in his verse. The change is evident in the last third of *The Miner's Pale Children* and in the first half of *Houses and Travellers,* whose prose pieces were written concurrently with *Writings to an Unfinished Accompaniment.*[4]

Unlike their predecessors, which circled about a situation enigmatically illuminated by oddities of language, these pieces unfold as developing narratives. Several even draw toward a particular point. In "The Nest," pigeons build a nest in an upside-down umbrella, but when their offspring leave home, they are fatally disadvantaged, for on the first rainy day, when umbrellas are opened, the world seems to have been overturned. Trying to fly upside down, they fall to the ground and are devoured. Yet the flaw Merwin reveals is not tragic; it is an error that can be rectified; it has a solution, one that requires a flexibility to slip free of conceptions that appear to guide (and that may have been offered with love) but only serve to entrap. The parents in "The Nest" who are puzzled when their offspring never return believe their children had to fly a long way to find a nest absolutely identical to their home. In this dialogue, Merwin identifies the flaw: their single-minded vision is the source of error, serving to blind their offspring and to cause their death.

The developing narratives of these pieces help undermine such rigidity. The truth, as the second piece in the collection, "Nothing Began As It Is," maintains, is that everything has its own story, and all the stories contradict each other even as they remain true to their origin. Whether each thing can find or maintain its own story becomes the critical question, but it is a moral with special relevance to Merwin. For unless he can conceive of the stories that other things are telling, then he is also constrained within his single-minded perspective, however brilliantly or originally he presents it. "The land of the fugitive is all around us," he says in "The Fugitive," proceeding to describe a world where "each of these rooms is a place of concealment, judged essentially in terms of how well hidden someone would be in it." And above all, the fugitive "hates his brother, the pilgrim, who walks on the ridges and rests under the trees, dissolves the rooms and the streets, and worships the rivers." But the piece ends with the fugitive waking into the pilgrim, as though the two were only opposite sides of the same sensibility.

The Miner's Pale Children was characterized by pieces, such as "The Animal Who Eats Numbers," that operated as riddles: if we could deduce the context from which the piece emerged, then that angle of vision illuminated the whole. In *Houses and Travellers,* Merwin moves away from depicting puzzles to portraying shifts that grow out of each other as narratives. In "The First Moon" a pebble is able to roll down a road by concentrating on that part of it which feels the sun; the act of concentration constantly shifts its center of balance and so it rolls: yearning is transformed into action. The pebble's shadow, its antiself, has only an indirect connection to the sun, and so it bounces along in terror, counseling caution, pleading with the pebble to stop. When night falls, the pebble halts, and the shadow immediately falls asleep; but by now the pebble has set its sights higher—it would turn into an eye, and at that thought, the first moon rises. Unlike "The Animal Who Eats Numbers," in which the momentum of the narrative is generated by the addition of information that fills out the context and allows the reader to draw nearer to appreciating it, in "The First Moon" the narrative generates its own momentum by changing from within: it is a parable that assures that support will be forthcoming if one continues to exert oneself. The pebble's shadow too timidly offers misguided advice. The shadow would merge into the darkness and the sleep of night. But when the pebble articulates its desire, then at once, as though a hand were being extended, the moon rises and the night is dispelled.

These later prose pieces, like their verse counterparts, swarm with transformations. Nothing began as it is—that is the unchanging truth. As a result, there is another side to everything, and Merwin delights in attempting to see it. In "The Footstep" noon is a moment of pure stasis, when all stands still: "The animals move into the shade of the trees, and watch, hardly breathing. The birds find a little darkness, and pause. A film like dust veils the shining leaves. In the unlit hives the bees dance more slowly and come to a stop. Silence leaks into the dream of the bats. The breeze dies. You shiver. He strikes. He is there" (HT, 34). But there is always a "but" close at hand, and just as noon fails to last more than a moment, so the piece continues forward: "But he is also one of the angels of turning, and we turn, and the air springs up again, and the day goes on, leaving behind it one more empty footstep, the place and the mark of no one."

In his earlier prose pieces, which mocked our vain pretense to impose control on eventful changes, Merwin focused on our weakness, our urge to trim and shape matters according to our own beliefs. These pieces focus instead on how much still lies before us. In "A Conversation" the garden and the wilderness endlessly converse with each other, each taking the measure of itself by contrast with the other, and Merwin presents this conversation as an endless continuum, beginning on the day of his birth. In "The Devil's Pig" the characteristics of the pig are in constant flux, and the pig slides adroitly in and out of a variety of situations. In "Martin" everything changes entirely if a single detail is altered. Quite unlike the earlier prose pieces that insisted upon reminding us of those inescapable truths that the culture seemed bent upon denying or evading, these pieces overwhelm us with networks of abundance and density.

5

Merwin's prose is his verse presented from one of those other perspectives that his verse is always urging us to adopt. And although Merwin has spoken of the differences between verse and prose as though they should be irrelevant, only a handful of examples exist in which a piece originally drafted in verse was changed into prose (fig. 17), and no examples remain of a piece drafted in prose then turned into verse.[5] In his verse, Merwin aims to write a wisdom literature; dealing in broad terms, he would discern a value or extract an insight, taking pride in his general language, in his economy of means. In his prose, he is writing a contemporary equivalent of the picaresque adventure; he expands a narrative to see how far it can go. To the prose, the verse is a key: the wisdom the verse uncovers is needed to appreciate the prose. To the verse, the prose is a test: the extensions the prose undertakes are the very material the verse must take into account. Prose and verse that follow closely on each other, literally written as companions, offer especially compelling examples of this interaction.[6]

In "The Bride of the East" a girl falls in love with the East. Every objection raised by her father only deepens her commitment to this impossible union, until she insists she is already married to the East. Her father responds by ordering her window covered with brick. Her position never changes; for years she remains at the window, long past the death of her father, beyond sieges laid to the city, until all but the bricked-in window has collapsed ("not a single brick had fallen, because scar tissue holds longer than the original"), and even after that has fallen. In a disjunctive turn, Merwin then reveals that you feel one of "her withered arms . . . occasionally on your arm"; she is blind, yet as she searches for that fallen brick wall beyond which the East lies, she leads you "to an unlit doorway" where a scorpion and a worm converse. They agree that they are fortunate to have no bones, but the scorpion thinks the worm should have eyes:

> "What would I want with eyes?"
> "You'd see."
> "Who needs to see?"
> "The bride of the East."
> "What for? Only the East can pass through this door and live."
> But you are not the East. You are subject to every wind that blows. And as you turn to tell her, she is not there (HT, 32).

This seems hopelessly enigmatic. Why two talking creatures? Why these addresses to "you" at the end? Why would a girl fall in love with the East?

Two days after "The Bride of the East" was completed, Merwin produced "The Day," a piece of verse as lucid as the prose was obscure:

> If you could take the day by the hand
> even now and say Come Father
> calling it by your own name
> it might rise in its blindness with all

its knuckles and curtains
and open the eyes it was born with (WUA, 14)

Features in "The Day" recall "The Bride of the East." Not a direct answer to the enigmas of the prose, the poem nonetheless comments on them. For the enigmas stem from misguided action, and if the tale grows progressively more distorted, it is because its characters set matters awry from the start. If the girl had been able to heed the wisdom in "The Day," then her story would never have taken place. The poem avows the forcefulness of empathetic action: by giving the day your name, you father it, and it flourishes. Neither father nor daughter in the story comprehends that truth. The bride is waiting for the East to arrive, never extending herself to the East, or to anyone. She brusquely rejects her father's inquiries, thereby hardening his position. As rigidity escalates, it proves enduring, like the scar tissue stronger than original skin. As the story maintains, traversing decades and then ages, the effects of a disagreement long outlast the original point of contention. The daughter, by the end, is no longer waiting for her true love but searching for the brick wall beyond which her true love is supposed to be. Lowly life-forms like the worm and the scorpion have the final word. They scorn bones because everything in the tale warns against fixity or firmness of any kind; eyes, however, may be valuable (as the scorpion suggests), but only if they are open and used (as the worm responds). And you, at the end of the tale, should be left grateful that "you are subject to every wind that blows" rather than stubbornly blind, devoted to one idea above all.

Merwin's prose and verse mirror each other. Sometimes they exchange roles. "The Vision," a prose piece, offers wisdom in a few succinct words, and "Foreword," a poem, tells a specific story. But for the most part, one learns in the poetry lessons that guide one through the prose, at the same time as the adventures unraveled in the prose call for the wisdom distilled in the verse.

"Brothers" tells of a man from the town of Lode who sets out to see his brothers in the war-torn town of Simburad, in a region whose language he cannot speak. The path he follows leads him to a swollen river, where he spots the distant figure of a man who suddenly grabs the body of a creature floating in the stream; the man then "drew a long knife, and cut a piece off the animal and began to eat it, just as it was." Unnerved by this barbarity, frustrated by the floodwaters, and frightened by something he sees in the man's face, the man from Lode decides to turn back. Walking back, he meets another man heading toward Simburad. Their brief attempts at conversation fail because each is ignorant of the other's language, but the first man realizes this second man will have the mistaken impression that he has come from Simburad, and he attempts to explain, by gesture and pantomime, what he has seen at the river, "though even as he described it he could not explain to himself why he had

Milk Spell

A fly may be waiting for the milk every day.
Then the milk changes but is it the same fly.
The milk that it's drunk turned into the same fly
and from then on it's the same.
so the milk changes
So the same hand puts a big white stone
in the same place.
The fly wants to fly away
after drinking the white stone
but it isn't a fly any more
doesn't have the soul of a fly
It's a stone with no color
* small dry stone in a desert
from then on with sand children
children who are not even children
even when they fall into milk they don't know it.
From then on there is no fly
and the milk stays the same

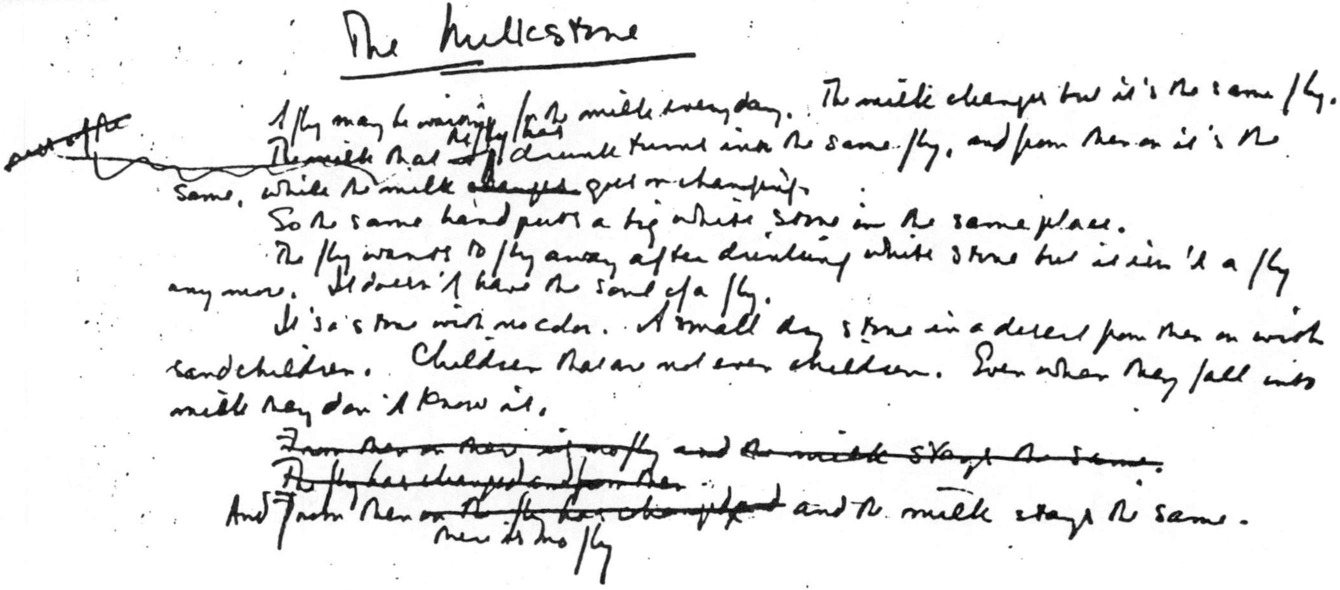

Figure 17. "The Fly and the Milk" (published in *Houses and Travellers,* p. 37) in its verse and prose versions, both written on the same day (MS. 21:13/025b,025c, d. Mar. 20, 1971).

hidden." The more he struggles to explain, the more bewildered the other becomes, until he breaks away in fear. Ultimately, the second man arrives at the river where he has the same experience as the first; he too is frightened by the appearance of the man by the stream. Like the man from Lode, the second man decides to turn back, at which point "it occurred to him that all this may have been what the man from Lode had been trying to tell him. He wondered whether he would ever see the man from Lode again, and whether he would recognize the man if he found him, and whether they would be able to tell each other anything" (HT, 91). The brothers in the story are, of course, the two men, identical in so many ways: both journeying to Simburad, both frightened by the same apparition, both turned away from their goal.

However, a poem completed just before "Brothers," "The Diggers," raises a set of questions that deepen the implications of the prose. The poem begins with an image that multiplies: one man with a shovel coming down a road turns into two men with shovels, then eight men, then seventeen men. As you see a stranger coming toward you on the road, your fear expands and multiplies as though you were no longer in command of yourself but responding as though one man were turning into many. Your first impulse is to wish everything were transparent, including yourself—to become invisible, that is, rather than greeting the man who, as he grows nearer, turns into two then eight then seventeen. By withholding any outgoing gesture, you only see the stranger as multiplying. That impulse to deny the event by wishing one were invisible results in only a momentary sense of protection that instantly gives way to an awareness of one's own withdrawal:

> yes that is what I would say but I would feel myself
> then like my hand in front of my eyes
> like this hand just as it is
> in front of my eyes (WUA, 50)

Withdrawn, one becomes all the more obvious, and the pausing and speculating here is not just to call attention to obvious failure but to stress that a hand is not for hiding behind but for opening. The proper response is to take down the hand, and to leave it open: "and I would try to take it down / before they saw through it and found me." The proper response, of course, is to be open to what is strange instead of multiplying fear by avoiding the strange.

"The Diggers" refocuses the meaning of "Brothers." By affirming the value, as well as acknowledging the difficulty, of opening one's hand to what is strange, it reveals that the two men in "Brothers" also share one other characteristic; a further question (that Merwin poses in his title) never occurs to either of them: Is the man by the stream also their brother? Both men make their decisions based on hasty, distant observations. The stranger is constructing something by the stream, though the "man from Lode could not tell whether the sticks were a shelter, the beginning of a bridge, or the materials for a raft or a fire." The second man confirms that the stranger is still active: he is "gathering sticks and bodies of animals." Why should this purposeful activity seem so fearful? For one thing, neither traveler is himself engaged in menial work; the two men can even afford, for example, to give up their ambition to reach Simburad. It never occurs to either that the stranger could be desperately at work to reach Simburad, and what may be frightening to both men in his face may be his determination. Merwin's poem, by speaking abstractly about the experience of fear that arises spontaneously when a stranger is seen, deepens the encounters in his prose piece. The lost connection noted by the second man at the end, wondering if he will ever meet the man from Lode again, is a superficial version of the deeper lost connection unknowingly shared by the second man and the man from Lode.

Merwin's prose and verse animate each other. Like a picaresque novel, Merwin's prose pieces unfold with apparent abandon, as though each sentence has been produced before the one preceding it was understood. Like wisdom literature, the verse seeks to crystallize an insight that reveals a principle that can be applied to the apparent disorder of the prose. But ultimately, such linkings are to be appreciated for their ability to remind us of the extraordinary diversity, the bountiful possibility, that surrounds us. We seem inclined to do all we can to escape this awareness, to wall ourselves up in authoritative categories that limit rather than extend understanding. By insisting there is always another angle from which to see, Merwin compels us to examine obstacles we erect with our assumptions. In every case, a barrier, from another perspective, may become a threshold.

PART THREE

Chronicles

12

In the Chambers of the Heart

"THE HEART" stands like a barrier before the entrance to *The Compass Flower,* proposing that we cross several thresholds, each more mysterious than the one before, until we reach the last:

> In the last chamber of the heart
> all the words are hanging
> but one
> the blood is naked as it steps through the door
> with its eyes open
> and a bathing bird in its hands
> and with its bare feet on the sill
> moving as though on water
> to the one stroke of the bell
> someone is ringing without hands (CF, 3)

In one sense, the poem is no more than its narrative, a staging of advances toward the "last chamber": as we continue, the activity of the hands, a bird, a bell rope, water, and one of the five senses increases. In another sense, the significance of these objects escapes understanding. Why these? As it proceeds openly, yet with images that remain enigmatic, "The Heart" displays features combined throughout *The Compass Flower,* a collection that will lead us deep into the heart's chambers, even as the precise meaning of what we find remains hidden.

Rather than judging *The Compass Flower,* as most critics have, as the anticlimactic ending to Merwin's exploratory free verse, it is more accurate to see it as a decisive break in his development, the earliest stage in what will eventually become his family writings, the memoirs in *Unframed Originals* and the poems in the first section of *Opening the Hand.*[1] Two occurrences caused an indelible change in Merwin's writing—the death of his father in June 1972, and that of his mother in September 1972. For the poetry of wisdom he had been so carefully cultivating through his open forms is simply inadequate to either. That it should be inadequate is proper, for the formulaic drive in the late free verse, which converts closure into process, is based on a courage to move ahead even when one may be leaving behind what is close and familiar. But no impulse could be less appropriate to mourning. Now when Merwin considers taking action he is liable to follow the path in "A Contemporary," in which he imagines taking root rather than taking wing.

Quite the opposite of "The Dwelling," the opening piece in *The Miner's Pale Children,* in which the poet set out to enter a new world, this poetry views what has always been around him but what he had never noticed. Rather than slipping free of his assumptions, Merwin is now intent upon recognizing and understanding them. "There she is / where she has been all my life / the moon in mist" was a three-line poem once included in the original typescript of the volume.[2] That awakening is the poet's response to the abrupt absence of those close to him; by acknowledging aspects that had escaped his awareness, he pays homage to others whose absence goes unnamed. But his response is particularly indirect: writing of a bucolic love affair or defining the emptiness at the center of the modern city may incorporate into his work elements from his own life that he had previously excluded, but it does not address those whose absences are most sharply felt.

Although these poems appear to be the most straightforward of any by Merwin, they are in many ways the most indirect. As open as they seem, much in them remains hidden. Merwin offers invitations to enter his inner life; yet at the same time, his poetry suggests how much he values living outwardly, in the moment. On the one hand, the poems center on details of Merwin's daily life; on the other hand, they remain guarded about every disclosure. In "St. Vincent's," he includes himself in the poem from the start, confessing he has "lived daily and with / eyes open and ears to hear / these years across from St Vincent's Hospital." But when he opens his eyes and ears, he recognizes only the conglomerate of unrelated details surrounding the building. Even its facade remains intact.

As in "St. Vincent's," Merwin is ready in other poems to acknowledge much he has not previously noticed. Once specifics appear, however, the poems are quick to end, as though it were enough for them to refer to an actual event. Because of this, an air of uncertainty about how next to proceed often surrounds them. Speculating in "St. Vincent's," it seems natural to imagine the hospital's interior life—even to contrast the businesslike and almost banal interchanges on its outside with the dramas of life and death within. Such a passage existed in an early draft but did not survive later revisions.[3] Its cancellation suggests something of Merwin's uncertainty about disclosing an interior drama. At the same time, he is gravitating toward that drama. When he ends his poem by asking, "Who was St Vincent," another question also can be heard: Who was W. S. Merwin? Did he leave behind a monument over which someone else would someday pause and question whether his life had yet begun?

1

The most striking feature of the poetry Merwin writes after 1972 is how often it might be read as prose. The distinction between prose and verse had already grown tenuous in the give-and-take between *Writings to an Unfinished Accompaniment* and *Houses and Travellers,* but the poetry in *The Compass Flower* often trespasses into territory, such as the chronicle or the memoir, that is typically the province of prose. But the effect can be more disconcerting than illuminating, more blinding than revealing, as though Merwin drew upon the least useful element in the other medium. His poetry includes specifics that cry out for additional explanation; his prose presents details as though they were illuminations in themselves.

Just how radically new is this new poetry? The lines in *Writings to an Unfinished Accompaniment* lifted themselves free of a historical environment; events described could as easily have happened 300 years ago as today: birds sing at dawn, travelers set out on a path, boats enter a harbor. But *The Compass Flower* announces its contemporary setting. In "Junction" two men pass by "carrying loud radio playing music." In "The Next Moon" the last words he had heard from his mother were "even then on the phone." The paraphernalia of contemporary life is most evident in the city poems of part 2, which include "Those waiting in line / for a cash register at a supermarket," but even the bucolic love poems of part 3 have

> Wire trees
> days with telephones
> pronouncing into black lamps
> trying to get them to light (CF, 55)

Merwin abandons the belief that the poem should unfold in a timeless realm. Actively, he locates himself in a particular setting.

He also diminishes the extent to which he governs the course of his poem. His open-form verses commanded renewal by finding a way beyond habitual modes. Without the guidance of punctuation, the poetry defined itself surprisingly as it went along. By contrast, "Crossing Place" offers no such momentum:

I crossed the stream
on the rocks
in the summer
evening
trying not to spill
the pitcher of water
from the falls (CF, 42)

The signature of this poetry is the line devoted to the prepositional phrase. Just as the figure negotiating the crossing place must, in a manner at once anxious and delicate, decide his next step, so the lines duplicate that cautious interplay between figure and setting. The poetry, that is, continually embodies such awkward positions, midway between verse and prose, between lines that have been shaped and lines that seem shapeless, in a crossing place.

Activity in these poems depends upon the figure of the narrator accommodating himself to a setting that may require awkward steps. He appears in ways that are muted or particularly discreet. He even withholds signals that might serve to communicate his progress through the poem. In his two earlier books, Merwin deployed the stanza break as an especially active line break, a unit that signaled a distinct shift. Implying disjuncture, the stanza break could indicate either genuine progress or a new impediment. Of the ninety-six poems in *Writings to an Unfinished Accompaniment,* all but twenty-two employed the stanza break (and those unbroken were often a few lines in length). But over two-thirds of the poems in *The Compass Flower* unfold in one unbroken set of lines, with no stanzas. Dramatic turns are not just downplayed but discouraged. Even when making a significant change, Merwin never underscores it: he is more immersed in the occasion and less its master, steering his way through by acknowledgment and adjustment.

Finally, each poem connects with adjacent works. Yet in keeping with the narrator's inclination to withhold signals, it is unclear whether we should read the four sections of the volume as stages in an unfolding narrative or as four separate perspectives on the poet. The four sections can portray aspects of Merwin in different environments. Returning to scenes from his childhood in part 1, he is the son struggling to accept the deaths of his parents. He is the anonymous urban dweller in part 2. In part 3, in rural France, he is the bucolic swain, the impassioned lover. And in part 4, with its glimpses of scenes from a variety of places, he is the restless vagabond.

Yet such a grouping is too static, too disengaged from the disruptive events that occur, if fleetingly, in the opening poems. These four sections also ask to be taken as stages in a narrative that moves from mourning through acceptance to renewal and rejuvenation. At the center of this narrative is the poet struggling to get beyond the despair brought by the unexpected death of his parents. That loss, as well as Merwin's reaction to it, is set forward in part 1, in poems of open grief, such as "Apples," or in poems in which he would escape the black clouds that surround him, as in "A Contemporary." Part 2, which is composed of city poems, offers both a background that confirms his despair and a space in which he alone can take his mourning into himself. The healing process, postponed in the city, is undertaken in part 3, which pivots on the longest poem in the book, "Kore," a work that links the poems on either side of it. Here, Merwin rediscovers the simplicity of the natural world, a simplicity that deepens when he shares it with a new love. (In this respect, *Finding the Islands* [1982], a work written in 1975–77 and 1980–81, is an extended coda to part 3.) Part 4 represents his recovery, his return to various moments from his past. As a whole, then, the volume strives to arch from loss to recovery, the bridge taken up by the nadir of the city poems and the zenith of the love poems, in which vitality is regained.

2

Merwin's poetry in memory of his parents is intensely private—so private, indeed, that reviewers and critics have discussed this volume with no inkling that it has an origin in profound grief.[4] Yet Merwin's intent is not to grieve over his loss but to bear it with grace. In the days that immediately followed his father's death in June, he worked on an extended sequence in memory of him.[5] The seven-part, 101-line, untitled and undated poem is not a conventional elegy. As though he could at last speak freely to his father, Merwin writes in a way both conciliatory and confrontational:

> Forty days now you have walked in the desert
> without your feet
> but they were never much use to you
> those two white fish cast up and swollen
> staying with you it seemed even
> against your will

In recognizing his father's discomfort with his body, his disavowal of the pleasures of sight, sound, and touch, Merwin is reaching for a consolation that rests upon his opportunity to speak openly of differences between himself and his father. "It is certain now that your ears were never / to be for me," he says at the opening of another section, then adds:

> only now that you have gone may we begin
> to listen to each other
> in the same tense of the verb
> and questions rise that can be asked only now
> that you have no ears to hear
> Saturday the thirty eighth day
> if we loved each other in what did it consist

> in what does it consist
> it is even time to begin to ask who were you
> father
> who were you

From his loss he would extract an understanding greater than had been possible before, even as he accepts it as coming too late, "now / that you have no ears to hear."

The last of the sections completed presents the act of conception as a diagram sketched "on a school black board":

> while in a clear voice it was explained
> though I missed the beginning
> that the small shining cloud flying
> slowly along the tunnel
> was from the father
> that looked so fearful shy hesitant smiling
> scarcely visible
> hearing remorse yet dancing with affrighted joy

It is peculiar to have this moment of deepest intimacy between his parents represented through this framework of instruction; yet it evokes both the distance between his parents and his own wish to overcome that distance, to invest the "cloud" with gentle emotions, "so fearful shy hesitant smiling"—as though the distance had been all along a matter of modesty. What must his parents have felt, at one time, to have conceived him? But the crucial figure in this final section is the person implicitly present from the start. As the diagram is sketched, Merwin is accompanied by "a small round woman watching whom the knife opened / to bear her children her nerves every one awake / who knows it from of old and who loves me." What makes Merwin's elegy to his father genuinely consoling is that it is also addressed to one who still has the ears to hear it, who can appreciate his effort to speak across the void, his willingness to conciliate. As much as this is a poem to his father, it is also a poem to his mother. It may have been interrupted, impossible to resume, after the loss of that other person who deeply needed to hear these words spoken.

Merwin's poems in memory of his mother also address one who is no longer there; but now there is truly no one to overhear him. Unlike the lengthy, multisectioned elegy to his father, these poems are brief, sharp, etched, anguished. And they simply do not let go, as in "An Old Waiting," an unpublished poem that begins:

> To have been so near to each other
> and find that the hands are air
> that is how it is
>
> and why it is all still to be said

and why I am still sitting with you
alone by the prow of the boat
do you remember
and we are waiting
nobody knows how much younger we are
I have not yet even been born[6]

This second death, this additional irrevocable loss so hard upon the first, appears in its stunning finality here, as though his mother's absence now entirely undoes him. "The Pocket Diary" simply notes the gulf that has opened in just a few months:

In June I looked at the calendar for September
thinking of you being there like the days
now it is October
and turning to the calendar and seeing
how long you are not there
I forget what number this is[7]

Grieving for one loss is difficult enough; grieving for a double loss is almost unbearable, especially when cultural taboos discourage expressions of grief. "The Drive Home" is an almost perfect poem about the barriers we erect, albeit politely, thoughtfully, around those who have suffered an irreversible loss. Confessing that he was always afraid "of the time I would arrive home / and be met by a special car" he immediately adds, "but this wasn't like that / they were so nice the young couple." And the poem continues in that bland vein, as

they sat in their back
having a good time
and they laughed with their collars up
then we all laughed
we wondered if anyone would notice
we talked of getting an inflatable
driver
to drive us for nothing through the autumn leaves (CF, 6)

Mourning is not to be countenanced, even as Merwin's grief is exacerbated by the young couple's decision not to stray outside the bounds of sociable discourse. No one is driving, of course, because no one has taken charge, for the couple has decided to pretend the occasion does not exist. The "inflatable / driver" also suggests just what the value of a human being is, in this unbearable context, and the intent of having such an entity lead them all on a drive "for nothing through the autumn leaves" suggests that nothing of worth is available in this situation, only a desire to get away free and clean.

Outright expressions of grief never emerge. The poems written after these remain intensely private.[8] "The Next Moon" (originally entitled "The Second

Moon of Mourning") recognizes that a month has passed since "the last ear on earth / heard your voice," and though Merwin knows how that absent voice would advise rest, "for a month I have heard nothing." He may know the voice but he cannot hear it. "The Snow" is less anguished; he must turn, he realizes, as though roles had been reversed: "after you were unborn it was my turn / to carry you in a world before me / trying to imagine you." Yet both poems emphasize stasis. A month has passed with no change except a deepening loss, and at the beginning of winter the falling snow dominates the "green wheated hill" in a remote past of springtime.

"The Arrival," by contrast, is all motion, a series of journeys in the company of a parent. What Merwin seeks is confirmation that the sharp division between the voyages across water, in which he is "young together" again with his parent, and the pilgrimage up "over the leafless mountain / in the blood red evening," in which he embarks upon things entirely new, can be healed. For there is a further journey before the child, toward "meadows of loose horses / that I will ride in the dark to come." This last image is purposely ambiguous, both fearful and exhilarating—the future without the company of the parent, a "dark to come" in which he will be an adult. Whether there can be the continuity expressed in the poem, between the joy of the past and the difficult moment of the present and the uncertainty of the future, is the anxiety Merwin is both acknowledging and attempting to overcome.

Although Merwin applies words of consolation, telling himself that life is subject to abrupt shifts, that "we are words on a journey / not the inscriptions of settled people" (in "An Encampment at Morning"), or recommending that he should leave behind the dark clouds of the mountain and live as freely and innocently as "one blade of grass" (in "A Contemporary"), these poems are offset by others with a darker texture. "Robin," the retelling of a creation myth, offers itself for comparison with the free verse that preceded it. But this time the poem ends darkly, without consolation:

> when the world he knew was utterly destroyed
> many worlds before ours
> and he invented the day
> for a new reason
> and again we survived
> we survivors
> without knowing why (CF, 22)

The difference between this poem and previous free verse is that "Robin" is painfully and intimately related to Merwin's specific situation; like the robin's, his world has been destroyed. At the same time, the "new reason" cannot be understood; who can know why it is possible to survive? He is left as we all are, as a survivor "without knowing why."

3

The process of healing begins with the city poems of the next section and continues in the love poetry of the third section. But it is more accurate to consider the city poems as a pause and a respite, a change of scenery and a distraction. The relief the city offers is little more than a cloak of anonymity. Wordsworth was awestruck by the city at dawn seen from afar in "Composed upon Westminster Bridge." Merwin's updated version in "City" ends by observing that with "all the traffic lights dark" there is "never such temptation to drive too fast." This trivializes a moment of hushed stillness, even as it discloses what the city values above all: rapid transit.

But the problem with valuing speed, as is recognized in "Numbered Apartment," is that what passes with the greatest speed is just what one wishes to hold on to, and once it has passed it is as remote as the day of one's birth. In this poem, nothing turns out to be "here," as in this passage where Merwin appears to be only fussily correcting himself but is actually evoking distances that are opening before him:

> I
> was born here one William
> on the last day of one September . . .
> and though I say
> here
> I know it was not
> for even at that time it was
> ninety-nine streets to the north by the river (CF, 32)

Everything close is also remote; speed has been institutionalized—except that it is the enemy:

> the whole country has changed
> means of travel accelerated
> signs almost totally replaced traffic re-routed every
> love altered
> the stamps re-issued and
> smells of streets and apples
> moved on (CF, 33)

What continue to return in this context where things of the greatest value vanish ("and parents gone as though at once") are rubber bands, the most trivial of items, capable of flexing in any direction.

Merwin's presentations of the city have to do with entering it or navigating through it.[9] Transportation and exchange, noticed throughout "St. Vincent's," draw attention away from realities inside the hospital. Indeed, the city always directs attention elsewhere, designed as it is to expedite rapid movement, and actively discourages close attention to itself. St. Vincent's Hospital is like the "sirens' howling near through traffic," of which he can only say: "I learned not to hear them." The final version of this poem remarkably declines every gambit that could solicit projective empathy. A montage of random memories, it falls into questions about operating a hospital because all that can be observed are the technicians of the hospital or the city—nurses, deliverymen, firemen who arrive to extinguish a fire, police—or patients who appear only as "faces staring from above / crutches or tubular clamps" and "turtling wheel-chairs." The descriptions catch odd moments; they are just peculiar enough to justify a second look yet bland enough to warrant no more: "hot dogs were handed over at the curb / in the middle of afternoon / mustard ketchup onions and relish." Not a meal but an exchange with a vendor, an impersonal handing-over, at an odd hour—then the food dissolves into its accessories, like the hospital dissolving into the technicians that come and go, bees moving around a sill.

Nothing gets known in the city. Attempts to focus end with details raying out, like the nurses leaving after their shift, into arterial streets. Asking where the "hours of a city begin and end" (in "The Counting Houses") leads only to speculation about

> how many hands of timepieces
> must be counting the hours
> clicking at a given moment
> numbering insects into machines to be codified (CF, 29)

When day turns into night, the divisions the city endlessly propagates grow blurred—except that another feature of these poems is their tendency to shift abruptly from day to night, from sleep to wakefulness. "By day we pace the many decks / of the stone boat / and at night we are turned out in its high windows / like stars of another side," Merwin writes in "The Estuary." The helmsman of the day and the helmsman of the night never meet, and each knows of the other only through "rumors of resemblances"; if the two could be one, instead of just calling out as they "pass the same places the sunrise / and the sunset," then there might be a better chance of imagining "becoming one anything / once"—a statement purposely left abstract because it seems so remote.

Nothing could be a more complete contrast to the urban poetry of part 2 than the bucolic love poetry of part 3, which emerges from within the wintry setting of a city:

> and the sun as it sets through the forest of windows
> unrolls slowly its
> unrepeatable secret
> all the colors of autumn without the leaves (CF, 49)

But the sequence of events described in "Kore" can only unfold outside the disjunctions of the city, in a natural environment that sets a slower pace. The city, with its abrupt shifts, only serves to recall the abruptness with which lives can be taken away; the country, which unfolds along the cyclical turn of the seasons, establishes a wider horizon in which thoughts can recompose themselves.

Part 3 establishes its own narrative of rejuvenation, a subnarrative within the overall progression of *The Compass Flower.* Following the seasons, it opens one summer and closes the next July, a record of a year.[10] The section begins as Merwin describes with wistful pleasure a bucolic landscape of late summer and early autumn; in nature, he recognizes with delight, there can be a second flowering, a return of what seemed to have passed. "Kore" then introduces an actual person who can be associated directly with the natural landscape. The final poems of spring and summer present this other person as inseparable from the surroundings that she and the speaker share. Her presence embodies the second flowering Merwin had noted at the opening. Contrast "Working into Autumn," a pre-"Kore" poem in which details simply jostle against one another—

> Daylight clears after rain to show cool morning
> pools in the stones echo birds' water-songs
> new growth is washed on tall trees before the leaves turn
> hens stray across empty pastures jays ignore them (CF, 45)

—with the transparent simplicities of "June Rain":

> The rain of the white valley the clear rain
> the rain holding the whole valley while it falls
> the mountain rain the high rain onto the mountain
> as it rained on the mountain on the night we met
> the many days' rain shadowless rain (CF, 69)

"June Rain" works as gently as the rain. Feelings toward his beloved permeate the speaker's perceptions, and there is simply no need for the orderly progression of events that syntax usually marshals.

"Kore" is the transition between the sorrow of autumn and the joy of summer. Opening in a wintry city with nostalgia for moments in the country, its first recollections are just vague enough to suggest that the poet could be writing generically, remembering a "you" that is a deity, an invisible spirit that personifies Nature herself: "I walk a little ahead of myself touching / the light air where nobody sees you." But by the end of the poem, it is apparent that he is addressing an actual person who has transformed the poem: "you step to me through the rust / you step to me through the city of amber / under the moon and the sun." She has not only transformed the poem, she has been generated in the course of it, as though a deity had been incarnated through the writing. Organizing the generative growth of the sequence are variations on "all the colors of autumn" that recur in the gold, bronze, red, and amber colors that offset darkness: "The candles flutter on the stairs of your voice / gold in the dark"; "in your eyes the bronze ferns older than seeing / unfurling above the dark springs"; "We came to the red stone / that they call black in that country / because it fell out of the night"; "I burned up all the matches in the night / to look at you."

Part 3, as a narrative of renewal, confirms the promise of a second flowering touched upon longingly in the autumn poems that precede "Kore." These poems, which often appear to be little more than descriptive jottings or casual impressions, actually bear forward the grief never fully expressed in part 1. Or more accurately, they are the point at which grief is converted into mourning, for the second flowering of autumn is a wistful pleasure at best; it mingles return with loss and commemorates the transitory aspect of existence. This brief blooming is a fragile gift, haunted by death:

> the long grass lies pointing uphill
> even in death for a reason
> that none of us knows
> and the wren laughs in the early shade now
> come again shining glance in your good time (CF, 47)

The grass may be prone but it is still pointing, like a last message or a signal that outlives its messenger. But autumn is also healing because its losses mingle with the promise of return. The wren's laughter within the early shade is a reminder that, in its own good time, the "shining glance" will be back.

These autumnal poems of second flowering mix life with death. They are the moments of consolation Merwin has been yearning for. "Memory of Summer Facing West" hovers around the idea of a ripening that is both fulfillment and loss, and the ending to "Autumn Evening" defines the season as a second birth:

> half the bronze leaves still hold to the walnut trees
> marjoram joy of the mountain flowers again
> even in the light frosts of these nights
> and there are mushrooms though the moon is new
> and though shadows whiten on the grass before morning
> and cowbells sound in the dusk from winter pastures (CF, 48)

The weighty series of phrases added at the end nicely unbalances the poem; the phrases seem like hurried afterthoughts, as though the gathering dusk and winter pastures were drawing near. Without these qualifiers, "marjoram joy of the mountain flowers again" would seem too celebratory; it is not, however, because everything that still clings or flowers again is living out that precious and transitory moment that the poem portrays.

4

Between writing the autumn poems and the spring poems of part 3—a transition represented in *The Compass Flower* by "Kore"—Merwin composed one of his longest works in prose, "Aspects of a Mountain." This gentle reminiscence of two pilgrimages to Mt. Athos, the peninsula on the coast of Greece that has been the site of monasteries since the Middle Ages, was written in the winter of 1973–74, as the chronicle of a week between October 2 and 10, 1973, and it permits the recall of a previous visit in September 1972. The piece is deliberately not prepossessing; yet in the context of Merwin's overall development, its unassuming set of impressions represents one further stage in his recovery from grief. Later, in the final chapter in *Unframed Originals,* this same journey will be directly associated with thoughts of his mother.

In 1974, though, Merwin is more intent on getting outside of his own thoughts than on turning inward. He is determined that this piece be a correct, almost fastidious chronicle of the events of his week. And perhaps its most surprising aspect is the apparent absence of any concentrated attention on the works of art of Mt. Athos. From Robert Byron's irreverent *The Station* (1928) to Ralph Harper's meditative *Journey from Paradise: Mt. Athos and the Interior Life* (1988), the perennial reason for visiting Mt. Athos has been to view its celebrated frescoes and icons. From the outset, though, Merwin's descriptions, rather than singling out specific works of art, are more likely to orient us toward the works' physical setting:

> I came to a small chapel, the old plaster walls shadowed with age, the apse toward the sea, and a porch almost as large as the chapel, at the door to the west. Stone steps up to the porch, then down inside it again to the stone floor, as though into a pool; a railing around it to the west and south, to keep the horses out, perhaps. And a wall to the north, and benches of stone, rimmed with wood, like mangers on the four sides. The afternoon light came in the eaves under the western facade, and filled the cracks in the gray unpainted boards of the door. Empty niches to either side of the doorway, and above it a third niche filled with a dim fresco of St. Nicholas and a head of Christ above him. (RM, 157)

At such a passage, an art historian might despair. The portrait of St. Nicholas is "a dim fresco" and the head of Christ is almost out of sight. For Merwin, the powerful visual event inside the chapel is the afternoon light as it fills the cracks in the door's unpainted boards. He is more concerned about getting the walls related to compass points ("to the west," "to the west and south," "to the north," "under the western facade") than about the works of art; indeed, the fresco would seem "dim" in contrast to the afternoon light filling the cracks in the "gray unpainted boards of the door."

Time after time, artistic works that might have established themselves as a focal point fade into the background that encloses them. Placed in awkward corners or out of easy view, they slide out of sight, provoking scant descriptions: "The frescoes inside the church, some of them dating from the sixteenth century, are impressive works, but the upper parts are hard to see: those in the church porch get more light. They are cruder, but the themes that are traditional in that part of the building—the Creation and the Apocalypse—lend themselves to naive treatment, which in turn benefits by the conventions of ikonographic composition. Outside, the monk said I should sign the guest book . . ." (RM, 124). This is by no means encouraging. Indeed, Merwin often inspects art casually: "When I had finished the meal, and carried my plates to the kitchen, the monk met me again and led me down to the church, to give me a chance to look at the magnificent sixteenth century frescoes there. When we came out, the monk pointed up to the massive tower . . ." (RM, 147).

Why would this tour be so cursory? Merwin reports on works of art not, it would seem, to bring them forward but to underscore the way they recede back into themselves. At one moment he starts to reproach himself for not concentrating more responsibly on the art, but what begins as a reproof turns into an insight. He is drawn up short when he realizes all his visits to libraries in different monasteries have blurred together: "Which illuminated page (the only one that could be seen, lying open under glass) of which water-colored gospel had been where? How far away had I stood from each sample offered to view and how cursory had been each glimpse of things made to be looked at again and again through whole lives" (RM, 147). If this is a reproach, Merwin bears it lightly—because it pivots toward the insight that these religious images, whether icons or murals or watercolor gospels, are not self-consciously art; as "things made to be looked at again and again through whole lives" they are not to be fixed or focused upon, but regarded from within the wholeness of one's life. In one sense, there are practical barriers to scrutinizing this "art" with care: dim light, inept restoration, the dirt of ages, the solitary one-page example turned open forever behind glass. But a barrier more difficult to overcome is that the qualities affirmed in Athos are invisible, as Merwin knows from his introductory pages that contrast the surface splendor of Venice, sinking into the sea, with the austerity of Athos, raising itself on mountains to the light.

For Merwin, this art functions inseparably with its setting; the sign that it is working effectively may be the attention it draws to the afternoon sunlight filling cracks in a gray wood door. "The scholarly purist," writes Merwin, disclosing that he has read commentaries on the art, "does not always do justice to the peculiar importance, to the great works, of their settings, including, often, the humbler, cruder patchworks of the tradition around them, and the aging buildings of which they are a part" (RM, 119–20). He goes on to describe the protagonists of the Annunciation, the angel Gabriel and the

Virgin Mary, placed so as to be separated by the arch of a church apse; their living presence within the church is evoked as much by their placement as by their figures, for they remain "silently conversing across a dark abyss lit only by a gold crucifix" (RM, 120). He points out that this composition is "repeated, with greatly differing artistry, in church after church on the mountain." These figures, composed not just in relation to each other but in relation to the building, loom forward as the painterly qualities that compose them recede. These paintings naturalize the frame that surrounds them by extending that frame outward to the building as a whole, until it is uncertain where the composition ends and where the architecture begins. Not the brilliance of the individual works of art but the vividness of their arrangement is striking; or as Merwin says, "The ikonography itself, where the art is as rich and functional as it is on Athos, is sometimes rendered with great vividness by a painting which, taken by itself, would seem neither especially gifted nor forceful" (RM, 120). The pivotal word is "functional," defined in an exemplary way, for this art gains in spirit precisely as its visibility recedes.

What catches Merwin's eye as he travels is not the art but the relationship between buildings or between everyday objects: "A marble *phiale*—a cupola over a basin for blessing holy water—facing me, was tipped towards the door of the church: the streams running down the mountain and through the courtyard had softened the ground at its base, and over the centuries it had subsided into the grass" (RM, 123). The art of Athos tends toward homely objects built with care and devotion, with the intent of enduring; only as one walks about, outside, among these things is one fully in touch with values to be revered. And one of the vows Merwin has taken on this, his second trip, is to walk. Walking, he comes alive, so much so that the high points of the narrative arrive at unexpected times, when he has left one *skete* and is en route to another:

> The path splits off, without warning, from the new sand road and the swath for the telephone poles, and in a dozen steps leads over a bank out of sight of them, to where the woods seem not to have changed for a thousand years. Trickling sounds, in the granite rubble. Flurries of cyclamens, jays diving through the trees with light folded in their wings. A robin, keeping just ahead of me, then following just behind me. The sea appearing in patches, far below, through the branches and the mist. Slate roofs and cypresses on the lower slopes. Mushrooms, smell of chestnut mould in the early morning. Mingled sound of sea and wind in autumn leaves not yet dry. Where the path straightens and starts to drop, a narrow wooden flume, on rickety stilts, keeps it company, dripping all the way. Near one of the biggest leaks, a tin can suspended for drinking from. (RM, 140–141)

It is impossible to decide whether the inward and "functional" art of Athos elicits Merwin's appreciation of this vivid natural activity or whether the teeming life of the woodlands allows him to respond so freshly to an art that must recede into invisibility in order to be appreciated. What is certain is that his descriptions of the walk between each monastery are always events both sumptuous and simple, with a full range of visual, aural, and olfactory gratifications. Each time Merwin takes on the role of a genuine pilgrim, walking from monastery to monastery, he is born anew.

Yet the pathways between monasteries are rapidly vanishing. Time and again, Merwin is met with ignorance or astonishment when he asks questions about the way from one to another. The motorway or sand road has encroached on the peninsula, and the ease with which a traveler can now attain almost any monastery has resulted in disruption, so that "the monasteries' traditional hospitality, instituted in an age of foot travel and pilgrims, has been taxed to breaking in recent years by the swelling current of tourists brought by motors, each summer" (RM, 124). The old footpaths themselves are disrupted by roadways, which usurp their prerogative; one path gives way to "mutilated swaths hacked across the slopes for telephone poles, and bright new wires humming above them," which Merwin calls "the new divine right": "Made for wheels, and the body can feel it" (RM, 129). The contrast to that "divine right" (and its echo of bureaucratic intervention in religious matters) is the delight Merwin experiences as he leaves the road to Karyes and enters a path that descends to the shore along a "shingle of white marble": "Stones, of different sizes, at intervals of surprising regularity, broken in half, and the broken surfaces, worn slightly round, the shapes of soles of human feet" (RM, 145). The path may also be described as "rich and functional," a prototype of the genuine art Athos offers to those who can see.

But far more prevalent is the deterioration or absence of the path. The most famous of the monasteries is Simopetra, perched impossibly at the tip of a narrow pinnacle, and at one time it was part of a network of paths: "It was still possible, not long ago, to cross over the mountain, on that same path, to Simopetra on the western coast, but Father Mark told me that the forest has blocked the way now" (RM, 143). When, despite warnings and offers of extra hospitality, Merwin persists, as he has from the start of this second trip, in staying on the paths, he tends to receive extraordinarily detailed instructions, as these from an "old monk" who knew the way: "I was not to turn off to the *sketes,* uphill or downhill, nor to the *kellis,* which he named. . . . His hand wound in the air, taking all the right turns, and then he stood back and watched me climb, waving me on, each time as I looked back, until I took the right turn out of sight" (RM, 143). This watchful farewell is repeated at various monasteries, sometimes with variations that involve special aids and even gifts; such *bon voyage* gestures convey the rarity of pathfinding nowadays on Athos.

These paths were once contemplative places; the journey over them was a natural adjunct to the experience of the monastery. As Merwin uses them, they regain some of their ancient usefulness, midway points between the human and the natural, order and confusion, art and utility. Their dramatic deterioration emphasizes the hostility that has grown up among the various monasteries; not lively interchange but schismatic disputes exist among them. Father Paul "believed that Athos as a whole was degenerate: that most of the monks and whole communities (Pantokratoros, for instance) had fallen from the true faith, and that nothing could be learned from them" (RM, 167). Father Theodoros of Pantokratoros hears news of the outbreak of the Arab-Israeli War and "Theodoros' sympathies were with the Arabs, less because of any inherent sympathy with them than because of a frank Anti-Semitism, a prejudice not vehement but ingrained, obstinate, deaf and imbued with a familiar obscurantism" (RM, 158). The monasteries have become balkanized, and the deteriorating pathways that once linked them are an example not just of encroaching modernity, of roadways that happen to make walking less convenient, but of a return to a fundamental divisiveness fostered by isolationism. At one time, Athos must have overcome that. The iconographic art, repeated from monastery to monastery, is a testament to that moment in the past.

Though Merwin's presence is little in evidence in "Aspects of a Mountain," or evident only as that of a mild and placid tourist casually noting his impressions, the aspects that he considers turn out to form a clear and coherent pattern. What may seem to be only details noted in passing (descriptions of the paths, or the natural life along them) and what may seem to be eccentric omissions or idiosyncratic perceptions (the absence of lengthy descriptions of works of art, the emphasis on architectural arrangements) turn out to be judgments of value made with care and confidence. Moreover, the values he supports are reinforced by his own position as wandering pilgrim. Only the pilgrim has the capaciousness to see all, to weigh and to judge, and to experience the deeper harmonies to be found along the pathways.

Yet Merwin's view of the pilgrim is not a portrait of a restless wanderer: to the one who is truly at peace, place does not matter, which is why the searching of the pilgrim is necessary, a test of endurance and a validation of worth. The most impressive figure he meets is Father Mark who tries to explain what "good" the monasteries do: "'It is there,' Father Mark said, touching the air as though to wake it, trying to remember something. 'How do you say it?' he asked, as though we did; he was whispering Greek words, groping to bring them into English. 'The Good man . . . out of his heart . . . out of its good riches.' *The good man, out of the good treasure of his heart, bringeth forth good things.* I listened to him making his own translation" (RM, 140). The translation in italics is what Merwin hears as he listens to Father Mark, whose own speech stumbles; so it is just as though those lucid words fall out of the air itself or emerge from within the listeners themselves.

5

The poems in part 4 of *The Compass Flower* are best understood as emerging from an aesthetic like that evidenced in the works of art described in "Aspects of a Mountain"—art so absorbed in living events that it risks appearing negligible. These poems mark a distinct step toward memoir and autobiography, a second flowering in human terms, the recovery of events that were misunderstood or dismissed when they originally occurred. Yet what complicates these poems is that Merwin seeks an approach to his past that, at the same time, guarantees he will be free of that past. He returns to his past to see it anew, precisely to dissolve the claims it might make upon him.

The poems resemble notes and sketches, anecdotal fragments; but their casual appearance is misleading. Merwin is careful to touch upon them lightly because he wants the effect of a rapid revisitation, a quick return that lasts just long enough to produce a new understanding of a moment that, if it were not handled so deftly, might draw him down into labyrinths of meaning. His intent to lighten the scenes he is revisiting is emphasized in the opening poem, "The Coin," which both sketches a scene as he had always recalled it and questions the accuracy of what he had thought he had seen. It describes a visit to a fair on a riverbank opposite a church's

> green sagging balconies from which
> during the occupation
> the bodies of many
> of the men of the town
> hung for days in full view
> of the women who had been their wives (CF, 75)

The fair unfolds against this grim memory of the occupation. Yet what dominates the scene seems to be the bustle of commerce. The speaker is surprised to see, even in a cage of three turtledoves, "a coin in with their grain." The poem closes with Merwin noticing pigeons watching from the church windowsills—watching, as he has been throughout, as nonparticipants in the process. The statement of the final line—"all of it returns without a sound"—might be a judgmental sweep of contempt, a pronouncement against a scene so absorbed in commercial exchanges that it has forgotten the sorrows of its past.

Yet the poem evokes so crude a reading precisely in order to deny it, as though Merwin had carried this ugly portrait within himself for years, and only now came to appreciate the other elements at work in it. While the poem lists commercial exchanges, it is careful to diffuse the emphasis on money. The first sight of the fair is the somber one of men "in long black coats selling animals," but the next sight is a woman in white holding "white cheese / wrapped in white paper / out into the sunlight." The whiteness of the sunlight purifies and sensualizes. And the woman who is selling cut flowers seems remote from the taint of commerce. The coin in the cage with the turtledoves could imply their sellers' disdain for money. In short, as the scenes unfold, money loses its hold, and the poem expands into a series of living scenes, active social exchanges; the balcony corpses become phantoms as the town reconstitutes itself.

Merwin set out with an eye on the dark of the past, ready to condemn the commercialization that the fair displays—except it is the townspeople who have swept the darkness away. When the pigeons lift themselves off the balcony, they are not an emblem of a dismissive gesture of contempt; they exemplify the same freedom of movement the townspeople have learned. What begins as a morbid work burdened with the past becomes a series of scenes that increase in animation, as though they are shaking free of the weight of symbolic portent. Merwin enters the poem from one angle and leaves it from another, his convictions turned around. His statement "all of it returns without a sound" may be a judgment against himself for not having understood enough at the time. He can only revive the life in the scene visually, not through the sound of voices, because only now, some time after, he sees the error in his original condemnation.

The poems in part 4 are more than just returns to scenes of the past; they are returns that have folded within them ways of leaving behind that past. The poems are not simply revivals of what is gone but revisitations that affirm that the poet is not held within that past. The manuscripts of several reveal that many began with a short prose recollection, a series of phrases and sentences jotted down like notes in a diary, which then modulated into verse (fig. 18). The poetry replicates this reorientation. It slips out from under the weight of a situation that had been fixed and framed by enacting a series of gestural turns and shifts. "The Trestle" begins with a narrow focus on a small object, a postcard the speaker had as a child, with the smallest of details included ("one white thumbtack"). But it opens onto the vast scene of a "tall train bridge / trembling over the gorge / with the tracks far below there" until we learn the postcard illustrated a scene

> where we have just been
> by the glittering rapids
> under the black trees
> past the only inn
> we see it from here
> as it is now
> painted
> between the moving girders (CF, 90)

The prepositional phrases of the opening lines, each a corridor to the postcard from the past, are now overturned by prepositional phrases that yield new activity: "by the glittering rapids / under the black trees / past the only inn."

When I live on the mountain I keep thinking of a fishing village. I see the mountain when my eyes are open.

Closing eyes on the mountain only hearing then the sea

I went for a walk around the small harbor in the evening and thought of not

A series of fishing villages with small harbors. I had dreamed it before I saw it.

Village so small
you could imagine it
not being there

Since the years
Harbor Boats

I hear my feet resound on a wharf
echo from other wharves
the fishing boats are all around
in the evening
until again harbor dusk
shadows fill the whirlpools of ropes
yellow sand small waves
breaking on under the wharf
I go again around the harbor

ladders filled again in unloading
all cranes
nets dangling from creaking hooks

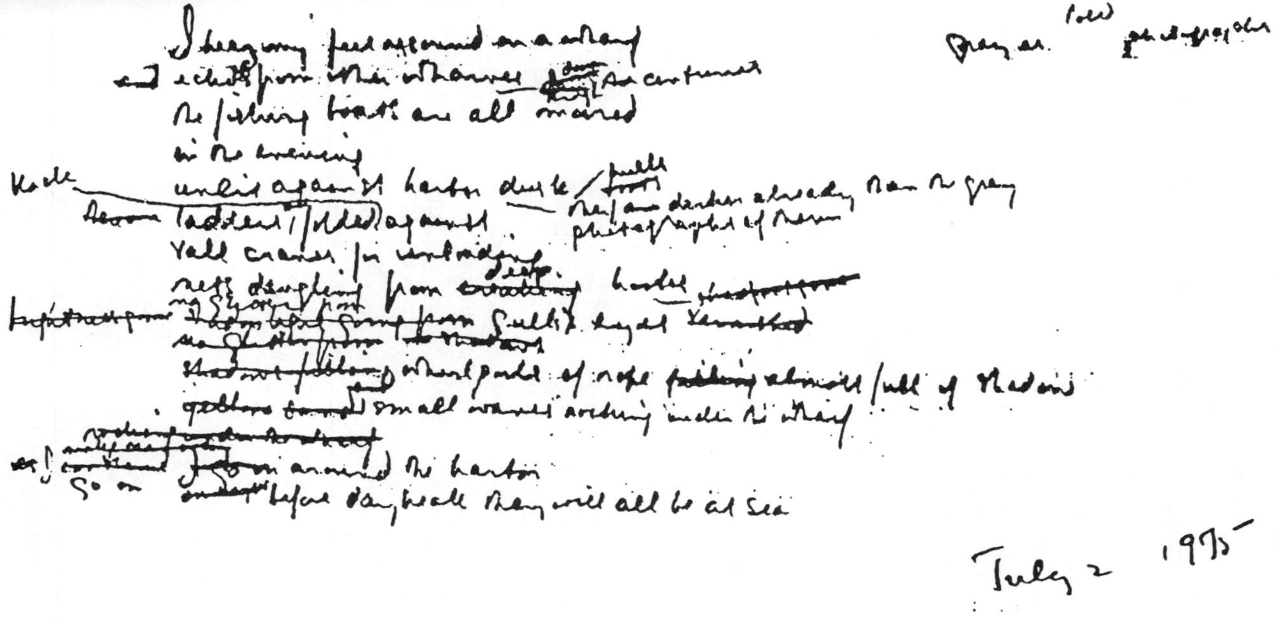

Figure 18. First and final draft with revisions of "Some of the Masts" (MS. 22:09/030, d. July 2, 1975), showing that the work began as a series of prose sentences.

More pointedly, the inn, a place to rest and a temporary home, is now revealed in this present moment; in the past, there had been only a gorge. And it is the inn that emerges in colors, "painted," not "in brown," "between the moving girders."

These poems crave such reversals. "Assembly" begins with a portrait of nomads who "gather in autumn / driving herds to the great auctions of animals on the gold earth," but after describing this autumnal landscape, Merwin suddenly shifts away from it:

> moments during the summer
> in upland pastures among the birds
> some play instruments
> others sing clapping their hands (CF, 85)

The conviction that a reversal can occur, that time can be shifted about, is essential if Merwin is to compose these works. Merwin may hold on to this conviction so tightly, because, as "The Banquet" reveals, he hesitates about returning to the past. In that poem,

> doors and windows from a childhood
> that was yours shrink
> seen again years afterwards
> for one moment late in the day
> when there is no time (CF, 78)

Windows and doors appear to be smaller to the adult who remembers them from childhood; but these doors and windows "shrink" as though to protect him from having to return, and, in any case, they are only seen for a moment, at a point so late in the day there is no time to visit. The end of this poem, which envisions a room from childhood now inhabited by "banqueters / raising their glasses // hours before the first star," imagines the past as though it had been erased, overtaken by changes so radical that it is all dissolved.

This is in keeping with the deepest conviction apparent in these poems: that traveling is preferable to homecoming. Not only is Merwin a traveler in virtually every one of the poems, but every time a homecoming looms, it is dissolved. In the final poem, "The Flight," Merwin sees a fire

> in an opening in the wall
> in another house and another
> before and after
> in house after house that was mine to see
> the same fire the perpetual bird (CF, 94)

But it is always "the perpetual bird" that appears in each: none of the houses is individuated, and the fire within each is conceived as "a doorway to see through / into the first thing." In "North Wind" the speaker confesses that he dreams of houses, but then quickly places himself imaginatively within not one house but three distinct settings. In "The Windows" the child is engaged in antics designed to thrust himself into a world outside his own home. He casts his gaze out a window while standing on his head, imagining that since he is

> hanging from nothing
> he might step down
> and walk on the old sky far down there
> out to the clouds
> in the far islands
> he might step on the clouds where they have worn shiny (CF, 88)

When he has tired of that game and returns "to a room full of his elders," he refuses to return at all, though he is now standing in the room: "without moving he flies." Merwin's sympathy with the child who would be free from his home is unquestioning.

When homes appear they are often formidably barricaded, as in "Service," where the gate house of a mansion has been turned into a gas station with a guard dog; its "shadow-bricked gardens" are empty, and there are "white / curtains drawn on all / the bay windows." Or the homes are helplessly frail, as in "Junction," with its "tin shack surrounded by / broken windshields" and its "far houses and red boats" that "float above themselves in gray sky." The poet is most comfortable walking around the harbor in "Some of the Masts," enjoying all the fishing boats "moored / in the evening"; part of his pleasure lies in knowing that "by daybreak they will all be at sea." The prim order of the boats is temporary, to be dissolved, perhaps to be reconstituted again tomorrow evening, though with a different set of details. The perfect home, sketched in "Sun," is a place where there is a "bird on south doorstep / poised like a stone"—but poised only for the moment, on the verge of flying away.

Merwin's idea of a satisfying place is not home, but a place to which one can return with another person, then take something memorable away. In "The Falcons," the three falcons that appear at dusk are emblems of their courtyard, and "this time they will come with us / when we leave the island / tonight for the rest of our lives." Now that the birds remain with Merwin and his companion, there will be no reason to return. This nomadic quality may explain why "Remembering a Boatman" presents an image that is haunting to Merwin yet one that he says he forgets "for years." That nearly invisible, almost-inaudible voyager crossing, with only traces visible as a flashing wake, is forgettable just because the figure is so thoroughly immersed in the specifics of his own landscape at twilight. In "The Fig Tree," what captures his attention, in a place notable for its ancient architecture, is the fig tree flourishing "against the south wall of a monastery / where it catches the first sun." Monastery law prohibits disrupting the growth of the tree: the secret, Merwin suggests, of a meaningfully enduring edifice is that it incorporates, welcomes, even nourishes (with the heat of its south wall) that living tree so utterly unlike its ancient foundations.

Although the poems in this section can be appreciated as a literal enactment of a second flowering, a chance for the poet to revisit situations he had once left behind, they remain disconcerting because Merwin insists upon maintaining so light a touch. In every respect, they celebrate the viewpoint of the wanderer or vagabond, who pauses for a moment but then passes by; his revisitations are not supposed to hold him or draw him nearer for an extended scrutiny. To return home is beyond comprehension; to continue voyaging is so ingrained it goes without question. Yet so determined a defense against being held by the past also implies a need to comprehend that past. At this point, he can project himself out of his home, like the boy in "The Windows," but when he brings his gaze back to the room full of elders, he always flies away. To remain within that room, to scrutinize and even interrogate his elders, will be, in fact, the task Merwin sets for himself over the next several years in his poetry, his short prose pieces, and his autobiographical reminiscences.

13

The Good of the Intellect

MORE THAN once after *The Drunk in the Furnace,* Merwin seemed on the verge of resuming the family poems broken off in 1958, as he was approaching his own immediate past. Around 1958, he revisited his home town, Union City, New Jersey, in a prose piece entitled "A View from the Palisades," but this never came to more than some detailed paragraphs in a notebook. In 1963, before *The Lice* was under way, he completed "The Garden" and "Offertory," two poems invoking his father's presence; in 1967, just as he was beginning *The Carrier of Ladders,* he completed a three-poem sequence more autobiographical than anything he had previously attempted. "The Piper" recalled a summer spent in Montreal in 1947 (where he had observed the sourdough miner of "Home for Thanksgiving"); "The Lake" returned to the vacation resort of "Stump Pond" (and the short story "The Barn"); and "The Church" revisited the setting of his father's parish in Union City, now a vacant lot (later described in a chapter from *Unframed Originals* entitled "The Skyline"). But neither set of poems prompted further work. Then in 1969, in an unpublished prose piece, "The Windsor Fields," written when *The Miner's Pale Children* was nearing completion, he tried a different approach: rather than returning to the past, he began to study why it was so difficult to do so.[1]

"The Windsor Fields" (at 7,000 words one of the longest of the short prose pieces) is divided into nine sections, each of which begins as a variation on the opening sentence: "It will be a long time yet before I can write about The Windsor Fields." But every new beginning is more disheartening than the last:

> I am sure it will be a long time yet before I can say anything about the Windsor Fields. . . .

> I realize that I am still far from being able to describe what I remember of the Windsor Fields. . . .
>
> I see that I have a great deal to learn before I can speak clearly and to any purpose of the Windsor Fields. . . .
>
> There is still something, perhaps there is a great deal, that I must learn, in the truest sense of the word, before I can give a simple and convincing account of the Windsor Fields. . . .

And so on, each new prologue growing increasingly tortuous. The more he writes, the less ground he gains, as the past recedes further.

Each section represents Merwin's renewed effort to grasp the significance of the Windsor Fields. Unremarkable except for their desolation, the fields are dominated at the west end by a "pale stone-faced embankment that rose, stately like one side of a pyramid, with a flight of broad stone steps running from top to bottom." At this pinnacle is a "little park full of lifeless privet bushes, rusted cans, empty bottles, newspapers, broken benches and a locked brick pavilion with an empty drinking fountain in front of it, cupping one dry-green metal heart." From here, one can peer out on the disappointing vista of the fields themselves. Whatever they were supposed to become, they did not. Perhaps a common pasture at the turn of the century, they were reclaimed in the 1930s as The Flats, then left undeveloped except for tennis courts in one corner. Marks of casual games are evident in cinders and dirt. After a heavy rain, a shallow lake appears at one end, explored at dusk by shadowy dogs. Gray houses, railroad flats, and tenements stretch eastward. As a child Merwin had been cautioned against crossing these fields. Warned by his father of the danger of the stone embankment, whose stairs lacked a railing, he only glimpsed these steps from afar: "I can see myself at the top of those steps, looking down, looking out eastward across the scuffed cindered flats, and the indelible lake, and then slowly, surreptitiously, withdrawing, like the sun." On the rare occasions when he disobeyed and trespassed, he experienced confusion and fear: "my occasional brief infringements of that command made the barren expanse suddenly broaden on all sides of me to huge horizons, a plain traversed by the lightning patterns of games which I did not understand and from which I somehow must keep my distance."

If the Windsor Fields summarize childhood as Merwin recalls it, they reveal a desolate zone of waste and indifference. But in the eighth section, instead of attempting one more description of the fields, he ponders why, when he approaches the stairs at the foot of the embankment, he stops: "What breaks off my impetus, and so far, at least without fail, there at the edge of the stone slope with the unguarded stairs plunging into the immense shadows at my feet? It always finds me in time. How can I trace it back, not knowing what it is? And if I try, it divides: it is legion."

What halts him at the edge is that these steps into "immense shadows" lead into his own past. The injunction that sounds in his ears as he approaches—"From those stairs, back"—originates with a childhood incident when he had fallen downstairs. Not just one flight of stairs comes to memory, however, but a series of three: "wooden stairs" surrounded by a formidable list of prohibitions, then "the darker stairs of an earlier house," which "curved in a manner that seemed to have histories of its own," and finally "outside stairs," where "on the top step, in still earlier days, I had been placed, seated, with the top buttons of my shirt undone, and allowed to stay by myself, quite still, once, just for a few minutes, to catch the sun." Each stairway promises a different past: stairs surrounded by what is forbidden, stairs that curve off into remoteness, and stairs that yield, however temporarily, to moments of joyous relief in which one can "catch the sun." Taken together, these memories, not the fields, summarize Merwin's sense of his childhood. Yet none of the stairways beckons him further. He remains overlooking a sprawling expanse, and the piece closes with uncertainty:

> I can no longer say with any degree of assurance whether [the fields] lie in the past or the future. I cannot tell whether the change that must take place before I can produce words to bear true witness to the Windsor Fields should be thought of as, essentially, a metamorphosis of the past as a revelation still hidden in the future. Every line of access to the fields ends before it reaches them. That is as it should be. My place is at the edge, forbidden, waiting to know. It would do no good to descend the stone stairs into the deepening tract of shadow, and start across to the shallow lake, now, this time. I cannot imagine my voice there.

He understands he is not yet ready to descend these steps. Yet "that is as it should be": it is proper that he should remain "at the edge," apart from what was forbidden, because that was exactly his position when what is now the past was then the present.

To approach the past, then, is genuinely intimidating because he was excluded from the past even when it was the present. If the truth is his exclusion, then not to descend the stairs remains true to the actuality of his past when he had been forbidden to descend the stairs. This tidy paradox ends "The Windsor Fields." Not to enter the past is as close as Merwin can come to entering a past in which his own curiosity and activity had been resolutely curtailed.

1

Yet Merwin's assumption that the past is impenetrable is recognized but overturned in a lengthy recollection written in the summer of 1973, "Mary" (fig. 19), the first of what would become a collection of memoirs, *Unframed Originals* (1983).[2] Initially, it could be mistaken for an apology, like "The

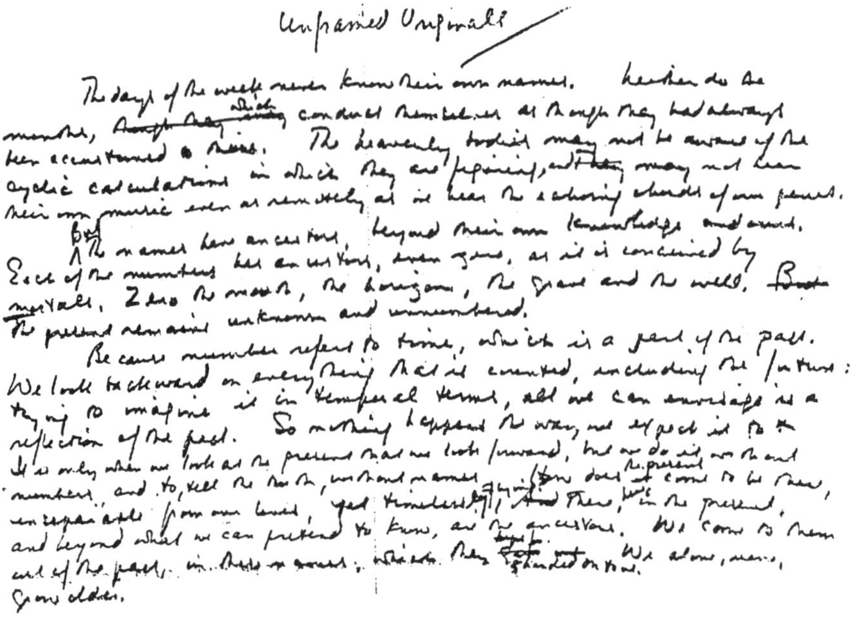

Figure 19. The opening paragraph, later canceled, of "Mary" (MS. 11:1250, d. June 29, 1973), which was originally entitled "Unframed Originals."

Windsor Fields," that explains why his family past must remain a closed book. The entrance to that past, through the recollections of older family members like his father's sister Mary, is blocked by the eccentricity of their personalities. Mary is so unreliable a witness, conveying information in a fragmentary and garbled manner, that family history grows hopelessly entangled. Merwin is careful to reproduce his own bafflement; listening to one story, he reports: "That was Jacob, I learned, later. But from the way she wandered into it, I listened to most of the story thinking it was William." In short, the past as a reasonable narrative is beyond reach. Just as Mary promises Merwin various daguerreotypes, souvenirs, and relics that are never produced, so her hints and allusions constitute a patchwork quilt of tales behind which history falls into obscurity.

Yet in another respect, "Mary" affirms that the past is not only possible but necessary to revisit. Merwin has good reason to begin writing these recollections in conjunction with Mary, for his contact with her literally stood at a threshold of his understanding of his family past. The memoir falls into two sections, one recalling the years from 1930 to 1936 when Mary spent time as an off-and-on member of the household, the other recalling visits to her in 1957, the year Merwin returned from his seven-year exile in Europe. These ancestral stories related to Merwin at thirty formed the basis for his aggressive, unsympathetic portraits in *The Drunk in the Furnace.* Threatened by some ancestors, appalled by others, Merwin moved against them forcefully, writing poetry that severed his ties with them (and redirected the heretofore benign course of his family sequence). In "Mary," then, he is returning to the moment when his own attitudes toward the past became congealed.

Recollecting Mary's stories seventeen years later, Merwin does not affirm a connection with his ancestors that he previously denied, but he listens to his father's sister in a way different from that in 1957. In an unusually harsh poem excluded from his 1957 family portraits, "Nothing New," he presented this snapshot of his great-grandfather: "Jake, who told little, and was murdered one night / Fetching home some coffee in a pillowcase, / And no one could say why the man hated him." Placed so resolutely in this way, Jake fits in with other portrayals of Merwin's ancestors as an unseemly, quarrelsome lot, "each one lost in the end // Without maps, in the niggard unlovely / Waste he had found for himself, sick of it."[3]

But when Merwin presents Mary explaining this same anecdote, it now becomes subtle, quizzical, evocative:

> Apparently he had been running for office, some kind of political office. That was behind it, some way. He had got mixed up in politics. Pawlitics. And this other man had shot him. It was at night, you know. And they never did see who it was. He went out to the store with a pillowcase to get some coffee. Cawfee. He'd took a pillowcase, to get it in. And they found him lying there. He was shot. In the top of his head. He'd been to the store and was coming back. There was coffee in the pillowcase. And there was a comb. (UO, 85–86)

This version is careful to incorporate the storyteller's voice. Odd mispronunciations intrude, like an overtone that blurs sounds: "Pawlitics," "Cawfee." One has to strain to hear the details beyond the voice. Merwin lets the story unfold with Mary's hesitations intact, as though she were rearranging pieces as she proceeded, returning to fragments like bits of a puzzle. Three times Mary returns to the most puzzling detail—coffee in a pillowcase?—as though this baffled her too. One expects the detail to fade away, or to metamorphose into something more appropriate (the pillowcase will turn into a sack), but it remains steadfastly itself, and nothing appears to explain it further. A new detail emerges at the end, but the addition of the comb, the new item we might have been anticipating as a key to the rest, unlocks nothing and only raises other questions: Is it a comb for his child? His wife? Or is it for someone unmentioned, at the edge of the story?

Merwin has added more than the sound of Mary's voice; he has added Mary's puzzlement as she retells the story, her awareness of the inexplicable quality of the events. She is searching for a way to make the details fit, and the sentences half-formed by her (and broken by Merwin as the oddity of her pronunciation overpowers his attention) create an effect of two persons united in following a puzzling story, both acutely listening even as they come up against barriers to understanding.

The long interrogation in which Mary is made to divulge her family's history will be an exercise in frustration if one is, as the younger Merwin apparently was, searching for a coherent, unified history. That coherent history is to be found in *The Drunk in the Furnace,* where women are stigmatized as manipulative and men apotheosized as martyrs. But if one approaches Mary's reminiscences as Merwin does at this later stage, regretting his earlier eagerness to make stories fit, then passages reveal that her struggle is not with fixed identities but with individuals against whom she reacts and who afford her the opportunity to display her own character. Even her reluctance to examine or to divulge certain aspects of the past becomes part of this struggle in herself. She often begins a story convinced she sees things clearly and steadily, but the more she speaks the more involved she becomes, and the hard personalities she sets out somewhat reluctantly to sketch dissolve into elusive human beings.

Her struggle becomes a prototype for Merwin's way of recollecting others. That his particular struggle begins with Mary—the source for his series, in *The Drunk in the Furnace,* of "Framed Types" rather than "Unframed Originals"—makes it a personal moment for him, an act of carefully undoing his mishearing of an earlier point in his life. He is not simply revisiting the past of 1957 but understanding his own failure to understand in 1957; the easy caricatures he took away from Mary melt back into the shadows in this revisiting of a past moment that had led to a sense of the past erected upon his own mishearing. In an unfinished poem, "Not a Real Relation," dating from the mid-1960s, he intimated that his presence at these meetings served to distort what he heard: "It was of course myself I was anxious to hear of / Among the forgotten forbears."[4] But the poem broke off before he explored the extent of his own distortions.

Now Merwin not only underscores his mishearing but makes amends for it: he rescues Mary from the oblivion to which he (and his family as a whole) had consigned her, by presenting her, in the first half of the piece, within a frame that he dissolves in the second half. At first Mary is cast in the role of an amusing eccentric, a perennial outcast, significantly deaf to the events around her. In the family, she is a liability, another person to take care of, her tasks strictly limited: "Mary could not be counted on to bear in mind from day to day everything that was not allowed: the list was too long, and she was too forgetful. If she felt that she had slipped up she might contribute some makeshift injunction of her own; it always retained the faltering accent of the hurried guess, and was obeyed out of general obedience" (UO, 62). Mary is more of a child than young Merwin. He knew the rules, as he indicates when he is recalls the stores that lined a particular street: of a barber shop he says "I knew one with a face of the sun smoking a cigar—a wrong thing to do—on the wall" (UO, 66). But this mastery of the family rules is now understood as a facile capability that helped distort his impression of his cousin.

Wry sayings are scattered through the text—"Give a dog a bad name" (UO, 65), "To the Greeks a stumbling-block" (UO, 66)—that reproduce the child's perception of the shorthand that adults resorted to, passing criticisms over his head, summing up Mary, backing her into the role of outsider, reducing her to an eccentric, turning her strengths into weaknesses. From his new vantage point, what he had been taught to think of as her liabilities now appear as virtues; it is not, for example, absurd to lose oneself in long walks, though to his family this had been a sign of grave incompetence. At one point, he is most explicit: "Doubtless what was more curious about her than any external feature was her curiosity itself, a current that twitched and drove her, apparently aimlessly, and planted her with feet apart and her mouth open, where nobody else thought of looking. She said she wanted to see. That restlessness of hers was something she shared with others of my father's family, but the fumbling inquiry that nagged her all her days had been born dead or pinched out or walled up in most of the others, and they never recognized it except in the way she embarrassed them" (UO, 66). This makes her interest, in later years, in the promises of the Jehovah's Witnesses something other than a stubborn assertion of piety. Merwin has the sensitivity to transfer her out of a situation in which her curiosity proved a handicap and to place her in a situation in which it can thrive. By shifting her from the family setting, with its explicit rules and devotional duties and inherent taboos, into a larger realm, that of the whole family stretching through generations, he frees her from her consignment to eccentricity, while at the same time he takes the measure of the repressive atmosphere of his own upbringing. He even mocks himself as a well-mannered child so adept at mastering the rules that it is not surprising that it took him so long to appreciate his cousin or that, back in 1957, he leapt so rapidly to definitive conclusions about his ancestors. But such mishearing is corrected in this piece, the first of the memoirs to be completed and the origin of the rest. The deliberate shift from a static portrayal of an eccentric toward a situation in which the clown becomes a sage, in which the certainty of the past is called into question, is necessary if Merwin wants to find an avenue into his past.

2

Merwin continues to question his fixed ideas about the past in sketches written from 1973 to 1976 that conclude *Houses and Travellers*, the most revealing of which is "The Ship from Costa Rica."[5] It hinges on a mistaken impression that turns out not to be a mistake. He begins by reporting on the appearance of a man identical in features to his father who emerges from a "sugar factory" at some distance from Merwin's observation post on a balcony overlooking a port. Though the man is distant, he is clearly observable, yet although Merwin addresses him with waves and gestures, he never responds and never looks up. He appears to be absorbed in his daily routine, which includes this short stroll. As he reappears, three times altogether, Merwin also remains convinced that his father, in fact, lives hundreds of miles away in another city. When he appears for the second time, Merwin responds: "As I watched, the same door opened, and he stepped out, in his shirt sleeves again, and put his hands on the balcony railing and stood looking down at the ship. I thought, as I had the first time, that he looked younger than he did at home. That, then, was the way he looked at the sugar factory—a life he never mentioned, a life of ships, distances, cargoes, easy-going gazes from balconies, without noticing the cold—whereas at home, in the life in which I was used to seeing him, he set the thermostat in the upper eighties and complained of drafts" (HT, 179–80).

His easy acceptance does not simply acknowledge that his father should have an alternate life: it accepts his father as having another life about which, until now, Merwin had been in the dark. And it is presented as perfectly natural: "That, then, was the way he looked at the sugar factory. . . ." It is a moment of surprise and understanding, as though this other aspect of his father was simply waiting to reveal itself at a special moment. In fact, at a later point, Merwin recalls having been shown a photograph of his father in the navy: "I had never been able to imagine him having anything to do with ships. When he had shown me, once, a photograph of himself and his friends on their ship, in the first war, he had to point himself out to me: sitting cross-legged, grinning, in a knitted hat, on top of a big tube called a ventilator. What he said was their ship looked like part of a building: a floor. When he showed me the brown picture I thought someone else was speaking to me, from behind him" (HT, 181). It is that "someone else" appearing now, years later, when Merwin is "older than my father had been when I was born" (HT, 181). His earlier inability or failure to see his father as having anything to do with ships still lingers in the way he recalls his surly reaction to looking at "the brown picture" and thinking that "their ship looked like part of a building: a floor."

What Merwin withheld from his own imagination, then, what he failed to glimpse in this photo, is that aspect of his father that had been present but that was neglected by a younger Merwin distracted elsewhere. The possibility for a radically new understanding of his father is left undeveloped in this brief piece, but its potential hovers at the close. The key to such a reversal lies in the passing phrase in which Merwin recognizes that he is now older than his father had been when he was born—a recognition that invites Merwin to consider his father not as a man at home, complaining of drafts, but as a person like himself, with his own inner life. Quite simply, outside of the frames in which they are customarily viewed, persons may reveal entirely new sides of themselves; moreover, such a discovery may place one's whole understanding of the past into question.

Though *Unframed Originals* opens with a chapter in which Merwin is searching his memory for the face of his grandfather—they met only once, briefly, when Merwin was nine, and no identifiable photographs remain of him—the face that is most difficult for him to recover is his father's.[6] The ideal is to see his father—as well as other family members—against their own sugar factories: as they were but as they need not have been. "The Skyline" (1977), the second of the pieces to be written, dwells longest on the relationship between father and son. This memory centers on Merwin's recollection of his father's church, from which his father was transferred when Merwin was nine. Although we see through a child's eyes, we also see what Merwin the adult is realizing as he recalls it—the way the child's perceptions differed so markedly from the father's. Details off to the side, things that were not intended to be noticed, all material that lacks a firm context—these Merwin recalls seeing as a child. He remembers the progress of a sunbeam creeping across the carpet during Sunday morning service; the sound of churchgoers clattering outside the door, audible to all when winter services were held in the basement; the dampness seeping through the walls, creating abstract shapes that waxed and waned with the seasons. But Merwin as a child is not simply alert to the offbeat: his alertness is the expression of his frustrated desire to bridge the gulf between himself and his father. The boy longs to share with his father what might be called the backstage life of the church; but his father is always onstage.

Much that his father instituted, as a new pastor, stresses this onstage element—for example, the new "glassed-in bulletin board facing the street: a flat box with a Gothic roof, the wood painted black every year. His pride. An innovation that he would bring his convocation, right from the start" (UO, 95). What Merwin recalls, though, is the backstage life—the weekly arrival of the bulletin for display, the color so fresh at first, then rapidly fading, the themes repeated from week to week. His interest only grows as his father, bound by precise notions of propriety, fails to acknowledge his yearning to participate and to understand. With delight Merwin recalls the one time he was allowed up in the organ loft with his father, but the memory is mixed painfully with his father's vexation and wrath:

> Don't touch anything—very emphatically. My father bending down, peering into boxes, dusting his fingers, puffing. Just stand right there and don't touch anything. Seeing the familiar church from that new height, it felt as though the organ loft were floating like a cloud, or as though I had suddenly grown out of the top of my head and were flying over the pews below. My father didn't seem to find what he was looking for up there. When I asked him he didn't hear, leading the way down the dusty stairs. (UO, 98)

There is no way to reconcile the opposition here. The offbeat view, astonishing for its forbidden rarity and the closeness it brings him with his father, is utterly lost on his father, who is irritated at being thrust behind the scenes to peer into dusty boxes. The question his son poses merits no reply, so this moment of shared intimacy, when both are backstage together, finds the father vanishing after enjoining his son not to move, not to touch anything—not to be there.

The one wholly positive memory in "The Skyline" recalls the time the boy's toolbox, a forbiddingly adult gift (offered one Christmas only to be taken away until a time when he was older), was employed as a prop in a marriage ceremony. The wonder of this particular ceremony is that so much of it defies established taboos; it is justifiable apparently because of the bride's vivacious personality:

> An evening wedding in any case (but it was really *night*, I thought) was heralded by a special wave of whispers and consultations in lowered voices. It was more than a rarity. No one could remember whether there had ever been one at the church. My father had probably never performed one. It was spoken of as something modern, and a bit fast. Everyone involved seemed to feel that they were doing something racy, and to be slightly surprised to find themselves getting away with it. But Mandy, the bride—they kept telling themselves—had very definite ideas. She was a character. She kept people waiting. My father said she was a clip. (UO, 103)

Merwin's connection to this rare occasion is secured when his toolbox is spirited away to be used, secretively, as a support for a cushion to kneel on in the wedding. Because the ceremony, with its air of forbidden gaiety, was held at night, the boy was unable to participate, but he remembers that "when I was told, in time, of Mandy's wedding, I imagined watching it from the organ loft" (UO, 106). This moment, one of the happiest in "The Skyline," depends on a series of taboos gently yielding to the insistence of a feminine presence. An object belonging to the child is integrated as a crucial item in the performance; most important, the object is hidden from the spectators, disguised as a kneeling cushion. This is as close as the child comes to participating in the backstage life of the church.

The sadness that dominates "The Skyline" can be traced to this fundamental opposition, an opposition not to be resolved except in Merwin's later understanding of it. In the closing paragraphs, Merwin looks out from the vacant lot where the Union City church once stood, and, finding the Manhattan skyline in the background, he can almost see the apartment where he has been living for years. It is the last, and most helpless, contrast between the backstage and the onstage: behind the vacant lot is the New York City skyline that Merwin inhabits now, even as the church is gone. But the gulf between vacant lot and skyline is also haunting because it evokes other rare moments, the times when the boy was allowed to accompany his father to his church study. There, truly backstage with his father, he was left to observe the workings of the harbor outside the window, against the New York skyline. But backstage together, the two face in opposite directions, his father immersed in preparing his sermon, the boy positioned to view the performance of the tugs and barges and ships. In this stylized arrangement, father and son reach a silent peace. In contrast, Merwin recalls being led to the church one time to act as an audience while his father tried out a sermon:

> Once he pushed back his chair and took me downstairs into the church and had me sit in a pew—any pew!—prickly with responsibility, to listen to a passage of sermons. For him to go over it, for his own purpose, and to see (he added) whether I was old enough to understand. Since I was the only one in the pews, and had been charged with this extraordinary and wholly unexpected office, I imagined that the rhetorical questions were addressed to me personally, and tried to answer them, which was a bad mistake. After that I became invisible, and a while later was summoned to follow my father upstairs again, to the window seat. He spoke well of how quiet I could be, there, but said that he could see that the sermon was still too old for me. (UO, 112)

To end this confusion about whether one is in the audience or behind the scenes, the young Merwin can only become "invisible" and eventually return to the window seat in the study where the harbor can be quietly observed—the pact of separation re-established.

Not only does "The Skyline" deal with the central conflict between Merwin and his father, it also reveals that such a conflict was never resolved; the solution that emerged was that precarious, temporary, rare arrangement that allowed the boy to remain with his father in his study, but with his back turned, eyes on the Hudson River harbor. "How often I was allowed up there, while he worked, I have no idea," Merwin says. "It may indeed have been only once. . . . But both of us came to speak of my going there to watch the river from the window, while he worked, as though it were a regular and cherished custom. Both preferred to think of it that way" (UO, 112). Each, that is, ultimately accepts his distance from the other, by embracing his customary role. But in the roles they embrace, the wrong parts are played. Merwin the boy, eager to reach out to his father, is prepared to act as an adult, wanting to participate in the backstage life of the church, to understand what goes on behind the scenes. For his father, though, the role of the child is always to be the son—obedient, well-mannered, a spectator appreciating a vista. The signals each sends the other are easily confused. And if Merwin the child is to act mature, he must adopt the role held out for him, to act as though he were onstage, even as his own intelligence, imagination, and curiosity drive him toward peering behind the scenes, seeking how and why things work. In a similar way, Merwin sees his father playing, much less adeptly, the role of the parent. Each, to his credit, is uncomfortable with the task he has imposed on himself and the other; but neither has an obvious alternative, at least that he can display for the other's acceptance.

3

A major exception to the narrowness encroaching on Merwin's youth occurs in "Hotel," the first to be written of the four chapters that would begin to shape "Mary" and "The Skyline" into *Unframed Originals.* The exception is major indeed: it depends on the intervention of a person outside the family. The hotel of the title is in downtown Pittsburgh, crisscrossed by Merwin at several stages in his life but never inhabited by him; the hotel serves to introduce family dwellings from which Merwin was more or less estranged: an enormous, ungainly mansion across the street from his father's West Scranton, Pennsylvania, church; an apartment visited briefly during his undergraduate years, after his parents had relocated; and still another apartment, lived in by his mother while his father was stationed in England during World War II. Most important, though, is the house Merwin did inhabit, an ancient, half-ruined stone farmhouse purchased in the 1950s, located in the south of France. When the story of purchasing this house was first extracted from "Hotel" and published as "A House Abroad" in 1981, it emphasized that everything happened felicitously and providentially.[7] He came upon the ruined farmhouse, struck up the right contacts, impressed the owners, and, most serendipitously of all, had the exact purchase price in an inheritance. The inheritance, a surprising gift from his aunt Margie, his mother's only close relative, was the most magical part of the story, underscoring a number of events coinciding in a narrative almost inexplicable in its coherence.

The same events, when unfolding against the background of "Hotel," emphasize the depth of connection between him and his aunt, one that rivals his relationship with his parents. The parents we choose for ourselves are likely to be more important, and certainly more revealing of our character, than the parents we inherit. In "Hotel" Merwin aligns himself with Margie rather than his parents. When Merwin is having difficulty with his homework his mother institutes a schedule: four arithmetic problems must be solved each morning before he can come down for breakfast. Why in the morning? "That is the time of day, she would say, when your mind is fresh" (UO, 173). By contrast, his aunt is free of such binding theories: "Margie sat with us over homework, and for me she added arithmetic exercises of her own. The time of day did not matter to her. She would sit with us not only after breakfast but also after we came home in the afternoon" (UO, 173). The mind, that is, can be fresh anytime; not confined to a routine, who knows when it will be alert? The point is to be prepared to seize that moment—and to shape one's life in accord with opportunities offered rather than by conforming to a schedule established by dictum.

Margie slices through stultifying, bewildering complexity, and her boisterous edge is felt not only after her death (Merwin's mother is scandalized by the fact that she has left all her belongings to her nephew), but in the months she spends as a family house guest. She believes any situation can be redefined according to one's own terms. Like Mandy, she is a character:

> Nobody else went to the Washburn Street cemetery just to walk around in there, but if Aunt Margie chose to do it that was one thing a cemetery was for, whether people realized it or not. Some days she had already been for her walk, by herself, when my sister and I got home from school. No doubt she needed an occasional outing to herself. The cemetery, when she walked in it, was her own place. I knew that when I was there. She did not read the tombstones. They were there like the trees. I did not ask many questions. I mentioned, at times, what I had been reading or thinking about, trying to catch and hold her attention. But I do not remember much about her conversations, if that is what they were. I doubt that we talked much. Cemeteries were also places to be quiet, out of respect, starting on the sidewalk before reaching the gate. (UO, 175–76)

These walks are neither traditional nor bound by rules: Margie sometimes goes unaccompanied, sometimes with the children. Nor is an effort made to ritualize this in memory, as with Merwin's visits to his father's study; all feels natural and appropriate, even though, as Merwin concedes, "nobody else went . . . just to walk around in there." Finally, the cemetery is a place "to be quiet, out of respect"—but the quiet is not demanded by a rule; it is a hush akin to inner peace. In the cemetery, inward feelings can appear in an outward manner; inner and outer need not always conflict, but can be held in balance.

This relaxation of the severe boundaries between inner and outer recalls Merwin's half-ruined French farmhouse, which itself overlaps and integrates an almost endless series of boundaries. Not only does it lie open to the creatures around it, but it stretches back into a past both ancient and current. On the morning after his first night spent there, Merwin is welcomed by an elderly neighbor who remembers the house as the local school during his youth. The house is the opposite, of course, of the public space of the anonymous hotel, exemplified by the postcard of it, lacking a message, that Merwin finds each time he is packing to leave for somewhere. Even more radically, the spaciousness of the farmhouse contrasts sharply with the clutter of objects found in his father's desk after his death. Merwin's listing of the bland contents of his father's desk drawer—"paper clips, gummed labels, key chains, emery boards . . . white plastic letter openers in the shape of files of elephants crossing bridges, hotel stationery, post cards showing airplanes motionless in blue" (UO, 139–40)—seems a terrible indictment: What is this if not a sign that his father has taken items intended to be useful and lively, and turned them into relics of the dead, mementos and souvenirs husbanded for some distant future? While Margie's acts turn the cemetery into a living place, where tombstones are no more fearful than trees, his father turns sprightly objects into a graveyard. This material pile, this clutter of junk that resists being transformed into anything personal, resembles the hotel's anonymity.

Looking for the person beyond their framework may issue in two kinds of discoveries, both distressing. The person may prove to be the clutter in a desk drawer, and the one sought—in shirt sleeves, lounging in the winter sun by the sugar factory—may turn out to be only a projection of one's own personality, an answer to one's own wishes and needs.[8] What may be otherwise discovered, with less dismay, is that persons have abandoned, for reasons of their own, what Merwin calls their "legendary" selves, to take up an existence in which the inner life goes underground, to be guarded with care. Speaking of his mother's family in his final chapter, Merwin views a lineage interrupted by mishap, ill fortune, persistent illness, and early death. For his mother, the death of Merwin's older brother, Hanson (who, named after his mother's father, had lived less than a day), appears as a turning point:

> Beyond the day by day aspect of her existence . . . there was always a trackless, twilit, secret country open to no one. Not a dreamland or a cherished mystery into which she retired. It has always been right there with her, like her shadow, whatever she has been doing or saying. It is still there, the real source both of her words and her silence, and Hanson's headstone marks one of its boundaries. To me it seems as though the whole of her life until his death was part of her legendary self, and everything since, whatever else it may have been, was history. (UO, 218)

For Merwin himself, one could reverse this distinction: everything in his childhood seemed like history, settled and fixed, while all that he did after was an effort to sustain his legendary self. The legendary self is what Mandy possesses when she convinces the churchgoers to accede to her unique standards; it is what Margie possesses when she redefines the cemetery space she walks through; and it is what Merwin possesses when he chances on his ancient farmhouse, or when he tours the monasteries on Athos, or when he returns to the dead past to discover the source of its deadness and its lost possibility of life.

4

At the ending of "Affable Irregular: Recollections of R. P. Blackmur" (completed in 1981, just after *Unframed Originals*),[9] Merwin recalled listening to Blackmur talk as they visited the Boston Museum of Fine Arts, years after graduating from Princeton: "That afternoon he seemed inexplicably yet unmistakably like a father. A father to me. Particularly when he was turned away, was looking elsewhere" (RM, 199). The parents we choose for ourselves are likely to be more revealing of our character than the parents we inherit.

This coda to Merwin's memoirs displays clear affinities with his family writings. "Affable Irregular" is rare for its portrayal of a person Merwin regards with unquestioned esteem, and it calls for a way of writing that will depict its subject with a special clarity. What at first appears odd in this writing turns out to be an approach essential if the particulars of Blackmur's character are to be presented. Blackmur's portrait emerges not through descriptions or anecdotes but through the way he compels Merwin to approach him.[10] Merwin's characterization, however, often risks seeming diffident. Notably absent, for example, is material proper to reminiscence about a great man. The piece seems lacking in dramatic encounters, memorable anecdotes, sharp details of conversation. It fails even to describe Blackmur's looks, except to note that he sometimes appeared older than he was. Although one learns how Merwin looked as a Princeton undergraduate—dressed in clothes borrowed from his father's army service and wearing a beard that his classmate William Arrowsmith likened to an armpit—one has no idea how Blackmur looked, whether he was thin or fat, elegant or disheveled.

Such absences are crucial to this piece. In this memoir, callow youth is marked by its love of clarity, its need to know what to do, how to dress, what to read. Maturity is knowing the unimportance of what passes for clarity or completeness or establishing a public identity. The moment of greatest naivete occurs just before Merwin meets Blackmur, from whom he hopes to receive an answer to a crucial question: "I wanted to know for sure how you could tell whether a poem you read, or (a little shifty) one you wrote yourself, was really good or not. Some of the professors pronounced upon specific poems and poets in categorical fashion, but when asked how the judgment had been reached their answers had not contented me. I suspected that they did not really know. And I thought it possible that this Professor Blackmur, who had no degree and was not a professor, might" (RM, 191). Merwin's naiveté is his need to know "for sure." Beyond his naivete, Merwin is right to believe that someone who is himself not clear in his identity, a professor "who had no degree and was not a professor"—a professor outside the framework of professorial authority—might be the one to answer a question that may have no clear answer. It is a key to Merwin's sense of value as learned through Blackmur: the understanding of what one does not know can initiate a love of curiosity and willingness to question.

From Blackmur, Merwin unlearns cleverness—an unlearning process reflected in this piece of writing, which will seem idiosyncratic until one realizes it is pervaded with Blackmur's ideals. The youthful Merwin believes in the need for a vivid identity: "I was in my third semester there, and I was busy being Shelley, mostly, and a bit of Beethoven" (RM, 190). By the end of his time at

Princeton, he has, by contrast, almost dissolved; he is a graduate student with no standing as a graduate student, no prospects for a job, not even a dim sense of the future: "I took it for granted that I did not know what I would do for a living, and even more strangely I took it for granted that I would not know, for a while" (RM, 194–95). And at this moment of high uncertainty, Merwin describes himself with the same term he reserves for Blackmur—an irregular: "By the time I sat in on his graduate seminar on the history of criticism I was no longer a graduate student and the irregularity of my presence in the course clearly pleased Richard" (RM, 195).

Rather than defining persons, Merwin's piece undefines them as it proceeds. Characteristically, his first encounter with Blackmur is almost no encounter at all. John Berryman (at the time, just past thirty) appears most distinctly, as befits his youth—"A severe, bony, superior figure all in browns" who may have been wearing the "long maroon-and-yellow striped knitted scarf" that became his hallmark. But Blackmur's first appearance could not be less dramatic. Merwin thinks he recalls seeing him, then wonders if he was actually there: "And was it not Blackmur, sitting behind a desk, smiling up in answer to questions, all but inaudible, and eclipsed, much of the time, by the students who came to register for the course?" Merwin delights in having no ready answer to his own question: "I think I saw him without meeting him, and he was out of the room before I knew it was he—if it was" (RM, 191).

No one but Blackmur could leave so distinct a doubt as to whether he was present. Continually, at the moment he is about to appear, in the early pages of the piece, he vanishes. After Merwin confesses that he never met him regularly, never took his courses formally, and wrote to him only sporadically, he says: "Gradually we circled a bit nearer to each other. The will was there. What I recall of Blackmur's speech during those years survives from such conversations, from the weekly talks on Joyce, Dostoevsky, Flaubert, and Mann that he gave regularly in the evenings in Clio Hall—one of the neo-classic temples in the middle of the campus, which were attended by a small fervent band of aficionados" (RM, 192). Just as he is circling closer, Merwin interrupts himself with a disconcertingly precise description of the architecture and location of Clio Hall. Everything and everyone has more of a completed, detailed, and visual presence than Blackmur.

As the piece progresses, however, what appears at first as privation turns into elusiveness, and what appears as elusiveness turns into a willingness to cherish what is, in oneself, as yet unfinished. In Merwin's final pages Blackmur appears as someone who hungers for situations in which one is called upon to display one's character. The idea behind the course Merwin attended in his final days at Princeton is that each week *Antony and Cleopatra* will be read from the perspective of a different critic. There is no single play, only these infinite, intelligent responses to it. It is no wonder, then, that, as Merwin points out, so little remains in anyone's memory of the exact content of these lectures. It is not simply that Blackmur "thought of a good critic as a house waiting to be haunted," though avoidance of any dogmatic approach is certainly a truth in the matter; but the deeper truth is that one's character can be defined depending on one's strengths or weaknesses on each occasion. Note taking is futile ("I think no one managed to keep up the practice constantly") because in this course, the listener loses his way, drawn into the encounter, thinking his own thoughts as he is engaged. "Some of the Blackmurisms promised to be inexhaustible," Merwin says, explaining how easy it was to follow neither text nor critic but one's own train of thought as engendered by the multiplying dialogues. "One heard them and missed the next fifteen minutes, or one went on listening and lost them" (RM, 196).

If the substance was lost, Merwin recalls two quotations that capture its essence. He remembers Blackmur's statement that Dostoevsky's characters acquired "potential reversibility": they were "able to act in ways inconsistent with what one had thought of, until then, as their true characters, without the reader's ceasing to believe in them" (RM, 197). What could have been decried as hopeless confusion becomes a moral decision sustained by the reader's commitment. The other fragment recalls Blackmur's fascination with Virgil's line to Dante in the third canto of the *Inferno* "explaining that the tenants of hell are those '*c'hanno perduto il ben del'intelleto*'—'who have lost the *good* of the intellect'" (RM, 197).[11] This, Merwin senses, was advice directed by Blackmur to Blackmur: it was his warning to himself of a danger into which he had fallen, a loss he had suffered. The good of the intellect, as defined through this piece, is nothing that can be possessed, but it is something that can be lost in thoughtless moments. Failing to rise to any necessary occasion can cause this loss, which is why its absence is marked so forcefully in one's mind. The long way Blackmur would follow is self-challenging, not an accumulation of triumphs. One's character exists only as long as one has the good to sustain it. Otherwise, everything else is a shell—patchwork clothes, mannered gestures, clever remarks.

Only in the final three paragraphs does Merwin bring together the memorable sayings, the bits of advice that Blackmur shared with him in these and later years. Only at the very end, that is, when we are in a position to hear these remarks in relation to Blackmur's beliefs and struggles, is Merwin prepared to present them. This withholding of what might be thought of as the best for last appropriately comes as an afterthought. One cannot cease thinking of a person like Blackmur, engaging with whom—even at a distance—prompts elaborations, twists, surprises of memory, additions, all of which are summoned by the haunting presence of the person. Since the memoir continues after it seems to be complete, Merwin can say unabashedly, "I still send him my poems"—a final sentence not sentimental but accurate. Blackmur requires this ongoing participation that continually forms around that "tenacious esteem not for the human alone but for the inchoate in humanity, as it struggles inexplicably to complete itself through language" (RM, 199).

14

The Broken Back Line

IN NOVEMBER 1976, as Merwin was completing the prose pieces that end *Houses and Travellers,* his poetry began to feature a device uncommon in its own right, largely untried by his contemporaries, and without precedent in his own work: a distinctive pause toward the middle of each line like a caesura, except that unlike a traditional caesura it was as apt to disrupt as to enhance the pauses in speech rhythms.[1] He has discussed this device in interviews, referring to it as "my 'broken back' line, the two-part line," but his comments have been impersonal, emphasizing historical antecedents. "The old Middle English line," he explains, has been "overlaid" by "Italianate iambic pentameter." Recognizing the caesura, then, draws attention to a melding that he would now disjoin. The caesura is an elemental recurrence, a deliberate atavism: "the caesura in the iambic pentameter line is like the ghost of the old Middle English line asserting itself all the time, saying I'm here all the time." But how does Merwin, whose work in iambic pentameter is limited to a handful of poems from the 1950s, find the device operating in his lines? He touches upon that only in a reserved summary, where the usefulness of the device is heavily qualified: "If you take up something that is like a continuation of it, it seems a little stiff, but it can do things that iambic pentameter probably can't."[2]

Merwin may be so diffident because he would reserve his enthusiasm for the unit that truly engages his interest, the line break. "One of the danger signs of recent verse," he has stated to interviewers, "is the demise of the clarity of the line." So important is that clarity that he urged workshop students to examine why a line stopped when it did, even "at the expense of losing a great deal of spontaneity": "there are two things that a line is doing—it's making a rhythm of its own by means of stopping here when it does; and unless you're doing it wrong, unless it's working against you and you've lost it, this *line,* it's making a continuity of movement and making a rhythm within a continuity."[3] The line pauses as it ends, but also continues, and one of these two movements inevitably dominates, a pattern that produces expectation: has the line come to a summary stopping point or is there a further elaboration ahead? The suspense of the poem hinges on this turn at the end of every line, a turn that is the point of every line.

Merwin's caesura, then, inserts another level of intricacy by doubling the potential for turns in each line. Why, at this point, would there be a need for greater complexity? One answer is that the caesura becomes valuable during a time of moving back and forth between verse and prose. The caesura is a sign of the poetic, an ancestral ghost reasserting itself; by reaffirming the line break, it recalls the one fundamental that distinguishes verse from prose—the need to make evident a series of turns as a work unfolds. Verse is lineated because the end of each line implies that a turn will occur that is at a level deeper than the turn after the end of a sentence. By including turns within turns, to evoke levels within levels, Merwin works within small intense units both rhythmic and meaningful. Yet the point of adopting this variable caesura, which occurs in each line whether or not the syntax calls for a pause, is not to elevate verse over prose. Rather, this device becomes beneficial if one is working *between* verse and prose, for it allows into verse the expansive qualities of prose discourse. The other side of the variable caesura is that it can relax meaning. Such semiturns as Merwin employs need not be emphatic; if they can add stress they can also relieve it by functioning in a minimal way. This option becomes especially important if one would include asides in the work but at the same time note their lack of relative importance.

1

The variable caesura addresses a problem evident in the verse of part 4 of *The Compass Flower* where, as Charles Altieri complains, "Merwin's cadences go slack":[4]

> we sit out in the late afternoon
> long grass and the trees of a park
> on the far side
> and a few cars on the hill (CF, 76)
>
> I hear my feet resound on a wharf
> echoed from other wharves
> through the centuries
> the fishing boats are all moored
> in the evening (CF, 80)
>
> some were still swimming
> in the short summer
> on the sand behind us (CF, 82)

To give over an entire line to a prepositional phrase is risky: if one expects a line to signal an authoritative turn, then the failure to turn with authority can weaken the poem. But the persistent appearance of the same kind of line suggests the effect may be deliberate: Merwin would drift back to some moment he recalls, with added dimensions slowly accruing, expanding the reverie but never sharpening it to a distinct impression. In a prose context, such asides would slip into the background as an element of detail; but in a verse context, with the reader's expectation that a new line promises an event, the line gains prominence despite Merwin's effort to weaken it with the prepositional phrase. Syntax, though a powerful ordering component in free verse, is still less powerful than the line break, a fundamental unit without which, of course, the verse would be prose.

The immense advantage of the variable caesura, then, is that it can orchestrate such a minor turn—not strong enough to deserve an entire line to itself yet indicating a distinct shift. Its inflection can be reserved for the turn that occurs within memory, the turn less active than the major turns unfolding as the poem develops. Although the caesura is exclusively associated with verse and related to the fundamental verse unit, the line break, it allows Merwin to borrow a feature from the spaciousness of prose: syntax can now be used adroitly, in the form of the prepositional phrase, to downplay turns, to render them less active.

One poem that draws on phrasings that might be considered weak, yet that serve to orchestrate the poet's feelings most precisely, is "Sun and Rain":

> Opening the book   at a bright window
> above a wide pasture   after five years
> I find that I am still standing   on a stone bridge
> looking down with my mother   at dusk into a river
> hearing the current as hers   in her lifetime
>
> now it comes to me   that that was the day
> she told me of seeing my father   alive for the last time
> and he waved her back from the door   as she was leaving
> took her hand   for a while and said
> nothing
>
>   at some signal
> in a band of sunlight all the black cows   flow down the pasture together
> to turn uphill and stand   as the dark rain touches them (OH, 10)

In the first stanza, the last halves of the lines form around prepositional phrases, weak turns that present Merwin's movement back into the past "after five years." In general, active statements begin after the line break, honoring its greater authority ("I find that," "looking down," and "hearing the current") while the afterthoughts, the deepening downward pull towards the past, occur in prepositional phrases that follow the caesura. Merwin conveys the sudden downward spiral of being overtaken by a memory of sorrow; the softening into darkness is palpable as we move from "a bright window" to the image of his mother looking "at dusk into a river" and "hearing the current as hers."

Against this emerges the saving gesture of the second stanza—hands held out for another and clinging to a long moment on the edge of death. The strength in the gesture is kept up in the forthright clauses that now begin to dominate and even spill over beyond the boundary of the caesura. This in turn leads back to the present, with the vivid movement of creatures that "turn uphill" in "a band of sunlight" and stand "as the dark rain touches them," as the hands of his mother and father once touched. It is a complex surrogate moment, in which Merwin's longing to reach out to his own mother is answered by this recollected moment in which his father had been able to overcome his own hesitancy to extend his hand to hers, and then comforted further by this encompassing vision of sun and rain mingling together. The vision is a gift much as his father's gesture was a gift to his mother; it keeps that gesture alive and recovers it for the present.

At its most effective, the caesura allows a degree of movement simply unavailable in verse with only one kind of pause within it. It allows for levels of activity within the activity promised by the individual line. Moreover, the flexibility of the caesura allows for exchanges of position: midway through the line, when we anticipate a weak turn, we may experience a strong one, and the reverse can happen at the end of the line. The line can turn intense or grow slack, within itself, according to the poem as it is shaped.

If the caesura introduces into verse some of the advantages Merwin recognizes as he writes in prose, with its greater latitude for digressions and asides, then it is fitting that the earliest work to employ the caesura was "The Cow," a piece that is entirely a narrative.[5] The poem is about the efforts of two neophyte to tend livestock and keep alive a cow that is too ill to live. It begins:

> The two boys down the road   with a vegetable farm
> they started from scratch   for their religion
> say they didn't know anything   when they began
> they had to pick it up   as they went along
> all about growing things   and they made a lot of mistakes (OH, 41)

In its first usage, the caesura is something of a novelty. It intrudes to modify the force of the line break for no reason other than that this poem, as a narrative, demands a line break not particularly forceful. Moreover, this first caesura generally follows speech patterns; it lends a rhythmic pace to the poem by distributing beats across the line. With a narrative that steers close to prose, the caesura lays a rhythmic path, gently suggesting that at least one beat should fall in each half of the line. The result lends movement to a story whose development might otherwise seem prolix. The reader's sympathy should be equally divided between the creature who dies through her owners' ineptitude and the owners whose well-meant convictions are difficult to fault. Merwin's own feelings are divided, and the equanimity he wants to achieve depends upon a narrative that blindly sets forward what happened in a blameless fashion.

If the first poem to employ the caesura uses it minimally, as a gentle goad to rhythm, the last poem to employ it virtually wields it as a scourge, terrorizing the reader.[6] In "Questions to Tourists Stopped by a Pineapple Field" (the earliest of Merwin's poems to register anger at the exploitation of Hawaii), the reader is thrown into the viewpoint of the hapless tourist. To be "stopped" means to be stalled or brought up short, as though tourists regularly expressed amazement that anything other than amusement and recreation might be a feature of the islands. In the barrage of questions directed against the tourists halted in their bustle from scenic site to scenic site, the caesura is a whiplash, speeding up the line or jerking it in a new direction:

> do you remember the first time   you tasted pineapple
> do you like it better fresh   or from the can
> what do you remember   of the picture on the can
> what did you feel   as you looked at the picture
> which do you like better   the picture or the pineapple field (OH, 43)

Physically halted by the appearance of a field of pineapple—not what one associates with a vacation paradise—the tourists nonetheless continue to be propelled forward under the goad of these questions. Their ability to endure the rapid-fire barrage, which goes on for 102 lines, is Merwin's testament to benumbed faculties. Here the caesura is a deliberate debasement that transforms the turn at the line break into a brutalizing shift of gears; such a desecration may have ruined the caesura for use by Merwin, as though it had been driven beyond its means in this one destructive outing.

In poetry written between these two extremes, from 1976 to 1979, Merwin remains entirely committed to the caesura, employing it in virtually all his poetry, though the extent to which it contributes to the individual poem varies considerably. At times, it verges on withering away: early drafts show it appearing in a more conventional typography as a half-line (fig. 20), though in final drafts it returns as a blank space near the line's midpoint. It appears least effectively in a group of poems about the city, several of which remain unpublished. A caesura poem, to be effective, should edge between prose and verse, able to counterpose moments of intense feeling with moments of release or expansion, as in "Sun and Rain." These city poems, however, portray a series of impenetrable facades that continue to resist the poet's considerations. In an earlier version of "Going" (entitled "If I Knew Why I Came Back to You") turbulent doubts precede the poet's description of the urban setting:

If I knew why I came   back to you
at any time even once   know instead of thinking
maybe I would not come back   any more again
maybe I would not be here   even now even now
but you are not something   I can know

always when I come to you it is   back from somewhere
I was born   into you I have
no beginning and I was   born into you
it is why you are never there   never were there never will be

but here I am after all   Haydn pouring from the walls
at night again   over the waves of the traffic
the noise the sound   the flowing drivers

faces all day reflecting   feet waiting feet in pairs
shut away simply from the logic   of ways of sitting in subways in silence
in positions of papers being read   papers flying in the squares
oh subways flying in the dark   all day
on glass in the streets broken   unknown
on spilled water before   feet hurrying homeward[7]

In revision, the first three stanzas were deleted, and the published version depicted the city as endlessly reproducing the least personal aspects of lives. Any thought of interpersonal communication is excluded. The obliquity of city life, "thinking of something else (/) that is elsewhere," is reinforced as faces are supplanted by papers held before them, which then reappear as scattered through the city, multiplied by the endless glass of skyscrapers, cast aloft and mirrored in casual spilled water that returns us to the endless multiple anonymity of "feet hurrying homeward." Because the poem emphasizes disengagement, the caesura has little opportunity to insinuate its turns and its reconsiderations, and it essentially dissolves in the course of the poem. Indeed, with the exception of the last line, the caesura discreetly shadows the syntax throughout, in many instances operating like a comma.

2

With the exception of verse in tercets—the three-line stanza used to convey natural descriptions in *Feathers from the Hill* (1978)—all of Merwin's poetry between November 1976 and June 1979 employed the variable caesura.[8] But it contributed most to the emotional series in which Merwin approached the memory of his father. In the opening section of *The Compass Flower* he had worked through the emotions of his mother's death, and in a sense, by leaving details unspecified, had included his father within that sequence. But the poems in section 1 of *Opening the Hand* specifically address his father's death, though as they do so the sequence becomes a homage to his mother. Intense, contradictory, and ambivalent emotions play across these works, which employ the gradations of the caesura most effectively.

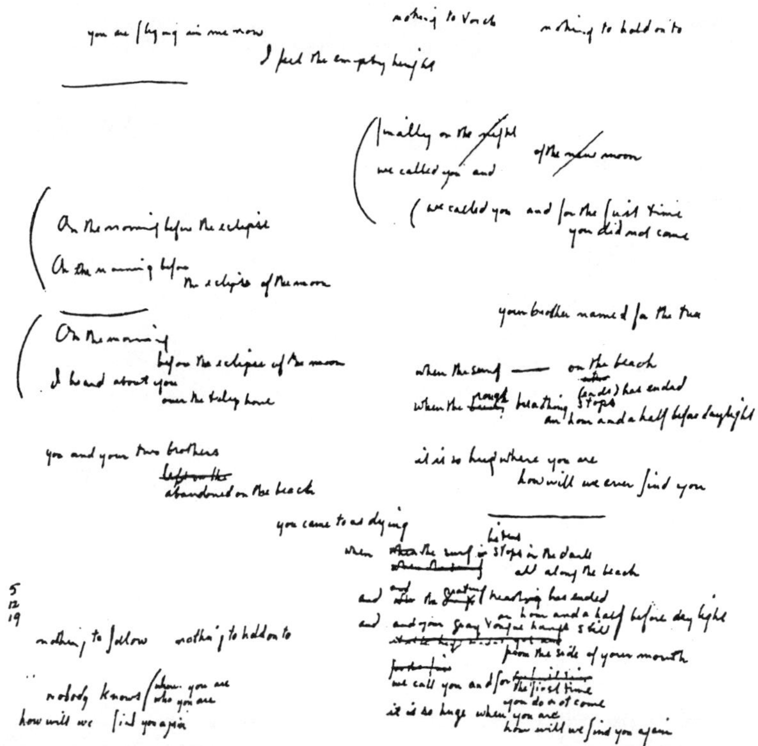
you are flying in one more
nothing to touch
nothing to hold on to
I feel the empty height
finally on the night
of the new moon
we called you and
(we called you and for the first time
you did not come
On the morning before the eclipse
On the morning before
the eclipse of the moon
your brother named for the tree
On the morning
before the eclipse of the moon
I heard about you
over the telephone
when the surf — on the beach
when the rough breathing (ends) has ended
an hour and a half before daylight
you and your two brothers
abandoned on the beach
it is so huge where you are
how will we ever find you
you came to us dying
when the surf stops in the dark
all along the beach
and the breathing has ended
and your gray tongue still
an hour and a half before daylight
from the side of your mouth
we call you and for the first time
you do not come
it is so huge where you are
how will we find you again
5
12
19
nothing to follow nothing to hold on to
nobody knows where you are
who you are
how will we find you again

Figure 20. Notes for "Ali" (MS. 22:20/039, c. 1977). Merwin's concern for the line break is evident in the way he tries several different breaks for one line. His earliest drafts of passages are punctuated somewhat conventionally, recording a semi-line break in the middle of each line. The caesura appears at a later point, as these passages are rewritten. As a caesura poem, "Ali" was left incomplete; it was finished at a later date as a non-caesura poem (MS. 22:20/047, d. Aug. 7, 1981).

"Strawberries" offers the best opportunity for a detailed consideration of the caesura's contribution because it is the only caesura poem to have been originally written without the caesura. This work went through an unusual set of variations before reaching its final state. Deeply embedded within the poem is a personal anecdote that Merwin mentioned in *Unframed Originals:*

> By the time I first saw Rimerton, the boat landings had gone from that part of the shore, but my father told me of seeing a team of beautiful horses, when he was a child, come down the road to cross the water on a flatboat, and on the way down the brake of the wagon failed, and the wagon rushed ahead, out of control, pushing the horses ahead of it onto the landing and the wharf, and off the end into the river, where they drowned before they could be cut loose from the harness. He remembered them being dragged out by other teams, and how he cried, and he showed me the spot where they had been buried—at least he

> thought it was the place. It is one of the handful of clear images of that time that he conveyed to me, something that continued to impress him. (UO, 30–31)

Although the story of this runaway team seems hardly related to the two mysterious horse-and-wagon appearances in "Strawberries," it is the source of that image, and its transformation can be traced to an early draft of his 1972 elegy to his father:

> Now that we can talk about anything
> I keep losing the beginning
> now that everything is clear to you
> you disappear
> I know it was your childhood I was sent looking for
> but all I see for a long time is a patch of surface
> of river
> words are no use there they only throw shadows
> they cast little silences before them
> when it is silent enough already
> does nobody ever laugh or sing there
> then the beautiful horses come down the hill
> as I alone see them they are everything you said matched and
> young and glossy in new harness
> but whatever you said their color is transparent
> I watch them without breathing
> down the slope under the shady trees in the ferry
>
> with the ferry
> and I see them plunge through the rail into the river
> with the wagon
> where the plowhorses drag them and later with chains as you said
> to the grave big enough to drive a team into
> but I cannot see them by then at all
> is that all you remembered
> the wagon also was raised you forgot to tell me
> they brought it up empty
> I know because I have seen it
> without horses entering the valley[9]

Merwin associated this story with his father's childhood, "one of the handful of clear images of that time that he conveyed to me." His recollection, then, is a bridge to his father's past, a past notable for its gloomy silence ("does nobody ever laugh or sing there"). The incident itself is the exception to that silence. It is so dramatic that his father had to relate it, and it linked father and son in one of their rare moments together. What Merwin brings to the story now is his sense of his own grievous loss. The empty wagon represents the desolation he feels, surrounded by the silence where there had once been a familiar voice.

That he can add a detail of his own to the story confirms how authentically he grieves, sharing with his father this moment of his own grief, in a story he had often heard but never felt so deeply as now. The poem folds within it communications that are frustrated—clarity that disappears, sounds that are silent, images that are transparent; they are all lost connections, their restoration now glimpsed just as they are broken.

In a later draft of this elegy in 1972, the opening section took a quite different form:

> Father after one day and night
> near the second dawn
> I too stood at the entrance to a deep valley
> that opens into darkness
> ahead of me an old wagon with no driver
> was carrying off a casket of the same parched wood
> into that valley
> while another wagonload laden with large berries
> of two kinds one of them strawberries
> the other unknown to me
> had emerged and was coming toward me
> with a horse but no driver
> where I was standing I have a little garden there
> in that sandy soil
> white beans a few young artichokes
> for my mother

As drafts of this elegy evolve, Merwin grows increasingly aware that his mother can hear these words that his father cannot. Her appearance, even indirectly, in this first section prepares for her reappearance in the final section. Her presence, offsetting his father's absence, is part of the balancing effect in this version. The horse-and-wagon incident has been removed entirely from the realm of family anecdote and now invites symbolic readings. His father's absence matches the drivers who are conspicuously missing. The wagons have doubled, and their twin movements, ingoing and outgoing, imply an exchange or a cyclical turn: something gone, something returned. Indeed, the very starkness of the narrative helps contrast balancing movements; down but also up—the casket departs, but berries arrive. The speaker first stands "at the entrance to a deep valley / that opens into darkness"; it resembles a hollow grave. He ultimately locates himself in a garden among vegetables he grows for his mother. The movement is away from darkness, narrow valleys, and caskets, and toward the fruits of the earth, cultivation, and fecundity.

Such starkness is appropriate as an introduction to an elegy in several sections: it sets forward opposing terms, death and life, that will broadly contend with each other. It would be less appealing if this were a separate poem, and when Merwin recast the section as an individual work in January 1973, first titling it "Berries," then "Strawberries," he thickened its texture:

> Working at night in my
> small sandy artichoke garden
> at the end of the valley
> where I was living with my mother
> one of those nights when everything is a shade lighter
> than its surroundings
> I looked up from the ground to watch
> a horse and wagon without a driver
> carrying an old wooden casket
> slowly into the valley
> and another wagon loaded with strawberries
> and some other unknown berry
> coming out
> my father was dead
> and in the morning there were strawberries for breakfast
> there would be strawberries for breakfast[10]

In this draft, a penultimate line has been canceled: "but not the other kind." If it had remained, it would have drawn a firm distinction between the familiar and the unknown. This draft is notable for Merwin's shifting attention to the one element in his previous draft that rested most uneasily in a pattern of death and rebirth—the two kinds of berries. This draft incorporates the recognizable strawberries back into everyday life, leaving the other berries unknown, like a persisting gap or absence, an indirect acknowledgment of his father's death. That sense of uncertainty as mingled inextricably with quotidian events is the burden of this early "Strawberries" (or "Berries"—Merwin's rejection of this title comports with his cancellation of its original last line). The poem now begins where the previous version ended, in the relative harmony of garden work. This version, rather than achieving a balance, unbalances itself; mysterious wagons intrude upon the gardener at work. The restoration at the end, incorporating the unknown with the known, is an uncertain or awkward balance, underscored by the peculiar emphasis of "there would be strawberries for breakfast," as though restating a fact one might not wish to hear.

As versions of the poem evolve, Merwin keeps refining the balance he achieves at the end. In addition, his mother exerts an increasingly powerful influence. What remains intact is the general pattern of ingoing-outgoing, of loss and replacement, in the example of the twin wagons. These features appear in the final version, now orchestrated by the caesura:

> When my father died I saw   a narrow valley
>
> it looked as though it began   across the river
> from the landing where he was born   but there was no river

I was hoeing the sand   of a small vegetable plot
for my mother   in deepening twilight
and looked up in time   to see a farm wagon
dry and gray   horse already hidden
and no driver   going into the valley
carrying a casket

                        and another wagon
coming out of the valley   behind a gray horse
with a boy driving   and a high load
of two kinds of berries   one of them strawberries

  that night when I slept   I dreamed of things
wrong in the house   all of them signs
the water of the shower   running brackish
and an insect of a kind   I had seen him kill
climbing around   the walls of his bathroom
  up in the morning   I stopped on the stairs
my mother was awake   already and asked me
if I wanted a shower   before breakfast
and for breakfast she said   we have strawberries (OH, 7)

"Strawberries" is, in fact, punctuated quite intricately with a number of typographical features not used by other caesura poems.[11] It is, first of all, divided into three verse-paragraphs that distinguish among temporal events: "When my father died," "that night when I slept," and "up in the morning." Moreover, the last two verse-paragraphs, which are not further separated into stanzas, are thereby presented as related to each other. By contrast, the first verse-paragraph virtually stands alone: it expands through three stanzas, the last of which is interrupted by a dramatic break that falls across the caesura. That dramatic break, moreover, initiates a turn away from the oppressive landscape of "a narrow valley." After the break, the gray wagon is replaced by "a gray horse," there is a boy driving the horse, and the wagon is laden with "two kinds of berries (/) one of them strawberries."

Merwin uses typography to punctuate two different patterns, which follow each other to form another, more inclusive pattern. Within the first temporal event (in the first three stanzas), a reversal occurs between "carrying a casket (//) and another wagon." Ominous, fearful, mysterious images are transformed into a version unthreatening and understandable, as the gray of the dry wagon, for instance, now appears in the gray of a living horse. In the verse-paragraph shift between the second and third temporal events, a similar transformation occurs: the son has nightmares "of things / wrong in the house" that center on the bathroom and the shower, but the next morning, he finds that his mother is already awake, that the shower is unthreatening and breakfast is on the way. Both redemptive transformations are related by the offer of strawberries for breakfast, as though the assimilations of the dream landscape and the assimilations of the nightmare both cohered into a general pattern. Revival and renewal still constitute the theme of the poem, as has been the case since the final draft of Merwin's elegy to his father, but rejuvenation now takes place on a larger scale, in a variety of settings. More pointedly, the role of his mother has been amplified. Her spoken words initiate the most powerful assimilation, one that connects the dream landscape and the nightmare. "We have strawberries," then, are words that offer special reassurance. The second, unknown berry almost passes unnoticed in this final version, perhaps a mark of how completely the unknown has been assimilated into a redemptive routine.

When the caesura is operating to full advantage, it fosters a complexity to which it also provides access. It increases movement on the level of the individual line, while organizing those movements into larger, overall patterns that lead toward appreciating the movement of the individual line. Consider the difference between the two stanzas of "The Oars":

> My father was born   in a house by a river
> nobody knows   the color of the water
> already seeds had set   in the summer weeds
> the house needed paint   but nobody will see
>
> after the century turned   he sat in a rowboat
> with its end on the bank   below the house
> holding onto the oars   while trains roared past
> until it was time for him   to get up and go (OH, 4)

Merwin deliberately aborts what might have been a delicate turn from line 1 to line 2. "Nobody knows" does not refer to "a house by a river"; rather, it is "the color of the water" that "nobody knows." The pivoting relation between the first two lines is no sooner offered than it is withdrawn, and the first stanza resolutely truncates each of its lines as a full sentence. This severe restriction explains why line 3 can be affecting: the possibilities implicit in origins and beginnings, in the new seeds, have already set early, locked in a battle for survival with the undergrowth. There will be no wanton flowering here. In turn, this suggests that the general air of dereliction in the fourth line stems not so much from poverty as from an attitude of deprivation. The setting is barren because persons within it withhold their attention from it. The house needs paint because no one will see it is starved for color, just as nobody knows the color of the water because no one has ever cared to look at it.

Given the inertia depicted in this first stanza, then, his father's achievement is to take a cue from the century that turns and the modern trains that roar by, rendering the river obsolete as a passageway, and to leave behind the rowboat and "get up and go." That inertia, to some extent, carries over into the one extended sentence that makes up the second stanza, with the decision to leave only occurring at the very end. Moreover, the caesura in each line draws attention to the conflict between going and staying with which his father must have struggled: the century turned but he sat in a rowboat, the rowboat was apart from the house but it was still on the riverbank, and the trains roared past but he was clinging to the oars. Inertia and momentum contend with each other over the caesura, just as the entire stanza must overcome the weight of its one long sentence to arrive at the breakaway point. It is true that "get up and go" is just enough like a slogan or catch phrase to imply that his father had no genuine sense of direction after he left home. But given the obstacles before him, enacted so powerfully in these lines that are crisscrossed with burdensome opposition, it is impressive that he can summon the energy to leave at all. By itself, this image of a man stuck in a rowboat while the century turns about him might appear to be a critical caricature; but the image cannot be separated from the activity of the caesura, conveying that mixture of inertia and momentum that is the key to this portrayal.

3

Outside the family poems, the variable caesura can still invite complexity into poems. It offers conflicting approaches to composition, depending on whether it is asserting itself microscopically or macroscopically. Microscopically, it is a verse device related to the line break, allowing for a minor turn within a line. Such an allowance raises intricate questions of orchestration: Is the caesura a minor or major turn? Is it affirming the break at the end or undercutting it? As a variant of the line break, its effect is to draw us closer to the activity in a line, inviting attention to minute detail. Macroscopically, it is a device that presents the work as a narrative. It resembles the pause of medieval epic narrative, which relates the two separate halves of the line by implying a parallel construction. By suggesting a resemblance between the halves of the line, it goads the poem forward, even increasing its pace. Halves of the line, as events, pass quickly because they are the same occurrence seen from a slightly different view. As in narrative poetry, there is an amount of "filler," but it is rapidly digested, further increasing the speed of the line.

"Sheridan," written in September 1978 and one of the last of the caesura poems, not only steers between these opposite features but is literally generated by the conflicting opportunities that so idiosyncratic a device offers. Although work on "Sheridan" began in conventional lines without the caesura, Merwin quickly began to recast his opening to include it. The result was a poem that could encompass a spectrum from the narrative and descriptive to the poetic and lyrical. At one end there is a literal narrative poem, "Sheridan's Ride," by Thomas Buchanan Read, a popular nineteenth-century poem describing a legendary twenty-mile night ride made by Civil War General Philip Sheridan. It reproduces the excitement of that ride in a tetrameter line of galloping anapests and iambs:

> But there is a road from Winchester town,
> A good, broad highway leading down;
> And there, through the flush of the morning light,
> A steed as black as the steeds of night,
> Was seen to pass, with eagle flight.
> As if he knew the terrible need,
> He stretched away with his utmost speed.

That is one extreme: quintessential narrative verse, driven by a rapid pace, fusing man and steed in a nighttime ride to save the day. Its opposite is Merwin's recollection, at the exact midpoint of the poem, of hearing "Sheridan's Ride" read to him as a child. These five lines appear forty-seven lines into the poem, and after them, forty-seven more lines will follow:

> I know because afterward   it was read to me
> already in bed   my mother in the chair beside me
> cellos in the avenue   of a lighted city
> night after night again   I listened to your ride
> as somebody never there   had celebrated it (OH, 54)

Unlike the ride itself, however, they are cozy and intimate, the child in bed, his mother beside him, listening to a story heard before as reassuring as the ground bass of a cello against the discord of the city, a spectator sharing the ride at a safe distance. The central line of this sequence, "cellos in the avenue (/) of a lighted city," is, moreover, a lyrical expression of inward harmony unlike any other in the work.

The contending opportunities posed by the variable caesura allow for such a range: echoes of a popular narrative poem, out in the world, and recollections of a personal moment in the past, an interior scene regarded with tenderness and fondness. To hold these two together seems difficult, but Merwin is, from the start, uniting the impersonal rush of events unfolding rapidly with the recollection of a moment of quiet harmony by focusing his work on Sheridan Square in New York City. Sheridan Square is an oasis surrounded by the city's energy, like a lyrical moment in a narrative poem:

> everyone knows the place   by your name now
> the iron fence   dry drinking fountain
> old faces from brick buildings   out for some sun
> sidewalk drunks   corner acquaintances
> leaves luminous above you   in the city night
> subway station   hands at green news stand
> traffic waiting   for the lights to change (OH, 55)

The last line holds together opposites that have crisscrossed the poem: traffic held in check, suspended like each line or half-line of description, but about to burst into motion. Like the caesura, liable to turn in a new direction or extend the first half of the line into the second half (either "the iron fence [/] dry drinking fountain" or "old faces from brick buildings [/] out for some sun"), motion is arrested but only for an instant.

Merwin brings his poem to a delicate close, but "Sheridan" is more than an elaborately indirect description of a park. This is a poem that, like the ride itself, goes on and on, disclosing subtexts within subtexts. One situation recurs frequently enough to form a center for the work: eyes suddenly open, but find nothing of what they expect. "The battle ended (/) the moment you got there," Merwin begins, setting in motion this pattern of anticlimactic arrival. The battle, when Sheridan arrives, is "gone as though you (/) had just opened your eyes / and there was nobody (/) who saw what you had come to see." At the end of the poem, Merwin underscores the point: Sheridan's aides rush to him, "telling you everything / that you had not seen could not see (/) never would see." Still closer to the end, Merwin portrays Sheridan's statue as though it conveyed that air of surprise: "only you are there / still seeing it disappear (/) in front of you."

This dissolving is even more remarkable because so much of the poem is based on detailed, dramatic descriptions of what appear, at first, to be scenes of battle:

> and they had broken upon   you they were long past
> your picket lines they were at large   in your positions
> outflanking outweighing   overrunning you
> burning beyond your campfires   in your constellations (OH, 56)

But Merwin is careful to state that Sheridan only imagined these scenes from a distance. In Read's poem the sound of a battle prompts Sheridan to mount up and head for the fray. But the excitement of the ride, not the horror of the battle, is what Read emphasizes; predictably, his poem romanticizes war by supplanting the battle scenes with Sheridan's own extended cavalry charge. All the confusion of war—troops in retreat, smoke clouding the field, enemies confused with allies—is overlooked. Merwin, by contrast, stresses the gap between Sheridan's conceptions and the actuality of war. However, he does so not by realistically portraying battlefield confusion but by stopping his poem at the very point when such confusion might appear:

> there was the smoke   and someone with your head
> raised an arm toward it   someone with your mouth
> gave an order   and stepped into the century
> and is seen no more   but is said
> to have won that battle   survived that war
> died and been buried   and only you are there
> still seeing it disappear   in front of you (OH, 56)

Sheridan's character undergoes a series of transformations: from the romantic night-rider feverishly caught up in imagining the battle under way to the figure who is literally someone else, the figure from history who "stepped into the century / and is seen no more" but about whom things are written in history books ("is said / to have won that battle"), to a final incarnation in a public statue in New York City, blinking with startled surprise.

These transformations ultimately bind Sheridan to the modern city, in which he is less of an anomaly than he at first appears to be. The question underlying "Sheridan" is, Why is it right for there be a statue of Sheridan in New York City? (In *Opening the Hand,* "Sheridan" is placed as the seventh of eight poems about the city.) The confusion, noise, and speed of the city continue to connect Sheridan and his ride to the urban environment. At the opening of his second stanza, Merwin makes a series of statements, each one more emphatic than the last:

> this was certainly the place   there is no
> place like this   this is the only place
> it could have been   this unquestionably
> is where the message came from   meant for you only
> the touched intelligence rushing   to find you
> tracing you gasping   drowning for lack of you
> racing with shadows   of falling bodies (OH, 56)

The "place" is Sheridan Square, more generally New York City, even more generally the modern urban environment with its ambiance of noise, confusion and speed. The rush of the modern city is equivalent to the sounds of battle that, in Read's recounting, reached Sheridan from twenty miles away. Merwin in New York is at the source of a battleground, the discord of which echoes the confusion of war. His response to that unfocused hum recalls Sheridan, whose own hearing transformed that mixture into the symphonics of a nighttime ride; Merwin then reproduces these symphonics in the descriptions of his own poem, which include his own version of the steed racing through the night, the apprehensive visions Sheridan felt as he plunged through the darkness.

"Sheridan" is a surprisingly intricate piece that asks to be read in a variety of ways. In one respect, it is a poem that recaptures a memory from Merwin's childhood. The ride narrated by Read that held his youthful attention is now duplicated, but with an adult's perspective. Yet the excitement of the original persists, flashing out sporadically in stunning passages that evoke the glamor of the ride. The insurmountable barriers that usually prevent Merwin from entering his past vanish as he recalls Read's poem. In another respect, however, "Sheridan" is one in a sequence of works about the modern city in which Merwin confesses his attraction for the city but remains disturbed by its destructive aspects. Sheridan's ride emphasizes speed, much as earlier poems from another city sequence, part 2 of *The Compass Flower,* declared rapid transit to be the only value the city upheld. The other side of Sheridan's glamorous ride, as Merwin reproduces it, is that it falls just short of sheer hysteria. A relentless motion overtakes even the bucolic setting in which the sounds of battle arrive to Sheridan, so that natural rhythms are disrupted by being rapidly sped along: "Fields were flooded with evening (/) seasons were resolved / forests came shouldering back." Merwin's replication of Read's version of Sheridan's ride is an adult's version that both appreciates and criticizes the allure of rapid transit.

In still another respect, the entire poem remains intensely critical of the heroics of warfare. Indeed, once a critical edge is allowed to enter the poem, once the nighttime ride begins to seem not heroic but hysterical, then judgments begin to proliferate. Sheridan's relation to the battle is, indeed, nothing if not boyish—an extended cavalry charge in a straight direction, entirely unlike the truth of warfare. His view is above the fray. He literally sees nothing of the battle, conceiving it entirely in terms of his own heroics, just as Read saw nothing of it, just as young Merwin saw nothing of it. (Both Read and Merwin the boy are fused in the line "I listened to your ride / as somebody never there [/] had celebrated it.") For Sheridan himself to participate in such innocence is absurd, yet, as Merwin notes, Sheridan passes into the century, becomes apotheosized, and is honored with a statue. But the final irony is that, honored as he is, he remains entirely forgotten, surrounded by the ordinary activities of urban life—a double irony, indeed, because forgetting the truth of war is a habit we seem to cultivate with ease. In this respect, the harmonious placidity of the final stanza, in which order delicately reconstitutes itself in a series of prim scenes, is a judgment against us all, a condemnation of our own propensity to forget the past. Sheridan's appearing to blink in surprise, wondering what happened to the battle, is just the way we prefer to think of our wars: great men arrive on the scene, all is resolved, and we can continue to go on living.

It is difficult to know where and when to stop extrapolating from "Sheridan" as it shifts among its diverse facets. The disruptions of the caesura, which shift lines from microscopic to macroscopic attention, establish a dynamic large enough to include a number of individual views, all of which exert themselves at different points: Merwin as a boy swept up in the excitement of Read; Merwin as an adult recapturing that excitement but with a wider understanding of its source; Merwin admiring the city for its fund of energy and its pockets of repose; Merwin as a critic of the city for its air of forgetfulness and love of empty transit; Sheridan as a romantic, believing that war can be directed by great men; and Sheridan as one who blinks in surprise, wondering what happened to the battle he had conceived. Ultimately, the opportunities offered by the caesura as it reappears from one kind of writing to another increase Merwin's range. Breathtakingly, the poem recaptures a moment from Merwin's childhood by overcoming barriers between past and present, turns itself critically but appreciatively toward the ambiance of the modern city, and raises acute and disturbing questions about the role of the hero in warfare.

4

The sudden disappearance of the caesura midway through the family sequence collected in section 1 of *Opening the Hand* is one of the most dramatic events in the volume. The family poems without the caesura were written in 1980 and 1981, as *Unframed Originals* was being completed, and they signal a degree of freedom new to Merwin.[12] The poems in the first half, with the caesura, center on his father and mother, and emphasize the memory of his father; by contrast, the poems in the second half focus on his aunt, on his sister and him as children, and on other family members. The poems in the first half respond to a somber occasion, marked by deep personal involvement, scored with upheaval and uncertainty, and they demand that subtle shifts be made to accommodate their complexity. But the poems in the second half are fluent and straightforward. Neither absorbed in detail nor tangled in discord, they would be handicapped by the caesura.

When Merwin arranged his family poems for *Opening the Hand* he placed "The Houses" as a transition between the early and late works. Its format is unlike anything else in the book. After the initial three-line stanza, each stanza increases by one line until the central twelve-line stanza, after which each stanza drops one line until a final three-line stanza. This parabolic form is used to unite two incidents separated by years. As a child Merwin notices a house while wandering in the woods, but when he tries to show it to his father it is no longer there. The incident is duplicated years later when Merwin is visiting property his father has just purchased and he spots a house on the property; when he asks his father about it he is told no such house exists. The narrative has the unsettling quality of a dream. Father and son cannot share feelings; what exists for one is not only invisible to the other but, more harrowingly, what exists when the son is by himself actually vanishes when he tries to share it with his father. The house is an image of tranquil stability that is beyond this pair who cannot agree on even the most elementary of things.

Merwin's acknowledgment of this gulf is one sign of change. His previous poetry was never far from a compulsive desire to reach out to a father he is trying to understand even as that understanding arrives too late. But "The Houses" accepts that father and son were fated to be separate. The fact that the incident repeats itself uncannily, decades later, becomes a statement that the past is no longer fluid but fixed and completed. The poem's dream format permits this knowledge to emerge as though Merwin were its helpless spectator. The remorseless addition and subtraction of the format is almost opposite to the caesura poems, with their poet so intricately involved in shaping his work.

What gives the past an air of stillness and lingering mystery is that, in these later poems, all its unanswered questions now remain both unfinished and complete; they are never to be answered. This is central to "Unknown Forbear," a poem to the figure on the dust jacket of *Unframed Originals*. Even though Merwin does not and cannot know the man, the man himself, Merwin observes, "appeared to know where he was / whose porch that was" and even "who had opened the windows" (OH, 28). The man may have known the answers to the questions swirling about the poem, but Merwin knows these questions will remain unanswered. Accepting this is the burden of the poem. The touch of singsong in the lines—though these off rhymes are barely noticeable since they hinge on the commonest of words ("was," "whose," and "house," for example)—suggests the poem's circular movement, turning about its subject but never grasping it.

A striking characteristic of these poems without a caesura is that, in contrast to those with it, they are dominated by the sound of individual human voices. Even "Unknown Forbear," the quietest of poems, begins with Merwin's imagining a voice calling offstage:

> Somebody who knew him
> ninety years ago
> called him by a name
> he answered to
> come out now they said to him
> onto the porch and stand
> right there (OH, 28)

Although Merwin cannot hear the name, he can imagine the act of calling, and that suddenly animates the photograph. No such opportunity occurs in the caesura poems. Voices are reduced to murmurs or communication depends on a gesture. In "Sunset Water" (OH, 5) the sounds of children are heard indistinctly, as echoes across water. In "The Waving of a Hand," when Merwin wants to share a striking view of a cloud full of moonlight, he does not call out: "I tapped someone's shoulder (/) and we both stared" (OH, 6). This is followed by a conversation that goes unreported: "then we talked of other things." In "A Pause by the Water" Merwin anticipates breaking his isolation by meeting "the muffled couple"; but instead of conversing, "later they will show me (/) pictures of children" (OH, 8).

The lack of strong individual voices in the caesura poems lends an extraordinary power to the one voice that can be heard clearly. To be able to speak at all becomes an event of some magnitude in an atmosphere where voices are reduced to murmurs and where feelings run so deep they can only be carried by gestures. Thus the larger significance of the moment narrated by his mother in "Sun and Rain"—

> and he waved her back from the door   as she was leaving
> took her hand   for a while and said
> nothing

—is that she was strong enough to relate this incident, finding the words to tell of a moment profound enough to overwhelm any effort to speak.[13] In "Son," his mother again speaks directly, in the moment in the sequence that is most beautiful and most distraught:

> three times leaning forward   far off she called
> *Good night* in a whisper   from before I was born
> later through the burial   a wren went on singing

These are the only words spoken directly in the first half of section 1. They are addressed to another who may not be able to hear them, they draw on a strange voice from a remote past, and they do not include Merwin himself.

When a voice is heard within the caesura poems, it carries such complex emotions that it is almost unbearable; it is surely accurate to say that Merwin only hears the words spoken by the person he trusts the most. The proliferation of voices in the second half marks an emergence from isolation, an emergence that coincides with the abandonment of the caesura. The ease with which poems move after the caesura is dropped provides considerable relief, as though human speech itself offered a sustaining support, and as Merwin moves away from isolation, he hears the sound of voices with new delight and sensitivity. He talks about this in "Talking" and relishes his own surprised laughter. In "After a Storm" he states that "if I could take one voice / with me it would be / the sound I hear every day" (OH, 23). Ending "The Family," he holds out the promise of speaking the names of the farmer's children as a way of enforcing the reality of a scene that may seem too purely idyllic.

The poem richest in voices is "Birdie":

> how many times you may have been born
> as my father's other sisters would say
> in your bawdy nobody is interested
> in things like that in the family
>
> somebody wrote down though that you was
> born one time on April 20
> 1874 so that my grandmother
> at that occasion was thirteen and the hardest thing
> to believe in that account as I think of it
> is that she was ever thirteen years old
> the way we grew up to hide things from each other (OH, 17)

Even when he is looking at a transcript, he hears the sound of a distinctive voice, a voice that leads him to chime in with a comment. Such blendings recur throughout, as when the voices of his father's other sisters, mispronouncing "body," are cut off by an elder talking to an inquisitive child: "nobody is interested / in things like that in the family." Birdie, however, is interested in things of the body, which others find bawdy, so it is no surprise other family members regard her as an error. Her recorded birthdate is a mistake, but to the family in general she remains the wanton outsider. Raucous, ebullient, exuberant, she is a reminder of a lost liveliness. In a homage that also appeared in

Unframed Originals,[14] Merwin contrasts her manner with that of other family members:

> inviting them all in so unexpected
> and not heard of for so long your own mother
> younger brother younger sisters new nephew
> to breakfast laughing and waving your hands
>
> with all the rings and them not listening
> saying they was in a hurry to drive farther
> and see the family and you going on
> telling them everything there was to eat (OH, 18)

Birdie rises to the occasion "so unexpected" while the rest of the family sticks to the track. She is ready to greet the family before her; they keep looking for the family further on. She offers hospitality; they don't listen. Bringing voices forward instead of suppressing matters darkly, she is a kind of tutelary spirit to the rest of the family poems. While Merwin never duplicates her exuberance himself, her spirit is present in "The Cart," an amusingly quirky poem in which he recalls riding with his sister on a handmade merry-go-round.

It should be clear that the strength required for Birdie's voice to be heard, and for Birdie to speak, is radically less than that required for Merwin's mother. But to speak at all under difficult circumstances remains a value affirmed not just in the family poems but elsewhere in *Opening the Hand.* It is at the center of two of the strongest poems in section 3, "Ali" and "Berryman." Beyond its simple details relating the story of a dog too frail to live, "Ali" expresses a deep responsibility to speak for those who have no speech. As he speaks for Ali, he also speaks for that part of himself which cannot speak easily of his own sense of loss. In caring for the creature, he is in some way caring for himself, perhaps forgiving himself for being unable to speak in other contexts.

With "Berryman," Merwin's achievement, as in "Birdie," is to capture the sound of another voice, reproducing even a certain rumbling portentousness, as if Berryman had been consciously addressing a wider audience. But the power Berryman manifests has to do with speaking into an unknown void. At the end of the poem, in reply to Merwin's question "how can you ever be sure / that what you write is really / any good,"

> he said you can't
>
> you can't you can never be sure
> you die without knowing
> whether anything you wrote was any good
> if you have to be sure don't write (OH, 66)

One late poem that encompasses all these concerns is "Yesterday." Though not written with the caesura, it uses repeated phrases with a similar effect: they become persistent pauses that impede the poem's progress. The poem centers directly on the problem of speaking in a situation where it is impossible to speak, and while the father in the story is someone else's, Merwin's understanding immediately extends not only to his friend but to his father. More important, Merwin creates a space for the voice of his friend to speak, and even sets aside his own concerns for the duration of the telling:

> he says the last time I went to see my father
> I say the last time I saw my father
>
> he says the last time I saw my father
> he was asking me about my life
> how I was making out and he
> went into the next room
> to get something to give me
>
> oh I say
> feeling again the cold
> of my father's hand the last time

All the themes in *Opening the Hand* are present in "Yesterday": the difficulty of speech in an impossible situation, a difficulty addressed not in a timely fashion but after the fact; the need for a sympathetic auditor whose understanding will extend outward to a situation and encompass it without judgment; the necessity of suspending one's own claims in an effort to allow someone else to speak, and to hear the words of that person in all their clarity. One listens in amazement to the experience as it is relived by Merwin, and one comes back to all the moments in one's own life when words could have been spoken but were not. It is one of a number of triumphs in *Opening the Hand*—a volume well named, for in it Merwin reveals his own involvement more openly than ever before.

15

The Words in the Language

SO DEEP are the connections now running through all of Merwin's recent writings, whether in prose or verse, that he may be doing himself a disservice by presenting them in individual volumes. Certainly the poetry written between 1982 and 1987 that appears in *The Rain in the Trees* (1988) is only enhanced by prose memoirs completed simultaneously. His recent work emphasizes the links that underlie apparently divergent occasions. A poem addressed to the woman he loves has affinities with a prose memoir of a year in rural France in the 1970s, which in turn can be linked to verse that derides contemporary urban architecture. For years, his inclination had been in the opposite direction, towards variety rather than homogeneity. Even in his cycles of poetry, there was little evidence of an underlying movement toward unity, only a willingness to explore a situation from as many different perspectives as possible. The impetus was to move along, to press toward the next discovery. His role was that of the pilgrim or wanderer, and he was delighted to follow the ruined pathways on Athos from one temporary lodging to the next. The first stage in his ending of his unsettled existence was his decision to build a home on the island of Maui in Hawaii, and that change has continued through a new marriage, on into further memoirs in both verse and prose, including a lengthy and candid deposition of events in his life from 1957 onward, "The Wake of the Blackfish," as viewed through his correspondence with George Kirstein.

One explanation for this new drive toward unity is that living in Hawaii makes him less isolated than he has ever been, far less than when he was dividing his time between New York City and rural France (or Mexico, where he settled for a few years in the 1970s). Hawaii, as he sees it, is like living at a crossroads. Though his home, as Edward Hirsch describes it in an introductory note to a 1986 interview, lies "toward the end of a winding, rocky dirt road that dead-ends at a cliff overlooking the Pacific," the island on which he lives is not only in the midst of rapid development but bears the scars of a long history of conquest and exploitation. Merwin's piece of ground acknowledges that history, for it is, Hirsch explains, reclaimed territory, land of "red volcanic clay ruined by fly-by-night pineapple farming fifty years ago."[1]

The centered existence of a single home has encouraged Merwin to reconsider his own position. When he was a temporary visitor or a pilgrim-tourist, he remained an outsider, and he took advantage of his position to welcome unusual angles of vision, delighting in whichever direction they led him. Now, however, as a settler on land that is his own, he is acutely dissatisfied with his position as the outsider. Earlier, he appropriated with ease the viewpoints of other cultures, especially in his free verse modeled on oral literature; the ideal poet was a citizen of the world. And since all poets were close to a point of origin through their own creativity, the poet could be happiest with those cultures that were young enough to keep close ties to their own origins. These convictions have been tempered by his current condition. For the Hawaiian culture, as he views it, is barely discernible. He has arrived, as another Westerner, at a late point in its destruction, long after much has passed into oblivion. He must engage himself with the depths surrounding him instead of following out the tourist's role as disengaged spectator freed from customary viewpoints.

Merwin's Hawaii, as he portrays it in *The Rain in the Trees,* is not at all the paradisal retreat glimpsed in the concluding poems of *Opening the Hand* or the perfect setting for the eroticism of "Turning to You" in *Finding the Islands.*[2] It is a well-traveled crossroads to which he comes as a late arrival. In his interview with Hirsch, a question about translating chants from the lost language of Hawaiian leads Merwin to consider "other kinds of extinction of various things": "Several species a week are now becoming extinct, and this is an accelerating process. It's all because of human action, entirely human action. It's natural for species to become extinct, of course, but not at the rate we have brought it about. Languages, cultures, and our own language are suffering the same fate. These aren't different processes. They're not different books on a shelf; they're all the same book. Any way of trying to turn that process around is useful."[3] Loss of such magnitude poses major problems. The need for urgent action is evident, yet such action must appreciate the delicacy of the steps to be taken—steps certain to be cautious, hesitant, reserved. Intervention must be undertaken with an almost unimaginable care, delicacy, and restraint. The procedures set forth in "Unchopping a Tree," impossible as they are, have become an actual standard.

1

The kind of delicate activism that Merwin now endorses is on display in "Shepherds," a prose memoir written in 1986 that recounts in detail events between the spring of 1973 and the fall of 1974 when Merwin lived in the hamlet of Barrade in southern France (not far from the house he had purchased in the late 1950s).[4] He recorded this experience once in poems collected in part 3 of *The Compass Flower.* Why has he returned? This new version adds a different level of detail. The poetry he wrote in 1973–74 while living in Barrade was heavily dependent on his current situation, in transit from the anonymity of the modern city and uncertain about how to live, seeking support from the rhythms of a natural cycle, a rhythm that ultimately offered the gift of second flowering. When he looks back at this time twelve years later, he concentrates instead on how he came to be accepted by a neighborhood in which he began as a stranger. As an exemplary record of how an intruder becomes a neighbor, "Shepherds" is intimately related to thoughts about his position in Hawaii.

It differs considerably from an earlier prose reminiscence of life in rural France, "Foie Gras," composed in 1984, a work that centers on the social life—as distinct from the neighborhood or communal life—as exemplified by a controversial figure.[5] Introduced in the opening sentence as "Fatty the Count," he is given, several paragraphs later, a title, "Fatty, le Comte d'Allers," and several pages further he appears in his given name, which even then hovers among several alternatives: "Pierre, M. le Comte, Fatty." His lack of a stable name is in keeping with his shadowy status. On the one hand, Pierre is the son of this region, devoutly attached to its ancient relics, while on the other, he has no compunction about removing and repossessing those relics that belong to others. He is at once high priest and grave robber, protecting sacred icons from those who would scatter them heedlessly, but attracted to recycling them for his own profit.

Though "Foie Gras" is as charitable a portrait of Pierre as one could conceivably muster, Merwin's portrayal of this region of France is less than sympathetic. This European past is difficult to admire, a difficulty acknowledged in the form of this work, which appears to ramble waywardly from one anecdote to another. But Merwin's distant approach is necessary: he cannot get too close because this past conceals a horror, a civilization carved out brutally in wars of conquest.

Merwin has, in fact, written of this region before, in a piece, originally entitled "Saigne," for a projected series of sketches started in the 1950s.[6] A forerunner of Pierre appears as a humorously disreputable "Marquis" who leads Merwin to a ruined castle with the dark motto "*Je fais saigner*"—"I draw blood"—hoping to convince him to purchase it. But Merwin is struck by a sinister gloom that pervades the ruins, and eventually the Marquis explains that during the Middle Ages, after the castle had been conquered by siege, its inhabitants were imprisoned in an underground keep and abandoned for weeks. When the new conquerors returned and opened the dungeon door, they found that "those who were not already dead had gone mad, and fallen to eating corpses, and each other, and in some cases themselves." Though this ghoulish revelation is the high point of the narrative of "Saigne," it is passed over dismissively by the Marquis who "simply said that the incident of the prisoners was 'typical.'"

Thirty years later, in "Foie Gras," the same incident is treated even more cavalierly; here, it is noted in passing, in three successive sentences: "Later, during the Wars of Religion, one army had locked up some fifty prisoners in the dungeon under the tower, which was still entered through a tiny door not four feet high, set below ground level. The prisoners had been abandoned there without food or water, in the dark. Weeks later someone opened the door and found the few survivors eating the bodies of the dead. In that same century, a scion of the family had been distinguished as an ambassador for Mary Queen of Scots. . . ." The incident is mentioned so briefly because it is so "typical" of what survives from this particular European past: quite simply, the ruin of this past almost always conceals a horror.

But "Shepherds," with a different cast of characters, presents a different past. To the extent that "Foie Gras" is urban, "Shepherds" is rural, its past less heavily scarred by barbaric efforts to achieve civilization. Indeed, it is close to an eternal present that is seasonal and natural, even preagricultural: "Gathering is older than agriculture and the gatherer knows it. Gathering is on happier and calmer terms with the unforeseen than are the later efforts of our kind to control the living world so that there can be more of us in every measured part of it. Gathering fallen fruit is a stage beyond picking it from its branches. When you pick you choose the fruit. With fallen fruit the tree and the fruit have made the decision before you. You have to find where the fruit has gone on its own." Gathering fruit depends upon alertness, receptivity to the moment. It is less a task than a joy, pleasurable work: "You stand up and the horizon is a surprise each time, and the size and color of the world come back to you." In "Foie Gras," the belief exists that valuables can be hauled away, even purchased; its very title points toward special refinements that mark off the socially superior. "Shepherds," by contrast, offers valuables that are fleeting, that occur at the cusp of a turn in time.

"Foie Gras" darts nervously from one vignette to another, as though exposing that the treasured artifacts that Pierre would exploit so shamelessly are in reality little more than junk, debris left over from the essential ruin of European history. But "Shepherds" moves lumberingly, with a slowness that reflects how carefully and by what stages Merwin enters into the community around him. Indeed, he is no longer the invisible narrator of "Foie Gras" who simply reports what happened next, but a participant whose presence alters the record. Though "Shepherds" spreads across a period of eighteen months in 1973–1974 and appears to be no more than a step-by-step report of one season after another, it unfolds in distinct phases, in each of which Merwin occupies an increasingly intimate position within the life of the region. Just as one learns, picking plums, to follow the course already set, so Merwin must proceed according to the customs that existed before his arrival.

Beyond its value as an exemplary record of how an intruder becomes a neighbor, "Shepherds" also bears a distinct message, though it only takes shape in its final catastrophic incident. Technological change, in the form of the railroad, eventually delivers a catastrophe—then passes on, oblivious to its destruction, leaving the older traditional network to begin the process of recovery. Significantly absent from the aftermath of disaster are the forces that represent change. In a bad time, technology provides no support; indeed, the bad time is brought about by it. Merwin reverses the usual thinking about the virtue of progress. Technological forces are inflexible, hardened, incapable of improvising a response—much like the mayor's idea of improved slaughterhouses, the success of which is contingent upon farmers altering their ancient methods of raising livestock.

By contrast, tradition is represented by forces that prove flexible. Merwin opens "Shepherds" by sketching two neighbors implacably hostile to each other. He closes it by showing the two, if not harmoniously working together, at least suspending their differences to help one another in a bad time. Their fundamental disagreements remain in place—but they can be set aside temporarily. Technological innovations, by contrast, require that an entire context change if they are to function; these innovations—which are touted as streamlined, efficient, and modern—are, in reality, cumbersome and crude. Traditional methods, which might appear to be hopelessly sluggish, are revealed as resilient; they encourage ways of improvising within a context.

2

Merwin is drawn, in 1986, to thoughts of Barrade in 1973—and his successful integration into that community—because in his new home in Hawaii such integration may be impossible: the traditional culture and its original environment have been thoroughly erased. Though he approaches his new home with an understanding of his intruder's status, though he is intent upon reclaiming what has been lost, his position is complicated by his late arrival. The catastrophe, which is still under way, began so long ago, and what is left of the network is now so feeble. The outcome cannot be resolved as neatly as the end of "Shepherds." Hawaii is not a secluded enclave; it is close to the rest of the world.

Late in his life Merwin has arrived at a place that he loves, a place that, even as he speaks, is vanishing. Love and loss are fatefully joined throughout these works, nowhere more helplessly than in "Koa," a poem not collected in *The Rain in the Trees.*[7] The occasion is the death of a beloved dog, and the loss suggests the terrifying idea that the moment one has it all, everything may be taken away:

> late I have come to live where I love to be
> with a woman I have looked for through all my lives
> and to work at what I have wanted to say
> since I was a child under the only tree
> about the given earth and now what do I know
> standing at night in the long wind without you

The poem may have been omitted because it is too personal, but the question it asks lingers in the other poetry.

An urgency, which results in activism as well as anger, all of it spoken in the name of love and protection, is the noble feature of this poetry. The book is organized around two cycles, one at the center of the collection, the other just before the end. The first is a group of ten poems of late love, prefigured in the three poems that open the volume, in which the last-minute quality of this love is almost overwhelming. "Everything begins so late after all," he says in "Before Us," a poem whose title deepens in meaning as the work progresses until "before" not only refers to the past but points forward to what is still to come. Though so the hour is so late—

> when the solitaires have already gone
> and the doves of Tanna
> when the Laughing Owls have
> long been followed by question marks
> and honeycreepers and the brown
> bears of Atlas
> the white wolf and the sea mink have not been seen
> by anyone living (RT, 30)

—there can still be a beginning, even if it is "so late after all," and the joy of the poem is in the moment of waking together in this instant, "and the world is here in its dew / you are here and the morning is whole / finally the light is young." He fashions a song of love out of "the brief air the vanishing green" at a point when the time still left, which may seem so little, becomes everything, made capacious by its beginning. This testimony answers the question raised in "Koa": even at a late point one can begin over and the light will be young.

This love poetry is markedly different from other pieces that Merwin wrote in a similar vein, most notably the "Turning to You" sequence of 1980–81, collected in *Finding the Islands.* There, the belief was that love erased ordinary time: "Once there were many days and nights / and then there was / only yours" (FI, 46). Beginning with the gift of a calendar, the "Turning to You" sequence insists that love continuously dissolves time's passage.[8] Although the closing tercet of the final poem can be read as an erotic declaration—"You can do it all with your eyes / you can do it all / with any motion" (FI, 71)—the reference to "it," as the entire poem suggests, is the beloved's ability to suspend the moment as though it could be eternal, to draw out time until it seems endless:

> the night is so still
> gecko cricket and an unknown voice
> we do not know our age
>
> I remember you talking
> to me a long time in whispers
> our early nights our late mornings (FI, 70–71)

But that attainment, as glorious as it once seemed, is regarded now as a facile thing: in these new poems, love, rather than expanding a moment as if it could endure forever, makes one intensely aware of time's passage, its utter preciousness.

A late recognition can force one to question one's own wisdom, as Merwin does in "Late Spring," the opening poem. In that poem and in the two that follow, one cannot see until one has learned to look; what was one seeing before? Merwin's willingness to doubt his ability to see because he may not yet know how to look or hear or even speak continues into the second cycle, eleven poems on Hawaiian themes. These differ sharply from previous poems in which Merwin appropriated the alien perspectives of different cultures. They resemble the slow immersion of his eighteen months at Barrade, except that in these he is quick to confess that he is often lost. They begin with his admitting he cannot control the ancient words of the Hawaiian language:

> behind the names that I do not have
> the color of water flows all day and all night
> the old man tells me the name for it
> and as he says it I forget it (RT, 60)

This reverses what has historically happened when an outsider from the West confronts an alien culture. Here the outsider attempts to learn the indigenous language, rather than expecting the natives to learn the invader's language. Here the native language is regarded not as crude or primitive but subtle, and the failure to grasp it becomes a judgment on the outsider. Indeed, Merwin's larger point may be that the Hawaiian language acts in a profoundly poetic way by apparently eliminating the gulf between signifier and signified. That language confidently evokes qualities that seem beyond words, or at least beyond the poverty-stricken sign system of English, which has no equivalent for "the color of water"—just as, in "Losing a Language," we begin to appreciate how much an alien culture might tell us when we learn that some of the Hawaiian words that have been lost are "the noun for standing in mist by a haunted tree / the verb for I."

It is important, though, that in this cycle of poetry Merwin draws attention to himself as the limited one, handicapped because he lacks the verb for I. In a 1984 interview, he singled out two characteristics unique to Hawaiian colonization.[9] Its language has been almost entirely erased: "There are no Hawaiians who don't speak English and many Hawaiians who don't speak Hawaiian." And the landscape has suffered a similar decimation: "Hawaii is unique. The flora and fauna that were there when Captain Cook got there were almost entirely exclusive to Hawaii. They had almost all evolved there. There's no other place on earth where this is true." Merwin is pointing to an inevitable circle: the language, responsive to its environment, dies as the environment is destroyed, and when the environment is gone there will no longer be a language to name its features. Merwin's role as he listens to an elder who is speaking a forgotten language that he can barely recall parallels his role in "Native" as a gardener intent upon salvaging remnants of native plant life. Here especially, his humility is very pronounced:

> Most afternoons
> of this year which is written as a number
> in my own hand
> on the white plastic labels
>
> I go down the slope
> where mules I never saw
> plowed in the sun and died
> while I was in school (RT, 63)

Writing the year as a number on white plastic labels may be distasteful, but the compromise is necessary, and compared to the devastation of the land, and the anguish of the mules "beaten to go / straight up the hill," Merwin's ordeal is nothing. He draws attention to himself as though a part of him were still in school, the child shielded from horrors. At its end, the poem celebrates a small triumph, the witnessing of these seeds from destroyed valleys opening late "beside their names in Latin / in the shade of leaves I have put there." The satisfaction of these closing lines is their link between language and environment: dead species named in a dead language, the two looking back at and animating each other, however modestly.

In this cycle of Hawaiian poems, the rain in the trees is a metonym for the words in the language: as trees thrive on rain, so language is nourished by words. The Hawaiian word Merwin cannot remember in "Hearing the Names of the Valleys" is "the name for the color of water." In an uncollected poem from this time, "A Last Look,"[10] he states that when there are no trees, when the rain has nothing to fall upon, language will wither and there will be no more words. But this play between words is more than a clever transposition. An absolute link between language and environment is necessary if he is to maintain his awareness of himself as outsider yet continue to seek ways of understanding from the inside. Language is a meeting ground, for it is the area in which he is adept, an expert, an insider; appreciating its use, he has a way of entering into a world whose alien qualities he will still respect. His own position is succinctly summarized in "Witness":

> I want to tell what the forests
> were like
>
> I will have to speak
> in a forgotten language (RT, 65)

The opening of "The Lost Originals" mordantly summarizes the position others hold: "If only you had written our language / we would have remembered how you died."

Merwin's scrupulous sensitivity to his own position as outsider is at the center of the most powerful work of the sequence. "Chord" is a fourteen-line poem with each line except for the last taking shape as a chantlike formula. It begins:

> While Keats wrote they were cutting down the sandalwood forests
>
> While he listened to the nightingale they heard their own axes echoing through the trees
>
> While he sat in the walled garden on the hill outside the city they thought of their gardens dying far away on the mountains
>
> While the sound of the words clawed at him they thought of their wives (RT, 66)

The first impression is that there are no connections, only stark contrasts. Keats, absorbed in his own poetic pursuits, ignores the monumental social change happening around him. But the contrast is soon blurred: "while he felt his heart they were hungry and their faith was sick." It is not that there are no connections—it is that there are missed connections throughout. That is the power of the poem: it touches on matters that might have yielded different results if a connection had been made. The interests of the unnamed "they" are the interests of Keats, and the interests of Keats are theirs. The activity at either end of the line takes place in distinct arenas, one unfolding in the world of a walled garden and travel to Italy and the tip of a pen, the other dealing with those uprooted from their homes and falling on faraway trails and surrounded by hateful cities. Yet Merwin's achievement is to evoke the similarities between these different realms. The poem recognizes that connections are missed, but also that connections exist to be made, though what outcome would issue is left unspoken because it is unimaginable. The visionary element in the poem is the possibility that the two ends might meet. The dying poet with no time to live his own life and those pressed into destroying what they loved most might somehow touch each other. Keats would live; they would return to their homes.

Merwin knows the world is not made that way. As he says in "Knock," speaking of passengers on an airliner, "they are hurtling toward the known world / which it is hopeless to reject / and death to accept." But there is a personal element here as well, with Keats as an analog to Merwin, who had at one time been immersed in his own pilgrimages and oblivious to the lives of those outside the walled garden or apart from the Grecian woods. The poem breaks down any belief in an easy division between the sophisticated and the primitive, directly questions the insularity of the Western perspective (even as it is careful to uphold the value of what Keats would do), and in every line, in the gap between the differences, visionary possibilities open, possibilities that might occur if connections could be made. It insists, ultimately, that the disjointed lurchings that together add up to the life of Keats, the erratic series of moments that begin each line, might be harmonized by way of the conclusions to each line: that the answer lies in one's insistent drive to unify one's own life not by concentrating on its particulars but by opening it to others.

3

Writing the poem "Trees" (from *The Compass Flower*) in 1975, Merwin insisted that the names of trees "have never touched them." But the specific names of a variety of trees are noted, repeated, and even savored throughout *The Rain in the Trees:* "they cut the sacred 'ohias then / the sacred koas / then the sandalwood and the halas" ("Rain at Night"), "the old leaves of the heliconia . . . the abutilons / the royal ilima" ("The Rose Beetle"), "under the Christmasberry tree / imported from Brazil" ("Empty Water"), "when the ailanthus leaves / went unnoticed" ("Sky in September"), "thorny / kiawas smelling / of honey" ("Term"), "the thrush on the guava branch in the shining rain" ("Before Us"), "like the great 'ohias and the honey creepers" ("The Solstice"), "the sandalwood forests" ("Chord"), "the small mossed oaks" ("History"), "under the apple trees" ("Pasture"), "a young mango tree" and "Here the 'ohia trees" ("Native"). Each tree, whether exotic or common, is provided with a name by which it can be known—a process of preservation that continues into poetry written after 1987. In "So Far," he watches a gecko not an hour old taking its first steps

in that shadow circling
the sprouting cycad overhead with its
single frond and its ancestry
older than the dinosaurs but now

a species rare if not officially
endangered named for one man Rumphius
who flourished in the Indies a mere three
centuries ago. . . .[11]

Now, names are not to be forgotten; they are to be rescued, revived, and appreciated in the course of the poem.[12]

To insist that one should know a tree has a name, that it can and must be identified, is new. This work emphasizes links—not only connections between trees and language or life-giving attributes shared by words and rain, but also the realization that our contemporary moment has its own history. We have been preceded by others, and to recognize that someone before us thought to find a word for a tree is to forge a continuity with that past. For Merwin, however, as that history opens, it serves to remind us of how briefly, in relative terms, the human species has flourished on this planet. To us, the three centuries that have passed since Rumphius lived are an almost inconceivable time span, but this period is nothing to the cycad, which predates the dinosaurs.

Underlying all of Merwin's recent work is an effort to redefine our sense of time. He wants us not only to understand how late the hour is, but also to comprehend how brief our time on earth has been. His sharp sense that so little time is left leads to an awareness of what a small segment of time has been occupied by the human species. "To the Insects" begins:

Elders

we have been here so short a time
and we pretend that we have invented memory

we have forgotten what it is like to be you
who do not remember us (RT, 49)

The insects, in "After the Alphabets," are the "tongues of the future," inhabitants of a world from which the human species has simply erased itself; such an erasure is a conclusion that asks to be drawn, for one of the achievements of the human species is its proven ability to eradicate other humans. In the city poems, Merwin leans heavily upon this perception until the monuments of civilization, the towering skyscrapers, the networks of transportation, seem perilously fragile, temporary edifices hastily erected. Two poems begin with a negative locution that eliminates any hope of meaningful development: "Nobody remembers / the original site / of course" ("Now Renting") and "There is no eye to catch" ("Glasses"). A related poem, "Airport," begins: "None of the computers can say / how long it took to evolve a facility / devoted to absence in life." "Glasses" absolutely reduces the inhabitants of the city to the series of protective windows in which they see other windows. "Now Renting" maintains that the city has been so often built over that scaffolding is the true architecture of New York. It reaches its apogee by erecting a scaffolding "with glass pictures on it" to commemorate a "glass building / never built on that site." The poems are not intended as satire but as straightforward depiction. This is what we want, what we deserve, a sought-after nullity.

The creative tension that existed between the city and the country in parts 2 and 3 of *The Compass Flower* snaps entirely. Whatever these two opposites had to say to each other before is now lost. Now the city and the country are set against each other as absolute contrasts. In a recent poem, "The River,"[13] crocodiles in a park zoo look out on the city that surrounds them. They are emblems of a patience so endless it seems unimaginable, imperceptible; they are denizens of "a dark river" that runs so deep it is "never forgotten / never remembered." Though they "appeared not to be moving / in the mud" they see everything in the city as "flowing shapes and colors," a transitory spectacle that, by their own inner time, is easily absorbed, easily forgotten.

If the city is to be derided, or simply ignored as inconsequential (as in "Summer '82"), the country, as represented by Merwin's memories of landscapes in Europe, is regarded with reverence. It is not just a place where the past intersects the present in a meaningful fashion, but the country is itself, for Merwin, a past that he now appreciates all the more in his own present, when it seems unattainable. "Notes from a Journey" presents scenes that blur any separation between inner and outer, human and natural, civilized and primitive. The shorthand notations are designed to sustain such an impression. A glimpse out a window is presented as though the sea were in the hallway: "from the end of the hall too / the sea shines." Or: "I saw that the wall at the end of the courtyard / was full of the sky from which the stones had fallen." This pleasurable confusion persists along more than one axis. As a foreigner, Merwin is different, but his very difference transforms him into an honored guest. When he is invited to share a meal with a family, "the daughters talk to me as though they knew me." A man and a woman invite him to sleep in a courtyard; he shares breakfast with a wagon driver's family. Walking by the shore he meets "a heavy woman in black . . . who knew everybody"—and now knows him.

Along with physical and social boundaries that dissolve, time also becomes fluid, approaching the condition that it enjoys in nature. He finds a port and experiences "the feeling that I once knew it / and that it has changed in the interval / like someone who remembers me as a child." Or he steps into a square and finds "the buildings around it / appeared to be melting like images on the horizon / and I thought it had happened before." Time literally dissolves: through the window of a flooded building a clock is "standing there / with its feet in water." Division between past and present melts away, like other distinctions between strangers and family, outdoors and indoors.

But these scenes that Merwin recalls with such nostalgia are marked by their inaccessibility. Each stanza in "Notes from a Journey" is like a moment framed, cherished, remembered, as though never to be seen again. It is a homage to a past more appreciated now than when it had been occurring. Its portraits resemble the long, drawn-out moment of farewell in "History," where Merwin takes leave of a region that is dear to him. (It is surely that moment in 1974 when he is leaving a Barrade to which he will not return.) But his farewell makes a larger point: he is leaving what could never be possessed by him or anyone, and the title of the poem calls attention to the tiny time span of any mortal being. The second stanza is unified by parallel syntax that employs "their" in order to stress that this region belongs to itself, not to anyone:

passing the last live farms
their stones running with dark liquid
and the ruined farms their windows without frames
facing away
looking out across the pastures of dead shepherds
whom nobody ever knew
grown high with the dry flowers of late summer
their empty doorways gazing
toward the arms of the last oaks
and at night their broken chimneys watching
the cold of the meteors (RT, 14)

This opens onto a cosmic time scale; what exists will continue without the shepherds, without Merwin, as though released from intrusion: "in the shade of black trees the houses were full / of their own fragrance at last." The notebook in a foreign language is "of course lost," though it was "a book full of words to remember." The poem is humbling, and Merwin's own intentions are seen as counting for little. When at the end he speaks the phrase that links up with the opening words "Only I never came back"—"I was not going to be long"—he is halted by the understanding that his own life, measured against this sense of natural time, is only a brief moment. His privilege is to have glimpsed, for this instant, like a gift offered to him as he was leaving, the life that will continue without him, independent of the tracings of humanity.

At his darkest, Merwin finds relief in conceiving a world from which our own species is absent. "The Inevitable Lightness" imagines the total destruction of the human world, as though in a nuclear holocaust; but what is left after is not an end but another beginning: "and the earth breathes naked with its new scars / and sky everywhere." It is typical, Merwin might say, of the self-importance of the human species, to believe that the earth could be totally destroyed by us; while we are easily capable of erasing ourselves, it is vain to think we have the power to destroy the earth. "Place," a companion-poem, makes an identical point: "On the last day of the world" he would plant a tree, "not for the fruit," but to declare a new beginning with this "tree that stands / in the earth for the first time."

Merwin's disgust at his own species is at times, as in "Thanks," so strong, so vexed with anger and dismay—

> with the forests falling faster than the minutes
> of our lives we are saying thank you
> with the words going out like cells of a brain
> with the cities growing over us
> we are saying thank you faster and faster (RT, 46)

—that it is tempting to decide that everything of worth and value inheres in the past. Southern Europe, after all, in "Notes from a Journey," grows more luminous with each vignette. "Pastures," a work that moves back in time through a series of natural enclosures, each one more wonderfully ideal than the last, skirts the nostalgic. The places to which Merwin is returning are only for children. The pasture, when ultimately defined at the midpoint of the poem, nourishes the perfect days of childhood:

> in the long sunset
> of an endless summer
> our thin voices
> spinning across the still pasture
> calling each other (RT, 20)

When "boys watching sheep" witness a man murder a woman, the pasture safely hides them in "flowering honeysuckle." He himself could only discover his first pasture when left to wander as a child, when "my mother / and the woman we were visiting / wanted to talk about things / they didn't want me to hear."

Although it is nostalgic for Merwin to return to a past that excludes everything but moments of loveliness, the poem as a whole escapes nostalgia because it recognizes how impossibly remote these moments are, as its ending confirms. His last words are spoken in sorrow, not for himself at the past he must relinquish, but for others; it seems to him that they will have no such memories themselves: "many / now do not know / any such thing." Giving "many" a line to itself (the only similar line is "the first pigs I had seen / alive / crowded to the corner / to look at me") requires a long pause, as Merwin, relinquishing his hold on his memories, turns away from his own regret to express sorrow for what others have now lost.

Epilogue

ENTERING HIS fifth decade of writing, W. S. Merwin continues to stand apart from his contemporaries as the representative of an unusual degree of freedom and independence. That independence is evident in his personal life. He has made his way on his own terms, much as he had hoped when, in 1949, with no prospects before him, he left America for Europe. He is one of the few American poets who have managed to support themselves through writing. But his independence is as evident in his work. Rereading the reviews prompted by Merwin's work, Cary Nelson and Ed Folsom were struck by the amount of controversy it had generated: "Perhaps no other contemporary poet has been as universally recognized as a major talent and simultaneously so criticized, prodded, reprimanded and challenged at every stage of his career."[1] Yet this is not surprising; indeed, it is almost inevitable.

For one thing, Merwin unsettles critics because each new collection is distinctly different from the last. The extent of his changes has, if anything, been underestimated by reviewers: they have perennially lagged at least one book behind him, expecting his latest volume to continue the tendencies of the one before. But his collections are organized with a break in their middle, a characteristic ever since the original typescript of *A Mask for Janus,* when a last-minute change included three new poems, among them the most untypical "Dictum: For a Masque of Deluge." As arrangements, then, his collections are designed to elude easy categorization; they begin at a point from which they have, by their end, strenuously departed.

The writing of poetry, for Merwin as for many of the American poets who began their careers in the postwar period, promotes active change. It is a commonplace that American poetry, especially after 1960, is exploratory, its form reflecting the writer's process of making a new discovery. But for Merwin, that discovery is frequently made against a specific background that represents the weight of custom, or the habits of the mind, or the pressures of authority. His discoveries, that is, are not entirely novel; what is discovered had been there all along, waiting to be found, perhaps even neglected by Merwin before. As a result, his poems can seem understated in comparison to those of his contemporaries. None of his poems in praise of creatures can compete for dynamism with Galway Kinnell's "The Porcupine"; none of his family poems are as immersed in regret, in seemingly depthless sorrow, as those by James Wright in memory of his ancestors and boyhood friends. None are as insouciantly dilettantish as work by James Merrill or, at another extreme, John Ashbery; nor are they as somber and rigorous as work by Philip Levine. These poets all work as master stylists, reconceiving language from deep within their own sensibilities.

By contrast, Merwin appears to have no style at all, or to take on whatever style suits the moment. In fact, this transparency is a clue to his effectiveness. His return to a scene discloses what had not been, he had thought, present before. The disclosure is often made through a detail that leads to a subtle shift in perspective that occurs as a surprise but that recasts the whole situation—expanding it, deepening it, widening it. The poetry, then, will always be vulnerable to the criticism that it is too delicate, for it depends on attention paid to small details or brief events. But however delicate those observations may be—and Merwin clearly appreciates their delicacy—their ultimate value is the shift they engender, and that dramatically alters the scope of the whole poem, opening to us realms that had not been otherwise available. The poems may be understated in their individual moments, but as whole works they are remarkably large, even sweeping, in their comprehension. From the minor to the major, from the customary to the rare, these poems repeatedly reenact a process of renewal that is the constant in Merwin's career. Creatures occupy, in their innocence, a fullness that constantly escapes our vain efforts at categorization. A frozen moth, out of place, in the wrong season, may return to life. Barriers become thresholds in his late free verse; outcasts and eccentrics become individuals in his family memoirs.

These renewals are not simply affirmations of the poet's vitality or ingenuity or passion, as similar rejuvenations are in the work of contemporaries. Indirectly, gently, but persistently, Merwin undermines the weight of authority. In this respect, his poetry has always had a social, political, and cultural dimension, although its emphasis has varied over the years. He is the gentlest of writers, but his gentleness has been prone to misunderstanding. In his early years, his light touch was mistaken for aloofness, or even a coldness, an inability to express emotions outwardly. Later, in his free verse, his deliberate simplicity was taken as a mark of withdrawal, even a denial that language could serve as communication. It is true that he is fond of the delicate turn of phrase, the graceful observation, the momentary glimpse and impression caught on the wing. But none of these is left to stand by itself. Each appears against its decisive opposite. To list those opposites would be a formidable task: they are everything we feel as the weight of the institution, everything that derives authority by generating an order that excludes accident, everything that unswervingly proceeds to a stipulated end. But the continual surprise in Merwin's work is that gestures contrary to these institutions, gestures that might be fragile, too fleeting to endure, too graceful to command, are rendered as though they were equal to powers vast, pervasive, dominating.

It is not Merwin's intent to arrange contests in which megaliths are toppled. But the distinction he tirelessly pursues is that between an orderly world, which is the invention of humans who hope to ensure stability through repetition, and that world's opposite, which cannot have a single name, which unfolds equidistantly through time and space and seems riddled with exceptions. The orderly world abounds in grammar and lexicons; everything there has been named and exists because there is a word for it. The other world is one of gesture and activity; it may be called silent but only because it will always escape from any name we give it. This other world is unimaginably innocent. Every moment in it is an origin. If any definition of poetry could be extracted from Merwin's work it would be the following: Poetry is the problematic area that breaks into existence when the poet once again realizes these two worlds as they intersect, overlie, and disrupt each other. One of the few predictable results is that our sense of scale will be subverted: what we had thought to be large diminishes, and what we had held to be tiny assumes cosmic proportions. And matters of scale become matters of value: what had seemed commanding reveals itself as bombast, and what had seemed the merest detail becomes a pivotal point for a vast new perspective. The three-line poem may equal the thousand-line poem.

Our assumptions about these two worlds, under Merwin's guidance, come to be reversed. We ordinarily think of the human world as that which is enduring, erecting stable orders resistant to change; indeed, our impulse to shape the world derives from our desire for such enduring stability. The silent world of immanent origins is viewed, if at all, as a matter of fleeting impressions, flashing glimpses, for that is the only way we can perceive its unimaginable wholeness. But for Merwin, the world that is silent and free will endure and persist while what we shape over and against it is subject to loss and decay. We may perceive that other world as utterly relative because of its ability to shift out from under our perceptions. But it is our own perceptions that are shifting and relative to it.

The gentleness that pervades Merwin's writing is not simply a character trait. Its higher purpose is to remind us that we are limited in the control we can impose, that the order and authority we take for granted are ultimately uncertain, liable to dissolve with a mere change in perspective. Poetry, for Merwin, can never be planned or conceived, only recognized when it occurs. "The encouragement of poetry itself," he writes in his 1966 essay, "Notes for a Preface," "is a labor and privilege like that of living. It requires, I imagine, among other startlingly simple things, a love of poetry, and possibly a recurring despair of finding it again, an indelible awareness of its parentage with that biblical waif, ill at ease in time, the spirit. No one has any claims on it, no one deserves it, no one knows where it goes." Merwin's position is not anti-intellectual. It is, however, intent upon incorporating the intellect into a network rather than establishing it at the top of a hierarchy.

By virtue of their intelligence, humans are forever estranged from the sheer innocence of creatures, from the seamless wholeness of the natural world. But the intelligence of the human species may become, in poetry, its own naturalizing context. The mind becomes complete, even in its incompleteness, if it can yield to its natural bent, which is that curious speculation that draws us toward what we do not know. Nature is always both different from us and hauntingly familiar to us, its innocence a trait we come closest to sharing when we are at our most curious and speculative. For Merwin, the poet is involved not in projecting himself onto his subjects but in making room for subjects to project themselves. The poet who can do that becomes the caretaker of thresholds over which subjects can pass without coercion, on their own terms.

Merwin's convictions have not changed, only acquired a new urgency in his most recent work, following *The Rain in the Trees.* His conviction that we must understand the limited time frame in which we, as a species, have operated is one of his most enduring beliefs. To understand that, to integrate it into our every action, is, quite simply, an expression of human thought at its highest, a use of the mind to check the powers of the mind, with the intent not of thwarting the intellect but of integrating it with the surroundings that should nourish it. The mind's power can be misused. The mind can adopt and enforce techniques that end in the blindness of routine procedures that control and even reshape the world, or it can remain in open contact with that which escapes understanding—that which always requires further understanding, with one horizon reached only to divulge another, and another.

"The Wars in New Jersey" considers what happens when we consign an area to oblivion by withholding our attention from it: "This is the way we were all brought up now / we imagine and so we all tell / of the same place by saying nothing about it."[2] The ruins of the Jersey flats are passed each day by thousands of commuters, all of whom studiously ignore the devastation beyond their windows. Merwin employs the first person plural, for these regions of devastation that we agree to overlook are everywhere and all around us. "We roll through them canned in a dream of steel / but the campaigns we know we know / were planned and are still carried out for our sake." Can we deliberately ignore even one element in our lives without ultimately infecting every aspect of our life? We may prefer to believe this area is just a dead zone, but Merwin portrays it as a complex battlefield, a war being fought in our own names. The insistent refrain "we know we know" haunts his descriptions; this is the portrait we have drawn of ourselves. At the end of his poem, he places the finishing touches on our self-portrayal:

> . . . we emerge into the old
>
> platform only a few minutes late
> as though it were another day
> in peacetime and we knew why we were there

The mindless destruction of the environment is the great issue of our time, yet it is a battle characterized by our refusal to acknowledge it. Consequently, we step out on a stage that is appropriately deserted, upon which we remain preoccupied with trivial matters, thinking we are "only a few minutes late" instead of realizing we may be the witnesses of the final days. The empty space and diminished time we passively inhabit reveal how severely foreshortened our perspectives have become. Our ignorance is complete, as Merwin icily remarks: we even act as though we know why we are there.

Arranging routines, establishing boundaries—these are, for Merwin, marks of a civilization that has lost its confidence and must nervously exert its authority. The danger of such a civilization lies in its indifference to everything but the dominion it occupies. In contrast, Merwin would remind us of the self-sufficient completeness of the natural world and what it offers as a perennial source of surprise and wonder.

The lesson returns again in "Among Bells." Climbing to the top of a belfry, he surveys the square of a foreign city below him; the objects there are intricate and elaborate expressions of a rich civilization. But the marvel of the poem, its governing force and reason for being, occurs when he discovers a bird huddled "above / one of the blackened cornices" and lifts it down as though it had perished there. The creature, held in his hands "like a bundle with no weight at all," then comes to life, escaping to a balustrade:

> for a moment glancing
> back as a black planet after which
> it was gone with a shriek into the long
> afternoon light that touched the net
> of wires
>
> the waiting aerials
> bare poles lines of laundry chimney flues
> patched roofs pots of geraniums windows
> standing open while in the streets
> the same

hats legs and wagons were
moving toward unchanging destinations
and at the station trains were arriving
on time without a sound and just
leaving[3]

The description of the city is changed by the escape of the bird, as though the authority of its parting glance ("as a black planet") passed to Merwin, altering the way he sees. Yet the alteration is subtle. On the one hand, after the lightninglike freedom of the bird, the objects of the city turn lumpish and clunky, separate but heaped together; moving objects seem to shift mechanically like toys. On the other hand, Merwin's descriptive lines also shake off the stiffness of a stark contrast—they even yield an opposite sense, as though the "bare poles lines of laundry chimney flues" were skimmed over rapidly, as seen by the bird, and the trains that arrive and leave soundlessly imitated the speed and flight of the chimney swift. Both perspectives remain present, each unsettling the other, as though Merwin held first one, then the other, as he sought to regain the balanced overview with which he opened his poem. But the point is that after the bird has asserted its autonomy, "Among Bells" is no longer exclusively his poem.

What Merwin would evoke, now more than ever, is the persisting presence of forces in the natural world to which we have grown blind. But these are the forces that endure, he would insist, representing a continuum that stretches beyond our understanding, that we must appreciate even as they judge us. We must submit to their judgment if we are to be complete, not submit them to ours.

In "The Blind Seer of Ambon," Merwin speaks in the voice of Georg Rumpf, the seventeenth-century naturalist (who loaned his name to a species of the cycad plant, as noted in "So Far") because the tragic events that disrupted Rumpf's life at every turn—the death of his wife and daughter in an earthquake, the destruction of his drawings and manuscripts in a fire, the extinction of the very species he had identified, and, finally, the loss of his own eyesight—are an unbearably complete record of the frailty that surrounds an individual life. Everyone and everything to which he was most deeply attached, all in his life that should have flourished and endured, has been taken away. Shakespeare's Lear went mad when stripped of the trappings of civilization and of everything he held dear to him. But Merwin's version of Lear is different, and Rumpf, although he has every reason to be Lear, is himself. Having lost all, what he discovers is how much still remains, the everything left to him that is the everything that had always been there, even in his blindness:

so this is the way I see now
I take a shell in my hand

new to itself and to me
I feel the thinness the warmth and the cold
I listen to the water
which is the story welling up
I remember the colors and their lives
everything takes me by surprise
it is all awake in the darkness[4]

The example may seem extreme; but given the lateness of the hour it is entirely appropriate. Merwin's aim, here as in so much of his work, is inseparable from his desire to transform the meager into the abundant, with the smallest, the gentlest, even the easiest of gestures, so that there can be no hesitation, no reluctance, no fear. He offers us what no one can ever possess, yet what should always be available to everyone.

Notes

Writings by W. S. Merwin in the University of Illinois Archives are cited according to the following method: a brief description of the material is followed by a catalogue number (if the work has been catalogued by number) and a date of composition (if Merwin affixed one—an estimated date is provided otherwise). For example, the holograph manuscript of the unpublished poem "Pigeon," dated March 20, 1955, in Merwin's hand is cited as: "Pigeon," unpub. MS. 19:12/029, d. Mar. 20, 1955. In another example, the undated typescript of a variant version of a published poem, "The Bones of Palinurus Pray to the North Star," is cited as: variant TS. 19:6/006a, c. 1950. Unless otherwise noted, all letters cited are in the Illinois archives.

Chapter 1. "Read Seeds Not Twigs"

1. See Glauco Cambon, *Recent American Poetry* (Minneapolis: University of Minnesota Press, 1962), p. 20; Cary Nelson, "Merwin's Deconstructive Career," in *W. S. Merwin: Essays on the Poetry*, ed. Cary Nelson and Ed Folsom (Urbana: University of Illinois Press, 1987), p. 81; Harvey Gross, "The Writing on the Void: The Poetry of W. S. Merwin," *Iowa Review* 1 (Summer 1970): 96; and Richard Howard, *Alone with America* (New York: Atheneum, 1969), pp. 355, 359. For characterizations of the early poetry that place it among the academic poetry of the 1950s, see Cambon, pp. 21–22; Nelson, p. 81; Gross, p. 93; and Howard, p. 355.

2. W. S. Merwin, "Introduction," *Four French Plays* (New York: Atheneum, 1984), pp. vii, viii, and W. S. Merwin, "Introduction," *From the Spanish Morning* (New York: Atheneum, 1984), p. viii. To my knowledge, Calvin Bedient was the first critic to have remarked on the medieval and pre-Renaissance influence in Merwin's early work in a review of W. S. Merwin, *The First Four Books of Poems* (New York: Atheneum, 1975) entitled "Horace and Modernism," *Sewanee Review* (Spring 1977): 366. Merwin's attachment to primal forms remains evident in poems written between 1947 and 1951 but not collected in *A Mask for Janus*. A villanelle, "Dirge," appears in *Perspective* 4 (Winter

1951), along with four sonnets, and medieval riddle poems are recalled in "Riddle Me," *Listener* 45, No. 1154 (April 12, 1951): 572. Among his unpublished poems from 1947–1951 there are several additional "Carols," a "Dirge for a Masque," an "Alba," a "Horaire and Prayer," a ballad, "Queen Helen," and several additional "Songs." For typescripts of verse for Merwin's first and second books of poems, see Illinois Archives 19:06/inclusive.

3. Richard Wilbur, "A *Mask for Janus* by W. S. Merwin," *Furioso* (Spring 1953): 59–62.

4. "[Untitled: 'Janus, at three the tide was filled']," unpub TS. 19:6/009j, c. 1947–1949?. In its early drafts, the poem printed as "Variations on a Line by Emerson" bore the title "Sestina for Janus."

5. Howard, *Alone with America*, p. 418.

6. Merwin requests the deletion of two stanzas from "Anabasis (II)" in an August 16, 1951, letter to the editor of the Yale University Press (carbon copy on the verso of the holograph manuscript of "To Brewster Ghiselin," unpub. MS. 10:17/13, d. Aug. 2, 1954). Also, the version of "Hermione on Simulacra" published in *Furioso* 7 (Spring 1952): 26–27 includes a stanza that the book version lacks.

7. First sonnet in "Three Sonnets About a Theme," *Perspective* 4 (Winter 1951): 23–25.

8. "The Bones of Palinurus Pray to the North Star," variant TS. 19:6/006a, c. 1950.

9. In the twenty-nine poems in the volume, "shadow" or its variant ("shadowy" or "shadowed") appears twenty-eight times and "stone" or its variant thirteen times. In poems written concurrently but uncollected, the statistics remain the same: in fifteen uncollected poems, "shadow" appears twenty times and "stone" nine times.

10. A related poem, close enough to "Hermione on Simulacra" to be a variant, is "Dance," which appeared in *Quarterly Review of Literature* 6 (1952): 365–66. "Dance" is an amoebean in which a man and woman exchange solemnly flirtatious remarks in sixteen four-line stanzas. The man would escape attachment to the woman by taking various new guises; the woman promises or threatens to react by always following him:

He: I shall become an image
More still than sleep, a stone;
Puritan then were your rage:
You would cast me down.

She: If you became a door,
A key I am to open;
Kindle to fire,
I shall fall as rain.

When Merwin recasts the poem, the man-woman interchange is still present but the work is dominated by Hermione's all-encompassing perspective.

11. In a letter to Yale University Press dated May 15, [1951?] (2:11/2161), Merwin made some last-minute substitutions in the edited copy of *A Mask for Janus*. He excluded "Alba" (which had been published in *Perspective* 5 [Winter 1952]: 44–46) and "Ode to Evening" (an ambitious, lengthy poem that exists in several typescripts [see TS. 19:6/003c, 004, 014a, and 014f]) and cut "Epitaph" to four lines. The letter does not name the three poems he is substituting, but one must have been "Dictum: for a Masque of Deluge," MS. 19:6/008a, d. April 25, 1951.

12. Sketches and ideas for plays begin appearing in Merwin's notebooks as early as 1948–49, with early drafts of a play based on the Admetus and Alcestis story; these later evolved into his unfinished verse drama "Shadows of Horses." See notebook 09:1150, and "Shadows of Horses," MS./TS. 10:1160, 1161, 1162. Merwin's 1949–50 notebooks (09:1149) also contain a short verse drama, "The Burial of Judas," and a lengthy sketch for a farce about a bewildered detective and a brush salesman. Another verse drama (undated but presumably from the early 1950s), "The Double Kingdom," was left unfinished; its extensive first act exists in holograph only. Merwin notes that his text is based on a play, which he does not name, by Calderón; see MS. 08:1130.

Chapter 2. Appreciations of Innocence

1. The earliest scholarly study of Merwin's work, Alice N. Benston's "Myth in the Poetry of W. S. Merwin" (in *Poets in Progress,* ed. Edward Hungerford [Evanston, Ill.: Northwestern University Press, 1962], pp. 179–204), begins the linkage: "[E]mphasis on the word, on the necessity as well as the creative power of language, is constantly stressed in Merwin's first two volumes, *A Mask for Janus* and *The Dancing Bears,* where metaphors based on language are pervasive" (p. 182). Richard Howard continues, in *Alone with America,* by describing the first six books of poetry as (emphasis his) "three *pairs* of volumes" (p. 351). Most recently, Paul Breslin, citing Howard's observation, has stated that the "first two volumes . . . are very much alike" (*The Psycho-Political Muse: American Poetry Since the Fifties* [Chicago: University of Chicago Press, 1987], p. 139).

2. Merwin may have seen, in manuscript (or heard in the classroom), R. P. Blackmur's allusion to Flaubert's words: "Those of us who are lovers of words . . . know very well that words are merely one medium in which we express our crying-out and our salutation, our discovery and our assent. . . . We have merciless compassion for the dancing bears—the ballet of our best words—because we understand they would if they could have been the moving stars—moving in their own drift and also our own. We are not lovers for nothing, but for life itself" ("The Language of Silence: A Citation," *Sewanee Review* 63 [Summer 1955]: 382).

3. In the fall of 1951 and winter of 1952, Merwin composed a series of poems, the majority of which were not collected in *The Dancing Bears;* these form a transition between his first and second books. Though they continue to display interest in the primal forms of pre-Renaissance verse, taking shape as ballads ("Queen Helen"), carols ("Canticle for Dido"), and dialogues among generic figures ("Four at the Crossroads"), virtually all are love poems. Nonetheless, the language in which they are written often tends to be restrained and severe, in the manner of Merwin's first book. That most were excluded from his second collection suggests he came to believe that expressions of love were more suited to language that was lavish and extravagant. See TS. 19:6/005a through 005e and TS. 19:6/015a through 015i. In addition, TS. 19:6/019a through 019j may be an early assemblage of *The Dancing Bears.*

4. Merwin infrequently experimented with composing in strict syllabic verse in 1951–52. The third "Canso" is one of his most intricate and successful compositions in that mode. Its eight stanzas follow a rigorous scheme in which odd stanzas have 14, 14, 14, 14, 7, 9, 10, 12, 10, 10, 7, 9, 12, 7, 12, 12, and 14 syllables in their lines, and even stanzas have 10, 10, 12, 7, 14, 14, 8, 7, 9, 12, 14, 14, 14, 14, 12, 10, and 7 syllables in their lines. Working through strict syllabic verse may have helped Merwin decide to

shift to strong-stress meter, for the odd thing about syllabic verse is that its structure remains virtually invisible and inaudible to the reader (especially when the syllable count is so high, as in the third "Canso"). After expending much labor, the poet produces a result with the effect of free verse. Recently, Merwin has taken up the technique again: the eighteen six-line stanzas of "Among Bells" (*New Yorker* 64 [October 17, 1988]: 38) have 6, 7, 10, 8, and 2 syllables in their lines.

5. W. S. Merwin, *The Dancing Bears* (New Haven, Conn.: Yale University Press, 1954), p. 4. The note, which is found among the acknowledgments, is not reproduced in *The First Four Books of Poems.*

6. "The Wood of Women," act 2, scene 1. MS./TS. 09:1163, c. 1953. Not surprisingly, Merwin was aware of at least Molière's version of the Don Juan legend: the quoted line that opens "Tobacco" (collected in *Green with Beasts)* is the first line of Molière's *Don Juan ou Le Festin de Pierre.*

7. W. S. Merwin, "The Neo-Classic Drama," *Hudson Review* 2 (Summer 1949): 259–300.

8. "Shadows of Horses," MS./TS. 10/1160–62, c. 1949–1952?; "The Wood of Women," MS./TS. 09:1163, c. 1953; "Darkling Child," MS./TS. 08:1108–1129, c. 1955; and "The Monument," MS./TS. 09:1148, c. 1954. "Darkling Child" is the only play that exists in a complete form; the other three have first and second acts in typescript but only scattered notes for a third act. All four are composed in verse. "The Monument" is the only play to be dated; it has the note "Begun April 12, 1954."

9. Alice N. Benston was first to claim that in "East of the Sun" "Merwin retells the Psyche legend" ("Myth in the Poetry," p. 184). Harvey Gross, in "The Writing on the Void: The Poetry of W. S. Merwin," *Iowa Review* 1 (Summer 1970): 94, traces the further connection to Apuleius by describing the tale as "a Norse version, with embellishments such as Trolls and large White Bears, of Apuleius' tale of *Cupid and Psyche.*" Mark Christhilf, in *Merwin the Mythmaker* (Columbia: University of Missouri Press, 1986), p. 9, alludes to Robert Graves' involvement when he states that the poem is "Merwin's most sustained illustration of the White Goddess myth"; he adds that the poem "can be read as a version of the Cupid and Psyche tale." For Graves' translation see Lucius Apuleius, *The Golden Ass,* trans. Robert Graves (New York: Straus & Giroux, 1973), pp. 96–143 (reprint of original 1951 edition). In a 1986 interview, Merwin explained that his relationship with Graves grew strained over the course of their time together: "we didn't part on the best of terms" ("The Art of Poetry XXXVIII: W. S. Merwin," interview with Edward Hirsch, *Paris Review* No. 102 [Spring 1987]: 69). To know of this discord between Graves and Merwin adds a layer of complexity to the source hunting: by telling the Norse version, which is the childhood version, of the Cupid and Psyche legend that Graves had translated (in that very adult book, *The Golden Ass*), Merwin takes on the role of apprentice to Graves at the same time as he circumvents the master.

10. See George Webbe Dasent, ed. and trans., *East o' the Sun and West o' the Moon* (New York: Dover, 1970), pp. 22–35 (reprint of 1859 edition); see also Andrew Lang, ed., *The Blue Fairy Book* (New York: Airmont, 1969), pp. 27–37 (reprint of 1889 edition).

11. Bruno Bettelheim, *The Uses of Enchantment: The Meaning and Importance of Fairy Tales* (New York: Vintage, 1977), pp. 296–97. The text Bettelheim studies is the

version by Andrew Lang. Bulfinch's retelling of the Cupid and Psyche legend is in *The Age of Fable* (Garden City, N.Y.: Dolphin, n.d.), pp. 95–105.

12. The original "East o' the Sun" tale falls into two awkwardly stitched parts. The first half draws upon the Cupid and Psyche legend; the second half (commencing with the heroine's trials after the Prince disappears) is virtually identical to "The Lilting, Leaping Lark," tale no. 88 in *Grimms' Tales for Young and Old,* trans. Ralph Manheim; its plot is synopsized in Maria Tatar, *The Hard Facts of the Grimms' Fairy Tales* (Princeton, N.J.: Princeton University Press, 1987), pp. 117–18.

Chapter 3. "Physiologus"

1. All but two of the bestiary poems were published in various journals: "Toro," *Poetry* 83 (November 1953): 72–74 and *Listener* 52 (July 1, 1954): 17; "Spider," *Poetry* 83 (March 1954): 320–22; "Cormorants," "The Hydra," *Botteghe Oscure* 13 (April 1954): 286–90 ("Cormorants" also appeared in *Harper's Bazaar* [April 1956]: 194); "Bear," "Camel," *Poetry* 85 (January 1955): 228–29; "Sow," *Paris Review* No. 11 (Winter 1955): 70–71; "Snail," "Leopard," *Sewanee Review* 64 (Winter 1956): 120–24; and "Toad," *Listen* 2 (Summer 1956): 14–15. Two poems not published were "Mouse," unpub. MS. 19:10/014, d. Mar. 30, 1954, and "Pigeon," unpub. MS. 19:12/029, d. Mar. 20, 1955.

2. The prose accompaniment to the bestiary was published as "The Ark of Silence" in *Western Review* 23 (Autumn 1958): 75–82. The manuscripts are not dated, but because at least two prose pieces were worked up from drafts of poems and notes that Merwin had on hand in England, it seems likely the prose was written after the winter of 1955–56 (when *Green with Beasts* was in galleys) and before August 1956 (when Merwin left England for a two-year stay in America).

3. Rejecting the submission, Merwin's editor at Knopf, Phillip Vaudrin, explained that too many of these poems had appeared in *Green with Beasts* printed only the year before. But publication prospects may have been harmed by Richard Wilbur's anthology, *A Bestiary,* published in 1955. Before submitting the manuscript to Knopf, Merwin had, in July 1957, discussed publishing a limited edition in England, but the small press that had been considering the manuscript lost interest.

4. For a history of the Middle English texts, see "Appendix," *The Bestiary: A Book of Beasts,* ed. and trans. T. H. White (New York: Capricorn, 1954), pp. 230–70.

5. Richard Wilbur, *Things of this World* (New York: Harcourt, Brace and World, 1956), pp. 31–32, reprinted from *A Bestiary* (New York: Harcourt, Brace and World, 1955). For a prose version of "Pelicanus," see White, p. 132.

6. "Introduction," Craig Williamson, *A Feast of Creatures: Anglo-Saxon Riddle-Songs* (Philadelphia: University of Pennsylvania Press, 1982), p. 5.

7. *Poems from the Old English,* trans. Burton Raffel (Lincoln: University of Nebraska Press, 1964), p. 56. For another version of "Ship," see Williamson, *Feast,* p. 90.

8. No final typescript of the bestiary has come to light, but on three occasions, Merwin arranged versions of the bestiary. Column 1 is the sequence of poems in the BBC broadcast of 1954, in which the poems were divided into two groups; column 2 is a sequence deduced from the arrangement in the original manuscript of the prose pieces; and column 3 is the sequence that the prose pieces took when published separately in the *Western Review.* The most stable sequence is the five-poem unit that appears in all

three arrangements (and twice as the opening unit): Leviathan / Blue Cockerel / Two Horses / The Hydra / Toro (and the first three poems remained a unit in the five-poem *Green with Beasts* excerpt). Note, however, that the first and third arrangements could have been tailored for the demands of their occasion rather than reflecting arrangements under consideration. The first may represent the sequence as designed for a broadcast that required two performances and the third may represent the prose as designed to appear without accompanying poetry.

BBC Broadcast (1954)	Sequence of Prose in Archives	Sequence of Prose in *Western Review*
(I)		
Leviathan	Leviathan	Cormorants
Blue Cockerel	Blue Cockerel	Sow
Two Horses	Two Horses	Spider
The Hydra	The Hydra	Leviathan
Toro	Toro	Blue Cockerel
Snail	Mouse	Two Horses
Cormorants	Cormorants	The Hydra
Mouse	Camel	Toro
(II)	Sow	Mouse
Sow	Spider	Camel
Spider	Pigeon	Pigeon
Dog	Dog	Dog
White Goat, Ram	Snail	Snail
Leopard	Toad	Toad
Camel	White Goat, Ram	White Goat, Ram
(Bear)	Leopard	Leopard
	Bear	Bear

9. The offhand reference to "St. Brendan's Islands" in the prose following "Leviathan" displays Merwin's familiarity with obscure medieval texts. *Navigatio Sancti Brendani* (The Voyage of Saint Brendan) was "one of the most famous and enduring stories of Western Christendom" in the Middle Ages, and "the most famous version of the story was done in Norman-French early in the twelfth century." "The Island or Islands of Brendan feature on many a map, chart and globe between the thirteenth and sixteenth centuries and beyond" (John J. O'Meara, "Introduction," *The Voyage of Saint Brendan* [Dublin: Dolmen Press, 1978], p. xiv). The narrative of St. Brendan relates the series of fantastic sights he encountered, sailing west from Ireland in search of the Promised Land; in fact, his stories have been traced to sources in European and Mediterranean folklore, making his text essentially a popular anthology of medieval tales and beliefs.

10. Originally, this prose piece was written as verse, as an unfinished third section (entitled "Cats at Home") to a three-part poem, "Cats" (unpub. variant MS. 19:12/028, d. Easter 1955), of which only section 2, "Burning the Cat," was published (in *Green with Beasts*). Merwin also shaped the prose piece that follows "Toro" from a note he

jotted on scrap paper and dated December 17, 1954; it is transcribed in Cary Nelson, "The Manuscript Archive at the University of Illinois," *Essays on the Poetry,* p. 318.

Chapter 4. Sea Poems

1. "The Monument," MS./TS. 09:1148, d. April 1954. There are first and second versions of act 1 and a substantial portion of act 2, but only scattered notes for act 3. The two versions differ considerably in details of plot, but in both Ascham's remarks to his mother remain virtually unchanged.

2. "To Brewster Ghiselin," unpub. MS. 19:10/017, d. Aug. 2, 1954. Brewster Ghiselin was director of the Writers' Conference at the University of Utah, and at this time had published a book of poems, *Against the Circle* (New York: E. P. Dutton, 1946) and an anthology, *The Creative Process* (Berkeley: University of California Press, 1952). Merwin's poem may echo the opening lines of the first of three poems by Ghiselin published in the Winter 1953 issue of the *Sewanee Review:* "I made a poem of fine shells and stones and glossy water / And a woman walking alone rose-gold among those dead things, naked" ("Poem," *Sewanee Review* 61 [Winter 1953]: 125). On a later occasion when Merwin offered a brief summary statement of his objectives, he drew on terminology like that in "To Brewster Ghiselin"; writing an introductory essay to *Green with Beasts* after the Poetry Book Society (in England) named the volume as a quarterly choice for 1956, he stated that "one of the few statements I feel safe in making about poetry" is that "it is a mystery. It is a metaphor of the other mysteries which comprise human experience. And it gives us the feeling of illumination—one mystery giving us a name by which we know another. . . . I think of it as a way of using what we know, to say what we do not know" ("Notes for the Poetry Book Society essay," MS. 10:1192, c. 1956). He restated this one more time in a passing remark while reviewing Hugh MacDiarmid's *In Memoriam James Joyce:* "Has not the subject of literature always been the abiding mystery of the human condition and what it faces, though the arts have tended to present, body forth, conjure up this mystery by means of minute details, particulars, familiars, the ephemera of more-or-less local mortality" ("Without the Reality of Music," *Poetry* 88 [April 1956]: 49).

3. A statistical portrait of Merwin's output at this time is not easy to assemble. A conservative estimate is that Merwin completed at least seventy-five poems between January 1953 and October 1955, the period he drew upon for *Green with Beasts.* Of these, thirty-eight were collected in the volume; of the thirty-seven left uncollected, fourteen had appeared in various journals and thirteen were apparently never published. These figures only give an approximate view, however; several poems of some length were heavily abridged, and one uncollected poem, "Don Quixote and the Knight of the Mirrors" (unpub. MS. 19:10/020, d. Jan. 7–13, 1954), a retelling of events in chapters 11 through 14 of book 2 of *Don Quixote,* is twenty-three twenty-three-line stanzas: at 529 lines, it is twenty-two lines longer than "East of the Sun and West of the Moon."

4. "Faces and Landscapes," *Nation* 182 (Apr. 14, 1956): 308; "Corps de Ballet," *Poetry* 87 (Mar. 1956): 325–27; "Catching Leaves in Autumn," *Sewanee Review* 62 (Summer 1954): 451–53; and "The Nine Days of Creation," *Kenyon Review* 18 (Summer 1956): 367–69.

5. "Stump Pond," unpub. variant MS. 19:10/038, d. Mar. 4, 1954. Two even longer poems were heavily abridged for book publication. "Saint Sebastian" was cut from 245 lines to fourteen lines (unpub. variant MS. 19:9/013a, d. Jan. 13, 1954). The twenty-one-line "River Sound Remembered" is a reprinting of the final seven tercets of an unpublished poem, "Views of the Delaware River from Morrisville" (unpub. MS. 19:9/001 and unpub. MS. 19:10/003), originally 180 lines long in sixty tercets. A segment of this poem was recast in free verse as "After the Flood."

6. "Cats," unpub. variant MS. 19:12/028, d. Easter 1955.

7. Merwin first began to consider a series of sea poems early in the 1950s. "Westfaring" would detail a series of sea voyages by ancient and Renaissance mariners (see "Notes for *Westfaring,*" MS. 11:1211, c. 1952?-54?). The first sea poem to be completed, however, was "To Brewster Ghiselin" (MS. 19:10/017, d. August 2, 1954), followed shortly by "Lee Shore and Cliffs," dated August 27, 1954. Others followed sporadically. "Two Poems for Alfred Wallis" and "Senility Cay" were completed in October 1954, and "The Fishermen" in February 1955. As a sequence, however, the group does not take shape until the fall of 1955, when *Green with Beasts* was being assembled. At that point, the number of sea poems (the majority included in *The Drunk in the Furnace)* markedly increases: "Fog" on September 20, "The Shipwreck" on July 21, and "The Eyes of the Drowned" on July 27. ("Mariners' Carol" is undated.) But the pace escalates dramatically after *Green with Beasts* has been assembled and submitted for publication: "Sailor Ashore" on October 18; "Sea Wife" on October 20; "Cape Dread," "The Frozen Sea," and "Whaler" (an uncollected poem, published in *Poetry* 89 [March 1957]: 346) on October 22; "Bell Buoy" and "Sea Monster" on October 23; and "The Iceberg" and "The Bones" on October 25—nine poems in seven days. The remainder appeared over the following weeks: "A Piece of Driftwood" (unpub. MS. 19:122/056, d. Dec. 21, 1955) on December 21, "The *Portland* Going Out" on January 20, 1956; "Fog Horn" on February 5; "Deception Island" on March 3 and "Odysseus" on April 24. Two other poems stand just outside these two sets. "Song of the Veiled Siren" was written in America, not England, at a later time, October 19, 1956 (unpub. MS. 20:3/018). Another unfinished poem written in America, "Chanty of the Middle Passage" (unfin. MS. 20:3/017, c. 1956), may have been composed for *Favor Island.* Finally, an unfinished and undated work, "Ballad of the Smiling Island" (unfin. MS. 19:12/074, c. 1955?-56?), sets out to describe the adventures of a salvage crew during World War II:

Things would slide up to us
Out of the mist
So that we seemed to be still
And the waters moving.

Would glide by on the sea-slick and be gone
Still unidentified,
So that we wondered where we were
And no instruments could satisfy us,
Wondered who were
That nothing recognized us.

While it touches on themes in the second set of sea poems, its flat and laconic tone is uncharacteristic of poems written in the fall and winter of 1955–56.

Chapter 5. His Bad Castle

1. W. S. Merwin, "A Conversation with W. S. Merwin," *Audience* 4 (1956): 6. The transcript of the original interview, with Merwin's later interpolations, is TS./MS. 10:1201, c. fall 1956.

2. W. S. Merwin, "An Interview by Michael Clifton," *American Poetry Review* 12 (July-August 1984): 18.

3. Act 1, the epilogue and a synopsis of act 2 of "Favor Island" were published in *New World Writing* 12 (1957): 122–54. Of Merwin's plays, only this one has an active publishing history. It was submitted to Harvard University Press but not published (see "Peter Davison to W. S. Merwin," May 7, 1957, Letter 02:0292/1873). At least four versions of the play survive in manuscript and typescript, MS. 08:1134 through TS. 08:1138; the earliest version contains significant variations in the plot. It was probably written in the winter of 1955–56, when the last of the sea poems were being completed and after he had been asked to apply for a grant as playwright in residence at the Poet's Theatre ("Donald Hall to W. S. Merwin," September 6, 1955, Letter 02:0158/1022). In an exchange of letters with *Partisan Review* editors Philip Rahv and Catherine Carver over a translation commissioned in February 1956 of Gregorio Maranon's *Gloriosa y Miseria del Conde de Villamediana*—which was published but, at Merwin's request, without acknowledging his role as translator (he objected to associating his name with Maranon's because of the inferior quality of Maranon's thought)—Merwin mentions he has interrupted work on a play to complete the translation. The Poet's Theatre production ran from May 20 to June 2, 1957, and the playbill can be found among the unclassified papers of the Cambridge Poet's Theatre in the Widener Library, Harvard. In addition, a version was performed at Cornell University ("Arthur Mizener to W. S. Merwin," March 27, 1957, 01:092/003) and the BBC Third Programme broadcast a slightly shortened text in 1958 ("Douglas Cleverdon to W. S. Merwin," March 13, 1958, Letter 01:064/343).

4. "Luzerne Street Looking West," *Hudson Review* 9 (Winter 1956–57): 509–10.

5. "After Some Years," *Harper's* 214 (June 1957): 45.

6. "Oh, Susannah!," unpub. MS. 19:12/059, d. Mar. 18, 1956. Susannah may have been a name for Merwin's great-grandmother. Although she is called "Hannah" in *Unframed Originals*, in "The Cemetery at Widnoon" (unfin. MS. 20:03/019, c. 1956–57), a stanza following a reference to "Old Jake" (his great-grandfather) begins: "Susannah his wife had skinny arms and three / Sons she farmed out over the river." See *Unframed Originals*, p. 29: "Old Jake's widow, Hannah, decided that she could not manage to bring up the three boys herself, and she farmed out Jim, aged seven, with the Heinz family at Widnoon."

7. "Flight Home," *Paris Review* 17 (Winter 1958): 236; rep. in W. S. Merwin, *Regions of Memory: Uncollected Prose, 1949–1982*, ed. Ed Folsom and Cary Nelson (Urbana: University of Illinois Press, 1987), p. 187.

8. "Rimer, Penna.," *Harper's* 215 (Nov. 1957): 72.

9. "The Cemetery at Widnoon," unfin. MS. 20:03/019, c. 1956–57.

10. "Nothing New," *Paris Review* No. 18 (Spring 1958): 91–92.

11. "W. S. Merwin to Arthur Mizener," Sept. 16, 1956, MS. Q.811 M559m.

12. "Uncle Cal," *Nation* 184 (March 2, 1957): 190.

13. "Aunt Alma," *Paris Review* No. 18 (Spring 1958): 90.

14. For reviewers (all of them poets) who saw no link with *Life Studies,* see Peter Davison, "Self-Revelation in the New Poetry," *Atlantic* (Nov. 1961): 174; James Dickey, "The Death and Keys of the Censor," *Sewanee Review* (Spring 1961): 329; Thom Gunn, "Outside Faction," *Yale Review* (Summer 1961): 589; Jon Holloway, *London Magazine* (January 1961): 76–77; Elizabeth Jennings, "Searching with Words," *New Statesman and Nation* (Oct. 15, 1960): 576; and Louis Simpson, "Important and Unimportant Poems," *Hudson Review* (Autumn 1961): 464–65. However, Robert D. Spector did describe the set as "unsentimental ancestor portraits (suggestive of those of Robert Lowell)" in "A Cloud of Quiet Terror," *Saturday Review* (Jan. 28, 1961): 30. For later critics who note the resemblance with Lowell, see Jarold Ramsey, "The Continuities of W. S. Merwin," *Essays on the Poetry,* p. 20; Richard Howard, *Alone with America,* p. 369; Marjorie Perloff, "Merwin and the Sorrows of Literary History," *Essays on the Poetry,* p. 124; and R. W. Flint, "Exiles from Olympus," *Parnassus* (Spring-Summer 1977): 97. The issue of indebtedness can be resolved by studying manuscripts. Merwin's first ancestor poem was "John Otto," dated April 22, 1956 (MS. 19:12/067); his next-to-last was "The Drunk in the Furnace," dated December 6, 1957 (MS. 20:3/026); and his last was "Grandmother and Grandson," dated January 2, 1958 (MS. 20:3/004). The majority of Merwin's poems were written in England in the spring and summer of 1956 and in America in the winter and spring of 1957. By contrast, Lowell began a prose autobiography in 1955, but his poetry came later: "From mid-August through October 1957, Lowell completed eleven poems in free verse" (Ian Hamilton, *Robert Lowell: A Biography* [New York: Random House, 1982], p. 233). Then, "Lowell spent the summer of 1958 completing the manuscript of *Life Studies*" (Hamilton, p. 258). That is, Merwin had completed all but two of his family poems before Lowell began his first in August 1957. Moreover, from October 1956 to March 1958, Merwin was living in Boston and socializing with Lowell (Hamilton, p. 239); if there is a line of influence, it runs from Merwin down to Lowell.

15. Merwin's father, a minister, raged against the insatiable appetite of the coal-burning furnace in the family's Scranton home (*Unframed Originals,* pp. 179–84). Thus the poem also asks to be read as a family joke, and as a distorted communication between Merwin and his father. Merwin's father used the costly furnace as an excuse to keep temperatures lower in selective parts of the house, in order to discourage a house guest of whom he disapproved and whom Merwin loved as a child.

Chapter 6. Lost Voices

1. "Interview with Michael Clifton," p. 18. Merwin's reticence is all the more striking because Clifton purposely set out to solicit information about the period just before *The Moving Target.* Merwin uses similar generalizations to describe his years of dissatisfaction in Jack Myers and Michael Simms, "Possibilities of the Unknown: Conversations with W. S. Merwin," *Southwest Review* 68 (Spring 1983): 169. The Clifton interview occurred in 1980, the Myers and Simms in 1982.

2. "[Untitled] Essay on Public Speakers in the Boston Common," in Notebook #1, unpub. MS. 11:1216, c. 1957–58. The notebook includes drafts of book reviews published in the *Nation* in 1958 and 1959.

3. "Hangman's Helicon," broadcast MS. 10:1182, c. 1959.

4. See W. S. Merwin, "The Wake of the Blackfish" (*Paris Review* 32 [Summer 1990]: 267–318) for a description of his friendship with George Kirstein, who had just purchased the *Nation* in 1957, the year the two met. Shortly after their meeting, Merwin began contributing a number of book reviews to the *Nation,* all of which testify to his deepening interest in political matters. These form a sharp contrast to his previous work: in 1957 and 1958 he contributed seven reviews to the *New York Times Book Review,* all on contemporary books of poetry or criticism by British and Americans; from 1958 to 1961, he contributed eleven reviews to the *Nation,* none of which treated contemporary poetry, and all of which displayed a growing involvement in cultural and political concerns. Within the elastic genre of the book review, Merwin could discuss matters of social concern, even when he had not yet imagined how to include them in poetry.

5. "Star," *Chelsea* 11 (Mar. 1962): 25.

6. "Arrival," *Chelsea* 11 (Mar. 1962): 25; also, MS. 20:06/028, d. Feb. 9, 1960.

7. "A Peacock at the Door," MS./TS. 09:1154 through 09:1157, c. 1957. "The Gilded West," MS./TS. 08:1139 through 08:1144. Like that of "Favor Island," its plot is based on fact. Late in his life, Cody was attracted to Katherine Clemmons, a British actress of little talent; he financed her theatrical tours in England and America, both failures. "She afterward married Howard Gould, who sued her for divorce in 1907, naming Cody. Dan Muller tells a story of Gould's attorneys coming to Cody at a time when his financial situation was desperate to offer him $50,000 to testify against Katherine. Cody told them to get the hell out of his tent, and meant it" (Don Russell, *The Lives and Legend of Buffalo Bill* [Norman: University of Oklahoma Press, 1960], p. 433). There are two undated fragments of plays, perhaps begun when Merwin was in Boston or at a later date, which suggest efforts to probe beyond the limits of conventional theater. "The Academy" is set on the urban streets; it opens with panhandlers instructing a novice in techniques of begging. The other, "*Jamais le Gars,*" subtitled "A Spectacle in (Two) Acts," is Beckett-like; Merwin's notes explain: "The play embodies the desires and fears of all the characters, but least of all of the second man. Situations and bits of dialogue keep repeating themselves and then developing differently. Most obvious of the repetitions is the reappearance, at least twice, after the opening, of the first man at the top of the stairs. . . . All the characters are dead (in their own and the others' fears and wishes) at least once in the play but the only character who ever disappears from the stage is the first man." Only the first man remains a stable personality; of the second man, Merwin says, "In the course of the play he may become: policeman, father of the first, brother of the first, father of each woman in turn, and of both of them at once." Of the two women, the first plays multiple roles and the second is described as "the object of [the first man's] desires and the spur to his dread." See MS. 09:1145. The title comes from a ribald chant Merwin jotted down among notes for poems: "Fous-la au lit fous la par terre / Fous la ou ce que tu voudra, / ni par devant ni par derriere / jamais le gars n'en jouira."

8. "Grant Applications," unpub. MS. 09:1190, c. 1957.

9. "Lost Voices," *Nation* 188 (February 14, 1959): 143; also, uncol. MS. 20:4/002, d. June 2, 1958.

10. When silence occurs it is dissolved at once. In "Backwater Pond: the Canoeists" (an earlier version dated March 4, 1954, with the revision probably in the fall of 1955), fishermen "drop their voices as they glide in from the lake." But the stillness is only a prelude to new sound, so when a turtle dives suddenly, the effect is startling: "and then there is a faint breeze and echo of laughter." As nature abhors a vacuum, the poet abhors silence; forces regroup and sound begins again. "River Sound Remembered" (the original version is undated; the revision was probably made in the fall of 1955) begins with the sound of water drowning "all voices until / It seemed a kind of silence unbroken / By anything." But after escaping the "kind of silence" of the roaring water, noises so ordinary they would usually go unnoticed are heard with a new sensitivity. Roaring silence is a framework that enhances true sound. Silence as a void never presides.

11. "On a Sacrifice of Darkness," *Poets and the Past,* ed. Dore Ashton (New York: Andre Emmerich Gallery, 1959), p. 36; also, uncol. MS. 20:4/004, d. July 16, 1958. The poem was custom-written just for the occasion; originally, Merwin had answered Ashton's request by offering "Tamburlaine in Persepolis" (unpub. MS. 20:03/021, d. Oct. 17, 1956), but the poem was rejected as inappropriate ("Dore Ashton to W. S. Merwin," June 15, 1958, 01:030/001).

12. "W. S. Merwin to Arthur Mizener," Dec. 6, 1959, Letter 03:0549/055.2483.

13. "W. S. Merwin to Arthur Mizener," July 27, 1958, Letter 03:0549/055.2481.

14. W. S. Merwin, *Selected Translations 1948–1968* (New York: Atheneum, 1969), p. viii.

15. W. S. Merwin, "The Translation of Verse," *Kenyon Review* 16 (Summer 1954): 500.

16. W. S. Anderson, "Introduction," *The Satires of Persius,* trans. W. S. Merwin (Bloomington: Indiana University Press, 1961), pp. 34–35.

17. These Neruda translations were dated 1959 when published in *Selected Translations 1948–1968.* Writing to his editor at Atheneum, Hiram Hayden, in January 1960, Merwin passed along some Neruda translations, praising Neruda as the "greatest Spanish poet of this century," then added that he was not proposing to translate Neruda because "Neruda's relation to my own poetry and what I want to do is too delicate and fraught for me to be able to definitely say right at the moment whether or not I'd like to translate a lot of him—I'm sure you'll understand that." This convoluted sentence is amplified in an even more extraordinary footnote in the letter: "All I really mean by this hyper hyper sentence is that I'd like to think about such a project before actually committing myself and because some of the things I've tried and still try to do could conceivably be influenced by such a project so I wasn't sure whether what I heard was me or not for a while" ("W. S. Merwin to Hiram [Hayden]," January 22, 1960, Letter 01:34/017.207). Merwin remained sensitive to the issue of Neruda's possible influence; he expressed similar reservations a few years later, when prodded by Nathaniel Tarn, then editing a collection of translations, to contribute further Neruda. Explaining that he was burdened with translations, Merwin added: "I'm trying to get something of my own done—and this last influences the possibility of work on Neruda in a number of ways. I'm sure you've the feeling that there are things of Neruda's that you'd simply not

want to be in touch with when you were trying to get on with some particular thing of your own" ("W. S. Merwin to Nathaniel Tarn," April 26, 1967, Letter 02:198/18.1242).

18. "Letter from a Distance," MS. 20:12/002, d. Sept. 8, 1960).

19. Anthony Libby, "W. S. Merwin and the Nothing that Is," *Contemporary Literature* 16 (Winter 1975): 27–28. Libby eliminated this portion of his essay when reprinting it in *Mythologies of Nothing* (Urbana: University of Illinois Press, 1984), pp. 185–209. Merwin's version of "Walking Around" is dated 1959 in *Selected Translations 1948–1968.*

20. See "Grant Proposals," MS. 10:1190 and 1191, for the proposed outline. See Ed Folsom, "'I Have Been a Long Time in a Strange Country': W. S. Merwin and America" in *Essays on the Poetry,* pp. 226–27, for further description of the Coxey's Army piece. The project held Merwin's interest, though erratically, for some time. The original proposals were made in the summer of 1959, in dual applications for a Guggenheim Fellowship and a Ford Foundation Grant; both met with no success. But a $500 advance he received in 1960 from his new publisher, Atheneum, for his next book (which would in fact be *The Moving Target)* was offered on the strength of his Coxey's Army project. In his original proposal, he planned to return to America in November 1960 to begin to trace the route of the marchers. Though his proposal was not funded, he returned to America in November, but soon wrote to Arthur Mizener in a December 12, 1960, letter that his plans for research had not worked out (03:549/55.2486). George Kirstein then helped arrange a grant from the Rabinowitz Foundation to defray the costs of research, and in a November 13, 1961, letter, Merwin thanks him for sending along some necessary material (letters to and from Kirstein are included in uncatalogued correspondence at the University of Illinois Merwin Archives). The project drops out of sight until August 30, 1963 (at the time *The Moving Target* was prepared for publication), when Merwin mentions to Kirstein, "I have been writing some new things, some poems, a story, some Coxey." It surfaces again in a June 5, 1964, letter to Kirstein that refers to work on "the long poem." A year later, in a July 24, 1965, letter to Kirstein, Merwin reports apologetically on his lack of progress: "I know there is the long poem, but I was somewhat embarrassed thinking of the Rabinowitz grant, and fearing that they expected that I would be able to finish the poem in some predictable time, whereas, I suspected, and am now convinced that it is something I will be some considerable time evolving, though the factual material has been assembled fairly adequately (and that was what the grant was given specifically for)." There is a last flurry of activity in 1967 (when *The Lice* was prepared for publication). In a February 6, 1967, letter, Harry Ford, Merwin's Atheneum editor, recalls that Merwin's 1959 contract with Hiram Hayden called for a $500 advance and another $500 to be paid on delivery of "the narrative poem" (01:128/67.712). Merwin answers on February 20, saying he has "no idea when the other half might be earned" (01:128/67.713). Yet Kirstein learns in an April 19, 1967, letter that Merwin has "looked up some things that have come up this winter in resumed work on Coxey." He notes on a June 26 postcard to Kirstein that he is in America, in a Citroen 20V, tracing the route the unemployed workers had taken across Pennsylvania. A month later, however, he is back in Europe and writing to Ford, on July 24, 1967: "About all I've done since getting back is to throw out several pages of the latest draft of that long improbable poem that your firm once unwisely invested good

money in" (01:128/67.721). Ford's reply is to send along a copy of a new poem by David Wagoner that Ford believes might be on a theme similar to Merwin's project, and Merwin's August 5, 1967, reply is the last word on the subject, stating that Wagoner's poem is "in no respect anything like what I've been floundering with—in case you might have wondered (again, where the hell am I with that)" (01:128/67.723).

21. For various drafts of "Congé" see unfin. MS. 20:5/001 and 002, plus unfin. MS. 20:07/003a, 003b, c. 1959–60. On one sheet, Merwin notes: "Now 32, till Sept.," placing the origin of the notes prior to September 1959. In an August 20, 1959, letter to George Kirstein, he looks forward to "two projects I've been trying to shape out a little." One he identifies as the Coxey's Army piece, the other is a "purely personal one, which I've hoped I might start this fall" ("W. S. Merwin to George Kirstein," Aug. 20, 1959, uncatalogued correspondence).

22. "Words for Departure," unpub. MS. 20:5/003, c. 1959–60; 20:7/006, c. 1959–60; and 20:13/003b, d. Jan. 27, 1960.

23. "Home for Thanksgiving," MS. 20:06/037, d. January 23, 1960.

24. "Wishes for Old Age," unpub. MS./TS. 20:06/016, c. January 1960.

Chapter 7. The Good Voyage

1. James Dickey, "The Many Ways of Speaking in Verse," *New York Times Book Review* (Dec. 22, 1963): 4; Joseph Bennett, "The Moving Finger Writes," *Hudson Review* (Winter 1963–64): 624–25; Ralph J. Mills Jr., "Some New Poetry," *Modern Age* (Fall 1964): 436–37; and David Galler, "Versions of Accident," *Kenyon Review* (Summer 1964): 581–83.

2. R. K. Meiners, "The Necessary and Permanent Revolution," *Southern Review* (Autumn 1964): 931–37.

3. Poems in the three stages are grouped together in the Atheneum text of *The Moving Target.* All the poems written in England and France in 1960 appear on pp. 2–34 of the volume, from "Home for Thanksgiving" to "October," with one exception—"The Poem," p. 41 (MS. 20:06/042, d. March 24, 1960).

4. "Unforgiveables," unpub. MS. 20:06/031, d. Feb. 4, 1960.

5. The poems of the middle third begin with "Departure's Girl-friend," dated January 16, 1961 (MS. 20:14/001), and end with "We Continue," dated April 10, 1962 (MS. 20:11/011). "We Continue" is the last poem to include punctuation. In the Atheneum text, the middle period begins on p. 35 and ends with "To Where We Are" on p. 61.

6. The revisions were probably undertaken along with the spate of new writing that initiated the middle period. After complaining to George Kirstein in a July 2, 1961, letter that he has not completed any writing of his own for months, he shortly thereafter begins the urban poetry that makes up the middle cycle of the volume. Living in France, in July he completes five poems, in August three, in September three, and in October two. These are the poems between pp. 37–55 of the Atheneum text of *The Moving Target* (generally grouped in their order of completion), with the exception of "Vocation" and "The Poem," written earlier. Before returning to New York in December 1961, he revised at least three poems written a year or so earlier: "Marica Lart," "Foreign Summer" (*Poetry* 99 [January 1962]: 209), and "Views from the High Camp" (*Contemporary American Poetry,* ed. Donald Hall [Baltimore: Penguin Books, 1962], p. 161). The

revisions are not dated, but as Brian Daldorph explains in a detailed discussion of Merwin's drafts and revisions in *The Moving Target* ("'The pulse / Of a stone was my flag / And the stone's in pieces': Merwin's Breaking Voice in *The Moving Target*," *American Poetry* 6 [Spring 1989]: 33–54], the time of revision can be deduced from Merwin's notes on the back of typescripts that list the journals to which the typescript has been submitted. As Daldorph explains with "Views from the High Camp": "Merwin dated the typescript 'March 15, 1960.' He did not date the revision written beneath it. However, it is possible to date the revision as post-July 1961 because on the back of the typescript Merwin wrote the titles of six magazines, dates, and checks by each one as the poem was presumably returned to him. The list ends with 'Poetry-July 61.'"

7. A published poem that Merwin set out to revise, "Views from the High Camp," proves even more intractable than "Foreign Summer." Its original version (dated March 15, 1960) is suffused with mixed regret, although its closing couplet—"Be assured that the rain will be released / Too late to save the harvest"—brutally cuts off the likelihood of any reconciliation. In revision, all traces of torment are eradicated. The original introduced the major turn into the third stanza by conceding an awareness of loss; in revision, however, loss appears abruptly, in passing, in one version ("—the sun / Moves over, loss peaks in the drapery") and disappears entirely from another (see TS./MS. 20:06/011 and 20:10/017). These 1960 poems cannot be salvaged through revision. Too intimately connected with quite particular moments in Merwin's evolution, they can be either printed as they were written or suppressed. "Marica Lart," an elegy for a friend, is shorter and about another person, and its revisions can proceed successfully.

8. The third phase begins with the first of the unpunctuated poems, "The Crossroads of the World, Etc." (MS. 20:11/001, d. Apr. 17, 1962) and continues to "Spring" (MS. 20:13/009, d. Jan. 21, 1963). During this time, Merwin was living in New York; he would return to Europe in the late spring or early summer of 1963. The final poem in the volume, "Daybreak," was completed on October 17, 1961 (MS. 20:10/019) and originally included punctuation; see Daldorph, "Merwin's Breaking Voice," for a definitive analysis of its various drafts.

9. The shift toward unpunctuated verse coincides with Merwin's interest in a plan to disrupt nuclear testing in the Pacific by sailing the *Everyman* into the test zone. The first unpunctuated poem was finished on April 17, 1962; the *Everyman* was scheduled for launching on May 8, 1962. "Act of Conscience" is reprinted in *Regions*, pp. 213–54.

Chapter 8. In a Clearing

1. Interview, Myers and Simms, p. 170. Merwin's insistence that he was striving to write clearly and directly in much of *The Lice* was reiterated in several places in correspondence written when *The Lice* was under way, as in this October 22, 1965, letter to George Kirstein: "I'm sure it sounds plain willful to you when I say that what I'm trying to do is to be simpler all the time, and in my perverse way I think I have been succeeding in doing just that, and that I suspect that it's strangeness rather than real difficulty which makes the poems seem incomprehensible." The letter asks: "But what is difficult about 'December Among the Vanished,' line by line? . . . Maybe you're trying too hard."

2. The riddle has another dimension: Merwin's translation stresses a battlefield

metaphor, and thereby draws attention to a society brutalized enough to assimilate images of war into its popular riddles. The original Greek is more neutral: "that which we have seen *(eidomen)* and grasped *(elabomen)* these things we leave behind, while what we have neither seen nor grasped these we carry away."

3. Jarold Ramsey, "The Continuities of W. S. Merwin," *Essays on the Poetry,* pp. 26–28. William Rueckert also is exceptionally sensitive to the role of nature in the volume as a whole; see "Rereading *The Lice*" in *Essays on the Poetry,* pp. 45–64, and especially pp. 57–60.

4. "Interview," Clifton, p. 19.

5. "Interview," Clifton, p. 19. In a 1984 interview, discussing the influence of surrealism on his poetry of the 1960s, Merwin acknowledged that the opening poems in *The Lice* reflected a surrealistic impulse: "There were definitely poems, particularly some of the first poems in *The Lice,* that were a deliberate attempt to use certain surrealist devices. . . . Those really might have been called surrealist, but they were seldom the ones that were talked about. For example, 'Unfinished Book of Kings.'" (David L. Elliott, "Interview with W. S. Merwin," *Contemporary Literature* 29 [Spring 1988]: 9).

6. "As the Dark Snow Continues to Fall," *Evergreen Review* 9 (March 1965): 50; also, MS. 21:01/006, d. February 19, 1963.

7. Hank Lazer, "For a Coming Extinction: A Reading of W. S. Merwin's *The Lice,*" *ELH* 49 (1982): 262–85.

8. MS. 21:02/015, d. May 1, 1964.

9. The typescript of the original title page is reproduced in *Essays on the Poetry,* p. 58.

Chapter 9. The Day for Carrying Loads

1. Work on Chamfort occupied Merwin during the beginning stages of *The Carrier of Ladders.* He was notified that his request to the National Translation Center for a commission to translate Chamfort's aphorisms had been accepted on November 3, 1965 (Letter 02:0254/1485). Work on it was interrupted by a sudden commission to translate Lorca's "Yerma" for a Lincoln Center Production in the fall of 1966. He returns to Chamfort in the fall of 1966, as *The Lice* was being assembled, and it reappears in his correspondence with George Kirstein up to September 1967, when the lengthy introduction was completed. The earliest poem in *The Carrier of Ladders* is its first, "Plane," dated December 30, 1966 (TS. 21:04/001d), and sixteen poems were completed in April 1967. Concluding work on Chamfort, then, coincides with beginning work on *The Carrier of Ladders.* A similar translation project, though much smaller in scope, Antonio Porchia's aphorisms in *Voices,* also overlaps this opening period; it was begun in May 1967 just before work on the Chamfort introduction.

2. MS. 20:017/001, d. "Dec. '64 / Apr. 25, 1967." 1964 versions of the manuscript (which can be distinguished from the 1967 versions because they still employ the convention of a capital letter at the outset of the line) differ considerably from the final poem of 1967 in their emphasis on a difficult quest: "Stars be / Auspicious and my masters // For the paths are tangled and / Lost with ancient disuse / I have pulled the ashes of the prophets' fires / I hope to set foot in new places." Howard Moss's request for an explanatory note was not untypical ("Howard Moss to W. S. Merwin," January 26,

1968, Letter 02:267/1698). Moss was sometimes made uncomfortable by the degree to which Merwin risked obscurity: he suggested changing the title of "Edouard" (CL, 25) to "Verdun Again." That would have clarified the poem, a wistful monologue by a French World War I veteran whose thoughts are fixed on the unbridgeable gulf between prewar and postwar days ("Howard Moss to W. S. Merwin," December 1, 1967, Letter 02:266/1696 and December 8, 1967, Letter 02:266/1697). Marguerite Yourcenar's description of *Les Tragiques* explains why this poem would hold Merwin's attention: "The work's subject involved, in effect, the perpetual contrast between the outbursts of man's ferocity, which derive from nature, and his outbursts of heroism, which proceed from the same source. . . . In a country where more than elsewhere poets turn from the actual and immediate, choosing to deal with a purified, distilled matter already over-refined by literary tradition, d'Aubigné's extraordinary audacity consists in having taken for his material the crude substance of his age. . . . [T]his epic is in reality wholly lyrical, unique by its mixture of transcendence and impassioned realism, sublime above all by its sudden outbursts and its sudden halts, by those verses which abruptly explode like voices, rise and intersect as though in a Renaissance motet" (*The Dark Brain of Peranesi and Other Essays,* trans. Richard Howard [New York: Farrar, Straus & Giroux, 1984], pp. 29, 38).

3. See Cary Nelson, "The Resources of Failure: W. S. Merwin's Deconstructive Career," in *Essays on the Poetry,* pp. 78–121, for the most eloquent presentation of Merwin as a writer exquisitely aware of the limitations of all language.

4. To my knowledge, the only critic to have taken note of at least one sequence in the book is Ed Folsom, in "Approaches and Removals: W. S. Merwin's Encounter with Whitman's America," *Shenandoah* 29 (Spring 1978): 57–73, an essay expanded as "'I Have Been a Long Time in a Strange Country': W. S. Merwin and America," in *Essays on the Poetry,* pp. 224–49.

5. While all the quasi-sequences raise problems, the "American" sequence is the most unstable. Folsom (*Essays on the Poetry,* pp. 241–49) sees the sequence beginning with "The Approaches," one poem earlier than I do, and running through "The Removal," a group of sixteen poems. My sense is that after seven poems on themes from American history, Merwin characteristically swerves toward another sequence on European immigrants and displaced persons in general that echoes the American history sequence. The point, however, is the instability of the entire movement; one can defend several different clusterings of the poetry.

6. See "W. S. Merwin to George Kirstein," April 11, 1968, uncatalogued correspondence. The publication of *The Carrier of Ladders* would be further delayed to coordinate with *The Miner's Pale Children,* whose last piece was written on December 31, 1969 ("The Roofs," TS. 21:07/065, d. Dec. 31, 1969). Merwin's uncertainty about the shape of the volume may explain the significant lacunae that exist in the University of Illinois Archives for this period only. No original manuscripts have survived from the period between late 1966 and April 1967, during which Merwin would have made his first assembling. (The dating of these poems is on record in the typescript of the final version of *The Carrier of Ladders,* TS. 16:16/1357.) However, typescripts of the poems in the first two-thirds of the book have survived, along with a dozen or so other poems, some of which ("Esther," "The Last Woman of Brunat") were published in journals. Among this group is a typescript of "The Removal" in a longer form, as a sequence of six

individual poems, and an unpublished poem addressed to Ezra Pound (without naming him), "A Homage." These typescripts may be all that remains of a first version of *Carrier,* scattered after work began on new poetry in June 1968.

7. Merwin not only displayed a new decisiveness in his poetry but also in his personal affairs. In the annotations to his correspondence with George Kirstein, Merwin explains that he and his wife Dido Milroy had decided to part in May 1968: "([Kirstein's] wife had died suddenly in July. On NY State reading tour my wife at the time and I had at least reached an agreement to separate as soon as possible; she planned to return to Europe.)" As Merwin remarked in his memoir of Kirstein, "The Wake of the Blackfish" (*Paris Review* 32 [Summer 1990]: 267–318), For years his letters carefully suppressed the discord in his marriage. The parenthetical remarks continue into another annotation for a letter of November 27, 1968: "(From Wash. D.C. on reading trip. From there, former wife, who had said she planned to stay in Washington, left instead as soon as I was gone, to spend time with my mother and build up semi-secret alliance with her 'for my own good')." Anyone currently reading Merwin's letters to Kirstein would find none of this information revealed; Merwin's running commentary on the correspondence alone makes it evident. Its absence underscores how difficult it was for Merwin to break free of this relationship that seems to have been over for some time, superseded by other relationships noted in letters to Kirstein. As an example of the difficulty of leave-taking, consider that *The Carrier of Ladders* is dedicated "to Dido." The nine love poems at the outset of *The Carrier of Ladders,* written from December 1966 to April 1967, do not appear to have been addressed to his wife; a July 19, 1967, letter to Kirstein announces that Merwin has returned to Europe and that a love affair has ended. In his memoir of Kirstein, Merwin often frankly notes relationships that proceeded independently of his wife.

8. MS. 21:05/019, d. June 5, 1968. The poem that was written immediately before this one, "The Hulk" (MS. 21:05/021, d. May 28, 1968), leaves Merwin at the end, clutching "my fear by the hand / by the hand / and no father."

9. Merwin at one time thought to continue the psalms. "The Way Ahead" (MS. 21:13/013, d. Feb. 21, 1971; published in *Writings to an Unfinished Accompaniment,* p. 63) was originally titled "Fifth Psalm: On the Way Ahead," then changed in typescript. It follows the same parallel structure of repeated formulas that one finds in the other psalms, but it differs in an important respect. The poet himself is not at the center of the conflicts it describes; the poem instead predicts the ruin to come if the culture persists in its destructive habits. In this respect, "The Way Ahead" only superficially resembles the other psalms.

Chapter 10. A Guide to This World

1. "If we ask why they are not more robust, they answer by a single eloquent finger pointing to sunless caverns where they were born: peaked and huge-eyed, like wizened English workhouse children, they stand in speechless reproach in the schoolyard, rebuking by their mere subterranean etiolation the boisterous ruddiness of the terrestrial." Helen Vendler, "The Miner's Pale Children," in *Part of Nature, Part of Us* (Cambridge, Mass.: Harvard University Press, 1980), p. 233.

2. The final poem composed for *The Carrier of Ladders* was "The Chaff," dated March 27, 1969. The first piece composed for *The Miner's Pale Children* was "The Bar,"

dated April 10, 1969. The prose pieces occupied Merwin exclusively from April into August of 1969, when the first of the poems for *Writings to an Unfinished Accompaniment* began.

3. "The Train for Camden," "Thaw," "A Friend of Bill's," and a fourth untitled, unfinished piece, in a notebook including a draft of a dramatization of Hawthorne's "Dr. Heidegger's Experiment," Notebook 08:1132, c. 1949–51. Evidence suggests the four stories may have been written at different times, though they follow one another directly in the notebook. "Thaw" is dated "July 8, 1949," but in a note for "The Train to Camden," where Merwin is calculating the age of one character, he uses 1950 as the year from which to subtract. And at the end of "A Friend of Bill's," a note pertains to "Dictum: For a Masque of Deluge," which was completed on April 6, 1951.

4. "The Parrot," unfin. TS. 11:1220, c. 1955–56.

5. "The Barn," unpub. MS. 10:1176, d. March 30-April 5, 1956. In 1957, the *Paris Review* accepted "Flight Home," "A Recollection of Stones" and "The Barn" ("George Plimpton to W. S. Merwin," May 14, 1957, Letter 02:0280/1830). Only "Flight Home" ever appeared in print.

6. "Return to the Mountains," *Evergreen Review* 7 (Oct.-Nov. 1963): 91–106; "The Museum," *Atlantic Monthly* 213 (May 1964): 68–73; and "The Church of Sounds," *Atlantic Monthly* 214 (Dec. 1964): 85–87. All three are reprinted in *Regions*, pp. 21–50.

7. "The Academy," "Campbell," and "The Flyover," *Quarterly Review of Literature* 16 (1969): 390–422. All three are reprinted in *Regions*, pp. 51–80.

8. Notebook 21:10/001, c. 1969–70.

9. On two earlier occasions Merwin adopted a similar tone, both times for essays that may have been conceived with *The Nation* in mind: "The Art of Giving," unpub. TS. 10:1172, c. 1957–59, and "A Progress Report, or the New Cock Robin," unpub. TS. 11:1227, c. 1958–60. "A New Right Arm" originally appeared in *Kulchur* 3 (Autumn 1963): 3–16.

Chapter 11. The Debt to Anonymous

1. Cary Nelson and Ed Folsom, "'Fact Has Two Faces': An Interview with W. S. Merwin," in *Essays on the Poetry*, p. 343.

2. Work on *(Asian Figures)* may have begun as early as 1968: a February 1968 letter from Bonnie Crown of the Asian Society awards him a grant to work on "Korean proverbs" ("Bonnie Crown to W. S. Merwin," Feb. 21, 1968, Letter 01:0031/0129).

3. Other activities attest to Merwin's interest in oral literature during these years. From 1971 to 1973, his second home was not his French farmhouse but a home he had purchased in rural Mexico. In his 1972 review of *The Book of Counsel: The Popul Vuh of the Quiche Maya of Guatemala* (*New York Review of Books* 18 [April 20, 1972]: 16–19 [excerpted in *Regions*, pp. 277–79]) he is quick to connect this translation with the work of contemporary poets, citing Jerome Rothenberg's anthologies. His unpublished and uncollected poems from 1969–1972 reveal that the only form that attracted his interest was the ballade. Along with the published "Ballade of Sayings" (which is composed entirely of proverbs and remains within oral literature), he also wrote two others in the same form, "The Inspectors" (unpub. MS. 21:16/024, d. Apr. 7, 1972) and "Ballade of the Unknown" (unpub. MS. 22:04/001, d. August 5, 1972).

4. Beginning in 1970, when *The Carrier of Ladders* and *The Miner's Pale Children*

appeared concurrently, the publishing history of Merwin's volumes makes for difficulty in tracking his developing concerns. The poetry collected in *Writings* begins in August 1969 and extends up to January 1972. The prose in *Miner's* begins in April 1969 and extends up to January 1970; that in *Houses* continues from January 1970 but extends all the way to July 1976, overlapping not only *Writings* but all of *The Compass Flower* (1977), the beginning of *Feathers from the Hill* (1978), two chapters in *Unframed Originals* (1982), and up to the first poems in *Opening the Hand* (1983). Unlike *Miner's*, which was a product of one concentrated period of less than a year, *Houses* is composed of material written at various times over almost six years. Moreover, *Miner's* is arranged almost entirely in its order of composition, whereas *Houses* often mixes work from different years. With some notable exceptions ("The Element," "The Great Union," and "Vanity"), the first two-thirds of *Houses and Travellers* is contemporary with *Writings to an Unfinished Accompaniment.*

5. Only four prose pieces seem to have originated as verse: "A Conversation" (variant MS. Arch. 21:13/016, d. March 6, 1971), "The Fly and the Milk" (variant MS. 21:13/025b, d. March 20, 1971), "The Lonely Child" (variant MS. 21:13/026, d. March 21, 1971), and "Watching a Train" (variant MS. 22:06/007, d. August 6, 1973).

6. In August 1970, for example, Merwin moved back and forth with great success among a variety of forms. Here is a chronology: the poem "Nomad Songs" (August 1), the poem "Ash" (August 4), the poem "Diggers" (also August 4), the prose piece "Brothers" (August 7), the prose piece "August" (August 9), the poem "Animals from Mountains" (August 11), the prose piece "The Bride of the East" (August 16), the poem "The Day" (August 18), the poem "Sybil" (August 25), the autobiographical memoir "The Hawk and the Mules" (August 28), and the prose piece "The Invalid" (August 30).

Chapter 12. In the Chambers of the Heart

1. If *The Compass Flower* had been published in the form in which it was originally assembled in 1976, it would have resembled Merwin's previous collection of free verse: initially, the first typescript of the book was a miscellany of work completed from mid-1972 through 1975, and it was not grouped in sections. Some time before its publication in 1977, the poems were divided into four separate sections, and seventeen poems were omitted. Merwin's editing seems intended to reshape his collection into a unified work, because the poems he excluded were by no means negligible. The majority had appeared in journals, and two were important enough to be included, some years later, as opening poems in subsequent volumes: "Time of Tree Cutting," in *Finding the Islands* (1982), and "The Waters," in *Opening the Hand* (1983). See TS. 16:1359 for the original typescript of *The Compass Flower.*

2. "The Moon in Mist," TS. 16:1359, original typescript of *The Compass Flower.*

3. For a detailed scrutiny of the revisions of "St. Vincent's" see Michael Greer and Cary Nelson, "'St. Vincent's': The Biography of a Poem," in *Essays on the Poetry*, pp. 296–316.

4. No reviewer recognized the poetry of grief in part 1 that establishes the overall framework Merwin is working within. As a result, the book tended to be read as though it were an extension of the preceding poetry. Poetry that fails to meet expectations can be judged by hasty reviewers not as propounding new standards but as failing to meet

established standards, and the most persistent claim was that Merwin had started to repeat himself (even though these poems were noticeably unlike any he had published before). David Bromwich, for example, suggested that Merwin was now producing poems by recipe, and he concocted his own Merwin poem, which he called "an *objet* by now as readily identifiable as an A. Calder or an R.C.A. Victor" (*Hudson Review* [Summer 1977]: 282). William Marling complained that "W. S. Merwin publishes too much" (*Southwest Review* [Spring 1978]: 198), and Harold Bloom stated that the book was "unlikely to alter the sense of decline that troubles some of his most sympathetic readers" (*New Republic* [Nov. 26, 1977]: 25). The most extended study was by Vincent Sherry, who further expanded his review in *Contemporary Literature* (Winter 1980): 159–70, into an essay, "W. S. Merwin's *The Compass Flower*: The Angles of Convergence," in *New Poetry* 26 (Apr. 1978): 44–54. He perceived the poetry in part 1 as detailing a love affair that prefigured the love poetry in part 3—an intuition not entirely incorrect.

5. Unfin. MS. 22:014/013b, c. Summer-Fall 1972. In two places Merwin refers to the "38th day" and "forty days" after his father's death, which would place work on the poem in August 1972. In August 1972 (while his mother was still living) Merwin also completed "The Heart," "The Wine," "The Drive Home," and "The Horse" (MS. 22:07/007, 006, 005, 002). He also wrote a number of other poems, all unpublished, that circumspectly refer to his own mourning: "Ballade of the Unknown," which begins "I don't know the way from here / as you do . . ." (unpub. MS. 22:04/001, d. Aug. 5, 1972); "Losing What Belongs to Someone Else," which begins "Amputated of a solid glass limb / I never felt / by a blade of twilight . . ." and ends "but it is now / now it is a limb of my own that has been taken away / when I go to use it" (unpub. MS. 22:04/004, d. Aug. 9, 1972); and "The Visionary Head of Dante" (22:04/003, d. Aug. 10, 1972). A section of the elegy was reworked in January 1973 as "Strawberries" (variant MS. 22:02/017, d. Jan. 23, 1973), and a later revision of "Strawberries" was published in *Opening the Hand.* (See Chapter 14 for a discussion of the variants of "Strawberries.")

6. "An Old Waiting," unpub. MS. 22:05/002, d. Oct. 11, 1972. This was the first of a series of elegiac poems written in October, from which "The Next Moon," "The Snow," and "The Arrival" were selected for publication.

7. "The Pocket Diary," unpub. MS. 22:01/009b, d. Oct. 14, 1972, and written on the same day as "The Next Moon."

8. For a slightly different arrangement of these poems that seems to be less private, more clearly a memorial sequence, see "The Arrival," "The Tree of Heirs," "The Next Moon," "The Snow," "The Drive Home," and "Migration," printed in this order (and presumably submitted as a group) in *Mundus Artium* 6 (1973): 112–17.

9. Two unpublished city poems also emphasize speed and transportation, as well as the blindness the city encourages. In "The Drivers" Merwin reconsiders the irritating noise of powerful trucks, deciding that while the trucks may be unreal, their drivers are not: they must rumble through "boredom sadness grease pay / kidney troubles abdominal deterioration / ulcer aches in bones / repeated advertisements radios / endless tunnels of noise traveled through" (unpub. MS. 22:02/010, d. Apr. 21, 1973). In "The Subway Paintings," also a poem of recognition, details of the subway, suddenly discovered ("nobody / paid mind until lately / but walked in and out / through them"), take on a flamboyant beauty (unpub. MS. 22:06/006, d. Aug. 30, 1973).

10. As evidence of Merwin's careful arranging of this section, it should be noted that the poetry itself was written over an eighteen-month period from spring 1973 to fall 1974, during the time he was living in rural Barrade, France (a period to which he returned in the prose memoir "Shepherds"). The poems were arranged not in the order they were written but to follow a seasonal rhythm. For example, "September Plowing" was completed on September 17, 1974, and "The Love for October" (which follows "September Plowing" in part 3) was completed on October 31, 1973 (MS. 22:08/001, and MS. 22:06/001).

Chapter 13. The Good of the Intellect

1. The early prose reminiscence was entitled "A View from the Palisade" in Notebook 11:1216, c. 1957–58 (see *Essays on the Poetry,* pp. 319–21, for excerpts and a discussion by Cary Nelson). "The Garden" was published in *KAYAK* No. 4 (1965): 20. "The Complaint of My Family" was published in *Evergreen Review* 9 (Mar. 1965): 50 (see *Essays on the Poetry,* pp. 344–52, for reproductions of the drafts of "The Complaint of My Family"). "Offertory" is an unpublished work (unpub. MS. 21:001/0088b, d. Mar. 20, 1963). "The Windsor Fields" (unpub. MS. 11:1258, c. 1969) is not dated, but the manuscript for "The Hours of a Bridge" (MPC, 187–88), (MS. 21:07/068, d. Sept. 26, 1969) starts with a variant of the opening sentence of "The Windsor Fields."

2. "Mary" is dated June 29, 1973 (MS. 11:1250) and was originally called "Unframed Originals." The sequence of composition of the other chapters is: "The Skyline" (MS. 11:1251), dated "Nov.-Dec. 1977"; "Hotel" (MS. 11:1253), dated July 17, 1980; "La Pia" (MS. 11:1254), dated August 8, 1980; "Tomatoes" (MS. 11:1249), dated November 6, 1980; and "Laurie" (MS. 11:1252), dated February 16, 1981.

3. "Nothing New," *Paris Review* No. 18 (Spring 1958): 92.

4. "Not a Real Relation," unfin. MS. 21:003.001, c. 1966–72?

5. For other short pieces that seem preparations for memoirs, also see "The Old Boat" (HT, 182–84), dated July 24–25, 1973; "By the Grain Elevators" (HT, 164–65), dated August 4, 1973; "On the Map" (HT, 185–86), dated June 25, 1974; "A Voyage" (HT, 173–76), dated January 21, 1975; "A Parcel" (HT, 192), dated June 19, 1975; "The Fair" (HT, 166–68), dated January 7, 1976; and "The Great Union" (HT, 59–61), dated February 3, 1976.

6. The original manuscript began with "Mary," followed by "Tomatoes," but Harry Ford suggested reversing their order. See "W. S. Merwin to Harry Ford," Sept. 23, 1981, Letter 01:131.0889.

7. "A House Abroad," *New Yorker* 57 (March 23, 1981): 36–41. "A House Abroad" excerpts pp. 155–70 of "Hotel" in the Atheneum text, adds a brief introductory paragraph, and omits the paragraph on p. 169 that describes a nightmare. Portions of both "Hotel" and "La Pia" also appear in "Anna," *New Yorker* 57 (August 3, 1981): 31–37, to create a composite portrait of his mother by way of her relationship with Margie. This version also downplays differences between the two women emphasized in *Originals.*

8. The most dramatic example of clutter dominating a person's life is exemplified by Aunt Alma, the center of "Laurie." It is fitting that this was the last of the pieces to be written, for it is the memoir with the longest genealogy. Under the name of "Gussy" or

"Gussie," Alma figured in two incomplete stories (an untitled story, c. 1949 [Notebook 08:1132], and "The Parrot" [unpub. TS. 11:1220, c. 1955–56]), one unfinished poem ("The Gadding Kitchen of Gussie Gardengrow" [unpub. MS. 19:11/003, c. 1953]), one collected poem ("A Letter from Gussie," MT, 4), and, under her own name, in one uncollected poem ("Aunt Alma," *Paris Review* No. 18 [Spring 1958]: 92). In 1949 or 1950, as Gussy, she appeared in an unfinished story about an elderly lady engaged in a lengthy conversation with an imaginary royalties agent. Merwin's note makes clear the connection between Gussie and Alma, for both share an obsession with an imaginary companion: "Gussy's sister—supposed to be or to have been staying with her. One is not sure whether the sister really exists or not. Maybe a sort of mad-true daydream but true to life enough to be terribly credible." By completing "Laurie," Merwin finishes redefining the axis along which he views the members of his family. In 1958, he decided that men were innocent vagabonds and women were possessive monsters, and his paternal grandfather and grandmother were the family archetypes. By 1981, the split is along paternal/maternal lines and takes a different form (and his grandfather plays a minimum role in the memoirs): his father and his ancestors (represented by Alma) consistently fail to unify their lives and lurk behind facades they have erected to assure their own appearance of normalcy, while his mother and her ancestors (represented by Margie) win through to an eccentric individuality in which norms and conventions are transformed. In one case, to step outside the frame leads to madness, in another to individuality. Alma serves as a double for Merwin's father and Margie for his mother, each extending the qualities of both parents, the polarity in Merwin's childhood. Although the story of "Laurie" can appear as an afterthought, it is useful in that it underscores this redefinition of the division within the family.

9. "Affable Irregular: Recollections of R. P. Blackmur," MS. 10:1166, d. Sept. 26, 1981. (The last chapter in *Unframed Originals* was completed in February 1981.)

10. In an early passage (later cancelled), Merwin contrasted the differences between Berryman and Blackmur, but this straightforward comparison presented Blackmur's features too starkly (as he is already beginning to note toward the end of the passage):

> When I think of [Berryman and Blackmur], I remember how I listened to them. And Berryman influenced my way of attending to the energies of words, the charge they generated in relation to each other, the presence of poetry in a line, the tension and ring of verse. From Blackmur, I was listening for something different, a way of thinking and being, a cast of mind and phrase. Insight and wisdom. Yet I never wanted to write like either of them. They were not models. There is no way, I see now, for me to assess the extent of the influence either of them has had on me but I know it is out of all proportion to how I knew them, or how much I saw of them.

Several early (and undeveloped) passages in the drafts of "Affable Irregular" dwell as much on Berryman as on Blackmur. As a gloss to the final sentence quoted above, for example, Merwin recalls Berryman explaining that "it was possible to be influenced by a single aspect, a fragment out of context, of someone else's work."

11. At a much earlier time, Merwin associated Dante's phrase with the other writer he adopted as the mentor of his youth; the words also appear in the second of eight

stanzas of an unpublished poem, "Satire (for Ezra Pound)," as drafted in Notebook 19:1149, c. 1949–51:

So am I clouded,
empty of celebration,
as a two-faced mirror
hung between smoke and ruin.

What news of morning?
What have the hours raked?
Has any rediscovered
The good of the intellect?

Chapter 14. The Broken Back Line

1. A similar device has appeared in the work of some contemporaries, notably James Dickey, Adrienne Rich, and Donald Finkel. However, it is almost always used as an extension of the caesura in classical prosody: as a natural pausing point in the line. As a result, in their work the device comes and goes according to the demands of the syntax. But Merwin adopts a caesura in every line, basing it on Middle English strong-stress verse (or the medieval epics he translated in the 1950s, one of which, *The Poem of the Cid,* employs the caesura as a typographical feature). In Merwin's hands, the caesura is not driven by the syntax of the line; indeed, it will oppose itself to syntactical structure: "A guest at Thanksgiving (/) said And you've got / a green water tower" (OH, 37). Merwin's caesura will also follow syntax at times, but Marjorie Perloff's remark that the caesura is "meant to mark the pauses in natural speech in what looks superficially like David Antin's 'talk poems'" (*Essays on the Poetry,* p. 142) considerably simplifies his use of the device. Two uses of it outside the 1976–1978 period, however, in "Kore" in 1974 ("one note under them [/] Full moon [/] The year / has turned" [CF, 52]) and in "The Salt Pond" in 1984 ("Mid September [/] my dead father's birthday" [RT, 28]), both employ it as an adjunct to syntax, a marker for the pauses in speech rhythms.

2. "Fact Has Two Faces," Nelson and Folsom, p. 358. Merwin made similar comments in a 1981 interview with Richard Jackson: "I believe that the parallelisms of Old English poetry and Middle English poetry are the underlying rhythms of poetry. Like any convention, the line I have been working with has its limits, but it seems to have many possibilities partly because it's been ignored for so long" ("Unnaming the Myths," in *Acts of Mind: Conversations with Contemporary Poets* [Tuscaloosa: University of Alabama Press, 1983], p. 52). As historically accurate as these remarks are, they still seem tangentially related to Merwin's writing, which has rarely employed the blank verse line.

3. "Fact Has Two Faces," Nelson and Folsom, pp. 354–55.

4. Charles Altieri, "Situating Merwin's Poetry Since 1970" (*Essays on the Poetry,* p. 194). Altieri's discussion of "The Fig Tree," which elicits this comment, reveals that the poems in part 4 of *The Compass Flower* easily seem negligible if they are regarded outside of the group as a whole. Within the group, a persistent theme is the contrast between permanent residents and vagabond travelers. The fig tree retains some of its status as a vagabond that happened to grow in one spot, honored by the rules of the

monastery—rules that in turn bring honor to the monastery. Viewed apart from its supporting poems, "The Fig Tree" conveys too little information, and readers would be driven, like Altieri, to rely on material that is extraneous to the work: Wordsworth's integrations of pagan roots and church customs.

5. "The Cow," MS. 22:13/014, d. Nov. 6, 1976.

6. "Questions to Tourists Stopped by a Pineapple Field," MS. 22:19/001, d. June 29, 1979.

7. "Going," variant MS. 22:14/003a, 003b, d. March 30, 1977.

8. The caesura poems were composed over a thirty-two-month period, from November 1976 to June 1979. Except for two poems, "Warm Pastures" (MS. 22:14/002, d. Feb. 28, 1977) and "Sheep Clouds" (MS. 22:17/002, d. Aug. 31, 1977), both continuing the tercet format begun in 1975 with "Time of Tree Cutting" (and collected in *Feathers from the Hill* [1978] and then in *Finding the Islands* [1982]), all poems employed the caesura, although some early drafts of 1977 work display it in a different position within the line. The poems were written in two lengthy sets, followed by a brief revival. From November 1976 to May 1977, Merwin finished twenty caesura poems, including most of his family sequence poems; three of the poems, all dealing with the modern city, and all written toward the end of the cycle in April and May of 1977, were left unpublished. (In November and December 1977, he completed "The Skyline.") From April to September 1978, he completed six more, among them the lengthy "Shaving without a Mirror," "Apparitions," and "Sheridan." In June 1979, he completed "Questions." ("Hotel," "La Pia," and "Tomatoes" for *Unframed Originals* were completed thereafter, between July and November 1980, with "Laurie," the final chapter, completed in February 1981.)

9. Unfin. MS. 22:04/013a, b, c. Summer-Fall 1972.

10. "Strawberries," variant MS. 22:02/017, d. Jan. 24, 1973.

11. The only other caesura poem to employ the verse-paragraph is "The Waving of a Hand" (OH, 6), MS. 22:13/011, d. Nov. 19, 1976, the day before "Strawberries" was revised in its final form. The family poems were not composed as a separate group from other poems employing the caesura. See MS. 22:13 for the poems in the opening sequence and MS. 22:14 for the closing sequence; the fact that the closing poems, all on the city, were contained in a separate order suggests they were composed in New York City, while the first poems were composed in Hawaii.

12. The latest poems in the second half of section 1 date from January 5, 1981 ("The Burnt Child") to October 4, 1981 ("Photograph"). Since the final chapter of *Unframed Originals* was completed in February 1981, the majority antedate Merwin's work in prose memoirs.

13. Merwin's sensitivity to voices speaking is also evident in a canceled passage from the second draft typescript of "Sun and Rain" (TS. 22:13/001, d. Jan. 28, 1977; reproduced in *Essays on the Poetry*, p. 284). The typescript of stanza two ended with lines reading:

> and took her hand for a moment   without saying anything
> here is what he did not say
>
>   in a band of sunlight
> at some signal all the black cows   flow down . . .

The typescript shows the following revision:

and took her hand for a while and said nothing
I know that and
at some signal
all the black cows in a band of sunlight flow down . . .

The final version suppresses entirely Merwin's effort to articulate what his father did not say; the voice of his mother alone is left to gain prominence.

14. See *Unframed Originals*, p. 51, for the prose version of events in "Birdie." This is the only significant passage that overlaps between the prose of *Unframed Originals* and the poetry of *Opening the Hand.*

Chapter 15. The Words in the Language

1. "The Art of Poetry XXXVIII," Hirsch, p. 58.

2. Numerous unpublished manuscripts written between 1980 and 1981 indicate that before Merwin developed his current relation to Hawaii in which he accepted his outsider's status, he tended to view it with an uncertainty that made him uncomfortable. The result was a number of poems, all unpublished and many unfinished, that strongly asserted that Hawaii was either a paradise or a hell, either a lush version of rural France or a California-like version of New York City, the two places where he had previously lived. (For this poetry, see MS. 22:18/inclusive and 22:20/inclusive.) In *Finding the Islands,* his radically divided vision is on display when the flat desolation of "Island City" is contrasted to the quiet beauty of "Mango Trees." A temporary solution, evident in section 3 of *Opening the Hand* (in "Palm" or "Listening"), is to focus on the landscape as a place from which one can extract a powerful and useful aesthetic. These works, however, seem somewhat rarefied. His current perspective has the merit of placing him in an accurate and dynamic relation to the islands in their historical evolution.

3. "The Art of Poetry XXXVIII," Hirsch, p. 79. The exploitation of Hawaii continues to this day, and Merwin is actively engaged in local struggles by native Hawaiians to retain control over their land. See his "Letter on the Wao Kele O Puna Rain Forest," *American Poetry Review* 19 (March-April 1990): 43–45.

4. "Shepherds," *Paris Review* No. 101 (Winter 1986): 68–181.

5. "Foie Gras," *New Yorker* 60 (Nov. 19, 1984): 46–85.

6. "A Recollection of Stones," MS. 11:1229, c. 1955–57. *A Recollection of Stones* may have been an alternate title for the whole series. The first page of the manuscript projects five pieces: "Slaughter-house," "Saigne," "Arguinaguin," "Posada," and "Santa Clara." Under the title "A Recollection of Stones," the first two pieces ("Slaughter-house" and "Saigne") appear in *Regions,* pp. 91–106.

7. "Koa," *Antaeus* 20 (Summer 1987): 131–34.

8. The tercet form was originally developed in 1975 as a vehicle for portraying a certain kind of perfection visible at moments in natural scenes—for conveying, in a glancing fashion, a complex living network of relationships that have an inevitable fleeting quality. Then, its characteristic trait was the abeyance of the definite or indefinite article. "Time of Tree Cutting" originally had this tercet—"Along the white mountain / an owl floats / weighted down with moonlight"—which became, by the

time of publication, "Along the white hill / owl floats / weighted down with moonlight." The singularity of any event is blurred into its generality, not "an owl floats" but "owl floats." Though on occasion the lines echoed the oriental ideograms transcribed in *(Asian Figures),* Merwin's primary effect was to minimize human intrusion: because everything is profoundly integrated in any natural scene, it would be an error—a human error—to enhance the individuality of any event: "Meadow of sagebrush in flower / cat sits in the middle / fur of morning sunlight." Taken up again in 1981 to deliver messages to a beloved companion, the form has the opposite effect: in 1975, the tercet's ability to change so radically and unexpectedly (yet with a growing completeness) within three short lines gave an impression of swiftness; in 1981, the tercet's movement is to absorb, expand, and reify, and by the time it is complete it is dense with memory and moving languorously. In its later incarnation, it banishes time.

9. "Interview," Elliott, p. 23.

10. "A Last Look," *Poetry* 151 (Oct.-Nov. 1987): 102.

11. "So Far," *Atlantic* 262 (October 1988): 64.

12. "Neither my father nor mother knew / the names of the trees / where I was born," Merwin writes in "Native Trees" (RT, 6). Merwin's tense relation to his childhood has relaxed in this volume. Knowing names his parents did not becomes, in fact, a declaration of his autonomy. It is as though he had previously feared that he would become an adult like his parents, but now understands that he has grown into an individual different from them. That may be why, when he sees himself as a small child in "Touching the Tree," he recalls his childhood self identifying the tree with a lion, an image of strength and potency. And in another poem, "After School," in which he recalls days at Princeton, he returns to the past, finds the way blocked by a "black wolf," "who snaps at my right hand." But he unties her and the two walk off into the night as companions in hunger.

13. "The River," *Grand Street* 7 (Summer 1988): 120.

Epilogue

1. Ed Folsom and Cary Nelson, "Introduction," *Essays on the Poetry,* p. 14.
2. "The Wars in New Jersey," *New Yorker* 64 (August 23, 1988): 22.
3. "Among Bells," *New Yorker* 64 (Oct. 17, 1988): 38.
4. "The Blind Seer of Ambon," *Atlantic* 261 (April 1988): 64.

Name Index

Index to the Works of W. S. Merwin

A Note on the Author

EDWARD J. BRUNNER is an associate professor of English at Southern Illinois University at Carbondale, where he teaches modern poetry. He is the author of *Splendid Failure: Hart Crane and the Making of "The Bridge,"* which won the MLA Prize for Independent Scholars in 1986.